HEART'S DESIRE

By the same author

Essays

THE COURAGE OF TURTLES
WALKING THE DEAD DIAMOND RIVER
RED WOLVES AND BLACK BEARS
THE TUGMAN'S PASSAGE

Fiction

CAT MAN
THE CIRCLE HOME
THE PEACOCK'S TAIL
CITY TALES
SEVEN RIVERS WEST

Travel

NOTES FROM THE CENTURY BEFORE:
A JOURNAL OF BRITISH COLUMBIA

AFRICAN CALLIOPE:
A JOURNEY TO THE SUDAN

HEART'S DESIRE

The Best of
EDWARD HOAGLAND

COLLINS HARVILL
8 Grafton Street, London W1
1990

COLLINS HARVILL
William Collins Sons & Co. Ltd
London · Glasgow · Sydney · Auckland
Toronto · Johannesburg

BRITISH LIBRARY CATALOGUING IN PUBLICATION DATA

Hoagland, Edward, *1932-*
Heart's desire: the best of Edward Hoagland
I. Title
814′.54

ISBN 0−00−272033−7

First published in the USA by Summit Books, Simon Schuster, 1988
First published in Great Britain by Collins Harvill 1990

Printed and bound in Great Britain by
Hartnolls Limited, Bodmin, Cornwall

FOR PAT AND BOB TOWERS,
AND LINDA GREEN

Contents

The Ridge-Slope Fox and the Knife Thrower • 9
The Courage of Turtles • 29
Home Is Two Places • 36
Mountain Notch • 54
Of Cows and Cambodia • 57
Howling Back at the Wolves • 72
Lament the Red Wolf • 78
Thoughts on Returning to the City After Five Months on a
    Mountain Where the Wolves Howled • 116
City Walking • 119
City Rat • 122
The Threshold and the Jolt of Pain • 129
In the Toils of the Law • 136
Virginie and the Slaves • 151
Mushpan Man • 170
Bears, Bears, Bears • 183
Hailing the Elusory Mountain Lion • 207
The Moose on the Wall • 221
A Run of Bad Luck • 228
Heart's Desire • 231
The Lapping, Itchy Edge of Love • 239
The Problem of the Golden Rule • 251
Bragging for Humanity • 261
Dogs and the Tug of Life • 274
Other Lives • 283
The Midnight Freight to Portland • 293
Fred King on the Allagash • 300
Walking the Dead Diamond River • 317
The Tugman's Passage • 333
A Low-Water Man • 347
Heaven and Nature • 354

Tiger Bright • 367
Dying Argots • 385
Two Clowns • 388
Should Auld Acquaintance • 391
Gods, Masks, and Horses • 397
Acknowledgments • 428

The Ridge-Slope Fox
and the
Knife Thrower

Saturday. I've finally fixed the water line and got the hot-water heater working and so will take a bath to mark the evening, although it's worth noting how many other treats of one sort or another I have at my disposal: wine, beer, vodka, whiskey, coffee, chocolate for cocoa, maple syrup, honey, jam, apple cider, just for starters. The pioneer whose cellar hole in the bramble patch I dig in occasionally for Castoria bottles and other curios might have had only a little sugar for his nightly tea and maybe a spare ounce of vanilla to spike his spring water for solace. He was a logger, down from New Brunswick, to judge from the lettering on the chemists' bottles, and had no lemon juice, no freeze-dried cubes of chicken broth or lamb tongues in Australian aspic to pique his palate. It is sometimes announced nowadays that we are becoming more and more specialized individually, because of the increasing specialization of the professions, but on the contrary, we are all becoming generalists—almost protean. We have the leisure for it; or if we like our work, our work may take us all over.

My dog outdoors is a sentinel in case somebody drives up from the highway, a rather formidable route until the road commissioner makes his yearly pass with the grader—although, of course, contrary to appearances, I *want* someone to come. Loneliness is my middle name just at the moment. Having driven for eight hours from the city in order to be alone, I'm "dying" of loneliness; can't seem to live with people or live without them. Lovers in comedies shout at each other, "I'll never speak to you again!" and the most abbreviated bout of lovemaking is much more cheering than masturbation. This need we have to talk continually, to rub or at

least bump shoulders, is of substantial significance. An anthropol-
ogist might claim that the habit of keeping company has been
graven into us as social creatures as a survival mechanism and
isn't in some sense a matter of immortality—soul next to soul. Perhaps, indeed, it isn't, but the fascination is that it *might be*.

A New York City editor has asked me for an article about
"the invigorating effects of silence," and yet I sometimes find silence enervating, and play the radio so much I fall asleep with it
still playing. These cutover New England woods are bilingual
when they do speak, as when one stumbles over an ancient scrap
of reddish barbed wire bound around a line of pasture birches
now lost in a new wilderness of outlaw growth. The sugaring trails
are all but effaced, and isolated, suffering apple trees, bloomless
lately, are slowly strangling to death in what was once a farmer's
water meadow but has become an alder swamp. Some coyotes and
a bounding white wolf-sized wild dog live here in this brief interval between the rival epochs of farming and of summer-home development.

In the silence in the house one hears the drumming-ticking of
the stove and an ovenbird's or veery's song. The wind sounds like
the brook and the brook like the wind, though from the way the
dog tilts his head I can infer the presence of a deer in the clump of
poplars below the house. It would be very well, except that the
birds give their best voice at dawn and the deer—a barren doe
whose fortunes I have followed for years (she is lonely herself)—
only comes down off my neighbor's land to mine to feed at 6:00 P.M.,
which leaves a lot of time to kill, and I'm a city man and life is
short to me.

City people try to buy time as a rule, when they can, whereas
country people are prepared to kill time, although both try to
cherish in their mind's eye the notion of a better life ahead. Country people do not behave as if they think life is short; they live on
the principle that it is long, and savor variations of the kind best
appreciated if most days are the same. City people crowd life when
they have the chance; and it is nonsense to suppose that they have
become "less observant," less alert than old-time country people
were. Even that pioneer, whose lumpy, sharp-roofed log house I
have a photo of, and who listened each morning for the location of
his big neighbor, the bear, was not more on his toes than the Los
Angeles denizens who, four abreast and tailgating, drive the Santa
Monica Freeway at seventy miles an hour. His hearing and eye-
sight may have been better, but the city dweller, it should be
borne in mind, wears out his eyes and ears from encountering so
much so fast.

Country people tend to consider that they have a corner on righteousness and to distrust most manifestations of cleverness, while people in the city are leery of righteousness but ascribe to themselves all manner of cleverness. The countryman in the meantime, however—at least in my experience—drops in his tracks from a coronary just as promptly and endures his full share of ulcers and nervous attacks, so that his famous procrastination, which is as characteristic a tendency as his righteousness, does him little concrete good. Whether it's the local lawyer you have business with, or the carpenter, the highway engineer, a nearby farmer with a tractor, the delays almost defy belief. Conventionally, most of us, both in the city and the country, say, "Oh, they enjoy life more upstate, and so naturally they work slower." More often, instead of that, it's the undifferentiated outlook they take toward work. Not that there is some fuzzy idea abroad in the country that every farmer is as good as any other farmer. But a cow is finally just a cow, a chore is after all a chore, there is small possibility of what is called in the city "advancement," and so many hard chores remain to be performed in a long lifetime that, even allowing for the satisfactions of craftsmanship, if you keep putting some of them off, you may get away with having to do fewer of them in the end.

What the countryman does frequently possess is a face more content with middle age; and this is an important phenomenon to try to understand, because one of the central questions—central in the sense that if we could ever answer it we'd know a lot—is why our faces lose so much of the hopefulness apparent in photographs taken around the age of nineteen. On our deathbed, in the last throes of death, a strangely convinced, calm, smiling hopefulness will capture our faces once again, if we are like most people, displacing the anxiety and pain that had been there and astonishing the relatives left behind. But in between, why is it "heartbreaking," as both my wife and mother like to say, to look at somebody's picture from a time when he or she was young instead of middle-aged? It scarcely matters who is pictured; a sorrowful, protective feeling sweeps over us as we look at his face then: "Little did he know."

The sag, the defeatism of the mouth, the calloused look about the eyes are not merely an instance of tissue wear and tear, and because older people in the country wear the same expressions that city people do when they get old, it may be that country folk, leading a life of less density, simply require longer to reach a similar point. Certainly the tenacity of grudges here in the country would indicate that life is slower rather than necessarily happier. My insurance agent hasn't said a pleasant word to me for six years because of a tiff we had, whereas no city man in his right mind would expend such a supply of bile on a single small affair; he'd have too many in hand. The finality of feuds implies a finality to life's possibilities too: a barn tying sixty-five cattle, one hundred thirty-five acres in pasturage and hay, a muddling spouse, four chubby children, seven good friendships, and three keen feuds.

But this analysis leaves out the sweetness of the mornings here, the mists swirling above the pond, the whap of a beaver's tail as you walk by, and what the postman means when he says he's "a rabbit hunter and a horned-pout fisherman." He means that he's not after bear or salmon; and he turned down the postmaster's job a couple of years ago for good measure, so that they had to bring in an outsider. Your true city man and countryman have become rare birds, in any case. Mostly now it's shopping malls, and the confusion is compounded by the fact that with the fanaticism of the convert, some of the most determined urbanites are really country boys who have fled from their boyhoods in the country, and many an overalled bumpkin maneuvering a Rototiller is chewing up two or three decades of city memories as he goes.

I get out of my car after the drive of eight hours, unbutton my fly, and piss on the lawn with a rich complex of feelings. The raccoons that very night take note that I have regained possession. In the country you know when your neighbor wakes up in the morning because smoke starts to waft up from his chimney. And we will always have that—those who want it. The mountain I look up at is late Devonian, when the amphibians were making news. Up top live black-poll warblers and golden-crowned kinglets that would fit the stunted spruces of a timberline more to the north or else much higher, and I am proud we have them. Still, the silence preys on me at times like noise, with the difference only that noise in its destructive impact is physiological and silence is harmless until the mind exfoliates ogres from it. Silence is exhilarating at first—as noise is—but there is a sweetness to silence outlasting exhilaration, akin to the sweetness of listening and the velvet of sleep. Particularly listening, because we listen for what we live for, which is to say, love and the peace of love and spontaneous joy. Maybe they never materialize, but the wood thrush's fluty cry, the hiss of the Coleman lantern at night are bridges of the sort that get us by meanwhile. It delights me to realize that right now a brown trout is filling her white belly with mosquitoes a mile down the road, that the glossy black sow bear who lives across the way has produced her biennial pair of cubs, to judge by the prints in the mud. At some point in the summer I'll put them up a tree and hear their peacock cries to her and her angry chuffing at me. Like the doe, she comes down to my bog to feed and I'm happy to pay the taxes on it so that, in this day and age, she can.

I'm surrounded by hatchlings—have scouted up the grouse that produces chicks each spring at the head of the upper field, to count how many she has: three black-brown feather-fluffs with needly beaks frozen as straight as ships in the short grass to deceive me. Two ravens have a nest on the cliff, around where the sunrise hits, and the pair of hawks whose presence I have enjoyed for years have safely returned, prudent in relation to a human figure on the ground. In incongruous mews and squeals they chat back and forth as they sail and soar. The hummingbirds, the bats, the man-prints of porcupines and coons—all as before, except that the bad winter appears to have cut into the population of bats. On the oak trees and striped maples flower tassels hang from the twigs; daffodils and shadbush blooms have given place to trillium, ground phlox, and cherry blossoms. I may miss seeing the ridge-slope fox, but glimpsed him last year with a tattered chipmunk drooping like a cigar from his mouth, tired and angling toward home, so I know where he lives. The white wolf-dog I've already caught sight of—watching me and watching his feet, he organized his escape plan as he fled—and my square house with its steep roof like a hat pulled low over the eyes: sometimes I would gladly drive for fifty hours to have these things.

The snow, which as a summer person I am content to miss, as not the least of its services, muffles the egos of people hereabouts, so that New Englanders are easier to swallow than a good many Californians or Texans (although the heat of the Deep South can do the same). The winter squats on them, much as the abrasions of city living are likely to moderate a person's self-esteem, not to rule him entirely but to keep him down to scale. Unfortunately, the snowfall can be so intimidating that it overly humbles people and turns them punch-drunk by the time spring comes. Besides, the tradition of self-deprecation has been institutionalized in New England to the point of absurdity. It's a relief in the autumn to get back to the smart-mouths of the city.

Of course my own "snowfall" at the moment is this upsurge of loneliness, in which a failure is implied: failure, to begin with, because one must dodge off to a solitary refuge. We like to blame the need for second homes on society, saying that our cities are unlivable, but the failure is personal, first of all. Alone at last, with the trees bulging above us in shapes that have defined and preserved the world, we find that we're incapacitated for living alone also.

Solitude is not a plaything. A friend of mine who is a professional explorer describes the violent seizures that have over-whelmed him on occasion—an irresistible shaking lasting for a couple of hours during which his body gradually fought off a nervous collapse. He lay in his tent, hugging himself and moan-ing, his best hope to give way to it until it stopped. These episodes have occurred not when he was absolutely by himself but, rather, when he was traveling with three or four morose and badly as-sorted companions, all of them hunkering around a greasy fire, rubbing soot off their biscuits, each hoarding a cup of smoky soup and facing in a different direction. Another veteran traveler has described for me the set of routines by which he wards off hysteria. Lunch is a production if possible, as a matter of habit; and then a nap; cocktails at five; note-taking during the morning; his diary in the evening—a fuss to record everything. Talk to your seatmate on the cross-Maharashtra bus—meals are always made much of— and in every city never refuse a gambit. *"Psst. Hey, mister,"* whis-pers a dragoman—go with him! He finds he gets a second wind; the loneliness strikes in several sieges, and to weather one means a respite, a spate of pleasures, before the next.

Both men are still fascinated, as I am, to speculate on what would happen if they were left on their own for many months. How soon and in what manner would they go mad? The wildlife biologists who are most inspired and acute turn out to be such isolated souls when one meets them in civilized surroundings that for them the seclusion of snow-leopard country in the Karakoram Range is hardly a departure. I know another individual (these peo-ple interest me) who, unlike the rest of us, doesn't worry that he might come unstrung in a situation of ultimate solitude. He has discovered that in the practical world there is no such circum-stance. It is his pleasure—when he has saved a few thousand dol-lars—to land himself at the north rim of the Sahara with a strapped suitcase in one hand and a windbreaker in the other and wait for his first ride.

Unannounced, with no expedition behind him, he will step from a pirogue onto the coast of one of the outer islands of Indo-nesia and see what happens. What does happen—either there, or back behind the wall of the Andes, or in Kurdistan—is that within several hours he is not alone; he is with a tribesman, then fifteen tribesmen, and the story continues familiarly. He has special quali-ties. He is a linguist, a sexual switch-hitter, and possessed of a sliding, enigmatic smile and the gift of equanimity in equal mea-sure with his fearlessness, and, like the other two, is an Olympic athlete at feats of solitude compared to you and me.

In Africa I've had my handwriting disintegrate at a border crossing from a case of bad nerves, so that I couldn't cash a traveler's check and was almost barred entry on grounds of illegibility. Even in these modest woods, loneliness muffles me like snow, and my sad penis at night, like a club in my hand—futile as a club, and a Stone Age implement for all of us, which is why we love it so—reminds me of many failings stretching far afield from sex. It is our saving grace that despite every social and scientific innovation and all our cumulative monkeying, if a man lays hands on a woman of his choosing and doesn't feel his penis swell with blood, his life can still be altered catastrophically. Though such is not my trouble, it's out here, holding this stubborn, thick appendage—never more impotent than when hard—that the relativism of the city appears in its full foolishness: the idea that anything goes.

The perception that our individual anguish is part of a tide of anguish and our exuberance part of a wave of joy is a religious one. We are all fragile—the health-food faddist down the road, throwing up his health foods now and submitting to anesthetic injections in the last stages of cancer; the counterculture young folk in the town knotting their brows at meetings of the Low Income Association, figuring how they, too, can become a clubhouse pressure group.

I went through a siege of cancer with a friend, and one of the spectacles that took shape in her mind as she waited between operations was an inspection of the raggle-taggle file of admirers with whom she'd shared a span of twenty years. No rosy glasses now: each was the subject of some hilarity, because trysts—just as in Chaucer—keep more kindly in the memory if treated as a stumble. As a Jewish intellectual, she had been lured by ethnic opposites or seamen, movers, actors, not seeking a mirror of herself but what she didn't already have, so that an obvious unconformity recurred. They weren't unlike a row of knotty "problems" as she ranged them up, trying to draw some conclusions. She could claim that she had left each of them a little better off than when she'd met him—his career clarified, perhaps, if he had one, his nervous system temporarily rehabilitated. To her surprise, the lover with the longest tenure had dwindled almost to a cipher in her recollection. Instead, her favorite was a motorcycling German who had joked with her and put her in the hospital and whom she hadn't taken seriously. At supper parties with his pals, she'd used to reach up her left sleeve and with a flourish remove her bra—but now girls had stopped wearing bras. Her former husband she had married on the rebound from another man, a man whom she herself had turned away, she realized, although he'd loved her endlessly and though indeed she may have loved him more than her husband. For having seemed to love her too much, at last he'd had to marry someone else. She remembered being told as a little girl by her aunt—the beauty in the family, whom she was thought to take after—to marry someone who loved her not only more than all the world but more than she loved him; and so she'd done the opposite.

Once I read about a medieval death imposed by a potentate on two lovers. He had their arms tied around each other and left them lying face-to-face to starve. Supposedly the horror of it was that they would grow to loathe each other, sweating in this mockery of the coital position, but I don't see it so; I remember my explorer friend shivering, hugging his ribs in a tent in New Guinea. Recently two revolutionaries were hanged in the Near East, and as they twisted, blindfolded, their hands tied behind their backs happened to touch, and touching, clasped, and so they died grasping each other.

Everything is so fragilely a matter of interpretation that we tread on the edge of mayhem or suicide if a tilt occurs in our minds. Sex and laughter were the original belly-pokers, and with inhibition came civilization, but there is such significance to loneliness that we still continue to suffer from it; we can't exist complacently, puttering about, watching TV, and sleeping, but instead are pulled together with an urgency, as if, apart, we had no skins. When it sets in, it springs up again although well placated only the day before: an awful ache, and what it partly is—as the anthropologists would agree—is the call of the wild, as one looks down at one's funny legs, which in their quirky shape have more to do with trotting across a grassy valley in company with a hunting party than accelerating a car. In the city, I live overlooking an elevated highway and can hear around the clock a rush of traffic, most of which cannot be going anywhere terribly exciting, but pressing, pressing, just the same. Once when the highway was out of commission it rapidly became populated with joggers, who also traveled up and down.

I don't stay still either, and give people that traveler's "Bye-bye" when I leave, though afterwards when I am under way I worry that I'm smashing up my life by my avoidances and indecisions. A friend who is seventy-nine, the only person hereabouts interested enough in scouting in the woods to pinpoint a den of coyotes that everyone was speculating about, whisks his hand lightly over his bald head to betoken the speeding years—says they go by for him like slices falling from a loaf of bread. He was born in his own bedroom, but never having left Vermont, he's brought the world to him. That is, he regularly sees in his wood-lot "tigers," "moose," "mountain lions."

I keep a turtle for the same reason. He hasn't surrendered to being a pet, and pauses in his escape attempts only long enough to eat a mouthful of strawberries. He may be as old as I am, to judge by the rings on his scutes, and as an experienced campaigner he knows that the hard knocks of captivity are not to be accepted as anything but temporary. I keep him in the rabbits' pen to confirm that, as in the fable, he covers much more ground than they do. To look at him, it wouldn't seem he could; and just as unexpectedly, his dogged efforts to escape—banging down on his back from halfway up the fence—are gradually accomplishing exactly what he seeks. I'm moved by his persistence and will soon release him. He looks like a brown chock of wood, and has a thumb-shaped head and mail-like, horny plates of armor on the front of his wide legs to shield them when he draws them inside his shell. But when he opens himself again—stretching out his legs and head—behind the head and sleeves of mail protecting his legs are a tender pair of shoulders, puffy with the fat that he has put on between escape attempts. Both these, and certain dashings on the previously hidden portions of his legs, are a passionate orange.

He lives under a roof of brown bone, on a hard bedboard, carrying his bed about with him, using it as a fifth leg in many of his maneuvers, as when he slides down off a log. He sleeps with his hind legs lolled out personably and his head poignantly at rest. His fire-colored shoulders must identify him to other turtles of the species, and it was probably his search for a mate that brought him out to the dirt road where I caught him. Otherwise he is remarkably footloose, has no social life to speak of (the rabbits are more interested in making friends with him), and seems almost as free from any knowledge of the pangs of hunger as of loneliness. He needs to be plump enough to survive hibernation, but shouldn't get so fat that his limbs can't pull wholly into his shell if a raccoon should happen to grab him and begin to scratch and gnaw.

Because turtles are willing to starve in captivity, their usual form of surrender is only to agree to eat. But his manner of pausing for a worm, casually letting the crumbs of it fall from the corners of his mouth as he continues to search for a hole in the fence, makes him seem more of a figure to me than merely fatalistic resistance by starvation would. Certainly his singular shell must have saved his life when he has been caught by human beings—as well as raccoons—before. For every dozen people who will immediately stomp on a snake, only one will want to kill a turtle.

He pumps his throat as he breathes, in an exercise reminiscent of cud-chewing, and expresses contentment by this, as dogs by the sounds of their breathing express affection to one another and to us. Even on his back after a fall, he rests, not panicked, because his mastery of the uses of his shell is like a hockey player's with a stick. He sometimes talks to himself with the thump of it, I think—employing or not employing the sound, choosing or not choosing to thump—and, like the elegant fire-flickerings of his shoulders and legs, it is a more eloquent statement than his official hiss.

A Friday, later.

I have a friend or two whose only response to adversity is to retreat to this same harshness of the woods to cauterize a failure or a wound. They buckle themselves into it like putting on ice packs. No doubt, like me, they go into the woods to celebrate also—the astounded feeling that you get from looking at a tadpole balancing in the water with his large tail, but sprouting four dark legs. Even a farmer hacking a path through a side of beef to stock his freezer is dismantling a structure of wonder and grace.

I cook rhubarb, nibble wood-sorrel, and steep the house with the smell of wild-meat roasts. Outward self-sufficiency, and yet I keep the radio on—women's voices from Canada announcing Schumann and speaking French. Whatever they are saying sounds loving to me.

In the past, when I have felt a divorce action drawing near, I've put a tent and sleeping bag in my car; a friend of mine sets a canoe on his truck—gestures about as germane as an Edwardian reserving a room at his club. But, sleeping bag and all, I am so lonely now that it is like a hemorrhage. Listening to the clicking noise of my dog licking his paws, feeding the stove past midnight till my hands sink and the knuckles get burned, I groan beastly groans or burst into loud phrases that might seem disconnected if they weren't embarrassingly transparent, with my belowstairs mind standing right in back of my tongue. A girl who lives as a squatter in a hut over the hill, when she gets into company where the talk is too much for her, makes a zipping motion across her temple to show that she has lost her way again. Chop-chop-chop she goes with her hips, in bed with the axmen who in payment will chop her winter's wood.

In midwinter the game warden, touring on his snowmobile, generally discovers somebody from the city still holed up in a cabin around here piled high with snow, a cashiered engineer from Boston, who used to work in aerospace but has denned up like a bear sucking on its toes and claws. The first woods travelers in America—men like Peter Kalm, William Bartram, and Crève-coeur—appear from their journals to have been a peaceable lot who, in exploring the God-given world, didn't find it necessary to become entangled overmuch with aborigines, as would have been the case on one of the hotter continents. Mostly they met other whites—energetic, appreciative souls, on the whole, who shared their gaiety. Now we are likely to lie low with our energies instead of walking, and do it in order to take stock, which is what we busy ourselves with a good deal anyway. Although the country hideaway, set in a kind of tuning-fork relationship of tension to the city, where the owner's money or reputation is actually made, is a new *modus operandi*, it is impossible to calculate the end of the effects of the closing off of all that old, free operating space.

At performances of the sideshow in a circus that I used to work for as a boy, I'd watch the knife thrower, after he had thrown at his wife (who was also the circus nurse), go into the second segment of his act, which was—to put it bluntly—to whip a series of women. He didn't need to ask for volunteers; he was besieged by them. In slacks and pleated blouses, cashmere sweaters and pedal pushers, they wanted the sensation of a horsewhip wrapping roughly around them, laid on by a black-haired, muscular man—the whole experience of a sexual lashing except (because of his skill) the pain. For him, too—both as a knife thrower who avoided murdering anybody and in the whipping performance—to go through the motions was sufficient.

There is a monster in me that I keep at bay by such reflexes as, for example, in the city, crooning to my young daughter while dandling her, "Your daddy is a monster to his little girl, so cruel to her." The true love in the voice vitiates the words; and I remember my own father gripping my arms fiercely at queer, furious instants when I was small and had done nothing especially wrong. I realize now that he was choking down a violence that did not really relate to me, lest I be hurt. He read sadistic popular fiction on occasion and must have been astonished by these impulses, as we all are, an astonishment which, at the layman's level, the science of psychology has not diminished. "Why are you watching this woman being whipped?" an inquiring reporter might have asked us at the sideshow; and as long as his expression

was serious and he approached us one by one, not trying to challenge us as a mob, we would have been utterly abashed, at a loss
to explain even in our private minds.

It's just as well, unless one believes in the perfectibility of
man. Besides, there is the complication that the wife of the woman-
whipper climbed off the platform—after he had thrown his knives
at her—and, in a perfectly unruffled, competent manner, she went
behind the hippo's tank to attend to a cage hand who was lying
in a pile of straw shaking with pneumonia. The husband did the
same when he was needed, and often stopped a minute in the
"whippings" he administered to ask her how the patient was
doing, when she emerged—seemed to care more than most of the
rest of us.

Diana, goddess of the woods, was chaste, but we who go into
the woods nowadays are as likely to be kinky as chaste. Still waiting to get to sleep, with this shillelagh or grease gun in my fist
(really like a little squirrel)—what to do with him?—I have a fantasy that at least has the virtue of logic. I am an itinerant slave
dealer and toward the end of the day I have the women walk in
front of my horse with their skirts pinned up so I can watch their
buttocks swing and pick a partner for the evening. Other fantasies, however, have me harnessed to a cart, instead of playing
the master; or where I wear a nose ring and am in bed attached
to a woman's necklace, like a kind of living bauble. And however
astutely you explain masochism, it is not logical.

Women after Diana have usually left men to their own devices in the woods, as perhaps we have wished. Nevertheless, we
do people it; and the recent fantasies I've had depict me lying
on my side on the bed with my hands tied behind my back and
fastened to a ring around the base of my scrotum. Helpless but
not in discomfort, I move about at times and am in use as a
sort of dildo by an amused woman, closer to forty than thirty (I
am identified as being "young"), who feeds me from her mouth
or with her hands, first fastening me between her legs with my
throat pressing against her so that she can feel me swallow. She
releases me to exercise but keeps the intimacy tight between us,
rationing my sexual activity.

I'm not unique in this variety of vision. The prostitutes are
telling the sociologists that they are being inundated at the moment by men seeking extreme humiliation. Is it death the customers are really after? The woman of my fantasy—self-besotted, like
the mannequin who stands in for me—does not resemble the women
who in fact inhabit my memories. I do still yearn to be initiated,
however, and try to manufacture opportunities for that in love-

making. I'm boyish, as if only through boyishness can I slip through the woman's resistance to win her indulgence.

There are two ways for a man to be boyish, both corresponding to a woman's "flirtation." One of them simply reclaims the years of first courtship, salting those blundering forms of appeal with irony and directness—the haste of people who recognize that they are mortal—and strikes the rest of us as pleasing because the person seems to occupy all of his life at once. But the other boyishness is compulsive, like a child's dizziness in the environs of Mum. In his abject imaginings, the prostitute's client gropes backward, I suspect, and not forward towards death.

It is marriage as often as bachelorhood that creates "dirty old men," or, for that matter, their counterpart, the "biddy." The person's inversion grows as a stain from his defeats, retreats, dysfunctions, and the gap between what life supposedly held in store for him and what life brought. Perhaps he gave himself over to his daydreams until the daydreams altered him, or found that his choice was between waking up in the same house with his children in the morning but living with a woman who would not sleep with him, or forlornly leaving them to go and live with somebody who would.

I used to ask the first girl I ever made love to to spread her legs as widely as she could and raise them high, as if to dramatize that the shut legs I had met with before had opened at last. But I have another memory, startling because it came back unannounced after a hiatus of many years. It's of my first wife, before our marriage, sleeping on the floor beside my bed—her bed, actually, narrow, in a narrow apartment—and the pretext was that there was just space for one. Such memories, a dozen or twenty of them, cast a greenish, unnerving light over one's past. I didn't need to drive so far, eat wild meat, live with a bat-faced dog, and burn kerosene in order to bump up against them, but here they stand in relief.

Only in a roundabout way are weeks spent in the wilderness "purifying," and then only when the affair is brought to a conclusion before the person is disabled. As in the old medical practice of leeching, the stamina has been bled out of me. I came here brim-up with city sarcasms and the woods soon overpowered these alkalis. If I stay on, as I've learned from experience, the woods will continue melting the edginess out of me, to a point of faith and glee and exultancy in the sailing foliage, the cut of the sunshine and rain—right on past this point of equilibrium, to my becoming runny butter on the ground. Arriving, I've had in me both the tigers that treed Black Sambo in the fairy tale and

Black Sambo himself. The tigers run around and around these trees, to which, terrified, I cling, until they (the tigers) gradually melt, and chastened—meek as Sambo was—I climb down, and, tiptoeing through a puddle that was a tiger once, steal away to the city again.

I get a glimpse, in other words, of what must have happened a good many times on the frontier. That pioneer in his uneasy solitude, with his vial of vanilla extract and endless spring water, for periods of an hour or two every few days began to imagine he had a brass ring around his testicles that his hands were fastened to. He was seven miles from a neighbor, two days' walk from town, and by stages these spells extended to several hours, almost daily, the daydream evolving into a hallucination he could no longer control. Though in his own mind he wasn't alone at all, month by month it reached such a pass that he could hardly snatch time to hoe his potatoes or hunt for meat. Eventually, walking around with his hands clasped behind his back, he stopped splitting wood. The fire went out, and one freezing night, lying with his hands that way, he died.

This is my one life and what is kinky in me worries me less than the dead spots. Kinkiness, like a reversible coat, can be turned inside out. A vulnerability, innocent as well as in despair, is represented, which, even if the opposite side is no more appetizing, makes for some leeway.

I have a clipping from Dien Bien Phu that shows a French major standing on a little rise with his arm raised to his men, more in salutation than command. He is leaf-thin, sleepless, soon to die. His hands sag exhaustedly. Like a leaf, he is beginning to curl at the ends, though his smile and long arms still carry the greeting, which is larger than his body.

It's incongruous that the older we get, the more likely we are to turn in the direction of religion. Less vivid and intense ourselves, closer to the grave, we begin to conceive of ourselves as immortal. But if the presentiment is even half correct, naturally, too, it would await our closer attention. The sweetness of ordinary people's voices singing together can be taken as evidence, for instance: the absolutely unearthly beauty they acquire in combining with each other, which has no relation to the honking quality each voice is cursed with, alone. In an era of canned entertainment, we hear one hundred voices singing together nowadays mostly in church, but whatever the setting, if the whole is so much greater than the parts, we might deduce the existence of God.

"Once I realized I couldn't rescue myself, an indescribable

feeling of calmness and serenity came over me," a man who had nearly drowned told two researchers from the University of Iowa. Interviewing more than a hundred survivors of near-death situations, they discovered that a slowing of external time "and a vast recall of happy events were generally linked and clearly related." Many people "described their emotional state as pleasurable, and 23 percent even acknowledged joy."

The very root of my own hopefulness is a long stint I spent working in an army morgue—the odd smiles of most of the dead as death had overtaken them and the nature of death had dawned on them. Or maybe, on the contrary, the revelation was not really so much of death as of the nature of life, as an extravaganza of glad scenes sped past their eyes. Either way, a simple explanation referring to the vicissitudes of evolution would not do justice to the sense of peace their expressions implied. We can argue that the reason women tend to forget the pain of childbirth is so that they can consent to have more children, but an epiphany arising from the convulsions of death itself bears no such interpretation.

Recently I went to Europe for the first time in ten years, sailing at night; and for me, on board, the event was rife with premonitions of living forever, although, of course, death is also pictured as being some sort of shipping out. Many people get these feelings—smiling at their enemies as at their friends, all of us to meet someday in a theater removed. I was ten years older, noticeably frailer on deck in the wind, and yet the sensation was as sharp as a yelp, compounded partly of my happiness and the ship's floodlit angles and New York City's big straight stripe of lights, which were yellow and hospitable-looking, stippled softly across a thousand buildings—as if, for me, this were not one of perhaps a last handful of trips across the Atlantic but one of an infinite number of sailings.

Manhattan makes a handsome showing from the water, with its streets orange slashes and the parcels of dark warehousing adding bulk and contrast to the lighted skyscrapers and apartment complexes, until the Battery and World Trade Center finish the narrative with a concentrated statement of what power is. Then the green, puff-chested Statue of Liberty, crusted with fame, and the green-lighted East River bridges, as you look back. I was on the *Queen Elizabeth II* for the fun of the voyage, the memories of earlier sailings, and the notion that crossing between continents ought to be a momentous undertaking. I wanted to feel the earth move under me and to rattle across a rough roadbed, because lying in one's stateroom in a light sea is rather like a railroad journey. I wanted to know for five days that I was afloat on the ocean, hearing not just surf sounds—which are a translation—but the immensity of the original source. Eighteen thousand feet of water below, and the grip of it insisting that one is not going to put one's foot down just any old where, but *there,* and now over *there,* and now over *there.* "Crossing the pond," the sailors say, with their faces belying the words.

And so, shivers of anticipation as we got under way, although, still the New Boy in middle age, I bumbled twice to the dining room with my briefcase bumping against my knee, being sized up humorously by the British waiters, before ascertaining that I needn't forfeit my dinner to watch the sailing. There were English round-trippers ("Oh, have you just come aboard?"), and English who had flown to America only the day before. Also a young fan of British shipping from Tooting who had gone to visit the *Queen Mary* in her concrete slip in Long Beach, California, having paid for the jaunt by running a roller coaster in Santa Cruz; and a couple of nurses who had been slaving away in Fort Worth, imported with three hundred of their country women to do a year of night duty. So many English don't like living in England, one meets them all over—English girls going out to Australia or veering around again.

In the rush on the pier I had kissed my daughter goodbye but had forgotten to kiss my wife and had tried to shout to her afterwards from the deck of the ship that I was sorry. Though, like most men, I have polygamous impulses, I don't generally try to "renew" myself by chasing after another generation of women—it is old friends I hanker after—and so after I had made a pass at one of the English nurses, I settled quite contentedly into the deck-chair society of other sedentary individuals. Even so, traveling is bound to be a polygamous experience, as one's memory works. My first wife and I had made a sea crossing, and she was here and would be again, I realized, in Orsini Castle, the Pitti Palace, and half a dozen other places. Both wives, with their poignant, slim necks—high collars—strolled the deck.

My father, too, was on the ship, because he'd always sailed off to an assignment in Europe on one of the Cunard *Queens* if he could. An exceedingly innocent man for a lawyer, he, like me, had been a little scared upon departure—you could see it in his back as he went up the gangplank—and sometimes did meet with adventures, such as returning to his hotel room in West Berlin to find four fishy fellows going through his luggage. His travels, like mine, were mostly alone, because my mother's romantic fancies led her elsewhere, but he was trusted on sight by most strangers, and I could envision him right now beginning the process of striking up with new acquaintances. Abroad, he was bad at learning the language of the country—the words just couldn't seem to jack themselves together in his mouth—but on his feet he had a fast sense of direction. He was reasonably tolerant of foreign customs, considering his intolerance of ethnic variations at home, but feared the germs on foreign money and disliked handling foreign currency; liked to "crack" bills in a mannerism I found irritating. He had bowel troubles, which he regarded so solemnly that the rest of the family took his alarums as a joke. (Once he flew clear home from Switzerland because of a case of constipation.) Then, however, he contracted bowel cancer, mourning his feet as they swelled up and died before his eyes, mourning his legs likewise.

I am evasive with people who are gravely ill, and what I most regret with respect to my father is not so much that secret hunchback residing in me who exulted to learn that he was dying—because the psychological phenomenon of sons set irremediably against their fathers is not something we are responsible for—but, instead, the genuinely grieving side that did wish urgently to help but miscalculated what to do. Sometimes when he sought sympathy, instead of mourning right along with him, I tried to "cheer him up." I remember him looking down at his legs, which were moribund and withering, and myself saying to him, "Oh, but you still have your brain!"

Swaddled like a sanatorium patient in the deck chair, drinking bouillon, chewing ship's biscuits, I couldn't fail to think of his last couple of ocean cruises; it seemed to be how he had wanted to go out of the world. Or maybe he'd felt convinced—like me in the excitement of the ship's sailing—that he would live forever if he was on the sea. Rattling along in a "ripple sea," with the broad band of white wake behind, an unvarnished stream of brown smoke above the ship in bright sunshine, and the vigorous longboats overhead as you paced the boat deck, it surely did appear as though, if God in the thrust of his vivacity were not benign, there must be multiple gods, because *one* of them was.

In a "moderate" sea, with thumps in it, knocking against three sides of the cabin, and the hull of the ship stretching and creaking, I had headaches and a weighty stomach, but this was part of what I'd come for. The steward kept four canaries, which he let fly in the corridor at night. He spoke of the ship as "goldier" than either the true-blue old *Q.E.* 1—which had just burned in Singapore—or the *Queen Mary*. Both had had portholes that opened, instead of air conditioning, so that a breeze blew through, and oak rather than plastic and alloy paneling. The two ships used to arrange to salute each other visually in the mid–North Atlantic, a ceremony I had witnessed from the *Mary* one morning. Indeed, to be "a good sailor" was socially important in my parents' day.

For entertainment in the Double Room, a silver-painted puppet danced from the strings of a taller puppet, clothed in red, which was worked by a green-suited puppeteer with wooden movements and a frigid grin—until he suddenly finished and bowed fluidly, a human being again. A few hours out of New York, I had woken with a nightmare from the whirling of Nantucket Light, but by the landfall off Cherbourg the city's tics had drained from my face and the ocean's surge had engendered in me the illusion of a whole family history of involvement with it. The sea is also a crocodile—in the agony of swallowing water overboard—but I was on the ship. I rocked ashore.

There are places in Ethiopia so high and silent that the villagers can listen to the wings of migrating birds miles away. They are roofless in the world, as we are too, if we remembered it. Digging earthworms for my turtle, sometimes I get the idea that nothing is more fleshly than worms are. Nutritionally, they are a quintessence of protein, and as white as one's secret flesh under one's pants. They are the flesh that fishermen root out before they go to try to catch a fish—and flesh is everything. To slide one's hand inside a lover's clothes is to want to leave it there forever—the buttocks larger than the hand. Life is at its sweetest when we have other flesh in hand besides our own. Vegetarians have often gone through some type of self-destructive phase before renouncing meat and are cleansing themselves, but we meat eaters eat to augment what we have, and, embracing, feast upon each other in order to amplify ourselves.

If human nature eventually is going to take the place of nature everywhere, those of us who have been naturalists will have to transpose the faith in nature which is inherent in the profession to a faith in man—if necessary, man alone in the world. It is not an impossible leap. I pick the sticks to cook my supper with, a ritual of intimacy with the fire and the wood, like my dog's delight in observing the chipmunks that he stalks. Like my handling a steak, there's nothing in his attentiveness toward what he hunts suggesting hate. Just now, I'm burning spruce floorboards torn up six years ago. Floorboards, like new birch logs, are made of sunshine too.

Outside, orange day lilies are in bloom, blue cornflowers, pink queen-of-the-prairie, rose-colored mallow, purple blossoms on the vetch, baby green apples, and red raspberries. On and on through the succession of quiet towns, the road from New York City seemed ready to lead me clear north to the Arctic if I kept driving. And yet I'm ready to retrace my steps awhile. City humor is expansive, New England's understated; New England humor is ironic, and the city's more festive. I want to sit down with some horse players again.

Country people believe they live close to the bone, close to the permanences, which, in the sense that nothing could be more evanescent than work accomplished in the country, they do. Their houses molder very promptly when unlived in. Their barns go broken-backed under the weight of the snow. Their fields quickly begin reverting to woods if left unmowed for more than three years in a row. Around here the most permanent work of inscription has been done by the bears on the beech trees.

Beeches possess a smooth, grayish bark, almost water-colored, which cuts as easily as the bark of paper birch, but doesn't peel as birch bark does. These were the trees that lovers carved their initials on back in the days when lovers knew the properties of different trees. The beech's skin, as tender as it is, will keep its scars right into old age, which may mean fifty or one hundred years or more, longer than the occupants of any house in this township will be remembered, even if the house continues to stand. In my junk woods of what the loggers call "widowmaker" stubs careening overhead and "schoolmarm" trees crotched so that no logger has wanted them, the marks of my friend the sow's climbs will outlive not only her own passions but mine.

The bears' favorite food in the early fall has been jewelweed, which is an orange-flowered, succulent herb that grows in clumpish profusion in wet soil until killed by the first hard frost. The same October frost will bring down heaps of small, triangular, thin-shelled beechnuts in spiny little open burrs that the bears dote on. The pioneers used to spread blankets on the ground to catch the nuts, from which they made beech coffee, as well as a first-rate salad oil and a cooking flavoring whose faint echo we taste in beechnut chewing gum. So far, beech is not a wood much in demand by the timber industry, and the bears, having the trees to themselves, and feeling impatient and proprietary, will climb sixty or eighty feet into the crown of the fall foliage to shake the limbs and hurry the harvest along. In doing so, they leave a ladder-like series of neat claw prints going up (going down, the bear will slide as if the tree were a firehouse pole), incised with a particular fingering that manages to create a personal image of the bear involved that, for anybody who visits here a half-century from now, will have outlasted the memory of Vermont's present governor or Gerald Ford.

These ladders up the beech trees have a logic to them and are precious for that. The bears are manlike and their marks manlike, and so carry an authority and resonance because they reach way back and yet one can ride forward on the memory of them for a good while.

The Courage
of Turtles

Turtles are a kind of bird with the governor
turned low. With the same attitude of removal, they cock a glance
at what is going on, as if they need only to fly away. Until recently
they were also a case of virtue rewarded, at least in the town where
I grew up, because, being humble creatures, there were plenty of
them. Even when we still had a few bobcats in the woods the local
snapping turtles, growing up to forty pounds, were the largest car-
nivores. You would see them through the amber water, as big as
greeny wash basins at the bottom of the pond, until they faded
into the inscrutable mud as if they hadn't existed at all.

When I was ten I went to Dr. Green's Pond, a two-acre pond
across the road. When I was twelve I walked a mile or so to Tag-
gart's Pond, which was lusher, had big water snakes and a waterfall; and shortly after that I was bicycling way up to the adventure-
some vastness of Mud Pond, a lake-sized body of water in the
reservoir system of a Connecticut city, possessed of cat-backed little
islands and empty shacks and a forest of pines and hardwoods
along the shore. Otters, foxes, and mink left their prints on the
bank; there were pike and perch. As I got older, the estates and
forgotten back lots in town were parceled out and sold for nice
prices, yet, though the woods had shrunk, it seemed that fewer people walked in the woods. The new residents didn't know how to
find them. Eventually, exploring, they did find them, and it·re-
quired some ingenuity and doubling around on my part to go for
eight miles without meeting someone. I was grown by now, I lived
in New York, and that's what I wanted to do on the occasional
weekends when I came out.

Since Mud Pond contained drinking water I had felt confident nothing untoward would happen there. For a long while the
developers stayed away, until the drought of the mid-1960s. This

event, squeezing the edges in, convinced the local water company that the pond really wasn't a necessity as a catch basin, however; so they bulldozed a hole in the earthen dam, bulldozed the banks to fill in the bottom, and landscaped the flow of water that remained to wind like an English brook and provide a domestic view for the houses which were planned. Most of the painted turtles of Mud Pond, who had been inaccessible as they sunned on their rocks, wound up in boxes in boys' closets within a matter of days. Their footsteps in the dry leaves gave them away as they wandered forlornly. The snappers and the little musk turtles, neither of whom leave the water except once a year to lay their eggs, dug into the drying mud for another siege of hot weather, which they were accustomed to doing whenever the pond got low. But this time it was low for good; the mud baked over them and slowly entombed them. As for the ducks, I couldn't stroll in the woods and not feel guilty, because they were crouched beside every stagnant pothole, or were slinking between the bushes with their heads tucked into their shoulders so that I wouldn't see them. If they decided I had, they beat their way up through the screen of trees, striking their wings dangerously, and wheeled about with that headlong, magnificent velocity to locate another poor puddle.

I used to catch possums and black snakes as well as turtles, and I kept dogs and goats. Some summers I worked in a menagerie with the big personalities of the animal kingdom, like elephants and rhinoceroses. I was twenty before these enthusiasms began to wane, and it was then that I picked turtles as the particular animal I wanted to keep in touch with. I was allergic to fur, for one thing, and turtles need minimal care and not much in the way of quarters. They're personable beasts. They see the same colors we do and they seem to see just as well, as one discovers in trying to sneak up on them. In the laboratory they unravel the twists of a maze with the hot-blooded rapidity of a mammal. Though they can't run as fast as a rat, they improve on their errors just as quickly, pausing at each crossroads to look left and right. And they rock rhythmically in place, as we often do, although they are hatched from eggs, not the womb. (A common explanation psychologists give for our pleasure in rocking quietly is that it recapitulates our mother's heartbeat *in utero*.)

Snakes, by contrast, are dryly silent and priapic. They are smooth movers, legalistic, unblinking, and they afford the humor which the humorless do. But they make challenging captives; sometimes they don't eat for months on a point of order—if the light isn't right, for instance. Alligators are sticklers too. They're like war-horses, or German shepherds, and with their bar-shaped, vertical pupils adding emphasis, they have the *idée fixe* of eating, eating, even when they choose to refuse all food and stubbornly die. They delight in tossing a salamander up towards the sky and grabbing him in their long mouths as he comes down. They're so eager that they get the jitters, and they're too much of a proposition for a casual aquarium like mine. Frogs are depressingly defenseless: that moist, extensive back, with the bones almost sticking through. Hold a frog and you're holding its skeleton. Frogs' tasty legs are the staff of life to many animals—herons, raccoons, ribbon snakes—though they themselves are hard to feed. It's not an enviable role to be the staff of life, and after frogs you descend down the evolutionary ladder a big step to fish.

Turtles cough, burp, whistle, grunt and hiss, and produce social judgments. They put their heads together amicably enough, but then one drives the other back with the suddenness of two dogs who have been conversing in tones too low for an onlooker to hear. They pee in fear when they're first caught, but exercise both pluck and optimism in trying to escape, walking for hundreds of yards within the confines of their pen, carrying the weight of that cumbersome box on legs which are cruelly positioned for walking. They don't feel that the contest is unfair; they keep plugging, rolling like sailorly souls—a bobbing, infirm gait, a brave, sea-legged momentum—stopping occasionally to study the lay of the land. For me, anyway, they manage to contain the rest of the animal world. They can stretch out their necks like a giraffe, or loom underwater like an apocryphal hippo. They browse on lettuce thrown on the water like a cow moose which is partly submerged. They have a penguin's alertness, combined with a build like a brontosaurus when they rise up on tiptoe. Then they hunch and ponderously lunge like a grizzly going forward.

Baby turtles in a turtle bowl are a puzzle in geometrics. They're as decorative as pansy petals, but they are also self-directed building blocks, propping themselves on one another in different arrangements, before upending the tower. The timid individuals turn fearless, or vice versa. If one gets a bit arrogant he will push the others off the rock and afterwards climb down into the water and cling to the back of one of those he has bullied, tickling him with his hind feet until he bucks like a bronco. On the other hand, when this same milder-mannered fellow isn't exerting himself, he will stare right into the face of the sun for hours. What could be more lionlike? And he's at home in or out of the water and does lots of metaphysical tilting. He sinks and rises, with an infinity of levels to choose from; or, elongating himself, he climbs out on the

land again to perambulate, sits boxed in his box, and finally slides
back in the water, submerging into dreams.

I have five of these babies in a kidney-shaped bowl. The hatch-
ling, who is a painted turtle, is not as large as the top joint of my
thumb. He eats chicken gladly. Other foods he will attempt to eat
but not with sufficient perseverance to succeed because he's so little. The yellow-bellied terrapin is probably a yearling, and he eats
salad voraciously, but no meat, fish, or fowl. The Cumberland
terrapin won't touch salad or chicken but eats fish and all of the
meats except for bacon. The little snapper, with a black crenel-
lated shell, feasts on any kind of meat, but rejects greens and fish.
The fifth of the turtles is African. I acquired him only recently and
don't know him well. A mottled brown, he unnerves the greener
turtles, dragging their food off to his lairs. He doesn't seem to want
to be green—he bites the algae off his shell, hanging meanwhile at
daring, steep, head-first angles.

The snapper was a Ferdinand until I provided him with
deeper water. Now he snaps at my pencil with his downturned and
fearsome mouth, his swollen face like a napalm victim's. The Cumberland has an elliptical red mark on the side of his green-and-
yellow head. He is benign by nature and ought to be as elegant as
his scientific name (*Pseudemys scripta elegans*), except he has contracted a disease of the air bladder which has permanently inflated
it; he floats high in the water at an undignified slant and can't go
under. There may have been internal bleeding, too, because his
carapace is stained along its ridge. Unfortunately, like flowers,
baby turtles often die. Their mouths fill up with a white fungus
and their lungs with pneumonia. Their organs clog up from the
rust in the water, or diet troubles, and, like a dying man's, their
eyes and heads become too prominent. Toward the end, the edge
of the shell becomes flabby as felt and folds around them like a
shroud.

While they live they're like puppies. Although they're viva-
cious, they would be a bore to be with all the time, so I also have an
adult wood turtle about six inches long. Her top shell is the equal
of any seashell for sculpturing, even a Cellini shell; it's like an old,
dusty, richly engraved medallion dug out of a hillside. Her legs are
salmon-orange bordered with black and protected by canted, heroic scales. Her plastron—the bottom shell—is splotched like a mar-
gay cat's coat, with black ocelli on a yellow background. It is convex to make room for the female organs inside, whereas a male's
would be concave to help him fit tightly on top of her. Altogether,
she exhibits every camouflage color on her limbs and shells. She
has a turtleneck neck, a tail like an elephant's, wise old pachy-

dermous hind legs, and the face of a turkey—except that when I carry her she gazes at the passing ground with a hawk's eyes and mouth. Her feet fit to the fingers of my hand, one to each one, and she rides looking down. She can walk on the floor in perfect silence, but usually she lets her plastron knock portentously, like a footstep, so that she resembles some grand, concise, slow-moving id. But if an earthworm is presented, she jerks swiftly ahead, poises above it, and strikes like a mongoose, consuming it with wild vigor. Yet she will climb on my lap to eat bread or boiled eggs.

If put into a creek, she swims like a cutter, nosing forward to intercept a strange turtle and smell him. She drifts with the current to go downstream, maneuvering behind a rock when she wants to take stock, or sinking to the nether levels, while bubbles float up. Getting out, choosing her path, she will proceed a distance and dig into a pile of humus, thrusting herself to the coolest layer at the bottom. The hole closes over her until it's as small as a mouse's hole. She's not as aquatic as a musk turtle, not quite as terrestrial as the box turtles in the same woods, but because of her versatility she's marvelous, she's everywhere. And though she breathes the way we breathe, with scarcely perceptible movements of her chest, sometimes instead she pumps her throat ruminatively, like a pipe smoker sucking and puffing. She waits and blinks, pumping her throat, turning her head, then sets off like a loping tiger in slow motion, hurdling the jungly lumber, the pea vine and twigs. She estimates angles so well that when she rides over the rocks, sliding down a drop-off with her rugged front legs extended, she has the grace of a rodeo mare.

But she's well off to be with me rather than at Mud Pond. The other turtles have fled—those that aren't baked into the bottom. Creeping up the brooks to sad, constricted marshes, burdened as they are with that box on their backs, they're walking into a setup where all their enemies move thirty times faster than they. It's like the nightmare most of us have whimpered through, where we are weighted down disastrously while trying to flee; fleeing our home ground, we try to run.

I've seen turtles in still worse straits. On Broadway, in New York, there is a penny arcade which used to sell baby terrapins that were scrawled with bon mots in enamel paint, such as KISS ME BABY. The manager turned out to be a wholesaler as well, and once I asked him whether he had any larger turtles to sell. He took me upstairs to a loft room devoted to the turtle business. There were desks for the paper work and a series of racks that held shallow tin bins atop one another, each with several hundred babies crawling around in it. He was a smudgy-complexioned, bespectacled, serious fellow and he did have a few adult terrapins, but I was going to school and wasn't actually planning to buy; I'd only wanted to see them. They were aquatic turtles, but here they went without water, presumably for weeks, lurching about in those dry bins like handicapped citizens, living on gumption. An easel where the artist worked stood in the middle of the floor. She had a palette and a clip attachment for fastening the babies in place. She wore a smock and a beret, and was homely, short, and eccentric-looking, with funny black hair, like some of the ladies who show their paintings in Washington Square in May. She had a cold, she was smoking, and her hand wasn't very steady, although she worked quickly enough. The smile that she produced for me would have looked giddy if she had been happier, or drunk. Of course the turtles' doom was sealed when she painted them, because their bodies inside would continue to grow but their shells would not. Gradually, invisibly, they would be crushed. Around us their bellies—two thousand belly shells—rubbed on the bins with a mournful, momentous hiss.

Somehow there were so many of them I didn't rescue one. Years later, however, I was walking on First Avenue when I noticed a basket of living turtles in front of a fish store. They were as dry as a heap of old bones in the sun; nevertheless, they were creeping over one another gimpily, doing their best to escape. I looked and was touched to discover that they appeared to be wood turtles, my favorites, so I bought one. In my apartment I looked closer and realized that in fact this was a diamondback terrapin, which was bad news. Diamondbacks are tidewater turtles from brackish estuaries, and I had no seawater to keep him in. He spent his days thumping interminably against the baseboards, pushing for an opening through the wall. He drank thirstily but would not eat and had none of the hearty, accepting qualities of wood turtles. He was morose, paler in color, sleeker and more Oriental in the carved ridges and rings that formed his shell. Though I felt sorry for him, finally I found his unrelenting presence exasperating. I carried him, struggling in a paper bag, across town to the Morton Street Pier on the Hudson River. It was August but gray and windy. He was very surprised when I tossed him in; for the first time in our association, I think, he was afraid. He looked afraid as he bobbed about on top of the water, looking up at me from ten feet below. Though we were both accustomed to his resistance and rigidity, seeing him still pitiful, I recognized that I must have done the wrong thing. At least the river was salty, but it was also bottomless; the waves were too rough for him, and the tide was coming in, bumping him against the pilings underneath the pier. Too late, I realized that he wouldn't be able to swim to a peaceful inlet in New Jersey, even if he could figure out which way to swim. But since, short of diving in after him, there was nothing I could do, I walked away.

Home
Is Two Places

Things are worse than many of us are admitting. I'm a brassbound optimist by habit—I'm an optimist in the same way that I am right-handed, and will always be. It's simpler to be an optimist and it's a sensible defense against the uncertainties and abysses which otherwise confront us prematurely—we can die a dozen deaths and then usually we find that the outcome is not one we predicted, neither so "bad" nor so "good," but one we hadn't taken into consideration. In an election, though, for instance, where it's only a question of No. 1 or No. 2, I confidently assume that whoever seems to be the better fellow is going to win. When sometimes he doesn't, I begin to feel quite sure that perhaps the other man, now in a position of responsibility, will shift around to views much closer to my own. If this doesn't occur either, then I fall back on my fuzzy but rooted belief that people of opposed opinions at least do share the quality of good-heartedness, of wanting good things to happen, and so events finally will work out for the best.

The trouble is that they're not working out for the best. Even the cheerfully inveterate sardonicists, whose chirpy pessimism is an affirmation of sorts, are growing dispirited and alarmed. And it's not just the liberals; the unease emanates from everybody, Republicans and Christian Scientists—the lapel buttons and bumper stickers and decal figures imply a kind of general clamming-up, a sense of being beleaguered, maybe a panic at the great numbers of people we each pass in a single day—this with the hardening of sects of opinion which have despaired of conversing with one another but only holler out code words and threats. Many people think about finding some peaceful holing-up spot, which may be in the suburbs, or if the individual has already opted for the suburbs, may be up toward Mount Katahdin. As soon as he can afford it he starts wanting a second home, a place to recuperate from the place where he lives while he works, and though it used to be that such a home was frankly a luxury, now nearly everybody who makes a middle-class living starts to think about buying a cottage in the woods or a boat at the shore, if just for the sake of his health. The thirty-hour week, so heralded, may mean three hard ten-hour days of work in the city and then a fast retreat for everybody (in shifts) to what will pass for "the country" in twenty years, there to lead the leisure life, building canoes and greenhouses and picket fences.

I grew up in the suburbs. My father left for New York City every weekday morning and got home about 7:00 P.M. The commuting was grueling and he liked a change of scene on his vacations in later years, but we didn't need to have a country cottage, since we saw deer in the evening and grew a Victory Garden during the war; there was a feed store in town, painted with checkerboards, where the local farmers talked about chicken diseases and trapping weasels. A man named Frank Weed trained pheasant dogs professionally, and my sister when she was growing up went across the road and watched a calf born every spring. Both she and I spent part of our childhoods developing a special sympathy for the animal personality. There was a magical fullness to my perceptions when I was with my dogs, a heat-lightning shiver and speed, quicker than words. Of course to rule is a pleasure, and yet as happiness, as intimacy, these interludes are not to be dismissed, and the experience of sensing other wavelengths in the world besides the human gabble needs woods and fields and isn't found as easily now.

The out-of-doors was everything to me. I spent the summer mornings on Miss Walker's big estate, vaulting the brooks, climbing the pines, creeping along the rabbit paths. Then I made lemonade for the afternoon heat wave and lay on the screen porch listening to Mel Allen broadcast the Yankee game. There'd be a thunderstorm and I would lie in the backyard for that, watching the black clouds brew, feeling the wind. Soaked, grinning, I'd go and sit inside the chicken coop for the clubbiness of the chickens, whose pecking order I knew all about. Later I traveled to prep school carrying my alligators wrapped in a blanket to protect them from the cold. But I loved Tommy Henrich too; I was a hero-worshiper. And at night, when I was jittery, I returned to the city, where I'd lived earlier; in the most frequent dream I jumped off the Empire State Building and flew with uneven success between the skyscrapers by flapping my arms. Winters were spent in galoshes, fooling on the schoolbus. Those bus rides were the best part of the day; we had no teacher accompanying us and the driver put up with anything. There was a boy who kept a Ford Model A to tinker with when he got home; another was the quarterback who won our football games; another the school mathematician or "brain." The mechanic has since turned into a clergyman, the quarterback works humbly for General Electric, the mathematician is mad. One nondescript goof-off has made a million dollars, and his chum of the period is a social worker with addicts. Of my own friends, the precocious radical has become a stockbroker and the knockabout juvenile delinquent journeys now in Africa. The same sea changes seem to have affected even the houses that I knew. Mrs. Holcomb's, where I took piano lessons, is now the Red Cross Headquarters; Dr. Ludlow's, where I went for inoculations, has become the town museum. Miss Walker's woodsy acres are the Nature Study Center, and the farm where my sister watched the calves born—Mr. Hulendorf's—has been subdivided into a deluxe set of hutches called Historic Homes.

Wherever, whoever we were, we've been squeezed out of the haunts of our childhood, and there is no reason why we shouldn't have been. The question is only whether we are gradually being squeezed out of all possible homes. To the fear of dying of the ailments that killed our fathers, of angina or driving badly, we have an added, overlying trepidation that life may be shortened anyway for all of us. Old age seems not to exist as a possibility culturally, in any case, and the generalized future seems incomprehensible—exploding, crazily variant developments to be fitted together. The more successful and propulsive a man of affairs is, the more freckled and browned he usually looks, so that when he finally folds up in exhaustion, he must correspond to a tree which has turned to punk inside the bark invisibly and which suddenly crumbles. Aging used to be a slow process involving wasting less and less of one's energy as well as having less energy, and so, for a long while at least, the pleasure in one's increased effectiveness just about balanced the sadness of winding down. And as a man lost some of his youthful idealism, he lost, too, some of the brutality that goes along with being young: a balance was maintained there also. Now he's either young or on the shelf, and if he's on the shelf he's savage.

When my father was dying I had a dream which amounts to a first memory, brought up intact like some frozen fossil which the ice has preserved. I was diapered, lying on my back in his hands, well before I could talk. By comparing my size in his hands to my daughter's right now I would guess that I was about ten months old. I was struggling, kicking, and he was dandling me, blowing in my ear, a sensation too ticklish, too delicious to bear.

Squealing, powerless to prevent his doing it, I loved it, though at the same time I was dependent upon him to stop before it became excruciating—I was waving my arms in the air trying to protect my ears. But the best, vividest piece of the memory is the whirring, vital presence of my father, with deep eyes and a humming voice, in the prime of life; I remember his strong hands. Even his early baldness seemed to add to his vigor because it made for more area of skin. He was several years younger than I am now, and so the continuity of seeing him then and myself now, and seeing him die, is startling.

This memory feeds on to the pinpoint events of a train wreck in Nebraska a year later, and to the familiar jumble of childhood. During the Depression we lived in the city; there were singers at the bottom of the air shaft whom the maid and I threw dimes down to, wrapped in toilet paper so that they wouldn't bounce too far. I pulled the bow of her apron twenty times a day to tease her, and she took me to Catholic church, whose mysteries I remember better than the inside of our church, though once recently when I was hurrying along Lexington Avenue I was brought up short by the sight of a mnemonic worn brick wall that shook me: Sunday school. My parents reappeared in youthful roles, and I could remember something about that whole extraordinary masquerade which one plays as a child—pretending to learn to read, as if we didn't know already, pretending to learn to tell the time, as if we hadn't known all about clocks for years and years.

My father was a financial lawyer. At first I went to an English-type school called St. Bernard's and to birthday parties at the St. Regis Hotel. I remember, too, watching King George pass in a cavalcade on Fifth Avenue from a dowager's wide windows. But Eisenhower, another wartime eminence whom I saw feted from those windows, represents much better my father's style. The side of Eisenhower that wasn't glamorous like Clark Gable resembled my father—the grin, the Kansas accent, the Middlewestern forehead, the level-headed calmness or caution, the sanguine and good-tempered informality. Each was a poor-boy democrat and a Republican; each stood out for rural, old-time values, though personally preferring to hang out at the golf club with industrialists; each was softer in manner than the average soldier or lawyer; and each had a Chinese face lurking behind the prosaic American bones which materialized inchmeal as he aged and died. My father worked in Eisenhower's administration, and Ike was the president he most approved of—an internationalist abroad, a gentle-minded conservative on the home front, who started, however, from the assumption that most people deserved to be liked.

Once when my father was leaving a Mario Lanza movie he stopped to hear one last aria again, and collapsed with emotion on the floor of the theater when it ended. And, if he hadn't much sense of humor (or it came hard to him), he laughed a lot, loudly, every chance he had. He thought that exercise, music and friends were the cure for mental illness: in other words, it terrified him. He thought homosexuality "sinister" on the occasions when he recognized it, and never drank much, and probably was sexually faithful, although I think he fooled himself about the nature of certain avuncular relationships he had; when one young woman married he tore her honeymoon picture in half. But his marriage wasn't unhappy. Quite often he ended his friendships with men who got divorced on what he considered frivolous grounds; he didn't swear or like swearing, although he liked vitality and a masculine air in his friends. He had the chest of a track man and may have read more passionately as a man of sixty than as a college boy, which is unusual—he was especially partial to translated classics and to looking at Renaissance art. Mother married him partly because of his idealism, she says, though naturally I didn't think him idealistic at all. I even went to a different barber in town as a means of delineating the difference between us. Mine was the Town Barbershop, which had *Liberty* magazine beside the chairs and a proprietor nearly eighty years old, wonderfully wiry and tall, with black hair, knotted hands and a sharp nose. For the many years I went to him he knew me as "Peter"—in the beginning I'd been too shy to set him straight. The Colonial Barbershop, which my father patronized, did a smoother job, and the owner, who was a worldly man, tried at one point to break out into the wholesale barbering-supply business but went bankrupt and soon was right back in the local shop. After that, he spent his weekends in New York, wandering reflectively among the skyscrapers, musing on the enigmas of fortune and wealth.

My father was battling for advancement at the same time, trying to rise from the position of a hired attorney to a directorship in the oil corporation he worked for. He wasn't an original type or a sparkplug—he seemed awfully meticulous—and so he lost. He went into retirement angry, though several offers came his way thereafter, such as to go to Hong Kong as consul or head a graduate school. Instead he drifted, wrote poetry, and went to Kyoto. When the World's Fair played on Long Island he drove out and roamed the cheerful pavilions, scanning the Midwestern faces, delighted by the accents, reminded of his boyhood; like the fair itself, he was hopeful. In manner, he was so deliberate some of the other commuters had called him Speed, and yet late in his life he traveled round the world, pulling my mother after him when her enthusiasm waned. He returned to Rome and Paris ten or twelve times, and he loved Florence—nothing that a thousand other men don't do but with as much intensity as any. Dutch Reform by background, he shifted towards agnosticism in middle age, joining the Episcopal Church as a form of neutralism. He liked to sail, sailed rather daringly, not with the caution that exasperated some business associates. He sent money to relatives who had hard rows to hoe and liked uninfluential people as well as the strong. For instance, when I was a boy he made me aware of a fellow at the oil company whose function was to meet transatlantic ships and speed the debarking of company bigwigs and guests—a tall, prudent, intelligent-looking man of mature years whom one would see standing among the crowd of passengers' relatives and friends as the ship docked. Noticeable for his banker's dress and for his height, he would step forward through the multitude and fix upon the personage he was supposed to meet (I suppose he studied photographs), bring over a Customs man, somehow accelerate the inspection, get porters, flag down a taxi, and see the mogul whisked away before most of the passengers were even off the boat. My father was touched by his plight.

When it was possible to procrastinate, my father did so, being a dreamy man, but he was decisive at the end. He went for a sail alone overnight in his little sloop before turning himself in, exhausted, to the doctor, with cancer signals, and while he was waiting to die, still ambulatory, he journeyed to Sarasota with my mother. She could scarcely get him to leave before it was too late for him to go under his own power, but then he settled into the house in Connecticut for the last siege with gallantry and gaiety, so that the big busty nurse, accustomed though she was to seeing men die, actually fell in love with him and became inconsolable. He enjoyed the ripening spring weather, the phonograph, the house he loved, and kept hold of his self-command (what, after all, can one do with one's time in those last weeks except to be friendly?). He talked on the telephone, blinked in the brightening sun—to overhear him in the final conversations he had with friends was piercing. And he did want the Church to fulfill its appointed duties, so when a cub minister was sent to visit him he wasn't satisfied with the small talk they were able to muster. Then an old senior minister, a tippler with a crumpled face, came and told him that he faced "a great adventure," which he accepted as being probably about as good a construction as anybody was going to be able to put on it. My mother saw horses with blowing manes climbing the sky for weeks after he died.

If we are to contrive to lead two lives now, one in the city and one near Katahdin, we can draw some quick assurance from the fact that our backgrounds individually are even more diverse than that. I've got millers, tailors, and outdoorsmen in mine, real outdoorsmen to whom the summer soldiers' Katahdin would be a tasty canapé. Though the two names, Morley and Hoagland, fit together neatly for me because I'm so used to them, the families—my mother's and father's—stretch back in complicated, quite disparate fashion, the Hoaglands to early Brooklyn; later they lived in New Jersey. They came out badly in the Revolutionary War—the branch of them I know about. A skirmish with the British a few minutes' walk from their farm put several of them out of commission for the rest of their lives. The ones who weren't too demoralized moved west and south shortly afterwards to Lexington, Kentucky, where they did fairly well, except that again my own ancestors after a generation or so migrated on by boat and wagon to the farming country of Bardolph, Illinois, where they spent the Civil War. One who had marched with Sherman creaked on from Bardolph by wagon to Hutchinson, Kansas, where he farmed a Soldier's Land Claim, kept a hotel, and worked with team and wagon on the construction of the Santa Fe Railroad, and wound up as the county agricultural agent and a Freemason. Though there were proud Eastern Hoaglands who belonged to the upper crust, and other Hoaglands who split away to seek lonelier, unknown destinies, most of my branch of the family were farmers consistently for two or three hundred years, right back to Brooklyn, and they appear to have filtered away into the soil finally, or else to have wound up in Los Angeles with the rest of the prairie farmers who scraped together a few thousand dollars, there joining the middling middle class.

One early pale fellow loyally fought cholera in the Kentucky epidemic of 1823, dying at his post, and my grandfather, who was a doctor too, died abruptly of meningitis in the 1930s after a bumpy career, mostly practicing obstetrics in Kansas City. He was a husky-faced, square-set man with a red complexion, certainly a kindly doctor, but he found it hard to make a living and for several interludes went down to the bayou lumber camps in Louisiana to work as a company physician. His oldest child died of a fever on one of these tours of duty; his youngest died in his arms after being hit by a trolley a little bit later. His wife, too, died young. I have the impression that his happiest years were while he was in the

Medical Corps during the First World War. He and my father got along quite well, and my father, despite his successes and travels later on, would have gone to the state university and presumably stayed in Kansas City if at the last minute he hadn't noticed a scholarship competition for Yale on his school's bulletin board. Being a lawyer and the son of a doctor, he thought of us as a family of professionals and hoped that I would enter one of the professions—if not either of those, then what he called "the cloth"—rather than be a businessman. When I wound up a writer he was utterly taken by surprise.

The Morleys, by contrast, were merchants instead of farmers for as far back as I am aware. They arrived in the New World after the Hoaglands did, and whatever matters they applied themselves to when they first got off the boat, they were in upstate New York for a while before settling in Painesville, Ohio, in the nineteenth century. The Morley burial plot is still in Painesville, along with a rambling white house with long porches and a poppy and gentian field in the rear—a sort of family "seat," which the Hoaglands lack. It was partly the Morleys' clannishness that put me off them when I was a boy. By 1900 they were worthy people with fat family businesses, big family weddings—the marriages were patriarchal; none of your warlike American ladies there—and they kept right on flourishing, until by the time Franklin D. Roosevelt campaigned through town, some of them wouldn't even walk down to the railroad depot just to set eyes on the man. Since I'd been brought up among the comforts my father's breadwinning had earned, these shrewd breadwinning businessmen from Painesville, and Saginaw, Michigan, and Aberdeen, Washington, seemed like vaguely unsavory bores to me. The family dinners, occurring whenever there was a visit, intimidated me; the questioning was bluff, immediate and intimate, as if blood were thicker than water. Yet I remember that when my great-uncle Ralph came east for the last time, knowing he was soon to die, he rented his suite at the Biltmore, invited my father up, and spent that last interview with us reading aloud with relish the notebook notations he kept in an inside pocket of what his stock-market portfolio was. My father, who had nothing to do with handling the Morleys' money, was astonished. This stingy or mercenary quality afflicting many of the Morleys is in me also, but they were a florid, varied crew whom a less Protestant person than myself would have found fascinating from the start, and next to whom we of the present tribe are insipid fellows. The Morleys are following the Hoaglands into modest extinction, part of the Johnny Carson family.

My mother's family's pride and principal vocation during the time between the two world wars was Morley Bros., a department store and statewide hardware dealership located in Saginaw. Before opening that, her grandfather had had a saddlery business in Chicago, after leaving Painesville as a young man. While getting his Chicago operation going, he married a packinghouse heiress, a Kelley (the family had sold out to Armour). Later, in Saginaw, he founded a bank as a kind of a sideline. Banking intrigued him, but during the 1929 boom he sold the bank to a big Detroit bank that was looking for mergers. He happened to be in New York City on a business trip in October during the first black days of the Crash. Realizing the seriousness of the situation, realizing that the Detroit bank was overcommitted and might have to close, he hated to think of his own town's bank collapsing along with it, and so he caught a Pullman home. The panic was spreading west, the officers in Detroit already saw the handwriting on the wall, and hurrying to rally the help of a few other Saginaw citizens, he was able to buy back the bank and save it, in a fine hour. Banks were still a centerpiece in the post-Victorian era and banks do figure on this side of my family; this same ancestor's daughter-in-law, my grandmother, had grown up in Homer, New York, the child of the local bank president. But they'd had to sneak out of town in sudden disgrace during the 1893 Panic when their bank failed. Her father's health foundered in the aftermath; he died, and she weathered some very hard years.

At any rate, Morley Bros. prospered. My great-grandfather toured the world with his beautiful chestnut-haired Kelley, leaving Ralph in charge of the Saginaw business and A. J., my grandfather, based in Chicago running the older saddlery firm. There were two other brothers, Walter and Paul. Paul was a Peter Pan type who loved combing my mother's hair when she was a young girl (it was the Kelley hair). An aesthete and idealist, he hobnobbed with landscape painters and portrait artists and married a girl of nineteen who was so very demure and Alice-like that she proved to be feeble-minded. He died at only forty-six, welcoming death, so it is said, and leaving behind five blighted children who suffered from Saint Vitus' dance, and worse. Walter, a more earthly man, was a gambler and womanizer, a failed writer, and, later in life, a Presbyterian minister, who lived in relative poverty, exiled by his father to the Wisconsin woods after some early miscues. However, Walter was the first of the Morleys to venture out to the state of Washington. He got mixed up in some kind of woman scandal and went badly into debt to the sawmill promoters of Aberdeen, and A. J. was sent west to buy them off. After Walter had been extricated, though, A. J. went to work investing in timber himself. Bored with Chicago saddlery, he became a pioneer businessman in the Gray's Harbor woods. When his first wife died in childbirth, he married my grandmother, whom he met in a tiny town where she was schoolteaching and where he'd missed his train. Soon he had three trains of his own for hauling logs, and a house on the hill, a yacht, a mistress in downtown Aberdeen (also a schoolmarm, oddly enough), a burro for his children and a black manservant, Tom. Land that he bought for seven thousand dollars and logged was sold recently for three million dollars. He was a careful, decent man with no archenemies, although he fought the Wobblies, and he and Ralph had pleasing sons. Both he and Ralph partook of the Morleys' honest but griping conservatism about money, which ultimately prevented them from getting big-time. Back in Michigan, Ralph turned down a neighbor named Henry Ford who wanted him to invest in a motorcar company, while out in Aberdeen a decade or two later A. J. declined the chance to buy into a new corporation called Boeing. His eldest boy had been killed by a falling tree, but he and his other two sons put their resources into timberland in the Oregon Coast Range instead. One was a financial man, at ease with the business community in Portland; the other, silver-haired before his mid-thirties, could deal with the loggers and union men and drove around through the mountains all day in his pickup truck. Unfortunately, the financial son dropped dead in church in his early fifties. Immediately the hard-nosed investors in Saginaw got scared that my silver-haired uncle would not be able to manage the business alone, and they made him sell out. He did enlist the women in the family, who were also stockholders, to help him stave them off when it came to a vote until he'd delayed long enough to get the proper price.

There is much to the Morleys that I don't know about and much to be said for them. Two women of Northern persuasion wrote action-filled, observant diaries during the Civil War, for instance—all about guerrillas and the battlefronts along the Mississippi. But for a long time, certainly throughout my teens, it was my wish to start from scratch and make my own way in the world without the help of relatives. The Morleys were always boosting each other, some were slightly Babbitt-like, and they assumed, aggravatingly, that any relative was fair game for their gregariousness. Besides, my socialist sentiments leaned more toward the Hoaglands on their dirt farms—they were pleasingly faceless to me, the few I'd seen having just been the Los Angeles transplants. Of course I'd traveled through enough Kansas farming communities to know how little tolerance people there would show for an oddball like me if they perceived my true colors. So, glad to let them remain faceless, I simply liked to think of myself as anchored—in theory, at least—in the heartland, in the Wheat Belt.

Lately it's become the rage to ridicule young 1960s radicals from middle-class backgrounds who pretend to themselves that they are black or are blue-collar, when actually all they need to do if things get tough is reach a telephone to raise bail money or be invited home. The ridicule has been a political weapon because what most bothers people about these young persons is their accomplishment in challenging the nation's stance. I was in their shoes in the 1950s, and we weren't challenging anybody successfully; we kept our heads down, lived privately, and we were few and far between; perhaps the troubles of the present time may owe a little something to our ineffectuality. But like these activists, I'm sure, I was aware of the inconsistencies in my own position—being only too eager to give my parents' suburban address to officialdom if I edged into a jam instead of my grubby Lower East Side street number. Despite the inconsistencies, it seemed to me then that I had the choice of either going out in the world and seeing what was foreign and maybe wretched, having experiences which were not strictly necessary in my case, and *caring*, however uselessly, or else of spending my summer on the tennis courts and terrace at the country club, as some of my schoolmates were doing. The head start they supposed they had on people born into different surroundings has often proved illusory, and anyway the effort to make a beginning on independent lines, not piggyback on one's father's achievements, seemed admirable, even traditional, in America until recently. It's just lately, with the exasperated warfare between the generations, that attempting to make a new start for oneself is ridiculed.

Apart from the fuss of being political, the reasons why I was so agitated as a youngster, so angry at my parents that it amounted to a fury lasting for weeks on end, are difficult to reconstruct; I was a bunch of nerves. My mother, who besides being impulsive and generous was a strangely warm woman at times, would ask me to eat dinner without my glasses on so she could look at my uncluttered face, and tried to insist that I move down from the third floor to the room next to hers. Sometimes after my father and I had had a conciliatory talk, she'd give me a quite opposite report of what he thought, or thought of me, as though to revive the quarrel. Later, in my twenties, looking back, my chief complaint against him was that he hadn't shielded me from some of her eccentric whims and decisions; yet I'd fought with him rather than her, especially when I was in earnest. She was my cohort, guiding me most directly, and now, when I put first things first and respond quickly to the moment, it's her influence. What I learned from him was not the Boerlike sobriety and self-denial he espoused but the qualities that I saw for myself: his gentleness and slow-tempoed soft gaiety, his equanimity under pressure. I liked the way he ate too; he ate like a gourmet whenever he could.

Although I would have been willing to ignore most facets of the life of the town where I grew up, luckily it wasn't possible for me to do that. So I have the many loose-leaf memories a hometown is supposed to provide—of the Kane children, whose father was a gardener and who threw jackknives at trees whenever they were mad, which, living as they did in other people's garages, was a good deal of the time; of setter field trials and local football; of woebegone neighbors and abrupt marital puzzles—a wife who rejoiced when her husband died and buried him before his friends knew there was going to be a funeral. There were some advertising people so rich that they lived in one large house by themselves and kept their children in another a hundred yards away. There was a young architect struck into stone with polio, and a lady who collected impoverished nobles in Italy after the war and whose husband, left sick at home, made the maid disrobe at gunpoint when he finally got lonely. On the dark roads after supper you'd see more than one commuter taking a determined-looking constitutional, walking fast for miles, as if to get his emotions under control.

After my father's death we sold our house and set about looking for new places to consider home, not an easy task. The memory was of twenty rooms, artesian water, a shady lawn, a little orchard and many majestic maples and spruce, all situated where an old crossroads stagecoach inn had stood. None of us came up with an arrangement to equal that, but my mother has a trim pretty house on Martha's Vineyard. My sister married and, with her husband, found a farmhouse in Connecticut near his work with five or six acres on which she put ten horses, in order to start a riding stable. These were snake-necked, branded horses that they'd brought in a van from California, right off the range, with a long winter's growth of hair. The neighbors, who believed that life ought to have a dual, contemporary character, rushed to the zoning board to express dismay that in a fast-developing, year-round community the regulations hadn't yet been revised to bar such activities, which seemed more appropriate to a *summer* home. They were right to think it surprising, and yet the board was awfully reluctant to declare once and for all, officially, that the era of farms and barns had ended.

I married too and live in western Greenwich Village, which is an ungeometric district of architecture in a smorgasbord and little stores. There is a massive wholesale meat market in the neighborhood, a gypsy moving industry, many printing plants and bakeries, a trading center for antiques, a dozen ocean-oriented wharves, and four or five hundred mysterious-looking enterprises in lofts, each of which could either be a cover for the Federal Narcotics Bureau or house an inventor-at-work. I like the variety (the mounted police have a stable two blocks away, the spice industry's warehouses are not far south); I like the low nineteenth-century houses alongside bars with rock jukeboxes and all the swoosh of à la mode. The pull or the necessity of living in the city seems only to grow stronger as every sort of development is telescoped into a briefer span of time. We can either live in our own period or decline to, and to decline revokes many other choices we might have. Mostly what we try to do is live with one foot in the seventies and one foot in an earlier decade—the foot that doesn't mind going to sleep and maybe missing something.

I've just bought a house of my own in Vermont, eight rooms with a steel roof, all painted a witching green. It's two miles from the nearest light pole and it was cheap, but it's got forty acres, extending in a diamond shape, that back up to five thousand acres of state-owned land, and stands in a basin just underneath the western-style peak of a stiff little mountain, Wheeler Mountain, that curves around in front. The Wheelers, our only neighbors, live next door on a three-hundred-acre farm, growing up in aspen, balsam, birch, and pine, just as our land is. Mr. Wheeler, in his eighties now, was a fireman on the Grand Trunk Railroad for much of his life but grew up here and returned during the Depression. His father had pioneered the land; the Butterfields pioneered mine. The Butterfields built a log house close to that of old Mr. Wheeler, for whom Mr. Butterfield worked. There was a sawmill, a sugar house, and even a granite quarry on Wheeler's place. The log house was really more like a root house than living quarters, to judge from the photograph we have, so in 1900 Mr. Butterfield and his three sons built this new home out of sawn spruce and big granite foundation blocks and plaster mixed from sand from the Boiling Spring over the hill. Their lame old horse did the hauling and pulled the scoop when they dug out the cellar hole, and young Wheeler, a schoolboy then, helped nail the laths.

Butterfield was a rough character, he says, "part Indian," as the phrase goes, but you could depend on him to do a job. His mother-in-law lived with the family, constantly fighting with him. She called him dumb and crude because he couldn't do sums, for instance; she wrote a column of numbers on the wall and watched him fail to add it. About 1909 he shot her, took his remaining relatives next door for refuge, and shot himself. There are bullet holes, stopped up with putty, and it is claimed that that nagging column of numbers on the parlor wall had finally been added correctly. Newspaper reporters buzzed around, the property soon passed to the Stanley family, and Burt Stanley, who was a stonemason, farmed it in his spare time until his death in the 1930s. Then a tax bill of thirteen dollars came due. His widow, Della, was unable to pay it (some say she paid it but got no receipt), so the town tax collector, a fellow named Byron Bundy, foreclosed and sold her home to a crony of his named Gray, who quickly reconveyed the place to Bundy himself. Bundy died, the house stood empty through World War II (the porcupines chewing away like carpenters at the corners and edges), and his heirs sold it to our predecessors at a joke of a price.

So I'm getting a grip on the ground, in other words—gathering the stories of what went on and poking in the woods. It's certainly not an onerous chore; I've explored so many wood lots which *weren't* mine. Up among the mountain ledges is a cave as big as a band concert shell, and a narrow unexpected swamp with pitcher plants growing in it, very lush, a spring that springs out of a rock, and a huge ash sheltered in a hollow which has disguised its height and kept the loggers and the lightning off. Not far away is a whetstone ledge where a little businesslike mining used to be done. And there are ravens, bats, barred owls, a hawk or two, phoebes under the eaves, and tales of big bears in the pasture and of somebody being cornered by a bull. Delphiniums, mint, lemon lilies, catnip, wild roses, and marigolds grow next to the house. Storer's snakes live in the woodpile, as well as garter snakes, brick-colored and black. In the spring dogtooth violets come up, and trilliums, Dutchman's-breeches, boxflowers, foamflowers, and lady's slippers, and in the fall the fields fill up with goldenrod and brown-eyed Susans, aster, fireweed. Raspberries grow in masses; also blackberries, blueberries, wild cherries and wild plums. The apple orchard is complicated in its plotting, because these farmers wanted apples in late summer—Dutch apples, Yellow Transparents, and McIntosh—and then another set of trees which ripened in the autumn, perhaps Baldwins or Northern Spies, and lastly the hard winter apples, which weren't sweet and which they canned or cooked as applesauce or "sulphured" to keep till spring. An orchard was a man's bequest to his children, being something that they couldn't promptly create for themselves when the land passed to them. I've got more going on that hill slope of apple trees than I know about, and when the fruit falls finally, the deer and

bears eat it—the bears when they have grown impatient waiting
have bashed down whole limbs.

In New York my home *is* New York; nothing less than the city
itself is worth the abrasion of living there, and the alterations go
on so fast that favorite hangouts go by the boards in a month's
time; the stream of people and sensation is the thing. But in the
country the one word is exactitude. If you don't like the barn
behind the house and the slant of the land and the trees that you
face, then you're not going to be happy. The Canadian climate of
north Vermont makes for an ideal second home because in four
months three seasons can be witnessed. June is spring, September
already is autumn. The moonlight is wheat-colored in August, and
the mountain rises with protean gradualism to a taciturn round
peak. On the east face is a wall which, if you walk around that
way, can look to be nine thousand feet; the granite turns ice-white.
The trees puff in the moonlight to swirling, steeplish shapes, or
look like ferns. During the day sometimes a fog will effect the same
exaggerated trick. High up, the wind blows harder, gnarling the
spruce and bringing clouds swiftly across like those in the high
Rockies; you seldom have a sense of just what altitude you're at.
Every winter the deer yard under the cliffs in a cedar copse, and
on the opposite side, the valley behind the hill that lies behind the
Wheelers' house and mine has never been farmed and is so big it is
called Big Valley. Vast and thick with trees, it's like an inlet of the
sea, sending off a sheen in midsummer as you look down on it.

Mr. Wheeler, the youngest in his family, went to school with
the Butterfield children in what is now the Wheelers' house, re-
modeled and enlarged. He is a broad-shouldered, white-faced man,
a machinist at one point, until the dust bothered his lungs. Now
he tinkers with his tractor and the power mower, listening to the
Red Sox games, although the only professional baseball he ever
saw was when he lived in Montreal during the early 1920s. He's a
serene, bold man who has survived heart trouble and diabetes and
says little but appears full of cheer even when he's angry. Mrs.
Wheeler is a dignified, straight-backed woman, quite a reader,
and formerly a psychiatric nurse. She once wrote a column for the
county newspaper, and used to brew a thousand pounds of cottage
cheese during the summer and peddle it among the vacationers,
along with strawberries, butter, and cream. She keeps a diary and
a record of the visitors who come to climb the mountain that we
look at, and keeps a calorie count of what her husband eats. She is
his second wife, ten years younger. They have a walkie-talkie for
communication with the world outside, and extra stocks of food,
and a 280-gallon tank of kerosene for heating, so that the snows

don't threaten them. The road plugs up but eventually it's plowed; the snow in the fields gets five feet deep and lasts so long "it mosses over—you always get six weeks of March." Being a vigorous walker still, Mrs. Wheeler is even less intimidated than her husband, and in the country style is reticently generous, as realistic as a nurse and farmer's wife combined.

In the old days there was a local man who could run down the deer and knife them, he had such endurance—he could keep up with their first dash, and as they porpoised through the woods, could keep going longer than they could. He hung the meat in a tree by his cabin to freeze, and liked raccoons particularly also, so that by midwinter the tree was strung with upwards of thirty raccoons, skinned and dressed, suspended like white pineapples. Another character, whose complexion was silver-colored, made a regual business out of bountying porcupines. The town paid fifty cents per pair of ears, and sometimes he brought in a hundred pairs. He claimed he had a super-hunting-dog, but actually he was cutting out triangular snips of stomach skin to make a dozen "porcupines" for every one he killed. He didn't do enough real work to break the Sabbath, as they say, and didn't lay in hay enough to last his cattle through the winter, so that by the end of February he would be dragging birch trees to the barn for them to scrape a living from. For spending money, he gave boxing lessons at night in the waiting room of the old railroad station at the foot of the hill. Roy Lord, who lives across from where the station was, learned to box from him. Lord has shot seventy-three deer in his lifetime. He lives with a sneezing parrot fifty-six years old, and a bull terrier who lost an eye in a fight in the driveway; he points out the spot where the eye fell. He can recite the details of the murders and suicides in the neighborhood going back forty years— all the fights with fenceposts, all the dirty cheating deals and sudden strange inheritances. He's learned the secrets of more than one suspicious death because he's made it a point over the years to get right to the scene, sometimes even before the police. Or they'd be gathering reinforcements, distributing riot guns, and radioing for instructions in front of the house, while Lord would sneak around to the back door and pop inside and see the way the brains were sprayed and where the body lay and where the gun was propped, and damn well *know* it wasn't suicide. There was a family of Indians here, who'd murdered somebody in Canada and buried him in their cellar and moved across the border. They slept on a pile of old buffalo robes laid on the floor. The daughter, a half-breed, went back into the woods in a fit of despondency and found a cliff and jumped. Then when the men had died as well, the last of them, a white-haired old woman, stretched out on the railroad tracks with her neck on a rail and ended it that way. (Lord tells these stories while watching the TV—sheriffs slugging baddies and bouncers punching drunks. His son was a sniper in the Pacific theater, stalking the Japanese like deer; is now a quiet bachelor who works in Massachusetts, driving home weekends.)

I'm transplanting some spruce and beginning to clear my upper field of striped maple and arctic birch. I'm also refashioning a chicken coop to serve as a playhouse when our baby is four or five. The barn is sturdy, moderate-sized, unpainted, built with used planking fifteen years ago. Although the place where I grew up probably had a better barn, I took that one for granted. Now I stand in my own barn and look up at the joists and rafters, the beams under the hayloft, the king posts, struts, and studding, the slabs of wood nailed angularly for extra strength. It's all in the same pattern as the other barns in town, and yet I marvel at it. The junk inside consists of whiffle trees, neck yokes and harness, a tractor and a harrow, neither functional, and painters' ladders, milking stools, and broken stanchions. In the attic in the house are smaller memorabilia, like fox and beaver traps, deer antlers and tobacco cans of clean deer lard, an old grindstone, an old bedpan, a pair of high green boots, a pile of *Reader's Digest*s, which when matched with our assorted miscellany and childhood books, stacked up, and different boxes of letters and snapshots (snapshots of the prairie Hoaglands seventy years ago, posed in joky insouciance—Hoaglands who would have felt at home here), will be the attic our daughter grows up to know.

Freight trains hoot through town; there is a busy blacksmith, a Ben Franklin store, and a rest home called Poole's, whose telephone is the night number for all emergency facilities. People say "the forenoon" and say a man whose wife has left him "keeps bachelor's hall." Our predecessors in the house, the Basfords, ate groundhogs parboiled, and deer in season and out, and, though we're easier on the game, we cook on their wood stove and light with kerosene, and just as in the platitudes, it's a source of ease and peace. Nothing hokum-yokum, just a sense of competence and self-sufficiency. Everything takes time—when it's too dark to read we cook supper, hearing the calling of the owls; then maybe I take the dogs for a walk, playing the part of the blind god. Of course I wouldn't want to get along with wood and kerosene all *winter;* nor do I want to turn the clock back. It's simply doing what is necessary; there is one kind of necessity in the city and another here.

The Basfords only moved around the mountain when we

bought their farm. The stove is one Mr. B.'s father bought in 1921—the salesman drove up with a team and wagon piled with iron stoves and told him that if he could break the lid of any of them he could have the whole stove free. The spring we pipe our water from Mr. B. found himself, using water-witching procedures. The first time that he dug a catch-hole he tried enlarging it with dynamite. One stick—detonated with the tractor engine—worked all right, but when he got greedy and wanted still a bigger source, he put in two more sticks and blew the spring away, tipping the base rock so that the water flowed by other routes. He had to go dowsing again, farther from the house, but found a new spot underground where three trickles joined together in front of a tree, and dug more modestly this time, although the overflow was sufficient for Mrs. B. to raise beds of celery there. She's English, once a war bride, now a giggly and seductive woman of about fifty. He is slow-speaking, sharp-witted, rather truculent and rather endearing. He doesn't vote, doesn't get along in town, doesn't work especially hard, doesn't look up to anyone, is an iconoclast. But she admires him. They seem to love each other in absolutely current terms. They're always having coffee, sipping wine, and talking endlessly.

Perhaps I might as well have begun this essay by saying that things are better than we think. In the public domain they're not, and we can't glance ahead with pleasure to the world our children will inhabit—more than us, they will have to swim for dear life. But middle age is the time when we give more than we get—give love, give work, seek sites. And sites can still be found, at least. You may discover you need two modest houses, but you can find your homes and set to work, living for the decade.

Mountain Notch

The little mountain in the Northeast Highlands of Vermont where I live is a knoll of low-grade granite and occasional schist more than three hundred million years old. One can date its origins, therefore, to about the time amphibians emerged on earth, and to the age of ferns. It stretches from west to east in the shape of a whale, with stunted spruces clinging in clefts of bare rock on the very top, and chatter marks gouged on the surface by the sole of the last glacier that worked it over, about twenty thousand years ago. At the whale's forehead are free-fall cliffs four hundred feet tall, so that, from a certain angle at a certain hour, at a distance of three miles, the mountain looks like a wave of breaking surf facing the rising sun. But on foggy mornings the clouds hide these dimensions and contours, making the mountain bulk bigger (if I want it to be bigger) than it really is.

A pair of bobcats generally dens in the jumbled boulders around the bottom of the cliffs. I encounter them by the evidence of their tracks, or when my dog trees one of them in the dead of night. An exasperated, rasping, extraordinarily fierce growl from a low branch overhead announces that this is not another of the local forest animals—no silent coon, or hissing fisher, or muttering bear. In high summer and in the mating season, in February, the bobcats will sometimes exchange a few loud, declaratory screams.

Fishers are large relatives of the weasel. Like raccoons, they den in hollow trees, and leave their five-toed tracks when they lope through our small valley, which is notched into the south slope of the mountainside. In the winter they are especially on the prowl for porcupines, which they strip so cleanly of flesh and bone that only the flat skin remains, inside up, on the ground. Coons try to hole up in snowy weather, but porcupines remain more active. Fishers breed in March, right after the female's previous litter has been born. Porcupines breed in December, the male performing a clumsy, poignant, three-legged dance while clutching his testicles with one front paw. The colony of porcupines then winter quite sociably among boulders underneath spruce and birch. The mountain's band of deer, in the meantime, have crossed a hardwood ridge opposite the cliffs and gone down into a cedar woods alongside Big Valley Brook, a thousand feet lower, where they can chew the cedar bark and other favored foods, and where part of the snow, caught overhead in the thick screen of boughs, evaporates.

The coyotes who raise their pups across the notch from my house howl in the fall and winter months, but carefully keep mum during their denning season so as not to betray the location of their pups. In the spring, only the pups themselves are likely to break the silence of the den—and then only to yap wistfully for a moment in the middle of the night in answer to the yapping of our dog pup, when we have one.

June is the best time to see bears. Every other year, males from far and near come calling upon the sow who seems to make her headquarters in this notch. They are great romancing bachelors, and they roam the road in broad daylight, too impatient to wait till dusk. Her yearling cubs, whom she has already ceased to mother at the start of the courtship, must cast about incautiously for new quarters; you see them grazing in the field well past dawn and drinking at midday at the brook. The old bears welt some favorite birch-tree trunk, standing up and scratching competitively. Walking, one will notice the dead logs they have beaten apart in search of grubs; and if I have gotten just muzzy-headed enough after a hike of eight or a dozen miles and lean over a bashed log, I find myself experiencing some of the same hungry, busy, humdrum interest in what is there that the bear must have felt.

Behind the rock crest of the mountain is a pocket bog with pitcher plants. Also a spring which tumbles in upon itself in the form of a whirlpool, so that any leaf that you drop in promptly disappears. The deer summer in this high mixed woods of fir and spruce and birch and beech and maple, descending maybe half a mile at night to browse the patches of moosewood, hobblebush, fire cherry, mountain ash, shadblow, vetch, and wild apple saplings at the edge of the fields. A pair of red-tailed hawks nests each year somewhere along the whale's back, in trees that I have never located. There are broad-wingeds, too, and once in a while a goshawk. Barred owls bark at night, and ravens inhabit the cliffs, croaking eloquently at midmorning and in the afternoon—but not the marvelous peregrine falcons, or "ledge hawks," as the farmers used to call them. Forty years ago they would stunt during the spring courtship season with flirtatious giddy dives down from where the ravens flap.

Woodcock do a more modest but still spectacular swooping

mating flight over a strip of alder thicket, where they later hunt earthworms. And below the alders is a beaver pond, which a pair of otters visits. Swimming playfully in sequence, they sometimes look to me like a sea monster. The patriarch among the beavers swims out toward them bravely and thwacks his tail on the water to warn his clan.

There are snowshoe rabbits, each intricately snug and custom-bound within the space of a handful of acres, bathing on a pleasant day in the same patch of dust that a ruffed grouse has used. And chipmunks—that courageous warning trill an individual, though hidden, gives, that may endanger it but save the race. There are congeries of songbirds, from indigo to scarlet-colored; three species of snakes in my woodpile; and trembling poplars, white-leaved in the wind, and all the manifestations of the moon.

Of Cows
and Cambodia

During the invasion of Cambodia, an event
which may rate little space when recent American initiatives are
summarized but which for many of us seemed the last straw at the
time, I made an escape to the woods. The old saw we've tried to
live by for an egalitarian half-century that "nothing human is
alien" has become so pervasive a truth that I was worn to a frazzle.
I was the massacre victim, the massacring soldier, and all the gaudy
queens and freaked-out hipsters on the street. Nothing human *was*
alien; I'd lost the essential anti-egalitarian ability to tune out on
occasion, and everything was ringing in my ears. Of course, even
my flight itself was part of a stampede of people who were doing
the same; and since my wife and I happened to be involved in a
kind of low-grade marital crisis, too, for all my dovish politics,
during my last few days in the city I had been going to mean and
bloody movies and reading dirty books, as I usually do when in a
trough of depression.

I have a hundred acres, mostly woodland, which I'm informed
is probably generating enough oxygen for eighteen hundred people
to breathe. I don't institute many improvements, both because of
my ignorance and because, for instance, instead of chopping dead-
wood for the stove, for twelve dollars I can buy sufficient stove-
sized scrap from the bobbin-and-dowel mill down the road to cook
and heat the house four months. A ten-mile stretch of Vermont
state forest adjoins my land, and there is more forest beyond, so
what I really do is walk. An old overgrown stagecoach road which
has been kept open by hunters' jeeps and loggers' wagons winds
with appropriate slow grandeur up through a pass and down into
a wild valley, where there are several ponds and much birdlife and
an abandoned log shack or two. A long brook rattles through the
undergrowth and evergreens for miles, and the ridges roll up to
haystack humps and aggregate themselves into the broad miniature

mass of Mount Hor, which on its other side looks off a giddy cliff into a spring-fed lake several miles long. There is a smugglers' cave beside the lake where silks and whiskey used to be stored; the Canadian border is only fifteen miles away, and for a whole summer a revenuer slept in a hammock in the woods along the shore, posing as a poet but listening for sounds. Another nearly lost, forgotten smugglers' camp—this dating from the Civil War, complete with cemetery and cellar holes—lies up behind an opposing mountain across the lake. Around on my side of Mount Hor a deep, traditional sort of cave corkscrews into the mountain a hundred feet or more, a place where hunters lived, and once an eccentric called Leatherman, who wore skins and lived off whatever he could catch or kill. Hor is a fastness for bears. I've heard descriptions of how six of them have died of gunshot wounds in the valley below. The surviving bears, like shy, fleet Indians still holding out, sometimes hoot to their mates at dusk in June—a single quiet hoot with a growl at the end, which distinguishes the sound from an owl's call. Plenty of deer skirt through, and on the mountainside you can find boggy glades where single deer have made their beds in the fine grassy patches, leaving the imprint of themselves after they run. There are frogs on the paths—occasionally a charged, invigorated snake with a frog in its mouth. I've seen mink holes along the brook, and glimpsed a pair of tiny shrews playing at the entrance to their burrow. The porcupines, after huddling in congregations through the winter, spread out and fight for territory during the spring, with piercing, nasty screams, though in the evening you can hear them chewing bark high in the spruces, their teeth sounding gravelly-voiced.

My collie, Bimbo, who accompanies me, tangles with mystery creatures like mother raccoons fifty yards back in the brush. He has enough finesse not to get torn by them or squirted by skunks, and kills woodchucks with a chop of his jaws and a snap of his head, mouthing them hungrily to break the bones, lingering over the body and salivating. But then he lets them fall and, trotting home, finishes off last night's helping of dry dog chow instead. Before I adopted him, he wolfed down crusts of bread on his visits to the house, running four miles for the privilege. Though he is uncompromising with strangers, he's almost overly loyal to me, having had so many other masters that he keeps a weather eye peeled for the day when he may find himself alone, starving again. He sticks beside me in the woods rather than ranging out, but chases any deer we see with businesslike directness, wholly wolfish for the moment, testing the air before finally lying down happily in a stream, and by his manner telegraphs the different creatures whose tracks he smells. He avoids gun-carrying people, having seen some shooting, and is afraid of thunder, indicating its approach before I hear it come. He is most cheerful in the morning, as if the day as it advances saddens him—he points up a somber nose. But he's a great ground-scratcher after urinating and a dramatic posturer with other dogs, his sense of self perhaps enhanced because he lives in isolation in the country and meets few other dogs. He fights sharply and seems to take a rich and realistic view of the citizenship of all the animals in the world, making no unnatural distinctions between those wild and tame. Cows, cats, and fishers intrigue him equally. Meadow mice are a pleasure to hunt, but in bear country he doesn't wag his tail as much and walks with gingerly circumspection through the smashed berry thickets, the rank and muddy wallows. When we set out, he springs with all four feet off the ground and catches my hand in his mouth, and when we get back to the house he pulls off the burrs that have stuck to me, breathing lovingly. There are two things difficult about him. He personalizes cars, and chases them with an inimical bold heroism, since he's been hit three times. And in an apparent attempt to aggrandize himself, he loves to roll on the moldering bones of redoubtable strange animals. Worse than just using a dead deer, he singles out a picnicker's ordure to roll in if he can, smearing his fluffy fur with excrement, wearing it like epaulets, as the most mythic material of all. Afterward he romps and struts; it gives him a tremendous lift to smell so thickly like a man.

Besides believing nothing human should be alien, we used to aspire to another condition: as D. H. Lawrence said, we must *live more intensely*. We thought that, vague and dreamy, we were letting life slide by. But I was joining a mass swing of people looking for country acreage who had begun to feel so hard-pressed that their main effort was just to disengage themselves. They were of different politics and different vocations, yet some of them felt that if they lived any more intensely, they might have to be hospitalized.

Although we're swamped in populace and intensity, a few ridges over from me was a commune—twelve or fifteen persons in their twenties whose response to these dilemmas was more hair of the dog. Instead of barricading themselves behind thousands of acres of forestland, as I was trying to do, they intended to chum and combine with some of these overnumerous souls. And with the aspens trembling, field flowers blooming, the blue sky and the lavish landscape, their admirable experiment seemed to be working out. The children were sunburned and muscular, doing without diapers and caring for each other. They lived in a Children's Tent, and while there was some uncertainty and ear-pulling, mostly they roamed between adventures, catching toads, feeding the hens. The grown-ups slept in pairs tucked into plastic lean-tos or hunters' tents under the spruces—there was one lofty-looking tepee. They had a geodesic dome which wowed their visitors and was intended to be transformed into a candle factory eventually, as well as a roomlike area covered with sheets of plastic draped over poles where the cooking was done, and a large produce garden that didn't succeed, owing to the acid soil.

Consistent with their life-style, they tried to welcome strangers, even explaining their beliefs to sightseers if asked to, or letting a hitchhiker camp with them for a week or so on a probationary basis. Since several were veterans of an ill-fated commune farther south in the state which had turned into a kind of motel for traveling hippies, this time they'd bought enough land for an agricultural existence, but without buildings, so that in these first months nobody could stay over unless he bestirred himself at least to pitch a tent. They built an outhouse, chicken house, and cow shed, repaired their road, attempted to incorporate as a private elementary school so they could educate their own children, avoided obtrusive drug use, helped their neighbors hay in exchange for the loan of farm equipment, and wisely went to meetings of the local Grange so that the local people could see firsthand that they were not dragons. The men were fit-looking—the long hair didn't appear to be a mark of bereavement—and the girls eloquent, graceful, appealing; they had big eyes, and as in many communes, they got the job of dealing with outsiders. I felt wistful when I dropped in. Obviously, no notable amount of work was being done. Everyone went off on jaunts into the countryside or swam or gathered firewood or sat talking all day in the cook tent, fixing salads of sorrel, lamb's-quarters, and wild mustard leaves with little berries and raw eggs stirred in. They made butter and ice cream and pots of sugared oatmeal, and boiled milkweed and fried cornbread. It was a summer idyll. Lying underneath the trees, they never did get the log house built that they had planned.

By October, like grasshoppers who'd danced the harvest time away, they were looking for winter quarters to rent, stung by the frosts, worried for their children's health. It developed that the townspeople were not so friendly after all; nothing was available. They were college folk, so they weren't really going to have to stay and freeze, but it was interesting to note that the most favorably disposed faction in town were older persons who could remember living off the land and looking rather ragged themselves during the Great Depression. Also, the oldsters connected the rootless appearance of these hip types with the itinerant loggers from French Canada in earlier days—longhaired, linguistically a puzzle, with underfed dependents—and therefore weren't afraid of them.

This corner of Vermont is without industry, and when a summer resident shows up again the following spring the winter news of friends and neighbors is likely to be bad—bad luck, bad health—because so many younger people clear out, and there is hardly any way for a man who has stayed around to have advanced himself. Seventy-five years ago the town had factories manufacturing cheese, knickers, shoes, and butter tubs, and what was then the longest power line east of the Rockies. Seventeen miles long, it carried eight hundred kilowatts and was the hobbyhorse of the inventive-minded middle class, although at that time farm boys still went into the woods after spruce chewing gum, which they cut off the trees with sharpened poles and steamed and sold downtown for a dollar a pound. Later they saved their gum money to buy battery radios and "windchargers," noisy windmills that turned and turned on the roof of the house and kept the batteries charged.

Since then whole settlements have disappeared in the outlying sections of town, and the country has grown so wild that one of the postal clerks has killed twenty-three bears so far. The saying is that you need only soak your feet in a bucket and set the salty water out by the back door for deer to drift right up to drink. A deer is just a joker like oneself; he's not much better at hearing a man move toward him in the woods than the man may be at hearing him.

Like most of the other abandoned farms, mine has its residue of projects that failed: a stunted orchard, an attempt at raising Christmas trees. The soil was marginal, and the family tried to keep goats at one time, and they had cows but the barn burned. Failure makes some men rough on their wives. There are stories of how the man who lived here during the thirties wouldn't bother to cut the stovewood short enough to fit the kitchen stove, wouldn't even cut down more than a week's supply, in case, as he said, he died; his wife could cut down her own trees after that. By and by he did die, and she moved off the place, saying that she was sick and tired of "staring at that damn mountain." Another, more sensible enterprise of theirs had been raising hunting dogs.

Woodcock fly up; a little fox runs down the road. In the springtime, when I arrive, being in my own fields is plenty for me—airing the house and stepping in and out, discovering again that the night sky exhibits stars by the thousand if they aren't blotted out by lights. No matter how brutal the winter has been (last Christmas fifty inches of snow fell in a single week), the grass is coming up like kettledrums; birches and pines, which grow as much as three feet in a year, are mustering themselves and shooting up. Goldfinches pick apart the dandelions; sapsuckers chisel for bugs underneath the maple bark. I roast potatoes to eat in their jackets like rolls and take walks on the drizzly evenings, listening to my brook, admiring the treetops against the sky, comparing spruce with fir, red spruce, white spruce, red pine, white pine. I watch the bats over Little Fish Pond, hearing trout jump that sometimes sound so big I step back under the trees, afraid somebody is heaving stones.

The young men hunt hard in season, turning their attention to the sport, but the old men think about it all the time; it is an elixir to them. They seem to feel they'll live longer if they are still able to shoot, as though in dealing death they are immortal for the moment. Far from shying from the ghastly antics of the dying deer, they recount these covetously, like a formula that may stave off the same collapse in themselves—the creature jerking its legs up as it fell, twitching and groaning on the ground. These tales can extend through half an afternoon, each man has killed so many deer, often outwitting the game warden too. Porcupines and groundhogs can be hunted much of the year, and some people do so when times are grim, either for the relish of the kill and as a means of staving death off, or else for food. When neighbors quarrel, they hear each other next morning out in the woods shooting small game; and in the fall, when the hayfields are mown and visibility is good, they both lay up a store of gutted groundhogs, later grinding the meat with onions, apples, and sunflower seeds into a matchless burger steak. Years ago people put up barrels of salted smelt caught in spawning season, bins of root vegetables, canned green tomatoes, and grated horseradish cut with turnip. Then in midwinter, after letting a barrel of hard cider freeze, they'd drill a hole in the middle and tap the nearly pure alcohol, which made a man's heart feel as if it were wrapped in soft cotton.

In farming country old people are not sequestered away, and when somebody dies nearly everyone knew him. Only last week in the drugstore he may have crossed his fingers and said with a mild smile that he was hoping for a clean bill of health from the doctor. The butchering, the weighing of each cow's fate every few months, also makes death a familiar companion. Not every cow that doesn't freshen promptly is sent to slaughter, but she goes "down the road," to bob in terror under the auctioneer's prodding. It's personal—rather like a slave auction, perhaps. "What a lovely lady this is! Look at the teats on her! Keep her in the pasture this summer, and then if you don't like her, cut her throat in the fall!" Milk farmers are involved in all the intricacies and ambiguities of life-and-death power, and generally are glad to be. Since they work mostly around the barn, they're paler than the farmers who grow crops. Not until the 1960 census did Vermonters come to outnumber their cows, and several say the reason they were in no hurry was that they simply *liked* cows. In the isolated gores and valleys cows were a kind of harem. They could withhold or volunteer part of their milk, and if well soothed and happy they gave more. Even with machine-milking, the udders need a good old-fashioned warm-fingered stroking beforehand, and when a cow is bred artificially, the technician massages her cervix as well as squirting in the semen. After he leaves, a skillful farmer will squat down for a while and in a friendly fashion rub and squeeze her teats.

Against the sense of exuberant release I felt on long walks in the woods was the knowledge that this in fact was just a hermetic patch of wilderness with highways on all sides, scarcely larger than a park: it was a ship in a bottle, and I was only hiding out. The commune idealists, who read *The Whole Earth Catalog* as a life's chart, seemed doctrinaire, not easy company, so on days when I wasn't out with the dog hunting for smugglers' camps, I started accompanying an artificial inseminator named Donald Nault from Newport Center on his regular rounds. I had the frivolous notion that I might be watching the way human procreation would eventually be carried on, each liberated woman choosing semen that suited her from a listing of donor traits. Instead, the cows, pinned in their stanchions, looked around at us like immobilized moose turning to watch the wolves approach to eat. But as Nault kneaded them the experience became less unpleasant or fearsome, obscurely peaceful. They visibly relaxed, as though an ill wind had blown through the barn but had left them unharmed.

Nault has five kids and lives in a frail-looking frame house, shingled gray and set on a hilltop that overlooks most of his working territory, which is twenty-five miles square. His wife is a stocky, pretty woman, an ironist, a pertinacious mother, who stuffs bitterns and flying squirrels to decorate the living room. He is a good explainer and seems to smile more than most people do, although he's perfectly prepared to yell. He's gangly and has short gray hair and the open-faced look of a high-school science teacher, with thin-rimmed glasses, a spacious physiognomy but narrow bones. His voice is flat-timbred and dispassionate-sounding; he breaks his vowels in half, twanging the halves in different tones.

He keeps bees and hunts with bow and arrow for hobbies, and works in the 4-H program, a much more freewheeling proposition than scouting, being geared to what farm youngsters can do off in the boondocks by themselves. Like the bulk-milk pickup drivers, the feed dealers and John Deere men, he's one of the county's peripatetics. According to tax figures, his corner of it has seventy-six hundred cattle, of which he services about half (the rest still rassle with his competitor, the bull). Even allowing for the heifers that are too young to breed, this means he services at least ten cows a day, because he does free repeat breedings when the first doesn't take. He's off three days a month, including Sundays, but gets no other vacation, and is paid at the rate of $2.80 per cow. The fee the farmer pays is $7.

I learned about the business, along with a good deal of outright gynecology, riding around with Nault from farm to farm, seeing the lightning rods atop red barns and white houses (Summer people reverse the colors—red houses and white barns.) The farmers took no more notice of us than of meter readers, and though the days turned out to be rawer than I'd expected, with sometimes afterbirths and once a dead calf on the floor, there was the pleasure of the pasturage and roller-coaster woods and the big-siloed, spruced-up farms lying in front of the dramatic silhouette of the Green Mountains, Jay Peak jutting up immediately in front.

Besides enjoying the guided tour, I was glad for the friendship between Nault and myself. We were contemporaries and whatever we didn't have in common tended not to come up. But the hard monotony of breadwinning communicated itself too, just as it does whenever one absorbs the routines that another person must live by. We'd pull up by a milkhouse, built of cement for easy cleaning, with cold spring water tumbling into black slate sinks and a torpedolike five-hundred-gallon milk cooler gleaming, milk stools hanging up beside breeding charts and bacteria counts sent by the creamery. The milkhouse is for people, but the dark barn, drafty and partitionless, smells of fermenting silage and wet, fleshly herd politics. The cows have topknots where they've been dehorned and side-set eyes, trusting noses, and flappy ears.

Nault steps into his rubber boots and syringes semen into a catheter, which he holds crosswise in his mouth while working with his hands. He is medical in manner, not chieftainish like the farmers, and though I admired the delicacy with which he handled the task, I pitied him the tedium of pounding round and round between a hundred farms year after year, none his. Some of the fellows envy him his free-lance life, however. Leaping land values, the overall slide toward change, cause a hollering across the countryside. Farmers think of retiring on the money their acreage would bring; yet dairying really has never been more profitable, they say. A hundred pounds of milk will buy two hundred pounds of grain, but a cow only needs to eat about a pound of grain for every three or four pounds of milk she produces during the winter months, or one to nine or ten pounds when she is pasturing. This is the ratio that matters. Also, about one acre of grazing ground and one of hay are necessary to support a cow in New England, and so if she brings in a yearly profit of perhaps two hundred dollars after all expenses, then each acre is worth a hundred dollars a year to the farmer and he will only continue keeping cows as long as that hundred dollars does not seem too paltry a sum when measured against the prices the land speculators offer him.

Whereas in the old days a man might dabble in winter logging or the Christmas-tree business or maple sugaring and take the chance that a few cows would catch pneumonia while he was gone, now it's best to be a specialist, with all the thorny breeding questions and mastitis and Bang's disease and vibriosis to watch for. Little farms must have the same expensive milk-handling equipment as big ones, so that the little operators are being bought out. Efficiency demands that they get rid of the mediocre milkers, then feed the good producers all the protein they will eat, whether in the form of short early-cut hay and high-value alfalfa and clover, or store-bought nutrients like beet pulp, citrus rinds, and chopped-up corn, wheat, barley, oats, and molasses ground together. Most of the cattle Nault breeds are black-and-white Holsteins, which yield an average of 14,900 pounds of milk a year, far outperforming the brown-and-white Guernseys or Jerseys. Genetically Holsteins are also more trustworthy than Guernseys and, being big, are worth two hundred dollars as beef just as they stand. Jerseys do keep a hold on some farmer's affections because they're quite emotional and heated, yet small and easy to manage, and their milk tests high in butterfat, which means a premium is paid.

The landscape grew more familiar as we tooled around Nault's territory. Sometimes, during the afternoon, we went right back to the same farms, driving through gray rain squalls, past fields of timothy, ryegrass, and vetch, and stands of lusciously foliaged trees in the townships of Troy and Coventry. We saw Canadian Frenchmen with de Gaulle's nose at the age-old New England occupation of gathering stones. We passed the house of the district's healer, a seventh son of a seventh son, who can cure everything from dropsy to the twist in the postman's hip, which got out of its socket as the poor guy leaned from his driver's seat to reach the mailboxes. This healer is a rough type and doesn't pray beside his customers; he simply puts his hand on the ailing area and holds it there for ten or fifteen minutes, telling raunchy jokes meanwhile.

Once we passed a mink farm, consisting of cage-filled sheds and several horses waiting in a vacant lot to be killed, cut up, and fed to the mink, then drove up the first grade of the mountains to a brown slumping home isolated in deep woods, with a toolshed in back where a brown cow was tied. No grown-ups were around. A girl of twelve, who had been left in charge, came out of the house, handed Nault seven one-dollar bills, and watched him work. Afterwards we coasted back to moneyed, rolling pasturelands, with immense barns equipped with stanchions by the hundred, all electrically hooked to the fire alarm so that the cows would be freed automatically in case of a disaster. Indeed, the latest innovation is to dispense with stanchions entirely, letting the creatures mill as they wish about the barn, only walking them through a "milking parlor" twice a day, because the more benign they feel, the more milk they will brew.

These new procedures naturally discourage the *machismo* bent of many farmers, which is why lots of them still keep bulls. The snorting beast costs hundreds of dollars to feed, more than the farmer saves in breeding fees, and it inhabits a stall where otherwise he could stable a milker. Yet some people will alternately utilize Nault's super variety of semen and their own yokel bull, and then, to his consternation, instead of raising the fine new calves which have the perfected genes for future stock and selling off the quirky local progeny, as often as not a man will keep his own bull's calves and send Nault's scientific infants straight to the butcher's block.

I am describing what I did in the aftermath of the Cambodia invasion, not a story with an end but of interest to me because it is what I would do again in the event of other invasions, or practically any other kind of trouble; it is the only thing that I can think of. I liked being poised near the Canadian border the way I was, and found that ducking quickly into the woods and living by myself had helped: up early, aware of other creatures besides man, with the sky-clock of sun and stars.

After hiking awhile around Mount Hor, I began going across the road to explore a large steep formless upland known as Robbins Hill, after a rifle-toting family of Raggedy Anns who have since disappeared. I'd been learning to recognize the common trees, and a riotous arboretum of these were crowded together on Robbins

Hill in what was an orgy for me. Young trees, particularly, send me into a hustle of needle-squeezing, bark-tapping, and branch-waggling. I can't believe how straight and true to type they are, how springy to the touch and brown and green. To discover so many examples together in deep grass—lacy cedars next to hemlocks next to wavy larch and beech and yellow birch and bigtooth aspen—was grounds for glee. Laughing to myself, I rushed from one to another, touching the leaves—perfect little maples, perfect little balsam firs and balsam poplars. There was a flowering shrub called moose missy by the old people and a flower that they called frog's mouth.

Now this was all escapism—a word that's going to lose its sting. I was escaping to recuperate, my ears grateful for the quiet of the woods. My wife flew up to join me as soon as she could, and except for her company, I found the old people best to be with, rather than those my own age, saddled with mortgages and emphatic politics. My neighbors told me about fermenting beer forty or fifty years ago that had a head so thick they could write their names in it or spoon it off for sandwich filling. They'd make next Christmas's plum pudding on Christmas Eve, to marinate in brandy for twelve months, and serve last year's. The husband remembers skidding logs down off Robbins Hill with oxen one winter after a forest fire. The fire leapt across the road on some loose birch bark that caught the wind, and he remembers how pathetically the porcupines squealed as it caught up with them. There was only one farrier in the county, a man named Duckless, who shoed oxen for icy winter work; he did it as a kind of stunt. Oxen are stiff-legged and can't lift their legs as a horse can, so he employed a block and tackle and canvas sling to hoist them up. Since they are cloven-hoofed, each foot needed two shoes. The dogs would collect from the farms nearby as if a bitch had come in heat. Dogs love a blacksmith's visits because they chew on the hoof parings—the parings are taffy to them.

My friend Paul Sumner went foxing with his dog as a youngster, following the fox for many winding miles and hours. He'd get twenty-five dollars for the skin at a time when the daily wage at the sawmills was less than a dollar and fifty cents. A fisher skin was worth still more. He had a Long Tom rifle which had a kick that knocked him down and a bolt action so loud that if he missed when he was deer shooting, the animal would stop running and listen, mystified by the strange sound. There were ten Sumner children, and necessarily the boys hunted for meat. They'd get one rabbit started, and in dodging about, it would scamper through every other good rabbit hiding place, scaring up a throng. After each snowstorm the father would tramp around the swamp, leaving a great circle of snowshoe tracks beyond which the younger kids were not supposed to go. Though they were very poor, the saying was that no woman could be admitted into heaven who cut more than four pieces from a pie. Paul still makes his own bullets, weighing out the grains of powder as some men roll their cigarettes. He used to make shot for his shotgun by mincing up a flattened pipe, and would hike off for days with a bait pail and traps into the Big Woods over in Essex County, carrying a few bottle caps with wax and string in them to heat the kindling for his fire on a wet night, later pouring his supper grease on the next morning's firewood. He remembers Halley's Comet in 1910, having climbed Mount Hor especially to see it, sleeping on the crest and watching a duckhawk fly up at dawn out of a tree and kill a fast-flying duck with such impact that both of them fell from the sky. He remembers fishing in Canada and catching northern pike four feet long. If the line broke, by jinks, he says, the fisherman jumped in the lake and wrestled with the fish, almost like another man. The blueberries were as big as thumbs and turned the hillsides blue.

He tells the legend of how oak trees acquired scalloped leaves. There was a man who signed a pact with the Devil according to which, after enjoying his handsome looks and riches, he would have to give himself up "when the oak lost its leaves." But oaks never do lose all their leaves; some cling stubbornly to the trees all through the winter until fresh foliage sprouts in the spring. And so the Devil, who was a bad loser, ran around and round the archetypal oak, chewing on its leaves, marking the edges with his teeth.

In the cavalry down in Brownsville, Texas, after World War I, Paul used to feed his horses sugar cane for a treat. His barracks mates kept an ocelot for a mascot; and there was a pet terrier in a bar they patronized which was so tough the customers would throw a tennis ball at it as hard as they could, down the aisle between the tables and the bar, and the dog, bounding in the air, would catch it on the fly. Back in Vermont, Paul, who was always a fisherman, located an old quarry hole with bass swimming at the bottom of it. A man lived nearby in a tar-paper shack, ten feet by six and all grown over with blackberries—"The house was only standing up because the termites inside were holding hands." It stood under a fine white pine that the fellow called his "sunflower tree" because the needles seemed so radiant when the light was right. He raised tomatoes on the remains of a defunct outhouse and baked his bread in loaves so big around a slice was the size of a pane of glass. He spent his days bucking firewood for money, though flourishing his rifle when people came to pick it up (he'd grab a broomstick and aim with that if they were kids). He was so fussy that he wouldn't let anybody touch his cartridges, afraid they'd leave some sweat on them and tarnish the parts of his gun, and yet his house was stuffed with junk, scarcely allowing room for the bed and stove. He never washed his dinner plate, just dumped more food on it, but every few weeks he would scrape off the detritus and fry that too, calling it "stodge."

Another character on that road was the Turkey Buyer, who ranged about the state in a truck carrying gobblers. When he passed a farm that raised the birds he would screech to a stop, jump out, run up to the door, and tell the farmer that one of the turkeys from his truck had got out of its crate and scurried in among the farmer's turkeys; would he please help catch it? Together they would catch one of the farmer's turkeys, and then the Turkey Buyer, with many thanks, would drive away.

Dan Tanner was a neighbor of Paul's too. Dan was a seven-footer who had once killed a bear which went after a string of fish he'd caught by stabbing it with a sharp stick of heartwood just underneath the arm. He was exceedingly tough; his wife, Abbey, used to wash the blood off all the men he licked. A good trout brook made up in their back field, most of it underground for the first mile. Nevertheless, there were some holes you could fish through and catch short little trout, discolored from not having seen the sun. Tanner ran a still that cooked his booze so hot, the pots and tubing jounced. He set aside a jug for Saturday and one for Sunday, but usually he'd finish Saturday's before sunset, vomit it up, and finish Sunday's too. He didn't trouble very much about the law and feuded with the game warden. One time in the winter when the warden was trailing him, Dan carefully tossed the doe he'd killed behind a rock and turned downhill, taking small steps, down to a brook, then walked backwards in his own tracks, stepping exactly in each step in the snow, and hopped behind a dead spruce on the ground, where he lay still. Pursuing him, the warden passed by and looked in vain for Tanner's tracks across on the other side of the brook. Thirsty, he stooped to drink, and Tanner fired a shot into the water just underneath his nose.

Paul, who is a father, a widower, is a less violent man. He suffers from angina but cuts pulpwood for a living at nineteen dollars a cord. One corner of his farm is about to be razed for an interstate highway, and parallel with that will be a power line, so his years of retirement will probably be spent between these fierce belts of activity. For much of his working life he was a lineman for a power company himself. The photos on the wall show him in climbing boots high on a leaning pole with a tree fallen on the line. He's got blue eyes and a jug-handle pair of ears, a puckery, sharp-witted face, a twisty smile. He jokes a lot, collapsing in laughter, swinging his arms, although he has a sense of misery as well. In wintertime he needs to shovel the snow from in front of his windows in order to see out; it gets so deep that he can walk right onto the roof when the ice must be scraped off. He grows winter apples, which are not picked until after the first snowfall. The frosts seem to condition them; that's when the deer prefer them too.

He who fights and runs away lives on, and that's what I had been up to. As the summer closed I went again to the roots of the brook under Mount Hor, finding the split-pear prints of deer and listening to the ravens honk. There is a "boiling spring" that Robert Frost used to visit, according to reports. The spring no longer boils, having become choked with leaves—it never did boil in the Westerner's meaning of the word; they don't have hot springs here—but it still tastes pristine and heads a cold and lively stream. Talking with the various old men, each one with a heart condition, I sometimes felt the need for haste in gathering information: even a sense that if the fellow should suffer a stroke before my eyes, I would bend over him, urgently asking, *Where was that cave? Who was it that you said lived there?*

Each of them, after his own manner of doing things, was in the process of selling off his land—at least the relics on it, like wagonwheels—pretending that he was just trying to "get rid of the stuff," impatient that the buyer hadn't come for them, and watching as his pastures, laboriously maintained since the nineteenth century, grew back to tangled wilderness. In September I accompanied a man I am fond of into the jungle that had formerly been his lower pasture and now was on the point of being sold to me. He was in his middle eighties and walked very slowly, like a frail Galapagos turtle, looking incongruously weightless but leaning heavily while I helped him to edge through the willow-alder thickets. We looked for the old fence line, where bits of barbed wire lingered on the trees, and the stump of a black cherry tree that he thought the bears had killed, and a round rock called Whippoor-will Rock, and a big butternut, and for the place beside the stream where his brothers and he had once successfully rigged a power saw operated by a waterwheel. The alders were a jungle, yet he struggled much farther into the center of the property than I'd expected, calm and slow about it, swaying a little when the wind blew. Many landmarks had been obliterated, but he found a few. The growth was swamp grass now, smothering in spiraea brush. Remembering as he went along, he persevered so far that I was afraid that even with my help he wouldn't be able to extricate himself again.

Howling Back
at the Wolves

Wolves have marvelous legs. The first thing one notices about them is how high they are set on their skinny legs, and the instant, blurred gait these can switch into, bicycling away, carrying them as much as forty miles in a day. With brindled coats in smoky shades, brushy tails, light-filled eyes, intense sharp faces which are more focused than an intelligent dog's but also less various, they are electric on first sighting, bending that bushy head around to look back as they run. In captivity when they are quarreling in a cage, the snarls sound guttural and their jaws chop, but scientists watching pet wolves in the woods speak of their flowing joy, of such a delight in running that they melt into the woods like sunlight, like running water.

The modern study of American wildlife may be said to have begun with Adolph Murie, who, writing about the wolves of Mount McKinley in 1944, realized there was not much point in a scientist's shooting them; so few wolves were left that this would be killing the goose laying the golden eggs. In those days even the biologists dealing with animals which weren't considered varmints mainly just boiled the flesh off their heads to examine the knobs on their skulls, or opened their stomachs to see what they ate. The scrutiny of skulls had resulted in a listing of eighty-six species and subspecies of the grizzly bear (it's now considered that there were a maximum of only two), and twenty-seven specified New World wolves (again, now revised down to two). Murie, in the field and looking at scats, could do a more thorough investigation even of diet than the autopsy fellows, who, as it was, knew almost nothing else about the life of wolves.

Murie and Ian McTaggart Cowan in Canada were the best of the bedroll scientists. They could travel with dogs all winter in the snow or camp alone on a gravel bar in a valley for the summer, go about quietly on foot and record everything that they saw. No amount of bush-plane maneuvering and electronic technology can quite replace these methods, by which the totality of a wilderness community can be observed and absorbed. Young scientists such as L. David Mech, who has been the salvation of wolves in Minnesota, which is practically the only place in the lower forty-eight states where they still occur, try to combine the current reliance on radiotelemetry with some of that old bedroll faithfulness to the five senses shared by a man with the animals he is studying.

Big game, like elk and caribou, and big glamorous predators have naturally received first attention, people being as they are, so that much more is known about wolves than about the grasshopper mouse, though the grasshopper mouse is a wolf among mice, trailing, gorging upon small mammals and insects; in fact, with nose pointed skyward, it even "howls." On lists of endangered species you occasionally find little beasts that wouldn't excite much attention on a picnic outing, but despite all the talk about saving the fruits of two billion years' worth of evolution, the funds available go to help those animals that tend to remind us of ourselves—rhinos, whales, falcons—and there aren't many lists of endangered plants.

So it is that the predator specialists are predatory. A hawk man drops out of the sky for a visit; he has radios attached to assorted raptors and albatrosses and swans, and flies around the world to track their migrations. During his chat about perfecting antennas it is obvious that he is full of what in an animal he would call "displaced aggression." The scientist Albert Erickson, who has worked on grizzlies in the north and leopard seals in Antarctica, was known as "Wild Man Erickson" when he studied black bears in Michigan. The Craighead brothers, Frank and John—territorial, secretive, and competitive—have been working on a definitive study of grizzlies (which are also territorial, secretive, and competitive) for umpteen years, scrapping with the National Park Service at Yellowstone and embargoing many of their own findings in the meantime. Maurice Hornocker, who is now the definitive mountain-lion man and who trained with them, is just as close-mouthed—as close-mouthed as a mountain lion, indeed. Down in Grand Chenier, Louisiana, Ted Joanen, the state's alligator expert, is equally able and reserved. One doesn't understand right away why he happens to be devoting his life to learning more about alligators than anybody else, rather than ibises or chimney swifts or pelicans, until he gets to describing how alligators can catch a swimming deer, pull it under the water, drown it, and tear its leg off by spinning like a lathe, and then points to one's own twitching leg.

Wolves *would* be more of a loss to us than some exotic mouse, because they epitomize the American wilderness as no other animal does, and fill both the folklore of childhood and that of the woods—folklore that would wither away if they all were to die, and may do so in any case. We know that the folklore was exaggerated, that generally they don't attack man, which is a relief, but we treasure the stories nonetheless, wanting the woods to be woods. In the contiguous states the gray wolf's range is less than 1 percent of what it used to be, and that patch of Minnesota wilderness, twelve thousand square miles where they live in much the same density as in primeval times, is greatly enriched by the presence of wolves.

Wisconsin didn't get around to granting its wolves protection until they had become extinct, but Mech got the Minnesota bounty removed and almost single-handedly turned local thinking around, until there is talk of declaring the wolf a "state animal" and establishing a sanctuary for it in the Boundary Waters Canoe Area. Mech is a swift-thinking, urbane, amused man, bald, round-faced, not a bit wolflike in appearance, although he is sharp in his rivalry with other scientists. As an advocate he knows how to generate "spontaneous" nationwide letter-writing campaigns and can gather financial support from the National Geographic Society and the New York Zoological Society, from Minneapolis industrialists and the federal government. He has a soul-stirring howl, more real than reality, that triggers the wolves into howling back when he is afoot trying to locate them, but his ears have begun to dim from a decade or more of flying all winter in flimsy planes to spot them against the snow. Sometimes he needs an assistant along to hear whether a pack at a distance is answering him.

That wolves do readily answer even bad imitations of their howl may have a good deal of significance. Observers have noticed the similarities between the intricate life of a wolf pack and the most primitive grouping of mankind, the family-sized band. Often there is a "peripheral wolf," for instance, which is tolerated but picked on, and as though the collective psyche of the pack required a scapegoat, if the peripheral wolf disappears another pack member may slip down the social ladder and assume the role, or a stray that otherwise might have been driven off will be adopted. The strays, or "lone wolves," not being bound by territorial considerations, range much farther and frequently eat better than pack wolves do, but are always seeking to enroll themselves.

What seems so uncanny and moving about the experience of howling to wolves, then hearing them answer, may be the envelop-

ing sense of déjà vu, perhaps partly subliminal, that goes right to
one's roots—band replying to band, each on its own ground, gazing
across a few hundred yards of meadow or bog at the same screen of
trees. The listener rises right up on his toes, looking about happily
at his human companions.

Wolf pups make a frothy ribbon of sound like fat bubbling, a
shiny, witchy, fluttery yapping, while the adults siren less excit-
ably, without those tremulous, flexible yips, although they sometimes do break pitch into a yodel. The senior wolf permits the response, if one is made, introducing it with his own note after a
pause—which is sometimes lengthy—before the others join in. Ordinarily pups left alone will not answer unless the adult closest to
them does so, as he or she returns to protect them. Wolves howl
for only a half-minute or so, though they may respond again and
again after a cautious intermission, if no danger is indicated from
their having already betrayed their position. Each wolf has a tone,
or series of tones, of its own that blends into an iridescent harmony with the others, and people who howl regularly at a wolf
rendezvous soon acquire vocal personalities too, as well as a kind
of choral sequence in which they join together—cupping their
mouths to the shape of a muzzle on cue.

I went out with a student of Mech's, Fred Harrington, who
records and voice-prints wolf howls. His wife was along, doing the
puppy trills, and so was the trap-line crew, who attach radio collars to the wolves they catch. We stood at the edge of a cutover
jack-pine flat, with a few tall spruces where the wolves were. The
sun was setting, the moon was rising, squirrels and birds were
chitting close by, and we knew that a radio-collared bear was digging its winter den just over the rise. Howling is not a hunting cry
and does not frighten other animals. The wolves howled as if for
their own edification, as a pleasurable thing, a popular, general
occasion set off by our calls to them, replying to us but not led by
our emphasis or interpretation. If they had been actively scouting
us they would have kept silent, as they do in the spring when the
pups are too young to travel. To us, their chorus sounded isolated,
vulnerable, the more so because obviously they were having fun,
and we all felt the urge to run toward them; but they didn't share
that feeling. A pack needs at least ten square miles for each member, as well as a deer every eighteen days for that individual, or a
deer every three days for a pack of six. The figure for moose is
one every three days for a pack of fifteen, Mech has calculated.
Thus, howling between packs does not serve the function of calling them to confabulate. Instead, it seems to keep them apart,
defining rough boundaries for their separate ranges, providing

them mutually with a roster of strength, though by howling, mates in a pack do find one another and find solidarity.

In Algonquin Provincial Park in Ontario thousands of people howl with the wolves in the early autumn. Whether or not it is a high point for the wolves, it certainly is for the people. I've gone to one of the favorite locations, where the ground is littered with cigarette butts, and tried, except the day was rainy and the wolves couldn't hear me. Nobody who has had the experience will fail to root for the beasts ever after. Glacier National Park in Montana is next to Canada, like Mech's country, and they may manage to become reestablished there; Yellowstone Park has a small vanguard. In East Texas a few survive, hiding in the coastal marshes. These are red wolves—relic relations of the gray wolf that inhabited the Southeast and lower Mississippi Valley and are probably now doomed, pushed up against the sea, with no reservoir such as the wildlands of Canada provide from which to replenish their numbers.

Apparently a special relationship can exist between men and wolves which is unlike that between men and any of the bears or big cats. One might have to look to the other primates for a link that is closer. It's not just a matter of howling; owls with their hoots and loons with their laughter also interact with wolves. Nor is it limited to the mystery of why dogs, about fifteen thousand years back, which is very recent as such events go, cut themselves away from other wolves by a gradual, at first "voluntary" process to become subservient to human beings as no other domestic creature is, running with man in packs in which *he* calls the tune. Another paradox is that the wolves which remained wolves, though they are large predators that might legitimately regard a man-shaped item as prey, don't seem to look upon him as such; don't even challenge him in the woods in quite the same way that they will accost a trespassing cougar or grizzly.

In the campaign to rescue the wolf from Red Ridinghood status, some scientists, including Mech, have overdone their testimonials as to its liberal behavior, becoming so categorical that they doubt that any North American wolf not rabid has ever attacked a human being. This does violence to scientific method, as well as to the good name of countless frontiersmen who knew more about the habits of wilderness animals than it is possible to learn today. (What these scientists really mean is that none of their Ph.D. candidates doing field work has been attacked by a wolf so far.) Such propaganda also pigeonholes the wolf in a disparaging way, as if it were a knee-jerk creature without any options, like a blowfish or a hog-nosed snake.

But the link with man remains. Douglas H. Pimlott, who is Canada's wolf expert, explores this matter in *The World of the Wolf*. He mentions behavioral patterns that are shared by man and wolf, and by indirection might have come to influence wolves. Both hunt cooperatively in groups and are nearly unique in that respect; both have lived in complex bands in which the adults of either sex care for the young. He mentions the likelihood that there are subconscious attributes of the human mind that may affect wolves. After all, the bonds between a man and dog penetrate far beyond the awe of the one for the other—are more compulsive, more telepathic than awe—and cannot be fully explained under the heading of love. Wolves, like dogs, says Pimlott, are excellent readers of signs because of their social makeup and their cruising system of hunting, which does not depend as much on surprise as the habits of most other predators do: "They instinctively recognize aggression, fear, and other qualities of mind which are evidenced in subtle ways by our expressions and actions. . . . In hunting we stalk deliberately, quietly . . . in winter we move through the woods and across lakes and streams deliberately, as a wolf does in traveling over his range, hunting for prey."

These movements indicate to wolves that we are superior predators—superior wolves—and not prey. It could be added that wolves, like dogs, take a remarkable delight in submissive ritual, ingratiating themselves, placating a bigger, more daring beast— this part of their adaptation through the millennia to life in a pack, in which usually only one or two members are really capable of killing the sizable game that will feed many mouths; the rest dance attendance upon them. Of course not only the stew-hunter prowling in the woods is predatory. In the city, when much more driving and successful men emerge on the street for a business lunch, their straight-line strides and manner, "bright-eyed and bushy-tailed," would bowl over any wolf.

Lament
the Red Wolf

Gas rationing is in order, the Environmental Protection Agency suggests. What will young people do? Ordinarily a fuel shortage accompanies a war, when they have various surrogates. It's not really that driving equals living dangerously, however. People drive more dangerously in the Alpes-Maritimes than in America, and in Italy a car itself perhaps can represent more precisely a man's own personality—at least, to hear the honking, it seems so. When I was living in a village in Sicily, the padrone of the lemon groves lying all around would wake up the populace after midnight with the peremptory note of his Ferrari's horn as he sped home. He was signaling to have his front gate opened, and to hasten the job, began a tattoo of toots right as he entered town. But distances, not speed, characterize American driving: trailers, campers, and the like. Or a retired couple, as their first project, will set out to tour from coast to coast, reserving a motel room each morning four hundred miles ahead. Youngsters, above all, start off, having the breadth and complexity of the continent to familiarize themselves with.

Geography has glamour in America. The whole excitement of driving here implies some opposite new place to reach, and other nationalities like us for this. The English, arriving in Boston, promptly want to head for Arizona to meet the Navajos. Thomas Wolfe celebrated the cross-country railroad, the auto's smoky, rumbling precursor; and how Walt Whitman would have loved to drive, finally to run plunk up against the shining Pacific! Although there used to seem to be no need to go beyond the sea—whichever sea—because almost everybody's ancestors had crossed over from the other side, those two grand bulky oceans, separated by such a spread of miles, did much to mute for us the sadness of the end of the frontier.

What is ominous is that we know that once they have been

instituted, alterations and restrictions in the scope of life are never quite relaxed. Actual rationing may not come to pass, but in the meantime the spontaneity of travel has become a privilege, not a right; a freedom that was traditional has been pinched off. It would be easier to assent to the call for a return to the simple life—long walks, and so on—if we hadn't already made so many localities uninhabitable, on the theory that everybody who lived in them could pop onto the freeway and drive someplace else for a day off. Nixon, jumping into his jet or speeding along the thruways near San Clemente to let off steam, was only a souped-up version of the rest of us.

I have driven clear from east to west and west to east half a dozen times, and yet this closing of the open road strikes me as an immediate personal loss. When my native iconoclasm builds up in me until I want to knock people's hats off, I pile into my car and drive away with the window open, and soon find myself singing "God is good, God is great!" at the top of my lungs into the roaring wind, looking out at the tire recaps along the highway in Pennsylvania—then, two days later, at alligators, which are the spitting image of tire recaps, in the watery Louisiana woods.

This trip I was wolfing, though. I had a hand-cranked siren in the trunk that wolves will answer to, and a wolfish, lunging husky along, whose beastly nostrils at my ear and boisterous snuffles from the backseat kept the car from becoming completely a car. I'd been to Minnesota to see how the black bears manage, because there is some hope for them, and now I wanted to have a look at an officially endangered species, and while I was at it, at the animal which in America is perhaps the worst off, Texas's red wolf. Even with the crush in the world, some creatures do thrive— the scavengers and compleat omnivores like possums and coons, and beasts that move into a disrupted habitat by preference, like cottontails and ground squirrels. Others, more conspicuous—the arrowy, showy predators and hearty herd creatures like buffaloes and prairie dogs—or animals that are too single-minded or delicately attuned, haven't much chance. One's interest swings back and forth between the two groups.

Conservationists assume that a day will come when we will all want to pick up the pieces—that if only they can hold onto such living entities as the green turtle and the right whale for a little while longer, the consensus of civilized opinion will swing behind them. It is a questionable assumption, and so the gloomier, more visceral individuals go instead on the hunch that something may happen whereby finally the saved animals will inherit the earth. This isn't sensible, is misanthropic, and is a view they keep to themselves, but the most vivid observation to be made about animal enthusiasts—both the professionals who work in the field and, in particular, the amateurs—is that they are split between the rosiest, well-adjusted sort of souls and the wounded and lame. (More professionals are rosy, more amateurs are lame.) Animals used to provide a lowlife way to kill and get away with it, as they do still, but, more intriguingly, for some people they are an aperture through which wounds drain. The scapegoat of olden times, driven off for the bystanders' sins, has become a tender thing, a running injury. There, running away—save it, save it—is me: hurt it and you are hurting me.

Wolves are well suited to cupping any wounds that we wish drained. Big and concise enough to command the notice of any dullard, they are aggressive, as the wounded themselves wish to be aggressive. Once passionately persecuted, in just the kind of turn-about which people relish, a wolf can now be taken to represent the very Eden we miss, and being a wolf, is thought to be the best at what it does in a world which demands that any creature to receive attention must be the "best." Although in fact red wolves are inferior to other wolves at wolfish deeds, their name "red" adds a cachet, concealing their ineptitude from everybody except their friends.

Luckily for me, the scientist working with these little wolves, Glynn Riley, was not under contract to *The National Geographic,* or otherwise operating under the notion that he should hoard his findings. On the other hand, he wasn't a certified scientist either, but a trapper who simply had interested himself and learned more than the degree-bearing scientists had been able to. This meant, in the first place, that he was suspicious of any writer from the big city because of the campaign of the urban humane societies against the leg-hold steel trap—a threat to his livelihood, as he conceived it, which loomed importantly to him, if not to me. Also he felt none of the curiosity in chatting with me that the full-fledged *National Geographic* biologists are likely to reveal, even as they hold back the yarns and lore they plan to jot down for their own profit at some future date. One can wheedle considerable information from them sideways, so to speak, and it is not as lonely with the *National Geographic* biologists because the rapport goes both ways, whereas after a week or two with a trapper, one begins wishing that maybe he'll ask a question about New York City.

Instead of growing less susceptible to the debilitations of solitude, as I get older I am more so. It's a peculiar life: Tuesday hurrying along Sixth Avenue in New York, Wednesday, after a flight, exploring Dog Canyon in the Big Bend country near the

Rio Grande, startling the vultures off a lion-killed deer in a dry streambed overhung with black persimmon trees. To drive the distances involved helps cushion the switch, but then one runs out of gumption that much sooner at the site one has come so far to inspect. More than once I've had to dash away from scenery that was unimaginably lovely because I knew my time was up, that if I lingered, my mind, like Cinderella's, would soon be crawling with transmogrified mice. I've had crying jags and such, once in the room which serves as office for water pollution control for the Louisiana Department of Wildlife and Fisheries, headquartered in Baton Rouge. It was an appropriately empty, watery spot for crying, and funny because to actually deal with water pollution in Louisiana would require an office site the size of the Pentagon. I'd spent a clutch of weeks with four French-speaking fur trappers in the Cajun salt marshes that front the Gulf in the southwestern part of the state, and now after my contact man here in officialdom got through arguing his budget request for the ensuing year, we were to set off on a night trip by skiff so that I could stay awhile with several freshwater trappers in the cypress-tupelo-gum-tree swamps between the Mississippi River and Lake Maurepas. I couldn't stem the tears.

Air travel and the telephone, too, make for hysteria. A few spins of the dial and we can talk to almost anybody in the world, and in towns like Hackberry or Buras, Louisiana, or Alpine, Texas, at the first strong pinch of loneliness I've known that I could jump into my Hertz Ford and hop a plane for home. The trouble is, at home I've often wanted to catch a plane for Alpine— to be back in Dog Canyon again listening to the javelinas yap and fuss; then, uneasy there, might want to streak for Philadelphia. A friend of mine does let this panic take possession of him. His acquaintances in Hawaii, Los Angeles, and London hear from him, the times being rough and events going badly. Since he is an endearing chap, they say yes, he can come, and await his next move. He's reassured by all the invitations and calls or writes his other friends to tell them he is going to Hawaii, London, Los Angeles, or Mexico City. He calls the airport for fare and time-table information, but in the end, more frequently than not, relaxed at last by the show of affection, he goes nowhere at all.

In Minnesota, Lynn Rogers, the bear expert, had been rather guarded with me, as though he were feeling vulnerable himself and did not welcome the possibility that somebody else might get a handle on him which properly ought to be his. By contrast, Glynn Riley had no suspicions of me as a lay psychologist, didn't care what I thought of him, and wasn't concerned with the riddles of motivation. Instead, he was alert to the good name of his profession, and while he told me freely about his boyhood, his screw-ups in school, and courting Pat, his wound-up, stringbean wife—she has a certain flash and dazzle to her eyes and hair, and used to fold herself into the trunk of his car to get into the drive-in movies when they were kids—with the equanimity of a man at peace with himself, he would do this only on his own front porch. Never would he let me bounce about the country with him on his regular rounds, as Rogers had, checking traps and palavering with the ranchers, lest I see a trapped creature and write of its struggles. I couldn't convince him that an exposé of trapping was very low on my list of priorities; I'd seen plenty of trapping and knew that if the fellow wasn't one of a kind, like Riley, he was probably by now a grandfather who wouldn't be around by the time the controversy resolved itself. Similarly, the trapper employed by the wolf scientists in Minnesota, an old-timer who catches the wolves that they can't, won't let anybody else watch how he works. If he is in his pickup with one of the Ph.D. candidates, he will drive past a likely trapsite, giving no sign that he has noticed it, and stop a hundred yards beyond, leaving the young man in the truck and walking back to set the device with his back turned, lest at this late date these doctoral scholars, discovering his secrets, might desert their latter-day vocation for the sake of becoming a master trapper and compete with him.

In spite of being thin-skinned, Rogers had liked lecturing on bears and appearing on television and in the papers, but Glynn Riley had let me drive down to see him solely in the hope that I might pry loose from the Bureau of Sport Fisheries and Wildlife in Washington his appropriated funding, and more of it too, so that he could put radios on the wolves and hire a spotting plane and someone to help him. As I had seen, they were being as slow as a taffy-pull up there, but he was also sick of blathering to newspapermen—sick of their errors, ignorance, perfunctoriness, misemphasis—and though I explained that letters might accomplish what he wanted, that I had hopes of doing more with the wolves than merely publicize them, he remained correct with me, not to be cozened.

The dog-wolf family is thought to have originated in North America, migrated to Eurasia, where the gray wolf defined itself as a prodigy of the Northern Hemisphere, and then returned. Some biologists think that red wolves may be descended from a primitive wolf that stayed in North America during this diaspora and were hounded into the southeast lip of the continent by the returning grays. Others speculate that they are an offshoot of a worldwide race of primitive wolves of the early Pleistocene which have disappeared elsewhere; or, on the contrary, that they are a product of the devious ice-age geography blocked out by the glaciers which did so much differentiating among animal species. Another theory is that the red wolf sprouted from a common ancestor with the coyote in the Pliocene, and is not directly from the gray wolf's line. Coyotes, like Old World jackals, are "brush wolves" that became miniaturized for pursuing smaller prey in broken country where a hefty predator might not operate as well. They can put up with hotter temperatures—ranging into Central America—but not with the deep snows and freezes that arctic gray wolves know.

Red wolves are short-coated and long-eared, with stilty, spindly legs for coursing through the southern marshes or under tall forests. They have the neck ruff, almond eyes, and wide nose pad of other wolves, but not the massive head and chest, and so their angular ears and legs seem to stick out plaintively. Anatomically their brains are primitive, almost foxlike among the canids, and they have impressed naturalists as being as rather rudimentary animals, fragile in their social linkups, not very clever, unenterprising and almost easy to trap. Besides the pacing gait that they share with larger wolves and a flat dash, they bound along like modest rocking horses, standing up on their hind legs to peer over a patch of tall weeds. They are an unemphatic, intermediate sort of animal, behaviorally like wolves, ecologically more like coyotes. They howl like wolves, not like coyotes, and snarl when threatened instead of silently gaping the mouth, as coyotes do. They scout in little packs, unlike coyotes, which have stripped away a good deal of the pack instinct for better secrecy in crowded country and better efficiency at gleaning small game. A grown male weighs about sixty pounds, midway between a coyote's thirty or forty and a gray wolf's average of eighty pounds; but skinny as he is, the red wolf can live on a coyote's diet of cotton rats and marsh rabbits, and whereas a gray wolf needs about ten temperate square miles to feed himself—coyotes can get along as densely distributed as one every square mile—the red wolf again is in between. Five square miles supplies his food, and ten to forty is enough to stretch his legs and psyche with other members of the pack, about half what a pack of Minnesota timber wolves requires.

The earliest observers—William Bartram in 1791, and Audubon and Bachman in 1851—were definite on the subject of a smallish, darkish, long-legged wolf inhabiting the region from Florida to what is now central Texas, and north to the Ohio River. It was primarily a forest beast, piney in its affinities. The first government biologists of this century, men like Vernon Bailey and Edward Goldman, backed up the idea of a specifically southern wolf still more strongly, although the animals on the eastern seaboard had been exterminated already, and were gone everywhere east of the Mississippi by the 1920s. They did range the Ozarks and the river bottoms of Louisiana and the East Texas prairies, but because some of these latter had started hybridizing with an invading legion of coyotes, a body of opinion claimed that red wolves might never have existed at all except as hybrids of a coyote–gray wolf cross, or maybe as local grays, colored to suit the climate, in much the way that "white" wolves developed in the north. Since gray wolves possess such a fastidious sense of self that a cross of the sort would be a rarity, the rival proposition was offered that though red wolves might have existed as a true species at some point, they'd crossed themselves into extinction even before white men arrived.

Wolves are special beasts, so variable genetically that they partly live on disguised as dogs. Dogs, too, dance attendance on a breadwinner, cheerfully accepting the ups and downs of life with a master just as wolves stick with the pack, and bark and rush at an intruder close to the "den," otherwise marking their passage through life semantically with squirts of pee. If dogs were to inherit the earth they would quickly turn into wolves again; and coyotes carry the flag for wolves most directly, becoming bushy-necked and wolfish in appropriately remote surroundings, or little more than wild dogs when they live close to a city. Indeed, gray wolves would need only a nod from the voters to get a foothold in corners of their old range—Maine, for instance. Brought in, they would soon be at home, parceling up the timberland wherever the human populace is thin, until the deer found themselves in a density of two or three hundred per wolf.

But red wolves are so far gone by now—none has been photographed in the wild since 1934, and they are considered present in pure form in only two of Texas's two hundred and fifty-four counties—that the main effort to protect them involves not only shielding them from human intervention but from encroachment and dilution by coyotes. This situation is unusual. The rarest breeds of ferret, parrot, and so on, even manatees and prairie chickens, depleted in numbers though they are, seldom require protection from other animals, and it is this peculiar rattle-headedness—that these last wolves will so amenably let a coyote mount them—which has called into question their right to be regarded as a species. Mostly the museum scientists, such as Barbara Lawrence of Harvard, rather than the outdoor workers, have been occupied with challenging them, but recently a formidable young taxonomist at the University of Kansas, Ronald Nowak, with a friend named John Paradiso from the National Museum in Washington, has computerized a much larger body of evidence than Lawrence's and has taken up the cudgels against her and for them. The current majority view is to return to the belief that *Canis rufus* (called *Canis niger* for a while, but scientific names sometimes change more frivolously than common ones) is indeed a discrete creature, only lately decimated.

Nearer the East Coast, there were no other predators to replace the wolves when they had been killed off, but west of the Mississippi, coyotes from the plains slid in as soon as the shattered packs stopped defending an area. Coyotes could withstand the poisoning and trapping campaigns better, and the hard logging that the settlers did among the old-growth trees actually benefited them by breaking down the forest canopy. According to the evidence of skulls in the National Museum, the red wolves of Missouri, northern Arkansas, and eastern Oklahoma met their end in good order as a species, not mating with the coyotes as they were superseded. (It is a textbook theory that a true species is supposed to preserve its racial purity even more stubbornly in a border area under pressure.) But around the turn of the century, on the Edwards Plateau of central Texas where the same blitzkrieg of white settlers from the East was followed by an invasion of coyotes from every other direction, the demoralized red wolves for some reason began to accept coyotes as their sexual partners, and in the delirium of catastrophe created with them a "Hybrid Swarm." This "Swarm" thereupon moved eastward slowly, as ordinary coyotes were doing anyway at every latitude clear into Canada—and naturally was irresistible. Bigger, "redder" than coyotes, with such a piquancy of wolf blood already, these hybrids absorbed the wolves of Texas's Hill Country and Big Thicket all the more readily. They bred with true wolves and true coyotes and wild-running domestic dogs (even a few escaped pet dingos)—anything they met and couldn't kill—becoming ever more adaptable, a shoal of skilled survivors in a kind of canine Injun-territory situation.

The beaver trappers in the West had hiked out of the mountains and switched to hunting buffalo when the beaver were gone. The buffalo hunters were soon wolfers as well, and bounty-hunted them for a living after they had run through the buffalo. They sold the skins and paved the mudholes in their roads with heaped wolf bones, so many thousands were killed. Throughout the 1800s strychnine was the poison used. Then a drastic potion, sodium fluoroacetate, known as 1080, was introduced, and by the 1940s, a device called the "getter gun," which when implanted in the ground fires cyanide gas into the animal's open mouth when it pulls on a trigger knob baited with scent. From 1915 on, most of the wolfers were employed by the U.S. Biological Survey, which under the umbrella of the Interior Department eventually metamorphosed into the Bureau of Sport Fisheries and Wildlife. Thus by a piece of bureaucratic irony the same corps responsible for reducing the Midwestern red wolf to its final extremity is now the agency in charge of trying to preserve it. Even some of the personnel have been the same, which gives credence to the frequent complaints of calculated foot-dragging that conservationists have made.

To a taxonomist who looks at skulls of the period the record now seems plain as to how succinctly coyotes supplanted wolves in the hardwoods bottomlands along the Mississippi and in the Ozark Mountains. But the salaried wolfers naturally preferred to continue to see themselves, like the old-timers, as dealing with wolves, and so they kept on toting up an annual kill of thousands of "red wolves" in the official tabulation. As late as 1963, 2,771 were reported to have been done away with in the federal program of control. The year before, however, an obscure dissenter, Dr. Howard McCarley of Austin College, Texas, had published his contention that many of these were either coyotes or hybrids, and that the red wolf was nearly gone. Once his discovery was confirmed, the received opinion among biologists, who had taken so cavalier a view of Canis rufus until then, reversed abruptly to the notion that the creature may well have existed, but no longer did. Since there was nothing to be done about it, the poisoning was allowed to continue, till 1966, even in the Texas coastal counties where in fact a few survived. Fortunately two Ontario scientists, taking the matter more seriously than most of the Americans, had journeyed about one summer in the meantime playing recorded wolf howls in wild places and listening to the answers that they got—sundry barking mutts, coyotes, and coydogs. They were privately financed and soon ran out of funds, but they did learn that while McCarley had been right about the broad belt of territory he had studied, down on the muggy coast between the Vermilion River in western Louisiana and the Brazos in Texas a tiny remnant of voices were answering their taped Canadian wolves in kind. What with the lengthy delay in publishing these findings in a recondite journal (like McCarley's, earlier), and of bringing them to the attention of the federal specialists, not until 1968 was an organized recovery effort initiated, and not until 1973 was enough money provided to really begin. The scientific method depends upon a scoffing skepticism on the part of rival investigators to puncture a weak argument, but one reason why the biologists did not do more for the red wolf is that so many of them dillydallied while they scoffed.

Part of the appeal of southeast Texas is that some of its residents tend to deprecate the charms of the place. They'll say that the landscape is mosquito-bitten and unlovely, the colors washed out, that a tourist who wants scenery ought to move on. For a hundred years an army of Texans have believed themselves to be a Chosen People on the grounds of their good fortune—rather like the Victorian British, and in contradistinction to the Jews, for example, who historically have interpreted *mis*fortune to be the insignia of blessedness. Many people have believed that they were Chosen, but none more baldly than the Texans. Standing one evening in the Chisos Basin, an old Apache stronghold which is probably the pearl of the western section of the state, I must have looked affected by the colors, because I heard a Dallas fellow drawl behind me, "Well, you think you'll buy it?"

Minnesota had seemed fairly familiar—bleaker and flatter than northern New England, wilder than around my home in Vermont, but not more so than northern Maine, which has a moose herd three times the size of Minnesota's and a wilderness region three times as large. Lakes were interspersed through a balsam fir and white pine forest, and the natives had that clamped-down modesty cold weather brings, because you can't cultivate too grandiose an opinion of yourself when at any time for half the year a three-foot snowfall may shut you in. In Isabella, Minnesota, there was an individual called the Pig Farmer because of his supposed smell, who when the spring floods came would slosh around in two feet of water in his swamp cabin, eat cold food, and sleep in a wet bed instead of bothering to move to higher ground. Maybe nobody else can be as glum as a Great Lakes Finlander, but near my own house in Vermont is a barn with a whole cavern smashed in it, fashioned by the farmer himself one night when he drove his bulldozer against the wall after hearing that his youngest son, too, was going to leave the farm.

People who are bundled up much of the time, with stacks of firewood half the size of the house, and the sense that things will most likely go wrong if they haven't already: this is the America which stretches from the Atlantic Ocean to the Great Plains next to the Canadian boundary. The warm-weather rain forest of the Pacific may alter a woodsman's outlook, and, otherwise, the Rockies will give him big ideas, but what happens where the plains begin is that all of a sudden there are no trees. *No trees!* People started wearing big hats not simply because the brims were shady and wouldn't catch in the branches, but to help break up the landscape. It was a vast change, and in a huge country without forests to enforce a different perspective, many of them got to feeling big in the britches. Indeed, the big got bigger. Whereas in the woods that fellow with the swamp shanty and two cabbagey acres owns everything the eye can see, on the prairie it takes a rich man to feel so proprietary.

Down in Texas, the hats, the vistas, the britches, and the distances to be ridden, were still more expansive. To be thirsty in Texas was a powerful thirst. The rich grew filthy rich, but before that the Indians, whom the Texans dispatched with an implacable efficiency that was the envy of Indian-haters everywhere, had included some of the continent's stiffest tribes. Not only Apaches, but Comanches, and not only Comanches, but the Attacapas and Karankawas of the Gulf Coast, who in the early years were rumored to enjoy a man-bake as much as a clambake, eating a castaway's buttocks and arms right in front of him as he died.

The "Kronks," as the white men were wont to call the Karankawas (or, in an earlier, more authentic spelling, "Carancahueses"), were a robust people described as standing almost seven feet tall, with slender hands and feet, sensitive faces, and hair to their shoulders, with snake rattles tied in it and bangs in front, who swam superbly and cruised between the islands and sandbars of Galveston Bay in little fleets of dugout pirogues. They communicated with smoke signals—Y's and V's, diverging, curling, spiraling columns or twin zigzags—and employed a six-foot cedar bow with a three-foot goose-feathered arrow. Two families might travel together in a pirogue with a small deck at either end and the baggage heaped in the middle, erecting a single shelter of skins thrown over poles on the beach at night. They worshiped the sun, and on ceremonial occasions blew the smoke of a fire in seven sacred directions. They had a personalized god named Pichini and a dread god Mel, in whose grim celebrations they played a dismal-sounding stringed instrument five feet long, which bellowed like an alligator. For gayer festivities they had a tambourine made from a tortoiseshell and a reed whistle. They talked in whistles and sign language as well as words, and counted on their fingers, going from the pinkie to the thumb, which was the "father." They were a voluptuous people, the women grabbing for the penis of an enemy's corpse. It was said that they masturbated a good deal, and the name Karankawa was generally translated as "dog-lovers," because of the horde of voiceless dogs they kept, though their detractors claimed that the love went to even further extremes. The Lipan Apaches called them "those-who-walk-in-water" because they shot fish while wading, rather than from a boat. The Tonkawas called them "the wrestlers" because they liked to wrestle and were good at it. They wore a breechclout of Spanish moss, with a wreath of palm leaves as a hat and perhaps a cock partridge's feather behind one ear. They slept wrapped in deerskins and kept their firesticks in a skin bundle, used wooden spoons and fishbone needles, and red and black pots with conical bottoms that would stand upright in the sand. They ate seafood and every kind of meat, from buffaloes to skunks and reptiles—nursing their children for years to shelter them from this rough diet. The children, their foreheads sometimes flattened as a form of decoration, played with wooden dolls, and the adults tattooed blue circles on their own cheeks, and lines from eye to ear or parallel lines descending from the mouth. With vermilion they accentuated their eyes and striped themselves red and black and white, unmarried girls with the simplest, thinnest line, but married individuals decorating themselves with flowers, birds, and animals, and hanging colored stones and conch shells from their ears and the wings of the nose.

The Karankawas smelled of alligator grease, which was their chief protection from the bugs. After the whites had outgunned them, they hid in the thorn-brush thickets and behind the endless screen of man-high roseau cane. Since they had fought against the Comanches and Jean Lafitte's pirates, as well as against more orthodox settlers, and since they had numbered probably only about four hundred warriors when La Salle first landed on the Texas shore to establish a fort in 1685, they were all gone before the Civil War, when settlement really started. The last canoeful of able-bodied men deliberately paddled for the open sea during a storm, the legend goes, and the few women and children left begged their way on foot along the coast to Mexico.

Wolves, too, were a force that molded early Texas, and the optimists would claim that if we can just hold onto a smattering of them, when the time comes that people want to pick up the pieces we will have them around as a force to observe once again. The difficulty is that though there are as many buffaloes alive as the buffalo reserves can hold, buffaloes are not a force anymore; indeed, buffaloes not in the millions may not *be* buffaloes. Neither are Big Brown Bears a force, nor Mounted Indians. That former midcontinental prairie community of mounted Indians, gaudily iconic big brown bears, and buffaloes and rattlesnakes and eagles and gray wolves that once existed centering around what is now Nebraska and Wyoming represents our idea of the pre-white New World better than the coastal or woodland aboriginal cultures do, and we all turn a bit sorrowful, reading of the buffaloes shot by the millions for their tongues, of whole dramatic nations of plains Indians starved or served up smallpox or ridden under the ground. Yet we wouldn't then and wouldn't now have had it any other way. What could we have possibly done with all those goofy buffaloes besides shoot them right off? Land of opportunity, land for the huddled masses—where would the opportunity have been without the genocide of those Old Guard, bristling Indian tribes?

A pause is necessary when speaking in defense of wolves for some mention of their fearful destructiveness. The settlers had good reason to be afraid of wolves, the same reason that the Indians had for howling to each other when they surrounded an isolated cabin: wolves digging under a dead man's cairn to wolf down his spoiling remains, wolves disemboweling the family cow, feeding on her thighs and abdominal fat, burying their heads inside her, although her entrails lay unbroken and she was still alive and watching them. When wild game was no longer available, wolves killed the new livestock prodigiously—such stupid, lavish, feasty beasts presented to them as on a tray. They soon cast off their wilderness inhibition against killing too much to eat; there was no sating them, and for a cattleman no living with them—at least the big buffalo lobos. It was either them or him. No honest-minded naturalist can peer at a caged wolf without recognizing in the old sense its wicked air. That sharp and fabled nose hooding the teeth, the bright eyes all the more dangerous for being downcast, the uncannily tall legs and twitching ears—these, with its lugubrious howl, were what the pioneers feared.

The first settler straggled into the wilderness with a single-shot rifle, leading a couple of mules, with a crate of brood hens on the back of one and two piglets in a sack to balance the load, some seed corn, potatoes and soldier beans, and dragging a long-suffering cow with a half-grown bull at her heels which the fellow hoped might manage to freshen her again before he butchered it. In the north, he settled in a beaver meadow where a little wild hay grew, and planted his potato peelings, living off boiled cowslips, sour dock, dandelion greens, Indian turnips, and goldthread roots in the meantime. In red-wolf country, he lived in a hot hut with a scrap of cloth hanging across the door hole to fend the mosquitoes off, and saw his cattle, too, turn gray with malaria or bog down dead. He was afraid of wolves. The prairie was theirs, not his, and if they swept through in cavalry style, mocking his gun, and killed his mules, he was in a bad way. If they killed his cow, his children would have no milk; if they drove the deer out of the neighborhood and killed his chickens and hogs, the whole family might starve. A bachelor mountain man, wrapped in hides, here today and gone tomorrow with a pack of curs, could afford to be more nonchalant; he had no kids wandering alone along the streambank poking at the muskrats with a stick, and if he stretched his lungs at night he could holler from his bedroll louder than the hooting packs. When he shot a deer he tied his neckerchief to it to keep the wolves away until he lugged the last of it to camp. Still, sometimes these self-sustaining hobos were the ones who reported the attacks; the wolves were hunting something else and in their speed and happiness (they have been seen to jump up on the rump of a running moose and briefly ride there) happened to blunder on the man and turn toward him. In Kipling's *Jungle Book,* wolves were "the Free People."

A real wolfer lived for his wolves, trailed them for days, smelling their pee and fingering their toeprints to distinguish the bitch from her mate, slept out in order to waylay them on the trail, and when he'd shot them both, walked from his hiding place to scalp them and strip off their skins in an act quick as sex, leaving the white frames grinning in the grass. That yodeling, streaking wolf— he strung up snares that yanked it into the air and kept it hanging there, upright as an effigy, choking, kicking, till he came in the morning and hugged and punched it and cut its throat, or bound its jaws with barbed wire and carried it home across his horse to tie to a tree in the dooryard to tease for a week.

Here in littoral Texas the pioneers found an old-growth forest of large sweet gums, elms, loblolly and longleaf pines, hackberry trees and beech and oak. Wild violets and blackberries grew where the trees gave out, and then the prairie extended toward the sea: bluestem bunchgrasses, Indian grass, gama grass and switchgrass, with bluebells and milkweed spreading blue and white during the spring and buttercups and Indian pinks under these, the terrain broken by occasional sand knolls covered with yaupon and myrtle brush where the wolves denned and hid out. Next came a marsh of spunkweed, cattails, cut-grass, and the same spartina that the colonists on the Atlantic shore had fed to their livestock. A bayshore ridge fronted the Gulf, beyond which the wolves and pioneers and Indians crabbed and beachcombed, collecting stunned redfish by the wagonload after a storm. Wagonloads of oysters, too; and in the bayous mullet seethed among gar, catfish, and bullheads. Out in the tides were weakfish, black drum, channel bass, gafftopsail cats, sand trout. Summer was the fishing season; in the winter everybody lived on wildfowl and game. Prairie chickens could be caught by hand when they got drunk on fermented chinaberries; so could the geese when their wings froze together when the rain blew cold.

There was yellow fever, and hurricanes that washed away entire hamlets, and influenza in the winds and hock-deep water that the cattle still stand in. The wolves fed on sick waterfowl from everywhere north to above Hudson Bay. They still eat sick birds, mainly cripples from the hunting months, which is when the ranchers make their tax money, charging ten dollars a day per hunter. Red-winged blackbirds and robins continue to flock in million-bird masses, and blue and snow geese arrive from Canada by the tens of thousands, along with teal, gadwalls, canvasbacks, pintails, shovelers, and widgeons. The federal government has a bird refuge at Anahuac in Chambers County and two near Angleton in Brazoria County and one in Cameron Parish, Louisiana. The managers of these burn over the brush to plant millet and other goose food, and bring in cattle to keep the grass cropped green and short and to chop puddles in the ground with their hard hooves.

It seemed unbelievable that these last uncompromised wolves should have been discovered here in the salt marshes—next to Houston, Galveston, and Beaumont, Texas's most industrial and populated section—instead of in the piney woods and hillbilly thickets always listed as their home. Metro Houston grew by six hundred thousand during the 1960s to a total of two million people, America's third-largest port by tonnage; yet the wolves had ranged within Harris County itself and beside Galveston Bay and over in Jefferson County, within sight of some of the new subdivisions, through intensively productive rice fields, next to several of the state's earliest oil strikes, such as Spindletop.

Oil wells pump like nodding grasshoppers, bird watchers creep about on the lookout for avocets and phalaropes, and now that the deer are mostly gone, the wolves chew on stillborn calves and the carcasses of bloated steers that died of anaplasmosis. It was the last place the authorities had thought to look (for the debunkers, still a debating point), but the industrial buzz, the waterways and highways may have served to delay the coyotes for a little while. The older wolfers I dropped in on mentioned animals weighing ninety pounds or more which they hunted half a century ago with their July and Goodman hounds—roping them or clubbing them in the water when they took to a bayou to escape the dogs. Nowadays the wolves altogether add up to only one or two hundred sorry smaller specimens, because these final marshes are so mosquito-ridden that a calf, for example, may smother from the balls of insects that fasten inside its nose. Heartworms kill or invalid the grown-up wolves, plugging up their heart valves so that they suffer seizures if they run, and hookworms starve the pups. Tapeworms, spiny-headed worms, and sarcoptic mange plague them indiscriminately, the spring floods drown their dens, the summer heat renders them somnambulistic, and the saw grass rips their fur until their tails are naked as a rat's. In Chambers County alone there are ten cattle ranches of better than ten thousand acres, but the only cattle that can survive the bugs and watery winter footing are an indigenous mongrel Brahma breed.

Still, the ranchers have built many windmill-driven wells that bring fresh water to the wolves and other wildlife as well as to the cattle. The U.S. Soil Conservation Service has constructed raised cow walks above the standing water, and the oil companies have laid oystershell-based roads running upon embankments which provide the wolves with direct access nearly everywhere. Where the sand knolls that used to be their safe haven have been bulldozed away, windbreaks of salt cedar, huisache, and Cherokee rose have been planted that fulfill the same purpose. Better still are the innumerable miles of canal banks channeling water to the rice fields, in which a pair of wolves will excavate their various emergency holes to foil a flood or hunter, a practice which also cuts down on puppy parasites.

Rice farming has introduced a "horn of plenty," as Glynn Riley calls it, in the way of rodents. The fields stand fallow every third year, and when they are plowed and reflooded the rice and barn and cotton rats and gobbly mice and big and baby rabbits must scrabble out across the levees to another field in a frenzied exodus which the wolves attend delightedly—just as up north in dairy country, coyotes will follow a farmer's mower at haying time to bolt the running mice, or follow his manure spreader to eat the afterbirths which are included in the mess. But the wolves' best staple lately is another creature tendered up to them by man, the nutria. Nutria are furry water rodents five times the size of a muskrat, and locally more catholic in habitat and diet. Introduced from Argentina to Avery Island, Louisiana, in the 1930s by a Tabasco Sauce mogul who dabbled in natural history, they escaped during a hurricane, and being tolerant of brackish water, made their way successfully along the edge of the Gulf and the Intracoastal Canal, reaching the Rio Grande around 1967. They are a resource in Louisiana—the pelts are worth four or five dollars apiece—but in Texas they are shot as pests because they burrow through the levees and breed exuberantly and eat a lot of rice. They leave fingery tracks—have delicate fingers which can pluck up a single grain of rice—though, when abroad, they are so clumsy that they have been a blessing to the beleaguered alligators as well as the red wolves. The gators grab them in the water and the wolves snatch them in the fields at night when they venture out to feed, and for the wolves there is a nice balance to it because whenever the water gets so high that the nutria achieve a degree of maneuverability, the dry-ground rats are in a panic.

In spite of this abundant provender, coyotes have now seized all but two of the last seven counties under study; there is talk of a "Dunkirk Operation" to salvage a few wolves and whisk them to some sanctuary island such as Matagorda (already teeming with coyotes)—or, as it soon seemed to me, there may be no hope. It may not matter much if we bear in mind the continentwide accomplishments of coyotes in resettling wild areas; these wolves have been grist for the mill, making them bigger and "redder." But such considerations did not temper my irritation at the officials I met who should have cared about what was happening and didn't. The arrangements of the national Wild Animal Propagation Trust to distribute red wolves for a breeding program among cooperating zoo directors had collapsed without getting started. A noted biochemist in Minneapolis who had been interested in doing blood protein studies of the species had been forced to quit for lack of funding. The State of Texas had made no move to resurrect the wolves from unprotected varmint status, or even to make legally permissible the little gestures of help that Riley was receiving from a couple of local enthusiasts. It was both sad and comic; he was entirely on his own—other federal agencies in the neighborhood, and even other chains of command within the Fish and Wildlife Service, seemed indifferent to the matter—yet, as a trapper, he had faith that here in Chambers and Jefferson counties his lone trapline could halt the tide.

Riley lives in the small town of Liberty, and grew up in Wortham in the East Texas brush not far away. His father did some trading in scrub horses and thin cows, and if there wasn't any money in the house it still was a good life for a boy. Now he's thirty-eight, calls his father Pappy, and has that cowpoke look of not putting much weight on the ground when he walks. His face is trim and small, his body slim, his hair curly and neat and his voice mild. Like many wildlife men, he prefers being inconspicuous, and nature has given him the wherewithal. After a good supper he'll say that he's "full as a tick." He hasn't finished college yet, having dropped out several times, and is country-religious, so that although he is subject to more than his share of professional frustrations, if he is speaking bitterly and doing a slow burn, suddenly in midsentence he'll undergo a change and say of the other individual in an altered tone, "But bless his heart." "The good Lord gave the wolf forty-two teeth to eat with," he says in the same folksy way; and broadcasts wolf howls from his tape recorder on the telephone to callers. "Sounds like a pack of Indians." He says a mountain with a wolf on it stands a little taller, and that a wolf represents everything a man wants to be. "He's free, he's a traveler, he's always on the move, he kills his food. He's *worth* three hundred deer."

With none of the pained air of a late bloomer, Riley instead seems simply different in this age of Ph.D.s, and himself suggests that someday his own head ought to be nailed on the wall at the Smithsonian Institution alongside the red wolf's. He is a first-rate trapper, has killed "a jillion" coyotes for the government, and therefore is as skilled at politicking with the old ranchers and trappers as any government agent is going to be. Since he is not a cosmopolitan man, his worst difficulty has probably been in dealing with what ought to be his natural constituency, the conservationists "up East," that redoubtable big-city crew of letter writers whom other scientists have rallied to the cause of the whooping crane, brown pelican, and whatnot.

From the start trapping has been his passion—on the first day of his honeymoon he insisted upon running his trapline—and he used to measure the tracks of the coyotes in Wortham against the sizable wolf tracks in Stanley Young and Edward Goldman's standard book, *The Wolves of North America,* discovering right as a teenager that these were no longer any variety of wolf, though everybody around still bragged them up as such. He knew of one old beech tree down next to the Trinity River which still carried the claw marks of a black bear that decades ago had climbed it, and knew an old hunter who as a boy had crawled into the briar jungle there after two hounds, thinking they had treed a squirrel, when, lo and behold, one dog jumped over his head to get away and he saw the bear sitting with its back against the tree, swatting the remaining pooch. Of course no bears are left in Texas now within six hundred miles for Riley to see, and his bitterest experience as a boy was when he had to sell his rifle and borrow a friend's one fall, in order to pay the landowner's fee, when he wanted to go hunting.

He loved the howling, the matching of wits, and went to work for the Bureau, eventually being put in charge of these last wolves because he'd grown so good at nabbing coyotes. He's in the position of knowing more about them than anybody else, yet watching a succession of schooled young men arrive to make their academic names studying the animal before it vanishes. They must turn to him for help, as do the cameramen and journalists who show up in Liberty, and he's evolved a quietly noncompetitive attitude, putting the fun of his work ahead of the rivalries of a career. He traps a few wolves to attach radio collars to, and traps calf-killing wolves when the ranchers complain, before they get caught in one of the mangling four-trap clusters that the ranchers set. (The old method was to drag a dead cow roundabout, strewing chunks of tallow laced with strychnine behind it.) Mostly, though, he traps coyotes, especially prophylactically along the edge of the Big Thicket where the middling tracks of the hybrid swarm already have met and mingled with the wolves' large pads.

WOLF AT WORK, says a sign in Riley's office. He claims he "probably would have amounted to something" if he hadn't become fascinated with wolves, but that the country "wouldn't be complete" without them. With people already wall-to-wall, he frankly couldn't comprehend why anyone who was enough like him to show up at his door in the first place would want to live in New York City for much of the year. He was uncomfortably amazed, and every morning talked to me at first as if he were seated in a dentist's chair—I being the dentist—so that his role in whatever I had in mind achieving for him professionally could be over and done with. My lunging husky did serve as a recommendation. Riley laughed at how very furry he was, although in Minnesota, where the dog had also served to break the ice with the predator men (everywhere he tended to offend the ranchers and the farmers), they would immediately begin to talk about a wolf pup they knew back in the bush that was about his size and shade of gray.

Another favorable factor for me was that I'd read some of the literature of this infant science of predator ethology. A poorly, skimpy showing it makes, on the whole—perhaps a good month's read—but few of the journalists who seek out these field men have bothered to look into it at all, and since the field men themselves are not readers outside the particular pocket of their specialty, they are impressed when somebody has taken the trouble. Besides, as boyish as I was (like Riley, I had the sense that these adventurous predators, just as they *eat* all other animals, somehow *contain* all other animals)—still trying morning and night to catch sight of a wolf, peering into the spoil-bank thickets in the rice fields just as I had done thirty years before, speeding across the greasewood West as a youngster en route to Los Angeles on the Super Chief—by midmorning he would have managed to relax with me.

As kids both of us had climbed to many "caves," which usually proved just to be stains on the face of the rock when we reached them, but hoping to find some magic beast, a cougar or a wolverine, whatever the continent's legends might contain. So now in the evening he took me out to a coyote family's rendezvous, where with the siren we got them howling. Out wolfing again at dawn, we tried to provoke the soundless wolves, but instead it was the snow geese from white-wolf country, wheeling in platters by the thousands, that answered us. We saw coots in the ditches and an alligator so long it looked like two, half in, half out of the water, and more serrate and flat-looking than I'd anticipated. We saw fish popping in Oyster Bayou, and crabs and fat brown water snakes, and an armadillo with a tiny pointed head and papery ears; saw pelicans flying, and wavy lines of white ibises and cormorants, and roseate spoonbills like scoops of strawberry ice cream high in the air, and plenty of mink and otter tracks. Otters lope in a way that even in the form of prints communicates their speedy eagerness.

Riley himself walked rapidly, hunkering down to feel the depressions left by a wolf's toes. He bent right to the ground to smell its scenting station—a wolf's squirt smells milder, not as musky as a coyote's—to distinguish how much time had passed. The far-flung spatters were a diagram for him. He loves toes, hopping with his hands, his fingers in the toes, and never now encounters a wolf or coyote that he can't catch if he wishes to. Often he chooses not to, unless he wants to shift them around, but in any part of Texas he can envision the land much in the way that coyotes do, knowing where to find their prints and how to catch those toes. He's like a managerial cowboy, with wolves and coyotes for his cows.

His traps have toothless offset jaws, with a long swiveled drag to minimize the damage done. He attaches a bit of cloth steeped in tranquilizer for the wolf to mouth so that it will sleep. Sometimes, too, he removes a spring to weaken the bite, and adjusts the pan until the jaws close at a touch, so not the slender leg but the resilient paw is pinched. He boils the traps in a black dye, then coats them with beeswax, and has a shed full of dark-glass bottles of wolf, coyote, and bobcat urine, with bits of anal gland chopped in, or powdered beaver castor and beaver oil—two universal lures from his old haunts along the Trinity—to sprinkle on a mudbank above the trap, although in fact the wolves are gullible enough to step into a trap lying open on the ground if it is placed well, and coyotes, though cleverer, are nearly as curious as they are clever, so that anything that stinks may draw some of them in.

Wolves scratch at a scent post after wetting it, whereas bobcats scratch beforehand, and neither is especially intrigued by the other's sign, but to trap either animal he employs the scent of an interloper of the same species. Wolves love to cross into the territory of another pack and leave their mark to razz the residents, like kids painting their colors on a rival school. Some of the feral dogs he traps run snapping at him, but wolves and coyotes are dumbstruck as he approaches, and after a bark or two will do anything to avoid offending him. Generally they hunch down, "sulling," facing away. I saw him bring a hybrid back and maneuver it into the netting of a holding cage, supplying a pan of water before he went to lunch. The coyote dipped its chin into the water to verify that it really was going to be permitted to drink, then held its head away from the pan until we left. He shoots these, saving the skull and skin and looking for any telltale vestiges, such as the placement of a certain vein on the rear ankle that red wolves bequeathed to the hybrids which neither gray wolves nor coyotes quite duplicate, or perhaps some feathers on the forelegs inherited from a stray bird dog. Or he may discover a coyote's little teeth set into a wolf's lanky jaw. The wear on the incisors will show its approximate age. Wolves have more forehead in their skulls than a coyote, and grays have more than reds, but dogs, which are dish-faced, have more forehead than wolves. Wolves boast big wide cheeks, big teeth, and a proportionately lengthier, narrower braincase than coyotes or dogs, and the sagittal crest along the ridge of the skull where their powerful jaw muscles attach is more pronounced, but a dog's crest is higher than a coyote's. Coyotes, though, like wolves, have more space provided within the margins of the skull for their hearing organs than dogs do.

Wolves' hind legs usually swing in the same line as their fore-legs—they single-foot, as foxes do—whereas dogs put their hind feet between the prints of their front feet and show a shorter stride. With his tape measure for checking tracks and a siren for censusing, Riley goes about looking at the feet of wolf-chewed calves to see if they had ever really walked or were born dead. If something did kill them, he sees whether they were pulled down by the ears, dog-style, or by the belly and the hams, as a proper wolf would. Everywhere he stops his truck to look at tracks—at the short feet of feral mongrels dumped sick originally from hurrying cars along the Interstate, at the wide feet of "duck dogs" lost during hunting season, and the big heelpad and long foot of a true wolf. For the record, too, he collects skulls and skins "off the fence," wherever the ranchers are still poisoning. When he catches notable beasts that please him—two black coyotes that I saw, for instance—he "transplants" them.

"You transplanted them to heaven?" I asked.

"No, no, somewhere that they're going to be real happy."

Texas contains considerably less state-owned park and recreation land than New Jersey, and for its size, remarkably little federal acreage too, because one of the terms of its annexation to the United States was that the federal government acquired no public domain. Its history has been all private enterprise, and whereas Florida and Southern California have fetishized their sunshine, Texas has promoted the notion of space. Conservation legislation of any kind has had a difficult time making much headway, and many a landowner profits more from selling his deer to the hunters, at two hundred and fifty dollars per season per man, than from his cattle. Minnesota's wolves range mainly on government land, but Texas's live on private property, which means that their fate is tied to the inheritance tax and the local tax rate on land. If the ranching oligarchies fare badly, if their oil runs out or the assessors decide to put the squeeze on them in favor of new industry or summer development, or if a younger generation, coming into possession of the key spreads of property, wants to be rich in money instead of open spaces and maybe live elsewhere, it will spell the end of the red wolves.

In 1803 the U.S. purchase of Louisiana brought Anglo-American settlers to the eastern border of what is Texas. In 1821 Mexico gained her independence from Spain and the first Anglo colonists received permission to cross the boundary and settle southward on the Brazos under a Spanish-type "emprasario" system, whereby one energetic, commanding man was given a land grant on which he undertook to establish upwards of two hundred families, exercising quasi-judicial authority over them. This was a different conception of how to do things from the homesteaders' democratic methods in the American Midwest farther north, but within fifteen years the population of Texas quintupled. By 1830 the government in Mexico City was trying to forbid new Anglo settlements, to restrict immigration to Catholics, and otherwise pinch off the fast-developing trade relations between these Protestant citizens and their former homeland in the States. The Texans' War of Independence followed in 1836, but the emprasario method of settlement continued, and by the time that Texas joined the Union in 1845, the population had again quintupled, to nearly a hundred and fifty thousand.

Thus Texas was annexed, but on its own say-so—take us as we are—its land its booty, and fashioned in its infancy by Spanish-

Mexican autocracy and in its adolescence by successful revolt and outlawry. In all the pulling and hauling there had been no eastern-seaboard counseling, no older-brother leavening by Virginia and Massachusetts army generals who supervised the birth of other states, or by a moderating president and Congress in Washington. In quick order the Civil War began, in which Texas, a slave state, went with the South, deposing its elected governor, Sam Houston, who was a Unionist, in the process. More revolt, hard riding, and bitterness through Reconstruction, until by the onset of the new century Texas's population had increased to three million, but the crest of settlement had included an embittered surge of Southern veterans—burnt-out families grappling for land to assuage their loss. The Mexicans had been bundled off or reduced to a serf class, the Indians done away with, the wildlife mostly extirpated, and in a pride-heavy, insular setting soon to be thoroughly lubricated with oil there was little influence to dampen the frontier swagger.

Booted boys and behatted giants fish from the boardwalk at Port Aransas, knifing the croakers that they catch with enthusiasm. Even Cokes look bigger in Texas; and eating habits remain Brobdingnagian, with funny consequences for the midriff. But in Odessa I went to a "rattlesnake roundup" advertised for the municipal coliseum, and found the entrance thronged with ticket holders. This seemed what I was after—the old Texas rite for ridding the calving range of snakes—except that the crowd turned out to be fans attending a rock concert. The "rattlesnake roundup" was way around in back inside an adjunct shed, with three cars parked at the door.

Texas is still a good place to be rich in. Money is the stamp of excellence, yet in the southeast sections a more rooted conservatism, involving the illusion of an old-family tradition, has been carried over from the states nearby. Since it is a conservatism essentially unburdened by the weight of tragic circumstance of the Old South, one needn't become a contortionist to imagine that this is indeed the good life. Part of a wolf-seeker's regimen is to visit these grand mansion houses, and everywhere he encounters gracious living in the form of magnolias and spacious acreage patrolled by black cowhands—peacocks, guinea hens, and fancy breeds of geese strolling the grounds, ten-foot alligators in private pools, pet deer in live-oak groves festooned with trailing moss. Quail and mourning doves, mimosas, pecans, orange trees, big-kneed cypresses, four cars in the garage, cool patios with iron grillwork, long lawns, little lakes, and girls and their daddies—girls so pretty Daddy doesn't quite know what to do with them.

These men of good fortune—men like Joe Lagow of Anahuac,

and R. E. Odom, who lives across the Sabine River from Texas in Louisiana—glanced at my Vermont license plates, New York face, and gray husky, and talked to me with caution. Lagow is a short jaybird of a man who serves as county commissioner and on a number of committes, and with his in-laws owns twenty-six thousand acres of snow-goose, red-wolf country. When I called to him across his aviary to ask if he was Joe Lagow, he swung around agreeably and said, "Yes, I'm what's left of him." Odom is younger and more reticent, even a little feline and courtly, in the Louisiana manner. We had tea in his jewelbox of a house, served by his white foreman. With his mother he owns a matchless spread of land in what is called Gum Cove, a luscious loop of grazing ground a few feet above sea level, enclaved within the badlands of Cameron Parish and reachable only by ferry across the Intracoastal Canal.

The time is past when Southern ranchers can be bamboozled into a reflexive show of hospitality, and various of these men gave me to understand, with conscious irony, that they were conservationists because they were conservatives and it would only be when new views took command that the ecology of their grasslands would be disrupted—smiling as they said this because of course a visiting Northern journalist was likely to represent those views. Nevertheless, the parade of exotic scribblers and photographers whom the environmental vogue is bringing to the door has started them thinking that the wolves that den on their mesquite knolls may be among the perquisites of wealth here on the Gulf; they've told their cowhands to quit killing them. It's the little operator, leasing pasturage for forty cattle that he has his hopes pinned on, who is still likely to put out traps, and if his few hundred acres happen to lie athwart a wolf run, it won't much matter how many thousands more stretch trap-free all around.

I went to Wolf Corner in Thompson, Texas, just beyond the Houston city line, where a trapper named Charlie Grisbee has nailed up as many as thirty wolves or hybrids at a time. Grisbee wasn't home, but on his starchy lawn a wooden wolf was chasing a wooden family of ducks. It was a suburban sort of house interfaced with stone, all spruce and neat, with blue Pullman curtains in the windows of the garage. I'd asked whether Charlie was married and people had said very much so; they didn't think his wife especially liked his trapping, but that it "went with Charlie." A single twenty-pound coyote was hanging on the rack at the corner of a field next to the highway—attenuated-looking, rotting, twitching in the strong wind off the Gulf, with its head and tail hacked off, its rain-stained, rabbity fur and rabbity legs no longer distinguishable as those of a predator. In the grass for yards around were tibias, scapulas, and backbone scraps, along with dewberries and Indian paintbrush, but some developers had now got hold of the field. I picnicked on the porch of a preempted farmhouse with a veteran fig tree for shade and honeysuckle all about.

In Danbury, in Brazoria County, I talked to Andrew Moller, among other old wolfers. Though Brazoria didn't bounty scalps, some of the fellows would deep-freeze what they caught and cash them in elsewhere. Moller is ninety-one. His grandfather jumped ship from a German whaler and bought land on Chocolate Bayou for five cents an acre, unfortunately sold off later. Once he was safely born, his father and his uncle had taken off for an adventure of their own, riding down the coast to Mexico for a couple of months, wading their horses across the many rivers they encountered at the mouth. And "in nineteen and eleven" he, a chip off the same block, had treated himself to a thousand-mile wagon ride around Texas, before paying thirty-five dollars for sixty cows, which over the next forty years he husbanded into a herd of fifteen hundred cattle. A traveling man, he mostly rented pasture for them. He trucked them to the Davis Mountains in West Texas, and to two decommissioned army camps in Arkansas and Oklahoma—unexpected long-grass pasturages on easy terms which he had hit upon during his hunting trips—always "keeping at least a nigger hired." Once he bought a thousand mares at four dollars a head, all of them running wild—he had to catch them—but sold them for ten dollars a head to a bootlegger who pirated them across the Sabine to Louisiana undipped and uninspected. Two of his old hands visited him recently in Danbury. He fed them catfish "and never heard two niggers laugh so much."

Using Walker hounds and Trumbulls, Moller caught little wolves in the nineteenth century when he was little and big ones when he grew up, till the barbed-wire fences were strung. A coyote, like a fox, will dodge into thick brush, he says, but a wolf "leaves the country." To catch him you first have to convince him that you are going to by running him ten miles through the sage and salt grass without letup. "Run a V on him" with other riders until his hind end wobbles and he hasn't gained a yard and begins to despair; then it may take another five or ten miles. Or if they could drive one into the Gulf of Mexico, they would keep roping him while he bit the ropes in two, until at last they drowned him. To run the wolves, even without a kill, kept the packs busted into isolated pairs which were less troublesome to the cattle, and generally Moller would catch the pups at the family rendezvous each fall. Sometimes, though, a varmint hunter would shoot a calf by mistake as it rose up suddenly in the grass. He'd had a couple of hog dogs as a boy that would chase any pup they came across, and with these he began wolfing on Chocolate Bayou, where the Amoco oil refinery now stands. In "nineteen and two" he was helping a trapper friend trail the wolves that hobbled off dragging the trap behind them, except it got to be such fun that they quit trapping and simply ran the creatures—ran them into swimming water where Moller would strip and grab a club and manhandle the wolf out to where the dogs could throttle it. Or he might rope it, haul it home to the hog pen, and feed it cracklings and offal until his wife complained about the stink.

Moller is a well-set-up individual with pink coloring, a long face, a big pair of ears and nose, and a mellow voice. In 1895 eighteen inches of snow fell and half his father's cattle died. They skinned two hundred hides that week that fetched a dollar a hide in Galveston, both working as dollar-a-day cowboys afterwards, his father eating alligator tails and getting a dollar apiece for those hides too. Or they would paddle down Chocolate Bayou with four deer carcasses, put them on the city boat, and trade them for a sack of green coffee in Galveston. In 1900 a hurricane blew down the house and washed away half the people who lived in the area, he says; one husband and wife held hands, grabbed hold of some driftwood, and floated for thirteen miles.

The game was so plentiful—from cranes to doves—that on their hunts sometimes they couldn't hear the hounds for all the birds hollering. Sometimes, too, there were so many wolves about that when they went out after geese they couldn't creep close to a pond where a flight had just landed before some wolf would bound into the water to see whether any cripples were in the bunch, putting them all to flight. Moller captured the spring pups by riding up on a sand knoll where a lot of wolf tracks converged and prancing his pony around until its hooves broke through into the den. Then, on the following day, he'd jump the gyp-wolf (mama) there, and the day after that the pop. Once at the South Texas Wolf Hunters Association meet at the King Ranch, the Mexican hands had butchered a beef and hung it up for everybody to help himself, and brought out horses—the members had only had to bring along their own saddles. They all painted numbers on their dogs to score them in the chase, and Moller and a buddy stayed out late hounding a wolf until at last the creature "set his bucket down." He was exhausted, so they roped him, whipped the dogs away, and tied his mouth and carried him back across a horse, and at the big bonfire slipped off the ropes and heaved him into the crowd of wolfers to start the hunt all over again.

The cowhands close to Houston are mostly black, not Mexican, as they are towards the Rio Grande, or white, as in the bulk of Texas. Slingshots, in the old journals, are known as "nigger-shooters," but since at least the work was manly in the old days, for some of them it may have been a tolerable sort of place to be a slave—alone on horseback hassling the cattle much of the day. It still would seem to add up to a better life than growing peanuts in Mississippi, although the shacks along the road look just as rickety as Mississippi's, and though many of the people one encounters have a peculiarly screwed-tight intensity to their faces—extraordinary faces that a traveler sees nowhere else in the United States— as if they had been scorched in a crucible, like black faces in Mississippi. Can it simply be the sun?

One morning I was chatting with a rancher who said he wanted to kill all the turkey buzzards in the sky as well as the red wolves. There are plenty of buzzards. We could count about fifteen standing about in the treetops and roosting on fence posts. Overnight the rain ditches had filled, the sky still smelled of rain, but as we visited, the sun broke through, lying at a cannon's angle, the kind of morning sun that made you answer to it, irradiating dead as well as living things. Greens bled into blues and reds, white was black and black was white: too much color and too bright. The wind, which had been chilly, began to heat. Then, in this incredible intensity of light, what the buzzards did, following some lead from an elder, was all at once to spread their wings, not in order to rise and fly, but holding them outflung to dry.

What we were witnessing was not unfamiliar. Everybody has seen pictures of a totem pole topped by a raven carved with its wings outstretched, the earth's creator, according to the maker of the totem pole. Ravens are the buzzards of the North. What we were privy to—fifteen buzzards spread-eagled, metal-colored in a violent sun—would have transfixed an Indian of the Northwest, would have provided a whole life's ozone to a woodcarver, a vision any warrior would have died for, if in fact his excitement didn't render him invincible. Fifteen images of the Creator in a rising sun would have propelled a great chief into his manhood after walking naked for a month; except we have no divine signs now.

I had settled in Anahuac at a café-motel where the owner displayed her late husband's Yale diploma in the office as a talking point. She missed Arkansas, claimed it had been an awful mistake for them to have left Little Rock nineteen years before, and looked that Southern mixture of left-over hopefulness and untidy despondency—hard shoulders and forearms but vulnerable breasts and soft hands. She served a rueful menu of chicken-fried steaks and heavy catfish to lonely oil workers and roaming fishermen. I was discouraged, angry at the way the wolf project was on the back burner for everybody but Glynn Riley. In Washington there was a mixture of flutter and indifference—even to get information had required a personal visit—and over the years Texas's Parks and Wildlife Department has taken what might politely be described as a minimum of interest. (Their black bears were allowed to fall practically to the vanishing point before receiving partial protection.) The wolves' blood characteristics had been studied not at a Texas medical center but in Minneapolis, and in Houston itself the concern, if possible, was fainter yet. The director of the Museum of Natural History, Dr. Thomas Pulley, an influential man, was not so much uninformed about the wolves as agin 'em. He hadn't exhibited the handsome skins that Riley had sent him, and liked to take the long view, speaking of man's impact on the world as related to evolution like the glaciers, belittling the notion of interfering as "causey, like preserving mustangs." He seemed bankerly in manner, a small-city, big-fish iconoclast with the mocking cast of mind that often develops in isolation, rubbing up against mostly laymen. He said that when he and his friends hunt deer they see plenty of coyotes.

The Houston zoo director, a civil servant, was not as self-assured. He had no wolves and agreed with me that though the zoos in San Antonio and Oklahoma City did keep one or two, it was incongruous that the only propagation program in the nation was way off in Tacoma, Washington. He said that to construct a "wolf woods" would cost only about seven thousand dollars, but that to raise such a piddling sum among the multimillionaires of Houston would be difficult because controversial, and so his efforts on behalf of disappearing species were devoted to the St. Vincent's parrot and Galápagos tortoise.

Riley carries hurt wolves to a veterinarian friend, Dr. Buddy Long, in the town of Winnie. Long pins together any broken bones (wolves will tear off a splint), administers penicillin and distemper shots, and worms them. He is a man who "likes old things," and is the angel of Riley's program, having sunk thousands of dollars of his own modest funds into the work. He has a scrunched-together, matter-of-fact face, the mouth creased for smiling, and propagandizes as he makes his rounds among the cattlemen, several of whom still trap but who will telephone him when they catch something, if they don't like the idea of inviting a government man to poke about their property. The animal is a sad sight, clinched into a clutch of traps, with its feet mauled. Whatever toes are left he tends, or if the wolf is dead, he leaves it soaking in a tub for whenever the scientific community gets around to wanting to know what a red wolf looked like under the skin. At the time of my visit he had no legal authority to keep wild animals, and when the wolves he treated were ambulatory not a zoo in the country was prepared to take them, and so one night he'd leave the door of the pen open.

Long is a bit older than Glynn Riley, well settled in one of those delicious marriages that are a pleasure to catch sight of, and, as luck would have it, has been bolstering to Glynn. Through studying blood parasites he had become interested in the wolves, and now kept captives of his own in a big breeding arena. White on the lips and chin, with broad cheeks, narrow noses, a pointed attention and that skittery bicycling gait—whirling, almost flittering away from me along the fence—they were still jazzed up from the courting season, when they had chased each other all over Chambers County. Unfortunately this same month or two coincides with the calving season in the region, so that the ranchers see more of the wolves when they least want to.

Long took me wolfing along Elm Bayou, East Bayou, Onion Bayou. A blue heron was eating baby alligators, though in a few weeks it might be summering in one of the suburbs of Chicago. The geese in their yapping thousands flew up from the fields around us; they would soon be on the tundra. Long said that skunks are thick, and that though a grown wolf would have enough sense to steer clear of a rabid skunk, a blundering pup might get bitten and carry the disease into the packs.

"Around here you can look farther and see less than anywhere in the world," he said. But we inspected the "swimming holes" where the stockmen swim their cattle across the Intracoastal Canal every fall, then in the spring again, bringing them back to higher ground. We saw the burros that they use to halter-break the yearling colts, tying colt and burro neck to neck. He spoke about the problems of a cow vet. "Sometimes they won't get well and sometimes they won't die." At the fence gates we found wolf tracks. Now that the fields were drying off for spring the baby rabbits were hopping from the nest, and the wolves had scattered off the levees to catch them. Long said that sometimes the wolves will run a ranch dog right through a screen door, and twenty cattle through a fence, and pass the house again that night, barking so as to rib the dog. When hunted, they will circle into a herd if no other cover is close, and hamper the men from getting a shot at them by sticking beside the cattle.

Among the many lice-chewed cattle we saw one fine high-horned bull with a long dewlap, ears that hung down at a steep angle, a hump big as a camel's, and a penis like a rhino's. He was a pretty mouse color, all the prettier for being so dangerous-looking underneath that comely pelt. "That one would try to get in your back pocket with you," said Long as we negotiated the gate.

The only other strong ally of Riley's I was able to find in Texas was Hank Robison, who sells cigarette lighters and ball-point pens in Houston. A lobbyist and crusader, he has worked to get the local bounties removed. He lives in a workingman's district, has gold in the front of his mouth, is self-educated and self-conscious about it, and financially must live by his wits, he says. But posters of lions and tigers stare off the walls of his small house; his blinds are dog-chewed. He talks like a dogged cross between a crank and social worker and is a fervid letter writer, keeping a file so that no officeholder can get away with not replying to him. He has a flatly single-minded fighter's face, taking you for where you stand, and when knocked down, obviously will not stay down, because his delight is just precisely to get up again. He camps in the Big Thicket on weekends and lives for his family as well as for wild animals, and yet in him I thought I saw what I notice in other enthusiasts and in myself: the injured man who recognizes in the running wolf his wounds.

Riley could comprehend a person preferring to live in the city if he liked going to the movies or had the money to eat in restaurants, but what he couldn't understand about the Eastern cities was the matter of muggers. Working with wolves, he wasn't afraid of muggers. "Why don't they clean them out of there?" Like Lynn Rogers in Minnesota, apparently he had a picture of himself walking down the avenues and, if he saw a mugger, punching him in the mouth. Of course, being familiar with firearms, he could adjust his image when I said that the mugger was likely to be armed, but he continued to presume that the solution lay in individual acts of heroism. What neither man could grasp was how *many* muggers there are.

Glynn has poisoned pocket gophers in East Texas and prairie dogs in West Texas, and out in Muleshoe in the Panhandle did rabbit counts for the Bureau, where he saw some odd spectacles: a badger and a coyote turning over cow chips in a partnership to eat the beetles underneath; an eagle snatching a duck from a windmill spillway. The eagles perched on the boxcars where feed was stored to spear the pack rats living underneath, and early one morning he watched a coyote filch a rabbit from an eagle, the coyote's chest fur shining nobly in the sun. Once in a while he'd drive a hundred miles or so to chat with an old wolfer who had shot the last gray Western lobos at their watering holes. One time the fellow had ridden here to the Gulf to dispose of a hog-killing red wolf: lay waiting for it behind the pen the night that he arrived, and when he heard the hog scream, shot the wolf, and the next day left—too many people here, not that big Western country. "We thought there'd always be another wolf. We didn't know they would ever play out," he told Glynn.

Riley's best thrill, when he has visited the study crew in Minnesota, has been to feel with his hands the outsized tracks the wolves make there in the fluffy snow. Gray wolves are real wolves in a way that red wolves aren't, and the black taiga wolves of the Yukon and the white arctic wolves are larger still. Someday he hopes to have a hand in studies of them all: jaguars too. He's a predator man and he wants size—dire wolf, cave bear! Then, because he was a novice on snowshoes, he began to make strange tracks himself, falling down and flinging out his arms. For days it was the joke in camp: *that's* where Glynn Riley from Texas fell down, and *there's* where he fell down again.

Like old-time trapping, Riley's is a lonely business. His best friend lives six hundred miles away in the Trans-Pecos town of Marathon, Texas. He's a mountain-lion hunter whom I'll call Mike Marfa, and the two of them became acquainted at what Marfa likes to call "rat meetings," where the varmint-control technicians of the Fish and Wildlife Service get together to talk shop, mostly about killing rodents and rabbits. But these two were men who had a penchant for pulling down a bigger creature, and, beyond that, were outdoorsmen with a vocation for it (Marfa likes to say that he's already caught enough coyotes to fill ten diesel trucks). When the two of them do manage a visit they can hardly contain their pleasure. They open the pungent brown bottles that Riley sets such store by, bobbing their heads like connoisseurs above the beaver oil and bobcat urine, two years in the brewing, though Marfa likes to tease Riley that it is where you put the trap, not so much what you sprinkle on it, that does the job.

Marfa is another man who knows more than many of the professors do who hold Chairs on the strength of their investigations into ethology, and sometimes comes back snorting from the symposia he goes to, saying he'd like to hear from the guy who *catches* their lions for them. For years he was the state's principal lion hunter, when the Bureau had a hundred and fifty trappers giving the coyotes a going-over. He was paid a little more and got up earlier too, he likes to claim, kidding Riley, and went out on muleback the whole day long, chasing after his hounds, instead of tooling about in a pickup truck like Riley and the rest, to prune the lions back to the edges of Big Bend National Park from a line which corresponded more or less to U.S. Highway 90. When I first met him he was on his way home from an excursion to Florida where he had demonstrated for the World Wildlife Fund that the Florida panther was rarer than Florida's wildlife officials had believed. His pack of mottled Walker hounds—a home brew he has bred and culled and whittled on over the years, and doesn't sell or swap or loan, he says, any more than a carpenter would his tools— were sleeping in a fresh pile of hay in the back of his truck, so placid after traveling so far that they spoke well for him. He and Riley took them for a run after bobcat along a bayou bank, but then, although Riley was eager to have him stay overnight and go to the Houston Fat Stock Show, which happened to be on that week, and although he himself was wistful about the possibility too, he said he had another twelve hours of driving ahead and didn't want to keep the dogs cooped up any longer than that. He's the type who scoops up every hitchhiker on the road, otherwise stopping nowhere, but compared to Riley, his mannerisms are gruff and harsh, and he is proud of going all day in the Big Bend desert without either water or food. Like so many other wildlife men, he was not in the Marines when he was a youngster and probably should have been. Where the bear man, Lynn Rogers, had made the burler's leap to city living in Minneapolis in the winter, Riley and Marfa had not. Riley had relinquished much of his hunter's spark, however, to a reflective attitude that suited his present work, but Marfa, whom Riley rather looks up to, was just as hot as ever; he had quit the Bureau and when he wasn't working on an experimental program to transplant mountain lions from the Big Bend country to South Texas, supported himself as a private lion hunter in the Big Bend region, and by trapping the last few lobo wolves down in the Mexican states of Durango and Chihuahua.

Marfa let me delve about with him a bit in his own territory, first wanting and then deciding that he didn't want a full-dress magazine article written about himself, but through both men I caught a sense of the cycle of wolf and coyote hunting.

The coyote is of course the "barking wolf," the Trickster of so many Indian tribes—a deity to the Chinooks and the Navajos, a subtle animal with a taste for the suckled milk in a lamb's stomach, for instance, which the simpler-minded bobcat does not share—the New World version of the jackal, and yet a creature so highly thought of that the pregnant women of certain Indian tribes would wear its testicles next to their stomachs to ward off difficulties. The fall is nonetheless the season when the guileless pups are dashing around; it is a chance to wipe out the year's crop while they are wet behind the ears, and was the season for the getter-gun until the getter-gun as a device was disallowed. Any witches' brew could be used to bait the knob—possum juice, rotted gopher, dead rattlesnake or frog—and since the pup took eight or ten leaps to die, more of the hunter's time was consumed in locating its little corpse in the brush than in any other part of the job.

In the winter the getters weren't as effective and the sort of man without any particular skill who had coasted along in the fall by putting out a lot of them took a back seat to the serious trapper. Winter is the mating season, and the emphasis is on catching the adults as they hustle about, pissing at scenting stations and trailing one another. Sex is what interests them, not picking up the quaint and curious scents that getter-guns are baited with. The trapper, milking the bladders, cutting the musky anal glands out of the specimens he bags, creates some scent posts of his own or activates others—a turkey wing lying next to a sheep path—that the smarter coyotes will step up to. In a bog in Anahuac, the fellow might set his trap at the end of a footlog, with a wad of moss under the pan so that a raccoon's weight won't depress it.

In the spring and summer the animals lose interest in everything except their pups, and travel in a beeline between the den and hunting grounds. Trotting back full-bellied from a long drink at a spring, they may stop for a moment and piddle at the turkey wing or even investigate the outré smells on the bait knob of a "getter," but generally this is when the professionals hunt for dens. Den-hunting is a specialty, intuitive, distinct. The steel-trap men are condescending about the cyanide go-getter—a kind of scattershot method, a glib, perfunctory tool—and yet compared with trapping, den-hunting is downright purist and arcane. It's catching the animals alive, by hand, in their hidden home, and some predator hunters hardly bother to trap at all, killing a presentable quota of coyotes just by finding and digging up the year's new dens. Usually they ride, because a coyote fears a man on horseback somewhat less, and what the hunter looks for is a bustling hodgepodge of tracks that, as he studies them, begin to offer evidence of radiating from a given point which the coyotes have tried to conceal. Often the den faces southeast from a slight elevation, and he may try to call one of the parents toward him with a "squeaker" made from a piece of a cow's horn which emits a rabbit's squeal. If, having dismounted, he sees the coyote first and holds his fire until it scents him, he will have the benefit of its last quick anxious glance in the direction of the den to guide him on, before it takes evasive action. If the grown-ups attempt to decoy him he shoots them, then looks sharp for the first pup, which will streak for the hole as soon as it sights him. He tumbles about in the brush, grabbing the pups and clubbing them, or if they are very young he must dig, hooking them out from underground with a wire prong twisted on the end. If either parent has escaped him, he will bury a dead whelp with one foot exposed and set traps alongside it and by the den.

In sheep territory the javelinas root holes under the woven fences that coyotes also make use of, and this is where the ancient craft of snaring can be practiced. Then, by contrast, there are hunters who are primarily marksmen and shoot the creatures from a helicopter. But none of these systems will suffice after the less vigilant 70 percent of the population has been eliminated. There are always a few coyotes which flatten down instead of bolting when the helicopter makes its pass over the chaparral, and which keep their pups clear of the getter-guns. For these holdouts some studying is necessary; the animal becomes individualized, and a Riley or a Marfa becomes interested. Or they may meet an animal like Adolph Murie's blithe classic coyote in the valley of the Yellowstone which trotted toward him carrying a sprig of sagebrush in its jaws that it tossed up and caught and tossed and caught.

When the Fish and Wildlife Service supervisors in San Antonio decided that the Big Bend mountain lions had had enough pruning, they set Marfa on a series of eccentric research labors, such as catching sixty coyote puppies "by Friday" for a sex-ratio study, collecting adults for a test of poisons, or gathering coyote urine and red-wolf skulls. (The number of red wolves killed in order to verify their existence as a species and then to train successive research cadres must surpass the number so far "saved.") Finally Marfa went into business for himself, charging the sheep ranchers two hundred and fifty dollars per lion, and more for the Sierra Madre lobos he has been capturing in Durango lately, working for the stockmen's association there. In some respects a wolf is more vulnerable than a coyote, because of the complexity of its social life and because it is bolder and therefore more accessible, but since it travels farther, in another way it is less so. These are "named" wolves, the last of their kind in an enormous spread of territory, in their way just as endangered as Riley's wolves are, and correspond to the famous "outlaw" wolves of the American Great Plains a half century ago. Like them, they're quirky, lonely, queer, atypical beasts, final survivors because they have allowed themselves only the sparsest pleasures. Marfa carries a handful of traps as he rides his mule around for a period of days or weeks to spy out some small chink in the precautionary tactics of the wolf he is after—some stray indulgence by which it still tries to amuse itself that has escaped the notice of all the other trappers who have had a go at it. These Mexican lobos have short pretty heads, and you must know the length of the neck and stride in situating the trap.

One such wolf, "Las Margaritas," took him eleven months to catch, humbling him, he says, and in the meantime, it was claimed, slaughtering ninety-six cattle on a single large ranch nearby. The only entertainment left "Margaret" after so many narrow escapes in a lengthy career was killing steers, once she was safely inside a pasture. She was poison-proof because she fed at her own kills and nowhere else, and never a second time at one of them. Already missing two front toes, she would follow a different route coming and going. If she arrived on a logging road, she exited by way of a cattle track; if through a canyon, by a high pass. She avoided other wolves, although from loneliness she sometimes would howl behind the ranchers' barns. She would not go close to the message stations of other wolves, but instead would squat wistfully to make her mark at a safe distance, so that he could not catch her by the ordinary technique of setting a trap at a scent post or manufacturing a bogus station with the urine of a foreign wolf. Some outlaws, he says, entirely give up trying to communicate with other wolves and use only their own scenting stations. Once, indeed, she did step in one of his traps, but the hole carved into her foot by the two toes that she was missing happened to fit across the pan and saved her. She jumped for her life.

She traveled continually, having often been hunted with hounds after a meal, and there was no predicting where she would go. Over the years, hundreds of traps had simply been left blind for her in paths across the mountainsides she ranged, which gradually had lost their human smell and any surface scars to show the ground had been worked on. But some of them had become boneyards for other animals that had been caught instead, and the rest she avoided by her spartan custom of stepping mostly on the rocks and stones, or else on ground too hard to dig in without leaving a permanent sign. On the road, if there was any indication that a rider had dismounted or that a man had left his truck, even the day before, she immediately veered off, not waiting to discover what he might have been up to. Without the fellowship of a pack, with nowhere safe enough for her to go to relax except among the actual cattle herds, killing was her life and her relations with her pursuers her only intimacy, so when at last Marfa did catch her— when he had almost given up—it was in a trap that he had left blind some weeks before next to a corral she liked to hang about. She pulled the stake out of the ground and painfully dragged the trap as far as she could, but all the ranch hands turned out to chase her down. Only then was it revealed that notorious "Margaret," so security-ridden that she squatted meekly to piss like a bitch, all along had been a male.

When this methodical search had palled, Marfa dashed off behind his light little slipping lion hounds—skinny so their feet hold up and so they can twist through the canyon cracks and into any boulder pile (for which he has a "climbing dog")—to run down one of the infrequent lions left. He sight-trailed for the pack over the alkali ground, where the scent, as dry as smoke, had blown away. Where there were grass and sticks again they'd pick it up. Salt blocks, windmills and fencing are what makes ranching here. Durango is also the starving country where wetbacks come from, and any deer whose prints show up is tracked relentlessly. There are human outlaws in the Sierra Madre as well, and Marfa, lean from his regimen of two meals shoveled in twelve hours apart, living very nearly on a level with a lion, with the two expressions that his face falls into—boyish and bleak—went about with his rifle handy and his bedroll and mule and dogs.

He caught another noteworthy wolf because his dogs showed him its single small inabstinence. It liked to go up on top of a mesa to a water tank with an earthen dam and wallow in that one soft place on a long-dead skunk lying in sweet-smelling grass. He captured a wolf called Wide Gait using a month-old turd which he had saved from its former lady love, whose Spanish name was Nearly Black and whom he had trapped previously with an old turtle shell. "Dead as a hammer," he says.

Turds represent survival in the desert or the woods and are beloved by animals for that: a meal put to use, the gift of life. Of a woodsman, too, you'll hear it said, "He was the best deer-hunter that ever took a shit in the woods." Marfa showed me how to distinguish a ringtail's scats (small-bore, on top of a rock, containing scorpion pincers and tails) from a raccoon's; a kit fox's fuzzy-toed, dainty prints from a gray fox's; and trundled me about, pointing out abundant lion scrapes in the sandy canyons we explored next to the Rio Grande. Lions scratch with their forefeet for their feces and their hind feet for urine, partly hiding the first but ballyhooing the latter. Their front feet make a bigger, rounder print, so people sometimes think one track is two.

This is country where one finds the arrows wetbacks put together in the dry streambeds with stones—where once in the Christmas Mountains Marfa found the skeleton of a "wet" who had gotten himself lost. He pointed out a mountain in Coahuila, a twelve-hour walk up a canyon tributary to the Rio Grande, which has a cave so big a plane could fly into its mouth, and cool high pine forests where a few black bears are still holding out. He spoke about another sanctuary, in Chihuahua, where until recently all the American cats could be found—jaguarundis, ocelots, bobcats, lions and jaguars—though now every such shangri-la in Mexico is shrinking faster than a puddle on hot city pavement. The last of the grizzly bears, he says, was blown up with nitroglycerin wired to a honey-smeared log.

An ocelot leaves more scent than a bobcat and doesn't fight the dogs as hard; a jaguarundi is lithest in the thickets and the toughest to trail, he said. Lions and lobos are a force, a *frequency*, if you will: once maybe the trombone, now the oboe in the orchestra. They are the Headless Horseman who, once he is gone, exists only in fairy tales, and although most of us can get along without hearing the oboe's note or seeing the Headless Horseman ride, in Riley and Marfa I had come close to locating the people who can't. Marfa, in particular, who has hunted jaguars in the jungle in Campeche too, talks about retiring to British Honduras, where in the wet woods he envisions the cats forever plentiful, leaving a trail for his dogs "as strong as a garbage truck." In the desert in the early morning he lets the vultures be his guide and trucks his dogs to where they are. Then, with the water *tinajas* fifteen or twenty miles apart, he gets his lion.

Red wolves howl in a higher, less emotive pitch than gray wolves and don't blend with each other quite as stylishly, though they do employ more nuances and personality than a coyote family's gabble. A coyote's howl sounds hysterical, amateurish by comparison, chopped and frantic, almost like barnyard cackling, or (in an early description) "like a prolonged howl the animal lets out and then runs after and bites into small pieces." The only likely-looking wild wolves I actually saw during my several visits to Texas were two smashed dead on the highway, which I passed at high speed as I was leaving. They were red, sizable, and somber, at least from the perspective I had by then accumulated. They were probably mates, the second having lingered alongside the first, and now were angled affectionately rump to rump—the copulative position—in death.

Once, too, alone one night along Elm Bayou, I howled up a wolf a quarter of a mile away that sounded querulous and yowly, variable and female. We were beginning to converse, but I left it to answer another wolf howling a mile beyond. This wolf and I talked back and forth, until I started to wonder. The sound jerked and creaked too unsteadily for a wolf and yet was pitched too low to be a coyote, and wasn't barky enough for a feral dog—almost like a windmill. In fact, that's what it was; I'd left a real wolf for a windmill.

In these inquiries I had begun to glimpse the noble stretch of science when it grabs hold of a sea of data and persuades it to jell. In a still-primitive, ambiguously motivated backwater area of scholarship there was nevertheless a majesty to the picture as it emerged. Predators are smarter than herbivores, usually need to sleep more, and possess the invaluable ability to vomit, and when the findings on these biggest beasts are combined, one understands better the grizzly with its "attack distance" developed for a life on the plains, the black bear thriving by gourmand eating and a love of holes, the mountain lion avoiding competition and starvation by avoiding wolf country and its own kind, the wolf avoiding competition and starvation by a hierarchal social existence. Unluckily, the very means of population control that had enabled each of them to prosper while ruling the roost—the graphic social life, in some cases, and the slow, problematical birth rate of more solitary creatures such as bears or eagles—is now depleting them. These discoveries were being made, on the one hand, by scholars many of whom might have been laughed out of the lab if they had been working in another branch of science, and on the other, by observers in the field whose woodsmanship was only a faint shadow of that of the centuries when the wilderness (and these animals) were real. But I'd met men like Marfa and Riley who wouldn't have done badly in any era of woodsmanship.

Thoughts on
Returning to the City
After Five Months
on a
Mountain Where
the Wolves Howled

CITY people are more supple than country people, and the sanest city people, being more tested and more broadly based in the world of men, are the sanest people on earth. As to honesty, though, or good sense, no clear-cut distinction exists either way.

I like gourmets, even winetasters. In the city they correspond to the old-timers who knew all the berries and herbs, made money collecting the roots of the ginseng plant, and knew the taste of each hill by its springs. Alertness and adaptability in the city are transferable to the country if you feel at home there, and alertness there can quickly be transmuted into alertness here. It is not necessary to choose between being a country man and a city man, as it is to decide, for instance, some time along in one's thirties, whether one is an Easterner or a Westerner. (Middle Westerners, too, make the choice: people in Cleveland consider themselves Easterners, people in Kansas City know they are Western.) But one can be both a country man and a city man. Once a big frog in a local pond, now suddenly I'm tiny again, and delighted to be so, kicking my way down through the water, swimming along my anchor chains and finding them fast in the bottom.

Nor must one make a great sacrifice in informational matters. I know more about bears and wolves than anybody in my town or the neighboring towns up there and can lead lifelong residents in the woods, yet the fierce, partisan block associations in my neighborhood in New York apparently know less than I do about the closer drug-peddling operations or they surely would have shut them down. This is not to say that such information is of paramount importance, however. While, lately, I was tasting the October fruit of the jack-in-the-pulpit and watching the club moss smoke with flying spores as I walked in the woods, my small daughter, who had not seen me for several weeks, missed me so much that when I did return, she threw up her arms in helpless and choked excitement to shield her eyes, as if I were the rising sun. The last thing I wish to be, of course, is the sun—being only a guilty father.

But what a kick it is to be back, seeing newspaperman friends; newspapermen are the best of the city. There are new restaurants down the block, and today I rescued an actual woodcock—New York is nothing if not cosmopolitan. Lost, it had dived for the one patch of green in the street, a basket of avocados in the doorway of Shanvilla's Grocery, and knocked itself out. I'd needed to drag myself back from that mountain where the wolves howl, and yet love is what I feel now; the days are long and my eyes and emotions are fresh.

The city is dying irreversibly as a metropolis. We who love it must recognize this if we wish to live in it intelligently. All programs, all palliatives and revenue-sharing, can only avail to ease what we love into oblivion a little more tenderly (if a tender death is ever possible for a city). But to claim that the city is dying, never to "turn the corner," is not to announce that we should jump for the lifeboats. There are still no better people than New Yorkers. No matter where I have been, I rediscover this every fall. And my mountain is dying too. The real estate ads up in that country put it very succinctly. "Wealth you can walk on," they say. As far as that goes, one cannot live intelligently without realizing that we and our friends and loved ones are all dying. But one's ideals, no: no matter what currently unfashionable ideals a person may harbor in secret, from self-sacrifice and wanting to fall in love to wanting to fight in a war, there will continue to be opportunities to carry them out.

My country neighbor is dying right now, wonderfully fiercely— nothing but stinging gall from his lips. The wolves' mountain bears his name, and at eighty-six he is dying almost on the spot where he was born, in the one-room schoolhouse in which he attended first grade, to which he moved when his father's house burned. This would not be possible in the city. In the city we live by being supple, bending with the wind. He lived by bending with the wind too, but his were the north and west winds.

You New Yorkers will excuse me for missing my barred owls, ruffed grouse, and snowshoe rabbits, my grosbeaks and deer. I love what you love too. In the city and in the country there is a simple, underlying basis to life which we forget almost daily: that life is good. We forget because losing it or wife, children, health, friends is so awfully painful, and because life is hard, but we know from our own experience as well as our expectations that it can and ought to be good, and is even *meant* to be good. Any careful study of living things, whether wolves, bears, or man, reminds one of the same direct truth; also of the clarity of the fact that evolution itself is obviously not some process of drowning beings clutching at straws and climbing from suffering and travail and virtual expiration to tenuous, momentary survival. Rather, evolution has been a matter of days well-lived, chameleon strength, energy, zappy sex, sunshine stored up, inventiveness, competitiveness, and the whole fun of busy brain cells. Watch how a rabbit loves to run; watch him set scenting puzzles for the terrier behind him. Or a wolf's amusement at the anatomy of a deer. Tug, tug, he pulls out the long intestines: ah, Yorick, how *long* you are!

An acre of forest will absorb six tons of carbon dioxide in a year.

Wordsworth walked an estimated 180,000 miles in his lifetime.

Robert Rogers's Twenty-first Rule of Ranger warfare was: "If the enemy pursue your rear, take a circle till you come to your own tracks, and there form an ambush to receive them, and give them the first fire."

Rain-in-the-face, a Hunkpapa Sioux, before attacking Fort Totten in the Dakota Territory in 1866: "I prepared for death. I painted as usual like the eclipse of the sun, half black and half red."

City Walking

There is a time of life somewhere between the sullen fugues of adolescence and the retrenchments of middle age when human nature becomes so absolutely absorbing one wants to be in the city constantly, even at the height of the summer. Nature can't seem to hold a candle to it. One gobbles the blocks, and if the weather is sweaty, so much the better; it brings everybody else out too. To the enthusiast's eye, what might later look to be human avarice is simply energy, brutality is strength, ambition is not wearisome or repellent or even alarming. In my own case, aiming to be a writer, I knew that every mile I walked, the better writer I'd be; and I went to Twentieth Street and the Hudson River to smell the yeasty redolence of the Nabisco factory, and to West Twelfth Street to sniff the police stables. In the meat-market district nearby, if a tyro complained that his back ached, the saying was "Don't bleed on me!"

Down close to the Battery the banana boats used to unload (now they are processed in Albany). Banana boats were the very definition of seagoing grubbiness, but bejeweled snakes could be discovered aboard which had arrived from the tropics as stowaways. On Bleecker Street you could get a dozen clams on the half shell for fifty cents if you ate them outdoors; and on Avenue A, piroshki, kielbasa, and suchlike. Kids still swam from piers west of the theater district in the Hudson and under Brooklyn Bridge, and I was on the lookout among them for Huckleberry Finn. He was there, all right, diving in, then scrambling up a piling, spitting water because he hadn't quite learned how to swim. In the evening I saw him again on Delancey Street, caught by the ear by a storekeeper for pilfering.

Oh yes, oh yes! one says, revisiting these old walking neighborhoods. Yorkville, Inwood, Columbus Avenue. Our New York sky is not muscular with cloud formations as is San Francisco's, or as green-smelling as London's, and rounding a corner here, one doesn't stop stock-still to gaze at the buildings as in Venice. The bartenders like to boast that in this city we have "the best and worst," yet intelligent conversation, for example, is mostly ad-libbed and comes in fits and starts, anywhere or nowhere; one cannot trot out of an evening and go looking for it. We have our famous New York energy instead, as well as its reverse, which is the keening misery, the special New York craziness, as if every thirteenth person standing on the street is wearing a gauzy hospital smock and paper shower slippers.

Edmund G. Love wrote a good city walker's book some years ago called *Subways Are for Sleeping*. Indeed they were, but now if the transit police didn't prevent old bums from snoozing the night away while rumbling back and forth from Brooklyn to the Bronx, somebody would set them on fire. Up on the street hunting parties are abroad, whom the walker must take cognizance of; it's not enough to have your historical guidebook and go maundering about to the Old Merchant's House on East Fourth Street. A pair of bravos will ask you for a light and want a light; another pair, when your hands are in your pockets, will slug you. If you're lucky they will slug you; the old bar fighters complain about how risky fighting has become. You must have a considerable feel for these things, an extra sense, eyes in the back of your head: or call it a walker's *emotional range*. You must know when a pistol pointed at you playfully by a ten-year-old is a cap pistol and when it's not; whether someone coming toward you with a broken bottle is really going for you or not. We have grown to be students of police work—watching a bank robber scram as the squad cars converge, watching a burglar tackled, watching four hoodlums unmercifully beating a cop until four patrol cars scream to a halt and eight policemen club down the hoods.

Nevertheless, if you ask people who have some choice in the matter why they live in a particular neighborhood, one answer they will give is that they "like to walk." Walking is a universal form of exercise, not age-oriented or bound to any national heritage, and costs and implies nothing except maybe a tolerant heart. Like other sports, it calls for a good eye as well as cheerful legs— those chunky gluteus muscles that are the butt of mankind's oldest jokes—because the rhythm of walking is in the sights and one's response as much as simply in how one steps. In America at the moment it may seem like something of a reader's or an individualist's sport, because we are becoming suburban, and the suburbs have not yet adjusted to the avocation of walking. But they will.

And yet times do change. Only this spring I was in a river town on the Mississippi, loafing on a dock the barges tie to, on the lookout for Huckleberry Finn once again. He was there, all right, with a barefoot, redheaded, towheaded gang. They had sandy freckles and wore torn pants; Miss Watson still cut their hair. They were carrying a pailful of red-eared turtles and green frogs from the borrow pit behind the levee, and were boasting about the garfish they had noosed with a piece of piano wire. They began daring each other, and what the dare turned out to be—the best they could think of—was which of them had nerve enough to reach down and taste the Mississippi!

Now, muggers are herd creatures like the rest of us; they too have a "rush hour." So if a walker is indeed an individualist there is nowhere he can't go at dawn and not many places he can't go at noon. But just as it demeans life to live alongside a great river you can no longer swim in or drink from, to be crowded into the safer areas and hours takes much of the gloss off walking—one sport you shouldn't have to reserve a time and a court for.

City Rat

Delightedly, I used to cross Park Avenue wearing an undershirt on my way to digs far to the south and east. I could remember waiting, as a boy of eight, on almost the same street corner for the St. Bernard's school bus in a proper tweed blazer, striped tie, and shiny shoes, and so this gulf between costumes seemed sweet. Sweaty, bare-shouldered, strolling the summer streets, I felt my class or creed unidentifiable, which very much pleased me. Physically I was in my prime, I liked to jog, and, long and loose like a runner, though still smooth-faced, I felt as if I were a thousand miles and a whole world away from that small boy. I'd sit around on door stoops after a walk of eighty blocks or so, up from the Battery or down from Yankee Stadium, and watch the world go by. If I'd been an out-of-towner, awed by the city, these walks would have been ideal for adjusting. Wherever I ran out of steam, I'd sit, keeping an eye peeled, and try to pretend that this was now my territory and I must figure it out quickly. It should be remembered that fifteen years ago violence in New York City was fairly well contained within a framework of teenage gangs attacking other gangs, not wayfarers; blacks' bitterness bore down mainly on other blacks, and though sometimes the Mafia in Brooklyn dumped a body on Avenue D, the Lower East Side itself and other such areas were quite peaceful.

I was in the theater district once, sitting on a stoop, enjoying the stream of life, when a brisk, well-preserved man with custom-fitted pants, a cane, and good coloring halted in front of me. "Young man," he said abruptly, "are you trying to break into the theater?" Aware that it was a funny question, he raised his eyebrows while he waited, as if I'd been the one who'd asked. I was holding my knees and looking up at him. He tapped my feet with the point of his cane as though he were buying me and I was supposed to stand.

I was too nervous to answer. Superciliously he stared at me. "You'd better come along. There are a great many young men trying to get into the theater. I'm in the theater." He tapped me again. I still didn't trust myself to speak, and he glanced at my army boots, laughed, and said, "Are you a paratrooper? Come now, last chance, young man. Fame and fortune. There are a great many of you and one of me. What's going to set you apart?" My embarrassed silence made him uncomfortable, as well as the possibility that somebody might recognize him standing there in this peculiar conversation. As he left, he called back, "Good luck, little friend, whoever you are." But I grinned more confidently at him as he got farther off, because a couple of months before I'd had my picture in *Time* as a blazing new author; perhaps he never had. That was the second fillip to wandering in my undershirt along Fifth or Park Avenue: the fact that on other days I'd be wearing a snaky gray flannel suit, slipping through the crowds in the skyscraper district, and shooting up high in a building for a swank lunch. I wasn't really masquerading as a carpenter; on the contrary, I'd made no choices yet—I was enjoying being free.

Banging around on a motor scooter down the length of Manhattan by way of the waterfront, I'd unwind in the evening after writing all day. New York was compartmentalized; Harlem was in Harlem, and on Delancey Street there were live ducks for sale, and in a shop with big windows, shoemakers cutting soles for shoes. I looked at coming attractions under the various movie marquees and watched the traffic on the stairs to a second-floor whorehouse (sailors coming down and a cop going up). Since I was both bashful and lonely, I would leave notes on the bulletin boards of some of the coffeehouses—"Typist wanted"—then wait by the telephone. The girls were under no illusions about what I was up to when they called, except that they usually did want some work out of the arrangement as well, and, unfairly enough, that's what I was reluctant to give. I kept my manuscripts in the refrigerator as a precaution against fire and was a nut about safeguarding them. Inevitably, then, the sort of girl who'd phone me blind and invite me over for a screw on the strength of a note I'd left in a coffeehouse was not a girl I'd trust my typing to.

One girl had a beachboy crouching naked on the floor painting her bathtub red when I arrived; the rest of the apartment was a deep black. Another, on Houston Street, immediately embraced me with her head swathed in bandages from the blows that her husband had bestowed the night before. Pulling the bookcases over, he'd strewn the books around, broken all the china, and announced he was leaving. Nothing had been picked up since. The baby, only a year old, cried desperately in the playpen, and though his mother naturally hoped I would be able to step right into the father's role and comfort him, I wasn't that skillful. A window was broken, so it was cold. She took me to the bedroom, moaning, "Hit me! Hit me!" When things there didn't work out she led me downstairs to a kind of commune, introduced me around, and announced to the members that I was impotent.

Still, I was busy, once sleeping with three different women in as many days, and covering the city better than most news reporters, it seemed to me, recognizing innumerable street nooks and faces which epitomized New York for me. Perhaps the air was rather sooty, but it didn't cause headaches or give people bleeding throats. Now I sometimes spit blood in the morning and feel raw sulfur in my gullet from breathing the air; in midtown or around Canal Street I breathe through my teeth like a survivalist who specializes in outlasting black lung. This morning when I went out to buy milk for breakfast I saw a clump of police cars and a yellow car which had slid out of the traffic and come to rest against the curb, empty except for a gray-looking dead man in his thirties slumped sideways against the wheel. I stood rubbernecking next to the delicatessen owner. One night last year I'd stood in a crowd and watched most of the building that houses his store burn to a shell, all of us—he wasn't there—as silent and spellbound as if we were witnessing public copulation. Though he is not a friendly man, I like his Greek bluntness and at the time I'd felt guilty to be watching as a mere spectacle what was a catastrophe for him. But here he was, rubbernecking at this fellow's death just like me, only less solemnly; he chuckled, shaking his head. I kept a straight face and felt a pang, but while I crossed the street with the groceries and rode up in the elevator the incident entirely slipped my mind; I didn't even mention it when I got home.

Such imperviousness is a result of changes in the city as well as in me. If I have lost my bloom, so has the city, more drastically. Among the beggars who approach me, almost weekly I see a mugger who is clearly screwing up his nerve to do more than just *ask* for money. I have the New Yorker's quick-hunch posture for broken-field maneuvering, and he swerves away. A minute later, with pounding feet, there he goes, clutching a purse, with a young woman in forlorn pursuit. Recently, riding in a bus, I saw a policeman with his gun drawn and his free hand stretched out tiptoe hastily after a suspect through a crowd and make the nab as the bus pulled away. It's not any single event, it's the cumulative number of them—shouted arguments, funerals, playground contretemps, drivers leaning on their horns, adults in tears, bums falling down and hitting their heads, young men in triumph over a business deal—that one sees in the course of a midday walk which veneers one with callousness.

We each work out a system of living in the city. With music, for instance. I put trumpet voluntaries on the phonograph in the morning, organ fugues after supper, and whale songs or wolf howls in the silence at night. I go to a Village bar which is like a club, with the same faces in it day after day, although as a hangout it does acquire a tannic-acid taste if you go too often because most of the people are divorced or on that road. The newspapermen see it as belonging to them; hungry poets and movie novelists view it as a literary saloon; the seamen, photographers, carpenters, folk singers, young real-estate impresarios, political lawyers, old union organizers, and Lincoln Brigade veterans all individually believe it's theirs.

I'm tired of Washington Square, Tompkins Square Park, Abingdon Square, even Central Park (I lived next to it for several years and found it to be ground as overused as the banks of the Ganges are). And the last time my wife and I picnicked in Van Cortlandt Park, which is more countrified, we needed to cut at top speed through the woods to escape two men who were stalking us. Space is important to me, and each of these public resting spots has its own character and defines a particular period for me. In the early sixties I was in Washington Square, watching, among other things, the early stirrings of black belligerence, still indirect. It seemed to take the form of their ballplaying, sometimes one man alone, throwing a rubber ball as high as he could and catching it on the second or third bounce. They were lanky, like men just out of the army or prison, and when they played catch they loped all over the park, taking possession everywhere. Already they had secret handshakes and contemptuous expressions, and this gobbling up the whole park with their legs and lofting a rubber ball into the stratosphere bespoke the blocked energy, the screened anger that would soon explode. The explosion is past; new developments are brewing in these parks, but I am fatigued with watching.

The Chinese laundryman we go to is mean of heart and keeps his children home from school to iron for him while he loafs. The two girls next to us are sleeping with the super, and sit in triumph while their apartment is painted, as a consequence. Perhaps he sleeps well, but I'm almost sleepless from fighting with my wife. And there are explosions going off nightly down in the street. I have no idea what they are; years ago I would have thought just firecrackers. New York is a city of the old and young, and looking out the window, I sometimes see old people fall. One man has cancer of the mouth. When he feels well he sits outside the barber shop or in the park, not looking up, withdrawn into his memories, but seeming tranquil there; certainly nobody enjoys the sunshine more. But the next day when you walk past he is sitting quietly hemorrhaging into his handkerchief, looking at it fearfully, then boosting himself off the bench to go back to the nursing home.

In the apartment on the other side of us are two young men who entertain a lot, and one day somebody leaned out their window with a rifle equipped with a spotting scope, searching the courtyard and the street. I assumed it was a toy, but in any case I simply pulled down the blinds; one can't react to everything. We'd had a stink in the corridor the week before that gradually grew stronger. It was a really hideous smell, subterraneanly terrifying, and we and some of the neighbors began to wonder whether somebody might not have died. It was pervasive, hard to isolate, and we were all city procrastinators—with so many emergencies, so many lonely people, why get involved? At last, however, where our consciences had failed, our noses got the better of us and we called the cops. It turned out to be a decomposing chicken which someone had defrosted before a trip and forgotten about. A month or so later the same putrid smell invaded our floor all over again. Holding our noses, we complained left and right, trying to ignore it. Even so, again the police had to be called. This time they found a young woman dead of an overdose of heroin, with her headband wrapped around her arm as a tourniquet and her cat still alive, having managed to subsist on her body fluids.

Year round, I keep my air conditioner on, its steady hum submerging the street sounds. But one of the neighbors upstairs, finding this noise, too, unnerving, has lent me a white-sound machine, an instrument which, like a sort of aural sun lamp, manufactures a sense of neutrality and well-being. Right now neutrality seems to be the first condition of peace; these devices have become commonplace. People are seeking to disengage, get out of town, or at least stay indoors and regale themselves with surfy sounds. The question everybody is asking is, Where does one live? New York is the action scene; one won't feel the kinesis of the 1970s in a Sicilian fishing village, and very few people are really quite ready to write all that off. Maybe the best of both worlds is to be a New Yorker outside New York. Anyway, I'm at my best as a traveler, and looking back when I am elderly, I may be fondest of some of my memories of hauling a suitcase along, grinning, questioning strangers, breathing the smoke of their wood fires, supported, although I was far from home, by the knowledge of where I'd come

from. Arriving in Alaska, straight from New York, one feels tough
as a badger, quick as a wolf. We New Yorkers see more death and
violence than most soldiers do, grow a thick chitin on our backs,
grimace like a rat and learn to do a disappearing act. Long ago we
outgrew the need to be blowhards about our masculinity; we leave
that to the Alaskans and Texans, who have more time for it. We
think and talk faster, we've seen and know more, and when my
friends in Vermont (who are much wiser folk than Alaskans) kid
me every fall because I clear out before the first heavy snow, I
smile and don't tell them that they no longer know what being
tough is.

Setting out from home for the landmark of the Empire State
Building, I arrive underneath it as a countryman might reach a
nearby bluff, and push on to the lions at the public library, and
St. Patrick's, and the fountain in front of the Plaza. Or in fifteen
minutes I can take my two-year-old daughter to the Museum of
Natural History, where, after waving goodbye to the subway train,
she strides inside, taking possession of the stuffed gorillas, antelopes, spiny anteaters, modeled Indian villages, and birds and fish—
the pre-twentieth-century world cooked down to some of its essen-
tials. Six or seven puppet shows and several children's plays are
being presented in the city this afternoon, and there are ships
to watch, four full-scale zoos, and until recently goats, monkeys,
chickens, and ten horses were quartered on an eccentric half-acre
a few blocks from our building. Just the city's lighted skyscrapers
and bridges alone will be with my daughter forever if her first
memories are like mine—she lies on her back looking upward
out the window when we ride uptown in a taxi at night, with the
lights opals and moons.

But is it worth the blood in the throat? Even when we go out
on a pier to watch the big ships, what comes blowing in is smudgy
smoke instead of a clean whiff of the sea. For me it's as disquieting
as if we had to drink right out of the Hudson; our lungs must be
as calloused as the soles of our feet. Is it worth seeing a dead man
before breakfast and forgetting him by the time one sits down to
one's orange juice? Sometimes when I'm changing records at night
I hear shrieks from the street, sounds that the phonograph ordinarily drowns out. My old boyhood dreams of playing counterspy
have declined in real life to washing perfume off my face once
in a blue moon when, meeting an old girlfriend in a bar, I get
smooched, but I still have a trotting bounce to my walk, like a middle-aged coyote who lopes along avoiding the cougars and hedgehogs, though still feeling quite capable of snapping up rabbits and

fawns. Lightness and strength in the legs are important to me; like the closed face, are almost a must for the city. There's not a week when I don't think of leaving for good, living in a *house*, living in the West, perhaps, or a smaller town. I will never lose my New Yorker's grimace, New Yorker's squint, and New Yorker's speed, but can't I live with them somewhere else?

The Threshold
and the
Jolt of Pain

Like most boys in their teens, I wondered once in a while how I would take torture. Badly, I thought. Later I thought not so badly, as I saw myself under the pressures of danger or emergency, once when a lion cub grabbed my hand in its mouth and I wrestled its lips for half a minute with my free hand. Another summer when I fought forest fires in a crew of Indians in the West, we stood up under intense heat and thirst, watching the flames crackle toward us irresistibly while we waited to see whether the fire lines that we had cut were going to hold. I've climbed over the lip of a high waterfall; I've scratched inside a hippopotamus's capacious jaws; I faced a pistol one day in Wyoming with some degree of fortitude. However, I knew that all this élan would vanish if my sex organs were approached. The initiation to join the Boy Scouts in our town was to have one's balls squeezed, so I never joined. Even to have my knuckle joints ground together in a handshake contest reduces me to quick surrender—something about bone on bone. I steered clear of the BB-gun fights in my neighborhood, and I could be caught in a chase and tied up easily by someone slower who yelled as if he were gaining ground, so I made friends with most of the toughies as a defensive measure.

As a boy I was much given to keeping pets and showering care on them, but I had a sadistic streak as well. In boarding school my roommate got asthma attacks when he was jumped on, and I always backed away laughing when his tormentors poured into the room. There was another nice boy whom I seldom picked on myself, and with sincere horror I watched a game grip the Florentine fancy of our corridor. Divided in teams, we would push him back and forth as a human football from goal to goal. The crush at the

129

center, where he was placed, was tremendous, and though no one remembered, I'd invented the game.

My first love affair was with a Philadelphian, a woman of twenty-seven. That is, she was the first woman I slept with. She was a love in the sense that she loved me; I was close and grateful to her but didn't love her—I'd loved one girl earlier whom I hadn't slept with. She lived in one of those winsome houses that they have down there, with a tiled backyard and three floors, one room to each floor. We wandered along the waterfront and spent Saturdays at the street market, which is the largest and visually the richest street market in the United States. I was not an ogre to her, but I did by stages develop the habit of beating her briefly with my belt or hairbrush before we made love, a practice which I have foregone ever since. It may be indicative of the preoccupations of the 1950s that I worried less about this than about any tendencies I may have had toward being homosexual; but the experience gives me a contempt for pornography of that arch gruesome genre, quite in vogue nowadays as psychological "exploration," where whipping occurs but the flesh recovers its sheen overnight and the whippee doesn't perhaps hang her(him)self, propelling the whipper into the nervous breakdown which he is heading for.

Seeing eventual disaster ahead, I didn't go deeply into this vein of sensation, just as I was shrewd enough as a boy not to be picked on often or to suffer more than a few accidents. Once I ran my hand through an apple crusher on a relative's farm, and once I imitated a child's stutter at summer camp, thereby—or so I imagined (remembering what was supposed to happen to you if you crossed your eyes)—picking up the malady at the age of six. Almost my only pangs, then, were this stutter, which still remains in my mouth. It may strike other people as more than a spasm, but to me it's a spasm of pain of a kind which I haven't time for, or time to regard as anything else. It's like someone who has a lesion or twist in his small intestine, which hurts him abruptly and of which he is hardly aware otherwise. The well-grooved wince I make in shaking the words out seems to keep my face pliant and reasonably young.

Somerset Maugham described his bitter discovery when he was a boy that prayer was no help: he woke up next morning still clamped to his adamant stutter. I was more of a pantheist; I kept trusting to the efficacy of sleep itself, or to the lilting lift that caused birds to fly. Also I went to a bunch of speech therapists. At the Ethical Culture School in New York, for example, a woman taught me to stick my right hand in my pocket and, with that hidden hand, to write down over and over the first letter of the word I was stuttering on. This was intended to distract me from stuttering, and it did for a week or two. The trouble was that watching me play pocket pool that way was more unsettling to other people than the ailment it was meant to cure. At a camp in northern Michigan I was trained by a team from the university to speak so slowly that in effect I wasn't speaking at all; I talked with the gradualism of a flower growing—so absurdly tardy a process that my mind unhinged itself from what was going on. In Cambridge, Massachusetts, a young fellow from the University of Iowa—and oh, how *he* stuttered—took the most direct approach. He got me to deliberately imitate myself, which was hard on me since I was already terribly tired of stuttering, and to stare, as well, at the people whom I was talking to in order to find out what their reactions were. I found out, for one thing, that some of my friends and about a fifth of the strangers I met smiled when the difficulty occurred, though they generally turned their heads to the side or wiped their mouths with one hand to hide the smile. Thereafter, life seemed simpler if I avoided looking at anybody, whoever he was, when I was stuttering badly, and I wasn't so edgily on the alert to see if I'd spit inadvertently.

Not that I lacked understanding for the smilers, though, because for many years I too had had the strange impulse, hardly controllable, to smile if somebody bumped his head on a low door lintel or received sad news. The phenomenologists say this is a form of defense. It goes with childhood especially, and I stopped indulging in it one night in Boston when I was in a police patrol wagon. A friend and I had been out for a walk, he was hit by a car, and as he woke from unconsciousness during the ride to the hospital and asked what had happened, I found myself grinning down at him while I answered. A few weeks later I was walking past an apartment building just as a rescue squad carried out a would-be suicide. He was alive, on a stretcher. When our eyes touched he smiled impenetrably, but I didn't smile back.

As a stutterer, I learned not to write notes. You put yourself at someone's mercy more when you write him a note than if you just stand there like a rhinoceros and snort. I could write a *Stutterer's Guide to Europe,* too: the titters in old Vienna, the knowing English remembering their King, the raw scorching baitings I met with in Greece, surrounded sometimes like a muzzled bear. The fourth means of effecting a cure I heard about was based on the fact that stutterers are able to sing without stuttering; hence, the victim should swing one of his arms like a big pendulum and talk in time to this—which again was a worse fate than the impediment. Though I didn't try it, I was sent to a lady voice teacher who laid my hand on her conspicuous chest so that I could "feel her breathe." For just that moment the lessons worked wonderfully; if I wasn't speechless I spoke in a rush.

Stammering (a less obtrusive word I used to prefer) apparently is not unattractive to women. It's a masculine encumbrance; five times as many men as women suffer from it. I was seldom alone while I was in Europe, and once or twice girls told me by way of a pick-me-up that they'd loved someone "for" his stutter. When I went into my seizures at parties, if a woman didn't step back she stepped forward, whereas the men did neither. The female instinct does not apply nearly so favorably to other afflictions. In our glib age the stutterer has even been considered a kind of contemporary hero, a presumed honest man who is unable to gab with the media people. Beyond the particular appeal of this image, it does seem to suit a writer. Publishers are fastidious types and some whom I've met have sidled away in distress from my flabbering face as soon as they could, but they probably remembered my name if they caught it. The purity image or Billy Budd stuff didn't intrigue them, just the hint of compulsion and complexity. Though I don't greatly go for either picture, in social terms I've thought of my stutter as a sort of miasma behind the Ivy League–looking exterior. People at parties take me for William Buckley until I begin, so I keep my mouth shut and smile prepossessingly as long as I can.

Being in these vocal handcuffs made me a desperate, devoted writer at twenty. I worked like a dog, choosing each word. I wrote two full-length novels in iambic meter and a firehose style. Three hundred review copies of the second of these were sent out, but I received, I think, only three reviews. This was new pain, a man's career pain, with its attendant stomach trouble and neck and back cramps. A couple of years after that I got divorced from my first wife, and bawled like a half-butchered bull for an hour, rolled up on the floor of my apartment, while the two homosexuals next door listened in silence close to the wall, wondering what they ought to do. It was a purge, but the pain of that experience I remember best was an earlier scene. I'd announced to my wife, whom I loved and still love, my belief that we needed to separate. The next time we talked she crossed the room to my chair, knelt down beside me, and asked what was going to become of each of us. That is the most painful splinter in my life, the most painful piece of the past. With variations the ache was prolonged through many fugitive suppers. In fact we still meet, holding hands and laughing at each other's jokes until we feel tears.

Who knows which qualities are godly? Pain probably makes us a bit godly, though, as tender love does. It makes us rue and summarize; it makes us bend and yield up ourselves. Pain is a watchdog medically, telling us when to consult a doctor, and then it's the true-blue dog at the bedside who rivals the relatives for fidelity. Last summer my father died of cancer. We had made peace, pretty much, a few years before. Although he had opposed my desire to be a writer, he ended up trying to write a book too, and he turned over to me at the last an old family history which he'd been hiding, partly because it mentioned a lot of muteness among my ancestors and partly in order to prevent my exploiting the stories. My voice and my liberal opinions grew a little more clarion in the household during the months he was dying. From a selfish standpoint, I suppose I was almost ready for him to die, but I was very earnestly sorry for every stage of rough handling involved in the process and for his own overriding regret that his life was cut off. Having lost our frank fear of death along with our faith in an afterlife, we have all adopted our fear of pain as a feeble alternative. Our regret, too, is magnified. When he was in discomfort I stuttered a great deal, but when he was not, when he was simply reminiscing or watching TV, I stuttered scarcely a bit. Then, as he was actually dying, during our last interview, he turned on the bed and asked me something. My answer was blocked in my mouth and his face went rigid with more pain than mine. He was startled because in the exigencies of dying he had forgotten that my infirmity was still there unhealed. He straightened, shutting his eyes, not wanting to end his life seeing it. Nevertheless, he'd often told me that it was my problems he loved me for rather than for my successes and sleekness. He loved my sister for being waiflike and my mother for being on occasion afraid she was mentally ill.

We were quite hardy while the months passed. Mother and he lay side by side on the bed clasping hands. Because of the pills, until nearly the end he was not suffering pain of the magnitude he had dreaded. The last couple of days there was a tossing, pitching, horrific pain, but the body more than the mind was responding— the body attempting to swallow its tongue. What I remember, therefore, of death's salutation to my father was that it came as a tickler, making his withered body twitch, touching him here and touching him there, wasting his tissues away like white wax, while his head on the headrest above looked down and watched; or he'd shoot an acute glance at me from out of the hunching amalgam of pricks, jactitation, and drug-induced torpor. Death tickled him in a gradual crescendo, taking its time, and, with his ironic attorney's mind, he was amused. His two satisfactions were that he was privy to its most intimate preparations, everything just-so and fussy, and that at last the long spiky battling within the family was over and done. The new summer blossomed. In mid-June I saw what is meant by "a widow's tears." They flow in a flood of tremulous vulnerability, so that one thinks they will never stop.

Most severe on the physiologists' scale of pain is that of childbirth. It's also the worst that I've seen. A year had gone by since I'd left the army and quit visiting my Philadelphia friend. She came to New York, looked me up, discovered me vomiting, thin as a rail because of woman trouble, and moved in with me on the Upper West Side, spooning in food and mothering me. Then, at about the time I perked up, she told me that she had got pregnant by a chap back in Philadelphia.

We drew out our savings and started for San Francisco, that vainglorious, clam-colored city. In her yellow convertible, with my English setter and her cocker spaniel, we drove through the South and through Texas, taking Highway 80 because it was the autumn and cold. I remember that whenever we stopped by the side of the road in Mississippi to let the dogs pee, and I shouted if one of them dawdled, any black woman or man who happened to be close by would turn to see what I wanted, quite naturally, as if I had called. It was a grueling trip. I'd begun vomiting again after my friend told me she was pregnant, and she was suffering mysterious pains in that region between her legs, which no druggist would touch. But we reached Russian Hill and established ourselves in one of the local apartment hotels. For a while during the seven-month wait this living arrangement didn't work out and she moved to a Florence Crittenton Home and I went to the beach, but we ended the period together. At six one morning I drove her up to a whelk-pink hospital on a breezy hill and sat in the labor room for eight hours, watching the blue grid of stretch marks on her anguished stomach: awful pain. She jolted and screamed, sucking gas from a cup, squeezing my hand and falling asleep between the throes. It took me three days to stop shaking, though it was a normal delivery throughout, and she, by the mental safety catch which women have, had blocked off most of the memory by the time she was wheeled to her room asleep. I'm ashamed to say that I'd spanked her a little the night before, not realizing it was the night before: I never spanked her again.

The contract she'd signed obliged my friend to relinquish the baby girl to the Home for three weeks, after which she could appropriate her completely as her own. I was privileged to keep her breasts flowing during those weeks, a luxury that would have been fitting for Zeus; and, to the astonishment of the Home, as soon as the interval expired we showed up for the child. This was so rare that they wondered whether we were kidnappers. Then we drove East. The baby acquired a stepfather before she was out of her infancy and is now about ten.

So, pain is a packet of chiseling tools. Women in labor make no bones about protesting its severity. Neither does a dying man once he has stopped lingering with the living—thinking of the memories of his behavior which he is leaving his children, for instance. It's when we have no imperative purpose in front of our sufferings that we think about "bearing up"; "bearing up" is converted to serve as a purpose. Pain, love, boredom, and glee, and anticipation or anxiety—these are the pilings we build our lives from. In love we beget more love and in pain we beget more pain. Since we must like it or lump it, we like it. And why not, indeed?

In the Toils
of the Law

Lately people seem to want to pigeonhole themselves ("I'm 'into' this," "I'm 'into' that"), and the anciently universal experiences like getting married or having a child, like voting or jury duty, acquire a kind of poignancy. We hardly believe that our vote will count, we wonder whether the world will wind up uninhabitable for the child, but still we do vote with a rueful fervor and look at new babies with undimmed tenderness, because who knows what will become of these old humane responsibilities? Sadism, homosexuality, and other inversions that represent despair for the race of man may be the wave of the future, the wise way to survive.

Jury duty. Here one sits listening to evidence: thumbs up for a witness or thumbs down. It's unexpectedly moving; everybody tries so hard to be fair. For their two weeks of service people really try to be better than themselves. In Manhattan eighteen hundred are called each week from the voters' rolls, a third of whom show up and qualify. Later this third is divided into three groups of two hundred, one for the State Supreme Court of New York County, one for the Criminal Court, and one for the Civil Court. At Civil Court, 111 Centre Street, right across from the Tombs, there are jury rooms on the third and eleventh floors, and every Monday a new pool goes to one or the other. The building is relatively modern, the chairs upholstered as in an airport lounge, and the two hundred people sit facing forward like a school of fish until the roll is called. It's like waiting six or seven hours a day for an unscheduled flight to leave. They read and watch the clock, go to the drinking fountain, strike up a conversation, dictate business letters into the pay telephones. When I served, one man in a booth was shouting, "I'll knock your teeth down your throat! I don't want to hear, I don't want to know!"

Women are exempt from jury duty if they wish to be, so usually not many serve. Instead there are lots of retired men and institutional employees from banks, the Post Office, or the Transit Authority whose bosses won't miss them, as well as people at loose ends who welcome the change. But some look extremely busy, rushing back to the office when given a chance or sitting at the tables at the front of the room, trying to keep up with their work. They'll write payroll checks, glancing to see if you notice how important they are, or pore over statistical charts or contact sheets with a magnifying glass, if they are in public relations or advertising. Once in a while a clerk emerges to rotate a lottery box and draw the names of jurors, who go into one of the challenge rooms—six jurors, six alternates—to be interviewed by the plaintiff's and defendant's lawyers. Unless the damages asked are large, in civil cases the jury has six members, only five of whom must agree on a decision, and since no one is going to be sentenced to jail, the evidence for a decision need merely seem preponderant, not "beyond a reasonable doubt."

The legal fiction is maintained that the man or woman you see as defendant is actually going to have to pay, but the defense attorneys are generally insurance lawyers from a regular battery which each big company keeps at the courthouse to handle these matters, or from the legal corps of the City of New York, Con Edison, Hertz Rent A Car, or whoever. If so, they act interchangeably and you may see a different face in court than you saw in the challenge room, and still another during the judge's charge. During my stint most cases I heard about went back four or five years, and the knottiest problem for either side was producing witnesses who were still willing to testify. In negligence cases, so many of which involve automobiles, there are several reasons why the insurers haven't settled earlier. They've waited for the plaintiff to lose hope or greed, and to see what cards each contestant will finally hold in his hands when the five years have passed. More significantly, it's a financial matter. The straight-arrow companies that do right by a sufferer and promptly pay him off lose the use as capital of that three thousand dollars or so meanwhile—multiplied perhaps eighty thousand times, for all the similar cases they have.

Selecting a jury is the last little battle of nerves between the two sides. By now the opposing attorneys know who will testify and have obtained pretrial depositions; this completes the hand each of them holds. Generally they think they know what will happen, so to save time and costs they settle the case either before the hearing starts or out of the jury's earshot during the hearing with the judge's help. Seeing a good sober jury waiting to hear them attempt to justify a bad case greases the wheels.

In the challenge room, though, the momentum of confrontation goes on. With a crowded court calendar, the judge in these civil cases is not present, as a rule. It's a small room, and there's an opportunity for the lawyers to be folksy or emotional in ways not permitted them later on. For example, in asking the jurors repeatedly if they will "be able to convert pain and suffering into dollars and cents" the plaintiff's attorney is preparing the ground for his more closely supervised presentation in court. By asking them if they own any stock in an insurance company he can get across the intelligence, which is otherwise *verboten*, that not the humble "defendant" but some corporation is going to have to pay the tab. His opponent will object if he tells too many jokes and wins too many friends, but both seek not so much a sympathetic jury as a jury that is free of nuts and grudge-holders, a jury dependably ready to give everybody "his day in court"—a phrase one hears over and over. The questioning we were subjected to was so polite as to be almost apologetic, however, because of the danger of unwittingly offending any of the jurors who remained. Having to size up a series of strangers, on the basis of some monosyllabic answers and each person's face, profession, and address, was hard work for these lawyers. Everybody was on his best behavior, the jurors too, because the procedure so much resembled a job interview, and no one wanted to be considered less than fair-minded, unfit to participate in the case; there was a vague sense of shame about being excused.

The six alternates sat listening. The lawyers could look at them and draw any conclusions they wished, but they could neither question them until a sitting juror had been challenged, nor know in advance which one of the alternates would be substituted first. Each person was asked about his work, about any honest bias or special knowledge he might have concerning cases of the same kind, or any lawsuits he himself might have been involved in at one time. Some questions were probably partly designed to educate us in the disciplines of objectivity, lest we think it was all too easy, and one or two lawyers actually made an effort to educate us in the majesty of the law, since, as they said, the judges sometimes are "dingbats" and don't. We were told there should be no opprobrium attached to being excused, that we must not simply assume a perfect impartiality in ourselves but should help them to examine us. Jailhouse advocates, or Spartan types who might secretly believe that the injured party should swallow his misfortune and grin and bear a stroke of bad luck, were to be avoided, of course, along with the mingy, the flippant, the grieved, and the wronged, as well as people who might want to redistribute the wealth of the world by finding for the plaintiff, or who might not limit their deliberations to the facts of the case, accepting the judge's interpretation of the law as law. We were told that our common sense and experience of life was what was wanted to sift out the likelihood of the testimony we heard.

Most dismissals were caused just by a lawyer's hunch—or figuring the percentages as baseball managers do. After the first day's waiting in the airport lounge, there wasn't anybody who didn't want to get on a case; even listening as an alternate in the challenge room was a relief. I dressed in a suit and tie and shined my shoes. I'd been afraid that when I said I was a novelist no lawyer would have me, on the theory that novelists favor the underdog. On the contrary, I was accepted every time; apparently a novelist was considered ideal, having no allegiances at all, no expertise, no professional link to the workaday world. I stutter and had supposed that this too might disqualify me—I saw homosexuals disqualified whenever their mannerisms gave them away—but, no, although to me a stutter in its way is as suspicious an ailment as homosexuality or alcoholism, these lawyers did not think it so. What they seemed to want was simply a balanced group, because when a jury gets down to arguing there's no telling where its leadership will arise. The rich man from Sutton Place whom the plaintiff's lawyers almost dismissed, fearing he'd favor the powers that be, may turn out to be a fighting liberal whose idea of what constitutes proper damages is much higher than what the machinist who sits next to him has in mind. In one case I heard about, in which a woman was clonked by a Christmas tree in a department store, the juror whose salary was lowest suggested an award of fifty dollars, and the man who earned the most, fifty thousand dollars. (They rounded it off to fifteen hundred dollars.) These were the kind of cases Sancho Panza did so well on when he was governor of Isle Barataria, and as I was questioned about my prejudices, and solemnly looked into each lawyer's eyes, shook my head, and murmured, No, I had no prejudices—all the time my true unreliable quirkiness filled my head. All I could do was resolve to try to be fair.

By the third day, we'd struck up shipboard friendships. There was a babbling camaraderie in the jury pool, and for lunch we plunged into that old, eclipsed, ethnic New York near City Hall—Chinese roast ducks hanging in the butcher's windows on Mulberry Street next door to an Italian store selling religious candles.

We ate at Cucina Luna and Giambone's. Eating at Ping Ching's, we saw whole pigs, blanched white, delivered at the door. We watched an Oriental funeral with Madame Nhu the director waving the limousines on. The deceased's picture, heaped with flowers, was in the lead car, and all his beautiful daughters wept with faces disordered and long black hair streaming down. One of the Italian bands which plays on feast days was mourning over a single refrain—two trumpets, a clarinet, a mellophone, and a drum.

As an alternate I sat in on the arguments for a rent-a-car crash case, with four lawyers, each of whom liked to hear himself talk, representing the different parties. The theme was that we were New Yorkers and therefore streetwise and no fools. The senior fellow seemed to think that all his years of trying these penny-ante negligence affairs had made him very good indeed, whereas my impression was that the reason he was still trying them was that he was rather bad. The same afternoon I got on a jury to hear the case of a cleaning woman, sixty-four, who had slipped on the floor of a Harlem ballroom in 1967 and broken her ankle. She claimed the floor was overwaxed. She'd obviously been passed from hand to hand within the firm that had taken her case and had wound up with an attractive young man who was here cutting his teeth. What I liked about her was her abusive manner, which expected no justice and made no distinction at all between her own lawyer and that of the ballroom owner, though she was confused by the fact that the judge was black. He was from the Supreme Court, assigned to help cut through this backlog, had a clerk with an Afro, and was exceedingly brisk and effective.

The porter who had waxed the floor testified—a man of goodwill, long since at another job. The ballroom owner had operated the hall for more than thirty years, and his face was fastidious, Jewish, sensitive, sad, like that of a concertgoer who is not unduly pleased with his life. He testified, and it was not *his* fault. Nevertheless the lady had hurt her ankle and been out of pocket and out of work. It was a wedding reception, and she'd just stepped forward, saying, "Here comes the bride!"

The proceedings were interrupted while motions were heard in another case, and we sat alone in a jury room, trading reading material, obeying the injunction not to discuss the case, until after several hours we were called back and thanked by the judge. "They also serve who stand and wait." He said that our presence next door as a deliberative body, passive though we were, had pressured a settlement. It was for seven hundred and fifty dollars, a low figure to me (the court attendant told me that there had been a legal flaw in the plaintiff's case), but some of the other jurors thought she'd deserved no money; they were trying to be fair to the ballroom man. Almost always that's what the disputes boiled down to: one juror trying to be fair to one person, another to another.

On Friday of my first week I got on a jury to hear the plight of a woman who had been standing at the front of a bus and had been thrown forward and injured when she stooped to pick up some change that had spilled from her purse. The bus company's lawyer was a ruddy, jovial sort. "Anybody here have a bone to pick with our New York City buses?" We laughed and said, no, we were capable of sending her away without any award if she couldn't prove negligence. Nevertheless, he settled with her attorney immediately after we left the challenge room. (These attorneys did not necessarily run to type. There was a Transit Authority man who shouted like William Kunstler; five times the judge had an officer make him sit down, and once threatened to have him bound to his chair.)

I was an alternate for another car crash. With cases in progress all over the building, the jury pool had thinned out, so that no sooner were we dropped back into it than our names were called again. Even one noteworthy white-haired fellow who was wearing a red velvet jump suit, a dragon-colored coat and a dangling gold talisman had some experiences to talk about. I was tabbed for a panel that was to hear from a soft-looking, tired, blond widow of fifty-seven who, while walking home at night five years before from the shop where she worked, had tripped into an excavation only six inches deep but ten feet long and three feet wide. She claimed that the twists and bumps of this had kept her in pain and out of work for five months. She seemed natural and truthful on the witness stand, yet her testimony was so brief and flat that one needed to bear in mind how much time had passed. As we'd first filed into the courtroom she had watched us with the ironic gravity that a person inevitably would feel who has waited five years for a hearing and now sees the cast of characters who will decide her case. This was a woeful low point of her life, but the memory of how bad she'd felt was stale.

The four attorneys on the case were straightforward youngsters getting their training here. The woman's was properly aggressive; Con Edison's asked humorously if we had ever quarreled with Con Edison over a bill; the city's, who was an idealist with shoulder-length hair, asked with another laugh if we disliked New York; and the realty company's, whether we fought with our landlords. Of course, fair-minded folk that we were, we told them no. They pointed out that just as the code of the law provides that a lone woman, fifty-seven, earning a hundred dollars a week, must receive the same consideration in court as a great city, so must the city be granted an equal measure of justice as that lone woman was.

Our panel included a bank guard, a lady loan officer, a young black Sing Sing guard, a pale, slim middle-aged executive from Coca-Cola, a hale fellow who sold package tours for an airline and looked like The Great Gildersleeve, and me. If her attorney had successfully eliminated Spartans from the jury, we'd surely award her something; the question was how much. I wondered about the five months. No bones broken—let's say, being rather generous, maybe two months of rest. But couldn't the remainder be one of those dead-still intermissions that each of us must stop and take once or twice in a life, not from any single blow but from the accumulating knocks and scabby disappointments that pile up, the harshness of winning a living, and the rest of it—for which the government in its blundering wisdom already makes some provision through unemployment insurance?

But there were no arguments. The judge had allowed the woman to testify about her injuries on the condition that her physician appear. When, the next day, he didn't, a mistrial was declared.

Lunches, walks in the Civic Center. I was reviewing two books and finding I could concentrate on them in the midst of the hubbub better than I might have under easier circumstances at home.

My ticket was drawn for another case. A woman carrying a year-old child had been knocked down (or said she had) by a parked car that suddenly backed up. Her attorney was a fighting machine, a fighting bantam—put him in a room and he would fight. His face in its heavy head flushed dark; one could see him as a child having temper tantrums. Combative as he was, however, when he wasn't raging he exuded geniality—genuinely wanted to be liked. Warm and *hot,* warm and *hot;* he whispered forensically. He was another of those veteran attorneys working for a contingency fee and sure that by now he knew a great deal about human nature and how to manipulate it, although in fact there was clearly some disastrous flaw in his judgment of people that he would never discover. Call him Fein (not his name).

His adversary—a word that Fein used with a smile, introducing Mr. Lahey (not *his* name)—was a man who disliked fighting. A ruined, short-nosed Irish drinker with a big seedy body, a bloated face, he held his hands tight to his chest or pushed them down hard on the table to keep them from shaking. He could no longer look anybody in the eye, not even the jury, and instead cast his gaze toward heaven when he made his summation, which, since his glasses magnified his pupils, was distressing. Besides feeling for him, I had the impression that he had not been a bad advocate in the beginning. As it was, he scarcely spoke in the challenge room, only shook his head when he wished to object to the other man's tactics. "You object?" Fein asked. Lahey nodded. Fein seemed fond of him, nevertheless, with that affection compulsive gladiators have for opponents who furnish the chance for a tussle, though his face lost its winning smile and flushed pugnaciously whenever he looked from us to him.

Lahey, who really seemed to know a little bit more law, so that even his minimal, unhappy, purely defensive efforts had some effect, did not return this friendship. Even asking us questions was burdensome to him. Here in the challenge room where the judge wouldn't intervene, Fein was going on and on, unimpeded, about the suffering of this mother and her tiny child. "But we don't want sympathy!" he said. "No," Lahey snickered. "You just want cash." Flushing plum-red, Fein told us that Lahey wasn't the insurance company's regular representative but just an "off-counsel."

Fein challenged a director of CIT, one of the nation's corporate giants, who may have been the richest man in the whole jury pool, exercised another hunch or two, then got around to asking about insurance stocks. Two of us, an IBM employee and myself, put up our hands as holders of bits of ITT, a conglomerate which has insurance interests. Lahey, silently shaking his head, objected to everyone being cast off the jury whose connection to the industry was as slender as that. They went upstairs to ask the judge. The judge ruled for Lahey, apparently, and told them that now only one of us could be challenged on peremptory grounds, so that Fein had to choose. The IBM man wore a rep tie and had hair that was as black and neat as his shoes. I wanted to stay on the jury, so I laid on my lap the books I was reviewing, which had identifying labels on them from the *Times,* figuring that if he was choosing between IBM and the *Times,* a plaintiff's attorney would pick the *Times.* That's what he did, looking sheepishly at me and stressing with some sense of theater that I must be fair enough to ignore the resentment which a juror is likely to feel toward a lawyer who wants him off the jury—not he but his client was the injured party.

So our group consisted of me; a round-faced black bus driver; a well-dressed real-estate broker who was carrying the *Wall Street Journal* and reading a skiing magazine; a brogue-speaking retired bank teller, who said that he had started out at the bank sweeping the floor and worked his way up; a cabdriver, formerly a bartender, who looked like the map of New York, had lived all over it, and was a philosopher; and the headwaiter on the milk run at a hotel. The court attendant who took us in tow was chuckling because he'd fixed the judge's wagon at lunch. The judge had sent him out for a sandwich and coffee, and in order to teach him not to do that again, he'd brought back two sandwiches, the wrong kind, instead of one, and no cream in the coffee. He was a limping old campaigner. The judge was an adequate little man who often stood up when he spoke, as lawyers do. His mode with the jury was like that of an optometrist explaining something to a customer. He was a stickler but always polite to the other participants too, though his job seemed to have lost much of its interest for him. Basically, no doubt, he was an impatient man, but by sixty had mastered this by hedging himself in with the precision of his job, by cramming his face with exaggeratedly pleasant expressions instead of scowling, and by whispering instructions as quietly as possible when he wanted to shout.

The plaintiff, being cross-examined about events that had occurred two years ago, screwed up her face and squinted determinedly, making a decided distinction between the lawyer who was working for her and the lawyer opposed. She was West Indian, dark, in her early thirties, not so much pretty as sensuous-looking, with an odalisque's walk and a thick coif of hair. Her baby, three years old now, was snoring softly on a bench. She compressed her lips with the force of her concentration after each answer she gave. Like the defendant, who was a private security guard, light-skinned, lean as a knife, wearing his pistol and handcuffs right in court, she had probably been coached. Both of them bumbled in testifying, however, and since the six of us on the jury turned out to be divided evenly about whom to believe, we kept reverting to those bungles, three of us excusing hers as signs of her sincerity, and three excusing his and criticizing hers.

She said that in crossing a street empty of traffic she had walked behind his parked car, which lurched back abruptly, knocking her screaming to the sidewalk and throwing the child out of her arms. She said she'd gone to the doctor seventeen times for her contusions and for medication, massages, and heat treatment of her shoulders and neck, and had taken the baby ten times. But she'd had no X-rays and had walked directly home to her other children, not going to the hospital for emergency treatment first. Her main mistake was to tell us she hadn't heard the car's engine and "would have" if it had been running. How could she have been hit if the motor wasn't running? There goes her case right there, said the jurors who were afraid the insurance company was being bilked. They had that sentence of testimony reread to us later in the jury room.

The man said that while it was true that he was sitting in his car, he hadn't started it; the car had never moved. The first thing he knew, out of the blue, this lady rapped on his door claiming she was bleeding and that he had backed into her; maybe she'd tripped on the curb. *His* blunder, which struck me as less a matter of verbiage than of veracity, was to give conflicting accounts of the distance he was from the nearest parked car. The avenue stretched downhill, and at first he said that if he'd wanted to move he had plenty of room just to coast away from where he was without backing up. Then it turned out that there was a car right in front of him. He was not a licensed driver, had only a learner's permit and was driving without the chaperon required by law. When the woman knocked on his door to claim that he had hit her (she said he'd hastily climbed out of his car as soon as she screamed), he gave her his name and address, offered to take her to the hospital, and then went across the street to find, as a witness, the girlfriend he'd been visiting; but they'd since broken up and she was not in court.

Although Fein at one point had managed to inform us that Lahey had been afraid that the defendant himself wouldn't put in an appearance, instead, his client's doctor was absent. For this reason, though he had been asking ten thousand dollars damages each for the mother and child, he felt it best to reduce the child's to four thousand dollars. In addition, he was asking a thousand dollars for the husband's loss of "consortium and services," which he gave us to understand meant sexual intercourse. In his charge the judge enlarged this to include "fellowship." The stenographer, a mannered young man with a Roman haircut, had forgotten to come back after lunch and needed to be summoned. But the charge was a conscientious one, not vacantly mouthed as if we on the jury were U.N. visitors. I'd come to like both Fein and the judge—Fein as a next-door neighbor whose barbecue smoke one would share, along with his pride in his kids and his delight in the sort of friendship that bridged disagreements. He tried to fix our eyes to his as he summed up, speaking hoarsely as though the trial had been going on for weeks, letting his voice sink and rise.

Then we were alone. We settled around the long table designed for a jury of twelve, in postures elaborately casual, as if we expected to battle the way movie juries do. The man who'd been reading the skiing magazine had dressed in loafers and chinos and a sport jacket today, and in educated accents he took the lead. He said the woman hadn't organized her thoughts or her case properly; otherwise she wouldn't have made the mistake of saying that the car which supposedly hit her wasn't running. And if your case isn't organized properly you don't deserve to win it. He owned property on Long Island and in Vermont, and the insurance premiums were too high. Also, why didn't the street fill with witnesses if she had screamed?

The peppy but retired teller, an endearing individual, didn't like the idea of paying out money on the unsubstantiated word of a woman who didn't have enough sense to get X-rays. Also, he regarded the driver's gun and handcuffs as a sort of character reference, because in his own line of work such licensed guards were trustworthy. Being nearly contemporaries, he and the cabbie had been at home with each other all along, trading jokes during every recess, he in an Abbey Theatre brogue and the cabbie in the accents of the Lower East Side. But, like me, though we didn't come straight out and say so, the cabbie was leery of the pistol and cuffs. He had once lived in East New York, where the accident occurred—just as he'd lived in every other known neighborhood—and he explained to the man in chinos that this was a tough neighborhood and didn't fill up with witnesses just because a girl screamed.

The teller then suggested that the girl had been jaywalking. The cabbie and I stressed that the defendant was driving illegally, however, didn't know how to drive in the first place, and that apart from his driving abilities we had difficulty believing him—was it really likely that this woman had stumbled on the curb, skinned herself, and simply looked around for somebody in a parked car to sue? If this character saw he was being set up like that, why hadn't he called the police?

But we want justice here, countered the teller. One-to-one testimony was no proof, and he doubted her. I said that nobody was going to jail, or even to have to pay a fine; this was a civil case in which the evidence, or our impression of it, need only be "preponderant."

The busdriver, who was wary—alone with these five white men—and had already heard some jokes about "witch doctors," referring to the woman's medical proclivities, had postponed giving his views. Now, nervously, speaking fast, he edged into a position of sympathy with her and raised an interesting question: why, if he hadn't really hit her, would this tough guy with his pistol and cuffs meekly hand over his name, address, and learner's permit to a woman who without reason tapped on his window for the plain purpose of victimizing him in a fraud?

Having waited all of us out, the headwaiter now said heatedly that he didn't trust any woman, that he "just used them and discarded them." He made a tossing motion, like throwing toilet paper into a john. His allies were a little taken aback, and I said (since I was providing the heat on our side) that if he had told that to the lawyers downstairs he wouldn't even be a member of the jury. He was a stiff, large, unusual man, a German, who pinned his ears tight to his head with the temple pieces of his glasses. In the challenge room he'd seemed like something of a caricature, talking about driving "only in Germany" when asked if he could drive, and about how as a European he always accepted authority, when asked if he would abide by the judge's charge; "in Germany it's not like here, you know."

We were released at five P.M. because the judge had a dental appointment. At ten the next morning, we greeted each other and found ourselves still lined up three to three. Just as the cabbie philosopher was best at arguing with the teller, I was more effective with the man in chinos, being the same age and from a background that he considered comparable to his own. He put his *Time* and *Wall Street Journal* on the table and I countered with my *New York Times* review books. In accents I remembered from prep school he complained about the amount Fein would receive from any settlement we gave the woman, but I brought in how much insurance lawyers were paid in a state like New York which lacks no-fault insurance.

We all recapitulated our reasoning, their side being fair to the driver, believing his version and dismissing his slips as honest ones; ours doing the same for the woman. As time passed, however, our side turned out to be more solidly aligned. For one thing, our sympathies were at least partly engaged; we had the confidence and expertise of two professional drivers operating; and then the headwaiter began to lapse into what might best be described as psychodrama. He told us that the reason he never believed any woman was that one had once accused him of indecent exposure— "showing his peeno"—and thereupon he began to imitate masturbation in a vigorous way. He also stood up and paced, though there was no room for pacing, and showed us the placement of his hernia scar, the injury having occurred while he was waiting on a governor's party of eight, with heavy silver service, and had tried to carry the entire main course on one tray, to spread it out all at once in grand fashion.

Other people also spoke personally. The busdriver, who was still wary of the rest of us, especially since both the plaintiff and defendant were black, mentioned times when fakers on the street had tried to stage incidents so as to sue him, making it plain that this story did not strike him as of that kind. On the Lower East Side the cabbie had once hit a girl on roller skates while hurrying home for services on Rosh Hashanah. The retired teller had ten grandchildren, he wanted us to know (the cabbie had six), and was not an unfeeling man—which nobody had thought. He was a dear; he simply was not used to giving out money so freely. The fellow in the chinos told us about a friend of his who had driven down Park Avenue drunk one night and hit three policemen. Although he was insured for five hundred thousand dollars, the jury awarded them 1.3 million dollars and he was bankrupted.

All of us, who might not have spent five minutes actually helping the woman at the scene if we had been witnesses, were invested with the law's solemnity and were spending what added up to five hours in these deliberations. But the night's sleep had made my friend the skier more amenable. Breaking the solidarity of his side, he offered to let the woman have one thousand dollars, not because he believed her but as a compromise. I'd suggested two thousand dollars for her and one thousand dollars for the child, the cabbie had said two thousand dollars and five hundred dollars, and the busdriver fifteen hundred dollars and five hundred. I said that if there had been any independent medical evidence we'd probably be asking for more, and that if we had wanted to bargain we could have walked in suggesting a figure double what we were ready to settle for. After all, her lawyer had first asked for ten times what we had in mind.

Now the cabbie really came into his own. In luckier days he had managed a taxi company which owned four hundred and fifty cabs, and in his soothing manner he began to recount the details of a dozen, two dozen, three dozen accident cases out of the countless assortment he'd dealt with, pointing out that the standard out-of-court settlement was five or six times the doctor's bills, declaring that he was convinced an accident had occurred, and that the learner-driver, scared because he was driving illegally, had begun by lying in his report to the police and so was lying still. With the broad, hospitable benignity of the old melting pot, for an hour or more he kept quietly filling in every silence with authentic street stories about New York accidents, making it all seem less exceptional to us, bringing it into perspective as a business risk for the companies involved. For every three cabs in a fleet, he said, a hundred dollars a week in insurance money was set aside to pay claims like this. In counterpoint, and maybe almost as effective in reducing the resistance of the other side, the headwaiter in his violinist's suit was striding along one wall of the narrow room doing unaccompanied cadenzas in a hollow voice of a sort that might have been interesting to scientists on the other side of one-way glass. It was an interior monologue, not without pathos. No, he wouldn't give any woman such an award.

Being a good fellow, the man relaxing in chinos agreed to come up to two thousand dollars if we who were above would come down. We did on condition that the teller would not require us to go lower. He was the foreman, by chance—the foreman is the man assigned to Seat No. 1—and remained wholeheartedly against any money at all being paid out. We recognized that in a practical sense we were a five-man, not a six-man jury, and that unanimity would be required. The man in chinos observed sarcastically that the baby didn't need money for candy and should no more receive a payment than the husband who claimed he hadn't been able to screw his wife for a couple of weeks. But I said that the baby had bled like anyone else, that you didn't have to be of voting age to suffer (the judge had refused to allow Fein to suggest "psychic scars"). I said that my first memory was of a train wreck, but didn't add that the memory seemed rather a happy one, because we were debating now, trying to score points, not even pretending to listen to each other judiciously.

Though the woman had spoken with the accent of the British West Indies, the cabbie explained her fluffs in testimony by going so far as to claim she was an immigrant new to the English language. He kept on with that legendary, big-hearted, big-city talk about every man getting a break, about generosity, a New York open to the masses of an older world. It was an unequal contest. By bringing in his six grandchildren he got the teller started again on his ten, and by and by the teller gave in, first to the extent of one thousand dollars, then one thousand five hundred, and then two thousand. He was so exasperated that he wanted to give half of it to the child just to spite the mother, and I, still resenting Fein's attempt to dismiss me from the jury—as Fein had suspected I would—thought that this sounded like a good idea because the cabbie had told us lawyers got less of a cut from money which was awarded to minors. The man in chinos shrugged and went along, so we'd reached our decision: a thousand dollars to the woman, a thousand to the child. We patted each other, brothers after the struggle.

"No!" said the headwaiter firmly in court when we were polled, not so ready to knuckle under as I'd imagined.

The last day or two, the jury pool swelled again to the initial crowd of two hundred, and people chatted in tête-à-têtes. When a new case was called nobody except the postmen and Transit Authority employees wanted to take the chance of being chosen for it and perhaps held over. One man told the lawyers that frankly he was sick and tired of hearing about auto accidents. I raised my hand and said I owned some ITT shares and would thus be biased in favor of the insurance company. The court clerks sallied forth from their inner sanctum to tell us about their six-week vacations. There was a sense of satisfaction and repletion at having seen some action and done some service. I had watched bits of trials from the spectators' section in the past, strolling out after half an hour if my interest flagged, but this was different.

On Friday I got home with a stamped receipt for ten days' work at twelve dollars a day, and found in my mail a stringent official warning that I must appear at New York's County Courthouse to explain why I hadn't shown up when called for jury duty and why contempt proceedings should not therefore be instituted against me. My answering note was lusciously righteous.

Virginie
and the Slaves

In New York City a white man meeting four blacks on a side street may quaver if he's alone, but the next day, flying to the Deep South, he sees fear on the faces of a group of Negroes on a country road when he stops for directions. They call him "Cap'm" and go right into the goofy set of mannerisms of song and story. The pretty girl among them has kinked her hair tightly into the waffle-iron pattern that slaves used to present to Massa at the commissary every Sunday before they got their pickled pork and kernel corn to last them through the week.

Traveling is not the undertaking that it used to be, when one progressed through every climatic, topographic change that finally culminated in the warm air or fine scenery we were in search of. By ship and train and jalopy we traveled as far vertically, just jouncing up and down. But now we jet abruptly into a softer climate, not ready for the balminess, which may seem unearned, or perhaps earned only professionally, like a stiff drink in the evening. And so in order not to feel like samplers, most of us manage to substitute for the old, flavorful, laborious transitions a kind of simultaneity of awareness: of what the Mississippi smells like at New Orleans and the face of the Rockies at Rifle, Colorado. When you go worldwide with this, meandering in Place St. Sulpice and thinking about where you'll be staying in Izmir tomorrow night, it creates an opportunity for either a catastrophe or a triumph of equilibrium.

To mention the Old South brings to mind plantation houses, just as "New England" calls up white steeples and green maples. But the South was quintessentially rural, and before the Civil War was more a matter of flatboats freighting bales of cotton on the rivers and canal excavations in the swamps than palace architecture. New England, too, was primarily a world center for sheep ranching rather than in the maple business; the occasional Greek

Revival house, with portico and fading pillars, was probably constructed with money from Merino wool at the same time as the South's cotton mansions. In the South there is a certain sisterly spirit toward New Englanders, so that when I've roamed about with Vermont license plates in the guise of a Yankee, although I've gotten gimpy glances from the carloads of whites who fought in the civil-rights fights of the 1960s, the older ladies of the upper-middle class were quite prepared to welcome me. Even today the War for Southern Independence, as they call it, preoccupies them, and any traditional foe of the Confederacy is to be embraced before the barbarians from Los Angeles and Phoenix who swoop through en route to Florida.

It is such older ladies who have bought and restored the mansions that remain along the lower Mississippi—a frighteningly accidental process. The Mississippi itself wiped out a good many houses that survived the Civil War, especially along the wet lowlands of the west bank and on the east bank below Baton Rouge where sugar cane was grown. Others were demolished when the high levees were built, or else have just lately fallen victim to the veritable Ruhr of industry—Exxon, American Cyanamid, and Union Carbide—which has usurped so much of the east bank. One sees cows on the levee, and cattle egrets that stalk along beside their feet to catch the grasshoppers that leap. Down next to the water are patches of willow and cottonwood, and sometimes bootleg little gardens with scarecrows with pie pans swinging from their fists, and the old "borrow pits," where the levee dirt was dug and where the fishing always was the best. Nevertheless, below Baton Rouge the bridges of the tankers and the crane booms of the freighters loom taller than the levee. There is the smell and steam of industry, jointed and shiny like a row of Erector Sets, and endless lines of tank cars waiting to be filled. This is the New South, which can be romanticized as foolishly as was the Old.

Throughout a tatty century these isolated, vainglorious houses were stoned and partied in by vandals, dismembered by treasure hunters; probably more of them were set afire by fraternity boys than by Abe Lincoln's soldiers. One looks for them between slag heaps and sulfur piles, and finds an upstairs now restored but the ground floor still scarred by campfires, the caretaker a stumbling, toothless white man who lives with his chickens in a shack in the yard. At Ashland–Belle Helene (twenty-eight white columns), which has for neighbors Shell, Texaco, and Allied Chemical and Borden Chemical, cattle were sheltering inside until only twenty years ago, when Clark Gable and Clint Eastwood came to make films.

Such houses are in a fix that might temper the wrath of even an old-time abolitionist, since their history concerns him too. Sometimes the sole trace left (and always the first sight one comes upon) is the splendid live oaks, boled like elephants and lavish in the reach of their limbs. But because the State of Louisiana has done nothing to assist in their protection—other than buying a house in West Feliciana Parish where John James Audubon lived during the summer of 1821 and another associated with the Longfellow-Evangeline State Park—they have become the hobbyhorse of individual women. In the course of touring a string of them, one hears about each new owner's Christmas customs, each new family's summer home. Alongside the Napoleon sofas, walnut armoires, and Italian altarpieces will be the son's silver costume from Mardi Gras, when he was Crown Prince of his dad's krewe, and Son himself in a kitsch portrait over the mantel of Carrara marble.

General Nathaniel Banks, who did most of the Union's fighting in these parts, has not the reputation of a Sherman, except that in 1864, in retreat through the Natchitoches district of northwest Louisiana after the defeat of his Red River campaign, he did some gratuitous burning. A party of hungry skirmishers would carry along a bucket of tar to brush against the walls of a house where they thought food should be obtainable, and if the residents didn't ante up they'd strike a match. There were two types of grand household: that from which the women had already fled in fear of the Union troops and their own servants, and that in which they stood their ground and saw their possessions fare well, on the whole. At Parlange the mistress feted General Banks at a fancy banquet and had her slaves barbecue a beef for the enlisted men under the looping oaks out on the lawn, so that she didn't have to stash her silverware in the stock pond. But slaves, envious neighbors, or white jayhawkers might loot or start a fire too, and as a Northern trooper named Lawrence Van Alstyne wrote in his diary across the Mississippi from Parlange, the sight of the scarred bodies of the field hands "beat all the antislavery sermons ever yet preached." This neighborhood was about as far down the river as anybody could be sold.

Vermonters have a saying when they hate someone: "I'd like to get him in my hog pen!" That regimen of slops and mud, and finally to be strung up by the heels and feel his throat cut. That there were few slaves in New England was fortunate both for the slaves and for New England, and certainly there is enough brutality in the famous parsimony of New Englanders to match up comparably with the bullying air of the young oil nabobs of the Gulf Coast. Still, since hogs are only hogs, and parsimony, hiding itself, continually dies back, as a practical matter nothing in the ordinary experience of a Yankee, I discovered, is going to prepare him for the extremes, as lush as nature's, of opulence alongside privation—the violent corrugations—of life in Louisiana.

Once the jungle had been pruned back, what this lower Mississippi region provided was topsoil from the nation's entire midsection, pilfered alluvially, along with sixty inches of rainfall a year and a 320-day growing season. But these benefits came accompanied at first by wolves and bears and panthers, fifteen-foot alligators, and fevers that killed more slaves than harsh treatment and more masters than feuding. The cypresses alone were so intimidating that a German immigrant who had for weeks been clearing a bank near the big river turned into the wrong bayou one morning, and every bend seemed perfectly familiar, every tupelo gum tree and cypress overhanging his canoe, lugubriously festooned with weeping moss, seemed like a specific adversary he thought he had laid low—until he recognized that the vindictive forest must have re-created itself overnight to stand just as it had before, and he gave up and paddled hard for New Orleans.

A man was known for his hound dogs—such a breed as the Catahoula cur or "leopard dog," which made the woods less formidable and routed out the hogs for butchering in the fall. After a plague of caterpillars in 1793, indigo faded as a crop (it was also rumored to have affected the health of the slaves). Then the wetlands were planted with sugar cane, usually by Creole settlers from New Orleans, a method for granulation having been invented at about this time. The hillier, drier country went into cotton. Being further from the river and the French city, it was occupied a little later, often by Americans of English ancestry who had journeyed across the Appalachians from the eastern states after the U.S. purchase of Louisiana in 1803. Rice needed such a thorough, constant wetting that it grew best along the stable bayous of southwest Louisiana—Bayou Teche, Vermilion River, and other Cajun strongholds. Therefore the cotton mansions naturally tended to resemble the great houses of Virginia, while those built with sugar or rice money might wear a French patina. The older French ones are influenced by Spanish architecture as well, especially with the feature of an outside staircase, because under Louisiana's period of Spanish administration (1764–1800) a house was taxed as a single-story dwelling as long as it did not boast a stairwell indoors.

The Spanish governors ruled rather benignly, considering that most of the citizenry were French. They even welcomed more Frenchmen from Europe and Canada, the "Cajuns" being Acadian refugees pushed out of Nova Scotia during and following the

French and Indian Wars. City Creole and country Cajun kept apart, and do so still. Besides them and the Spanish and Canary Islanders, the German settlers, the high-class, black-earth French, the high-class, black-earth English-Americans, the red-dirt, dirt-poor American backwoodsmen, and all the slaves, there was a substantial contingent of Irishmen, who bestowed upon downtown New Orleans its Brooklyn accent ("foist," "hoid," "boid"). No other Southern state remains such a crosshatch of bailiwicks, with blacks so black, French so French, rich so rich, and rednecks so redbone: a gastronomic, tacky city, surrounded by hardshell, die-hard hillbillies.

The different mansion tours are modestly priced and usually improvised. At the steamboat-gothic edifice known as San Francisco (not after the city but from the expression *mon saint-frusquin,* "my last red cent"—and indeed the young fellow who built it died soon afterwards), the lady in residence has "trained," as they say in the trade, two black servants to speak certain key phrases and herself sits downstairs to answer further inquiries. At Asphodel, on the other hand, the lady of the manor has said her piece into a tape recorder which the maid carries from room to room, plugging and unplugging it as you progress, meanwhile dusting and sweeping continually. Madewood, on Bayou Lafourche, is another house whose original owner, a Colonel Pugh—altogether his family owned eighteen plantations and three thousand slaves by the time of the Civil War—died of fret and yellow fever before he could enjoy the premises. The present cook, however, leaves her kitchen, wry and brisk, to show a visitor around. "Corinthian columns inside, Ionic columns outside in front, Doric columns outside in back." At Evergreen, near Edgard, Louisiana, even the brick privies were built like Greek temples. And the tour of Houmas House is led by a crisp young black woman. "Made by the slaves," she says, pointing at a pewter chandelier, her tone as noncommittal as two saucers clinking.

A bit of crewelwork at Houmas House gives the slogan of the day: "Yours is the Earth and everything in it." One sees a butterfly-pegged floor, a canopied bed of tiger maple, a kneehole desk, a secretary carved out of crotch mahogany. The wall ovens were fired the day before a banquet and then the fire removed for baking. The young white "gemmelmen" roosted on their own in twin white *garçonnières,* which they could spray with tomcat squirt at night, as rank as goats, and the ladies in the main house needn't know.

Rosedown, in the former cotton center of St. Francisville, is another product of the copious thirty years or so preceding the

Civil War. With its Versailles garden and eleven fireplaces in its sixteen rooms, it has been restored with Texas oil money and is in the custody of a squadron of retired schoolteachers who seem to have geared themselves to appear redoubtable enough to make the four-dollar fee worthwhile. The tour is roped and formal, and they exaggerate their accents for toniness even more than for geography. There are Aubusson carpets, a swan-shaped cradle, a Chippendale birdcage, Mallard and Belter furniture, smoke bells over the many oil lamps, a punkah, and pull ropes in most of the rooms that lead to bells of varying tones by which the servants could figure out where they were required to go. One prize bed, intended for Henry Clay, has bedposts nearly fourteen feet high; another is a sort of miniature fashioned from papier-mâché inlaid with mother-of-pearl. The prettiest room is the breakfast room, with a collection of green lacquer furniture and a wooden chandelier. The six columns in front of the front door are cypress trunks; the walls and floors are cypress. There are summer houses in the garden and a dovecote beside the pond, an outdoor furnace for boiling soap and scalding pigs, and an enormous kitchen shed. The ensemble was built to go with thirty-five hundred acres and four hundred and fifty slaves, and not till 1955 did the family finally "daughter out."

One can stay close by at Asphodel in a slave cabin, of all places, air-conditioned, where the food is good. The Cottage is the other fancy inn in the vicinity of St. Francisville. Built of cypress around an inner Spanish structure which dates to 1795, it has the loveliest possible setting and smells of jasmine and honeysuckle in the month of May. The floors are going cattywomp, the wallpaper is original; one sleeps in a hip-high, silken-canopied, 1810 fourposter bed, and a bandannaed black serves breakfast. The principal past owner was Thomas Butler, who owned twelve plantations across the Mississippi and was a member of Congress. Many of his outbuildings have been preserved—his law office, milk house, smokehouse, carriage house, commissary, and three of twenty-five slave hovels, each of which had two rooms and housed two families.

Oakley, the state-owned house memorializing Audubon's stay in Louisiana, was also begun around 1800. It was built for a plantation of twenty-nine hundred acres and a hundred and thirty-five slaves; outside, under loblolly pines, the cotton rows are still discernible. The Colonial Dames and D.A.R. have furnished it comfortably with Federal Period appurtenances, so that of all the restored manor houses it is probably the most natural. On the walls are Audubon's chipping sparrow, tufted duck, red-cockaded

woodpecker, and cerulean warbler, and there are leather fire
buckets, pewter plates (called "poor man's silver"), a spinning-and-
weaving room, and an inventory of slaves, in which I noticed that
a man in his forties like me was still considered to be worth the
top price of seven hundred dollars, as were others ten years
younger or even just nineteen.

Herefords and Anguses graze in the fields around town nowadays, because after the boll weevil's inroads in the 1930s, cotton
never did come back; the terrain defeated the modern machinery
that made cotton so profitable again in Mississippi's flat delta
counties north of Vicksburg. A lot of pine was planted instead,
Crown Zellerbach has erected a paper mill, and there's a sweet-
potato-canning factory and a concrete-mat-casting plant of the U.S.
Army Corps of Engineers at riverside. But all of this scarcely dents
the unemployment in this old plantation region, with more black
people than white and much miserable poverty. Even the panel
trucks that sell snap beans and tomatoes along Highway 61 bear
a scrawl on cardboard: "We accept food stamps." Vee's squatty 5¢–
10¢ store and the Boll Weevil Café with its planked porch are
something of a link to slavery if one reads people's faces aright—
screwed tight, as if they had been baked in a crucible. And when
a white man around here speaks of the slaves or the slaves' life, a
sneaky smile captures his mouth, as though he were remembering
a rich practical joke.

Sometimes I found my mind didn't take the tour as planned.
I'd look into the hostess's face—or another visitor's—to see what
kind of mistress she would have made, and it was never encour-
aging. Inside the house, with a forbiddingly unreconstructed ma-
tron speaking of the six hundred thousand homemade bricks
under one's feet—a platform eight feet high, before they'd even
started with the cypress and the *bousillage* plastering—all the while
pulling the bell ropes and pointing to a punkah fan and to a
water jar suspended from a hook in the ceiling, to be pulled a
thousand times and cooled, I would panic slightly; I wanted to be
out, as though some sudden reversion could cause these tasks to
be delegated to me. But then outside, beyond the Spanish dagger
and the century plants, the redbud and crape myrtle trees, I'd walk
around the immense house at a distance of a hundred yards, wanting painfully to get *in.* On the one side, the sweating discipline of
men, and on the other, the impossible discipline of women, while
in a wider circle all around had been the jungle, with cotton-
mouths, six-foot rattlers, and biting bugs. Even the runaways who
learned to live in it and fish and snare, putting the wateriest parts
between them and the master's hounds, seem to have been drawn

back, not only in order to resupply themselves, but for another look at that white, blinding, concise house.

Of them all, San Francisco alarmed me most, because of its pop-gothic gingerbread and rococo scrollwork, the fluted pillars' decorative iron devices on its double galleries, the snake-eyed narrow windows high up. I gazed at it from atop the Mississippi's levee, and walked around and around. It had a blaring quality, a fearful and tyrannical sense—even the looming twin cisterns built of cypress wood and holding eight thousand gallons apiece—because I couldn't possibly imagine myself as the master at such a place, only as a slave, and whatever mind had lived there as its master had been a tinkerer's, a monkey's.

The headquarters of the East Louisiana State Hospital for mental illness, at Jackson, is an imposing white plantation mansion, and so is the administrative building of the U.S. National Leprosarium at Carville, on the Mississippi, the only leper colony in the United States. Angola State Prison, at Tunica, which is close to St. Francisville, is another location to visit for a whiff of the old woefulness which accompanied this splendor; there you can still see Negroes crouch and scurry. The steamboat captains, with that waterman's relish for the high and low tidemarks of life, used to salute the lepers with three bawdy toots when they slid by, and no doubt did the same at Tunica when passing a convict gang. The river itself was so unpredictable, so rife with contradictions, that the savageries of slavery must have seemed less weird right alongside. And yet the best place for a runaway to head for is said to have been the woodyards on both banks, where a freemasonry of axmen and raftsmen existed and where he might manage to hole up successfully if he could hold his own.

From the army, some of us remember the sergeant's familiar warning, derived from slavery and hollered in the drizzly dawn: "I'll have your *ass*. Your souls may still belong to God but your ass is mine!" In fact of course it wasn't, but the most remarkable omission in American literature is the virtual absence of this unnerving and dramatic subject, going so against the country's grain. Melville and Hawthorne, Thoreau, Whitman, Emerson, and even Twain touched upon it only briefly, never finding it obsessive, compared to the nineteenth-century Russian geniuses, their contemporaries. Presumably serfdom seemed so much in character with the Russian national spirit to Turgenev, Chekhov, Gogol, Tolstoy, that to try to excise their continual pain and preoccupation with the question would be to rifle out the heart of much of their best work. By contrast, our Northerners could regard slavery as the plague of another region if they chose to, and something of an abstraction besides, because the slaves were Africans and black. More recently Willa Cather, Robert Penn Warren, and William Styron, writers with Southern roots, have tried to come to grips with the matter, but not convincingly. Faulkner, who with his marvelous imaginative grasp was the obvious candidate, seems to have flinched from depicting the reality of slavery, preferring to deal with it as a subsequent "stain," or, in his best brush with the idea, by means of another device of removal—the master being the comic obese Indian chief, Moketubbe, in the Indian story "Red Leaves." Thus, instead of a literature to set next to the Russian masterpieces which record the tragedy of serfdom, we have *Uncle Tom's Cabin* and *Gone with the Wind.*

Slaves who lived within the unit of a middle-class white family had a more interesting time of it, for better or worse, than in the regimented hoeing gangs, although the Big House gradually became the very symbol of slavery. A great house was cooler during the summer than an ordinary dwelling, and provided ways to employ a surplus labor force (those bricks!); also to consume slathers of money that otherwise might not have been so easily spent. Beyond that, it represented luxury and power and monumentalized the ego of a man and wife who lived like petty gods, a centerpiece to focus every eye on what the labor of the plantation was all about. The slave quarters were seldom far away, which indicates a continuing wish on the part of the white folk for intimacy with their darkies. Belle Grove, a seventy-five-room manor on the Mississippi constructed with sugar money, had dungeons with barred windows in the very basement. At Magnolia Plantation House in Derry, Louisiana, the stocks for those who were unruly still stand underneath the veranda. At Oakland, on the Cane River, in the cellar under the master's bedroom was a little room with a trap door for the girl who was kept there to respond to his summons at night. And in the formal gardens at The Shadows, on Bayou Teche, bordered now with hand-shaped bricks from the slave cottages, is a sundial on which is engraved the grim homily: "Abundance is the daughter of economy and work." David Weeks, who built the house, stood seven feet tall and must have been a frightening sight. He got hold of ten thousand acres of the most fecund sugar land in North America, which since his death has been found to overlie Louisiana's fattest salt deposits, if there is a lesson in that.

Many slaves, arriving in New Orleans as *Africains bruts,* originated in Senegal. (And some of the local doctors made their fortunes buying and speculating on those who'd sickened on the trip.) After 1808, when this import trade was banned in the United

States, Negroes were brought in coffles overland from Virginia and the Carolinas to Tennessee and down the river, as the old tobacco fields gave out and eastern slaves themselves turned into a cash crop. Men and women who were removed to the cane country by their own masters were aghast at the bodeful change in countenance that came over these individuals where so much money could be made. Wearing a breechcloth in the summer, in winter a woolen hooded monk's cape, they were worked from before sunup to dark, except in the fall, the cane-grinding season, when the sugar mills ran around the clock. Indeed, one can still see a cane-rich lady's mouth bulge full-of-nails when she speaks of that tough spell of the year. The cotton planter's reckoning with his slaves during the picking season came at the weighing scales, if he hadn't ridden herd on them rigorously enough all day in the field. And from boyhood on, it must be borne in mind, managing slaves encompassed all the macho importance of a cowboy out West cutting horses, or what is now entailed in driving a car well. For a severe beating, the person was staked to the ground in a St. Andrew's cross and whipped from the heels to the neck, a hole being dug in the ground in order to accommodate the stomach in cases of pregnancy.

"What is more remarkable is that the Creole women are often much crueler than the men," wrote C. C. Robin, a French diarist, in his *Voyage to Louisiana* (1807). "Their slow and soft demeanor, the meticulous tasks which they impose, are given in a manner of apathetic indolence, but if a slave does not obey promptly enough, if he is slow to interpret their gestures or their looks, in an instant they are armed with a formidable whip. No longer is this the arm which can hardly support a parasol. . . . Once she has ordered the punishment of one of these unfortunate slaves, she watches with a dry eye . . . she counts the blows and if the arm of him who strikes begins to falter or if the blood does not run fast enough, she raises her voice in menacing tones. . . . They require to see this horrible spectacle repeated at intervals. In order to revive themselves, they require to hear the sharp cries and to see again the flow of blood."

At several houses you can inspect the bronze bell which ruled the hours, as soft and greeny-looking as a melon now, but there is nothing else from that era, except the fruits of the women's shopping expeditions to Paris. No whips that paid the bills, no handcuffs, no belled iron collars, no wooden "goggles," which weighed three pounds and were attached to bands of iron around a runaway's ankles—a kind of caricature of Mercury's wings—to lash him if he trotted, and no immersion stool. "Tried the cold water on her Ladyship," wrote Bennet H. Barrow, a rather temperate fellow, a resident of St. Francisville, in his journal, after a whipping had not worked on a slave girl. With all the nostalgic exhibits of kitchen utensils, farming equipment, the dainty bibelots, the encyclopedia of gracious furnishings, I saw not a single whip preserved at the mansions I visited, though the state museum at Oakley did have a slave trap (unlabeled) outside—like a bear trap but without teeth so that the person's leg would not be pulverized.

In a cement-block restaurant on the highway, drinking Dixie Beer with rib-eye steak smothered in okra, I listened to several cattle dealers tell about the nigger who got treed inside a cattle truck when they had let a bull in when he wasn't looking—how he scrambled up the walls and along the ceiling, clinging like a monkey as it hooked at him, the whole crowd laughing till he saved himself. It wasn't that they had wanted him killed—he was popular enough—they had wanted him *all but* killed, reduced to a parody of any man's nightmare. Another fellow, a trapper, told how a nigger last winter waved his truck down and begged for the carcass of a coon he'd skinned. "Man, I just threw three coons away!" he'd yelled.

With the exception of those doughty Brooklyn Irishmen in New Orleans, the coastal and delta South still speaks with the drawl the African slaves fell into as they stepped off the boat and began to wrestle with the king's English. And since Southerners remain charmed by their own speech patterns (as, admittedly, most of the rest of us are charmed) slavery can be credited for that. It also bestowed upon them two centuries' worth of scapegoats to burlesque every other man's worst night sweats and dreads: of losing children, wife, and home, of hunger, cold, and being whopped and bestialized. Having before them a black populace who were actually undergoing, in a horrific kind of shadow show, events that are usually confined to one's bad dreams, Southerners as a group perhaps tended to become less introspective than Northerners. They were, in a sense, *released;* yet at the same time they were also mesmerized by the fact that they lived with the dream made real. Their "tragic view" has taken the form of an abstractedness, an absentmindedness which is peculiar to many Southerners and has been reinforced by the feeling, widely spread, that whatever the task, if somebody will just wait a little, other hands and other backs will get it done. Always, however, they reserved one province—violence—to themselves, which is why they still fly off the handle so extravagantly when crossed and why they fight for their country and love football.

But hot under the collar and abstracted as they got, it was

great fun being an old-school Southerner. This is evident to me whenever I go poking around with a white-haired gent I know, quail-hunting or netting half a pail of crawfish, and gossiping with the different landowners whose fences we must climb. Then after dark we go fishing on the bayou with a Coleman lantern dragged behind the boat on a raft made from a tire which draws thousands of bugs and slews of little fish and some fine big ones. He has his pal from New Orleans along, a white-blonde in her late forties with shrewd eyes and an aggravated mouth—a V-shaped, stripper's face—who's fat in all the right and all the wrong places, and splits her evenings and weekends between my friend and another aging tiger. She's a beautician, a soldierly and slangy woman whose freedom and friendship with men is her strength here in the back country, where the woodsy women seem either rather mousy or have the same jumpy appeal as deer. A Yankee like me she teases about putting the niggers "in a vat," and with her fantasy of riding in a carriage pulled by twelve chained bucks, and her with a horsewhip—nonetheless, it really *is* her fantasy. She says New Orleans is "careforgotten. We don't care who you are or what you have or where you come from if you know how to have a good time." She grew up in Biloxi, on the Mississippi Gulf Coast, feeling with her bare toes for soft-shell crabs hiding in the salt grass at night for Sunday dinner. She says her mother was Italian but at fourteen she "crossed the line" and captured a twenty-one-year-old Protestant of the old stock. In this town, she says, she would have left, by golly, at the age of five.

In the motel parking lot, when we pass another white-haired gentleman escorting a bleached blonde, my friend and he exchange meaningful nods. "Well, how are you? Good to see you. How you holdin' up?"

The other thing that my friend likes to do when visiting his boyhood stamping grounds is to chat with the "nigras," especially those who are his age. It's a man's business, fiddling and dickering with the nigras, and it is simply untrue to claim, as political liberals often do, that only the Negro in the parley realizes that the bonhomie is a charade. The grin my friend wears is ripe with import and his eyes shine, asking the "boy" where his boss is—a grin for back-of-the-barn—while the "boy," scattering yes-suhs, goes into a kind of stationary buck and wing. It's semisexual, not much different from when my gent is chaffing a "brown-meat-and-brown-gravy" whore, and even when there is no nigger around and he's just telling nigger stories, his smile is like that of a boy who's fingering his genitalia. Like frogging, fishing, shooting rabbits, masturbating, it is good country fun to hang about with the niggers—more a man's proper activity than a woman's, and more of a boy's than a grown man's. Niggers, or at least the fun of niggers, go so much with boyhood that this may be part of the reason why they are called "boy." And though most of the menace in the tone has waned and everybody knows nigger servitude is ending, men my friend's age know that just as it is surely going to end, it won't end so soon that they will have to do without it in their own lifetimes; they can relax in that regard. Besides the ripe, erotic grin, the other expression they wear when on the subject is vaguely secretive, like that which goes with talk of money corruption up North—that of a man who has "a good thing going."

As for the violence, recollections of Negroes tipped into the water and run down with a motorboat or beaten to death with an oar for crabbing in the wrong bayou (the offense also invariably boyish), one must eavesdrop on the poorer white men—top shirt button buttoned—or a man who began life poor and still sees no necessity to keep quiet about such incidents. "Oooo-oooo," he'll say, recalling with a small smile those good ole boys who'd got so *mad*.

To relive the relationship between owner and slave we can consider how we treat our cars and dogs—a dog exercising a somewhat similar leverage on our mercies and an automobile being comparable in value to a slave in those days. We can look in the big cities for the casualties or drive the back roads of the Black Belt where the stay-putters remain. Historically, there has been incredible procrastination on the matter, beginning with the negligence of Washington and Jefferson, who disapproved of slavery but made no provision for moderating it in the manipulative late 1780s before regional patterns rigidified. Because remorse has never been America's strong suit, Reconstruction had hardly got started before forced labor was reinstituted and, at least in the form of convict-leasing, grew so bad that in Louisiana the mortality rate reached 14 percent in 1881. Eventually there must be some provision for the other reality: the fact that these plantations were also archipelagos of suffering. There must be a "Blacks' Plantation" museum too.

As it is, Catalpa, in St. Francisville, and Parlange, which is across the Mississippi on an oxbow called False River, are occupied by descendants of the antebellum tenants, so that while listening to these old women painstakingly display their wares, one can catch a glimpse, even through the obfuscation of family folklore, of the strange feral existence led here before and just after the Civil War.

At Catalpa, Mamie Ford Thompson shows Audubon's portrait of her beautiful great-grandmother (for whose safety's sake he

was purportedly dismissed from his post as her tutor); then another
of her grandmother, who she says collected a hundred proposals.
She herself is a modest, hospitable woman in a drab blue sack of a
suit, and serves sherry to visitors, saying twelve of America's first
nineteen millionaires lived here along the lower river. There's a
Sèvres whale-oil lamp to prove it, an ingenious whale-oil coffee-
maker, Meissen and Venetian vases, a ladies' cuspidor, rose-petal
jars for scent, low chairs for small-boned people, numerous silver
services that were buried in burlap during the War, and the curved
silver crumber used at Rosedown during the seven-course dinners
when she dined there with her relatives before the family turned
land-poor. The pride of Catalpa is the elliptical quarter-mile driveway lined with live oaks planted as acorns in 1814, with circles of
conch shells under them, pink inside, most of which the tourists
have stolen but which the slaves used to wash regularly in the bass
pond. Azaleas bloom pinkly in May and hydrangeas and magnolias
in June, set off by the hanging moss.

Mrs. Parlange, across the river, is a tiny innocent, showing
silk-and-mahogany bookcases, swords, tea boxes, applewood beds
from Paris, a Boulle cabinet, candle vases that served the dual purpose of giving light and of keeping the night teakettle hot, a bub-
ble-maker for enlivening drinks, an ebony table inlaid with gold
and tortoiseshell. It's a winsome tour, comprising the usual mix of
gewgaws and museum pieces, good portraits and atrocious ones—
a belle forced into marriage who died of a heart attack on her wedding night and was buried in her white dress. The house was built
more than two hundred years ago of mud-and-deer-fur *bousillage*
framed with cypress posts on a cool raised brick base, with dove-
cotes set in front and a Southern garden of mimosas and camellias
(as well as chameleons). Mrs. Parlange speaks in New Orleans
Brooklynese of ice brought down the Mississippi during her girl-
hood for summer champagne balls, and about how no Creole
whose origins cannot be traced back to the eighteenth century is
clean of nigger blood. Her own mama married a New York Dutch
Yankee, because at the balls in New Orleans that season he changed
his white gloves before each dance and spoke French with the accent of France.

Across False River, however, is what Mrs. Parlange calls "the
chickencoop," where the *coureurs de bois* settled. These "runners
of the woods"—French trappers and woodsmen who rafted down
from the Great Lakes region instead of coming by sea through
New Orleans—have slivered the shoreline into splintery freehold-
ings, as along the St. Lawrence, through their practice of dividing
land into equal parcels for the next generation. By contrast, the

Parlanges struggled to save at least two thousand of their acres intact. One young man married the mortgage holder's daughter, and Virginie Parlange, a stylish *maman,* after having entertained both General Banks and then General Dick Taylor of the Confederacy in 1864, called together her slaves under an oak tree and told them Abe Lincoln had freed them but that she would hock her silver in New Orleans to feed them if they would stay put and work. This latest Mrs. Parlange's confused *pied noir* face so guilelessly recaptures that instant as she talks—a wildness, a pity, a misery which otherwise would be irretrievable—that somehow it is possible to stand in the shoes not only of Virginie but of one of the two hundred slaves: damned if they accepted, damned if they did not.

The South in the years immediately following the War dug down into its stock of rural savvy, scraping by on possum meat and poke salad, but later was to show off those white pillars as substantiation of the claim that this, like other slave societies, had been a golden age. The slave who dwells in me found it impossible to be inside the houses, yet impossible to be altogether outside, because it *was* a golden age for somebody, all right; there were happy people here. Apologists gloss over the wretchedness of the institution by pointing to the millhands of Massachusetts and to the European navvies who labored through these swamps, building roads and railroads where yellow fever was too pervasive to risk the health of a slave. But of course the well-turned-out visitors who drive up to Rosedown on their way to Florida are descendants not of the slaves but of the navvies and millhands. Sometimes, for a quarter of an hour, one feels in the position of the young gemmelman of the house, to whom every nearby creature belonged; sometimes like a traveler lodged in the "stranger's room" opening only onto the veranda (these levee grandees were so free with their hospitality that they couldn't always let the guest inside the house); and sometimes in the winter clodhoppers of a field hand glimpsing the hipped roof while marching to chop cane.

Sugar cane is sweetest if harvested after a cold snap—just as maple sap is best when a night frost has brought up the sugar content—and so the hardest work on a sugar plantation coincided with the end of the fall. Some of the landowners even concocted a ceremony to wind it up. The biggest cane-cutter would be set dancing around the final stalk, which was tasseled with a bit of ribbon, in what the overseers conceived of as resembling a tribal "dance." Then he cut the cane and carried it, with all the prime hands behind him, to Marse's house. Marse would come out on the white gallery with the mistress and Mizz Judith and Marse Alexander and raise a glass of wine to the good harvest in front of the hands, and let them each enjoy a cup of rum. Then they gave their massa a cheer and he had their Chrismus gifs distributed, which were the tow shirts, capes, pants and shoes that they would wear while plowing, planting, hoeing, chopping, and cooking down the sugar crop next year.

Once in Jefferson County, Texas, across the Sabine River from Louisiana, I stumbled on a ranch of umpteen hundred acres which struck a note of terror in me. I'd come there wolfing, and since there were few wolves, I'd had plenty of chance to see a more embracing predation. To catch a horse the cowmen mesmerized him with their arms extended, snake-to-bird, and when they waved their magic arms at a big bull, riding in irresistible circles around him, the animal soon folded.

Wolfing about the bends and elbows of the country, one has plenty of opportunities for recapitulating history. For blundering upon an alligator hunter with emphysema or a stick-up artist from the Depression, there's nothing like it. And on this ranch: no prurient guesswork about slavery, but a whiff of the real thing. The owner was a stony little man who consented to chat with me only because I was accompanied by a fellow whose grazing rights he hoped to lease. My companion, curly-headed, under thirty but already a smoothie, was in a race for City Council, mending some fences as we toured. The smell of spring was in the air, and it was time to think of bringing in the cattle that had wintered beside the Gulf to mark them up and doctor them. The old man had four of his blacks standing around, and he was fussing like a spinning flywheel on a motor that hasn't been greased—that never *has* been greased. Not for a minute did he stop issuing orders and then countermanding them. "Hey, get the tractor going; no, kick it off; no, get it going again. It sounds funny, don't it—no, turn it off. Catch that sorrel—not the one-eye. Get the tractor going, catch him with that. No, turn it off, you can catch the sumbitch just walkin' at him." He kicked the tire of his pickup truck as we leaned against it and told another black to run and get the tire gauge. He squinted at the roof of his machinery shed—this was a corner of the ranch, not where he lived—was that rooftree busted? He thought somebody ought to climb up and look.

A range cow and her calf ran by the fence but swerved when he turned toward them, his gaze like a squirt of acid that festered for a moment, his hand bouncing just a little, like a pistol, as he pointed. Though he had a friend visiting—a big-ribbed, frog-faced, impassive man who had retired from a career at one of the petrochemical plants, who did some poisoning for him as a hobby—he still burned openly with bitterness about the Civil War. He said his ranch had been larger then, and moved away from me until the only way I could hear what he was saying was to keep following him around the truck, sticking beside my City Council friend whose pasturage he wanted. In 1924, he said, a tidal wave and blizzard had killed two hundred cattle here; one hundred last winter had frozen to death. He buzzed in anger at the wolves as well—they bit his calves' tails off, or they would chase a calf until it panted and slash its tongue out so that it strangled on its blood—and at the rats in his oat bin, and at the vultures, which he said would flap around his cows when they were trying to drop a calf, scrapping with each other to do the honors on the afterbirth until the mama strained herself in plunging at them and never was the same again. Scrambling to her feet, she might step on her infant inadvertently and cripple it. In the bayou bottom along one of his boundaries lived a drove of razorbacks, rooting in the mud and weeds. They were a remnant that had escaped his previous expeditions to kill them, and thinking of them, he decided he'd get his guns out tomorrow and go in there with all his niggers and clean them out—hang 'em up and cut 'em up. His fury made him hum.

Probably he was too old to really go and shoot the hogs; the federal government had forbidden him the use of the familiar wolf poisons—he'd have to send his friend to Mexico to buy some—and with the bad winter's dead cattle sprawled about, the vultures were increasing. His Negroes also were older men, the top hand the eldest, with a smile incised on his wrinkled face by so many decades that it had become a snarl. This fellow chuckled, every few words that he mumbled, swaying with the dozen contradictory orders that came from Mr. Phil, but at the same time he was as immune as a weathervane, never moving far unless the instructions were given again, and then renewed. For me to have had to take orders from the man would have been like torture with electrodes, but Em farmed with them and never jerked as if they stung. Plum-black, a slim knot of a fellow, he displayed his calluses to us when told to, and had come to resemble his master a bit, as dogs are said to. None of the young help could climb a windmill or shoe a horse or mend a waterline like Em. Once he had loaded eleven hundred cattle into stock cars in an hour and three-quarters and sent the train highballing. He mumbled that he "need a li'l money," grinning. Mr. Phil laughed too and reached in a side pocket for his wallet, which was fat and which he handled as men do their scrotums when they soap themselves, and gave him two one-dollar bills.

But it was the fizzing of Mr. Phil that got to me, not the wages. He fizzed and his men twitched, and there was nothing comic about it. He was grim, mischievous, punitive, convinced that God had given him the land and the people to work it with. I could envision him deliberating on the question of whom to sell. We like to manufacture metaphors and say that slavery is the bondage of a bad love, or is the schoolboy who must grin along with his tormentors at his own clumsiness. But slavery is not as easy to re-create as that. Slavery was wiring that you were hitched to: wired to the acid batteries of a crazy brain.

Although he lived at the time of slavery, William Bartram had to go wandering among the Seminoles before he recognized the utter anxiety in which slaves lived; and here I was wolfing in Texas to discover the same thing. My rancher was perpetually disgruntled, inspecting the blossoms on his peach tree for a blight, looking at his horses for a limp. He was so accustomed to the luxury of company to blow off to that he would only have noticed if he hadn't had four men dogging him to ring his comments on. He had them catch the sorrel horse, then let it go because he liked the white-socks better. No, grab the sorrel again. There were limits that the man had had to adjust to—perhaps he couldn't point to the top of a tree and send somebody up to check the soundness of a high branch—but his matter-of-factness was the worst of it.

Some of the "old boys," he said (that Southern conjunction of two fond words, "old" and "boy"), would get after a horse with a quirt until it could read and write, or at least read the brands. He said that when he went out bulldogging he used to tie the steers right where they lay with their heads down between their legs and their asses sticking up above the grass so that you'd spot them easily when you rode back at the end of the day. I could envision him tending the fire while the young stock was marked, frying the "prairie oysters" that his black cowboys tossed him, and (to turn the clock back) some time during the hot afternoon pointing with a wink for his foreman's benefit at one of the blacks who had been feisty and having *his* balls in the frying pan too in half a minute.

In the early 1800s, jolly Jean Lafitte, the buccaneer of Louisiana and Galveston Island, used to sell the slaves that he was pirating to the settlers at a dollar a pound. His lieutenants, the Berthoud brothers, would race in longboats with slave crews and with a pistol nip a snip off someone's ear if he broke the stroke. Phil said that fifty years after the import business in slaves had been proscribed, bootlegged blacks were still being spirited into the estuary of the Sabine River here and auctioned on its banks. "We put their first clothes on them."

As I left Texas for Louisiana and New York again, an old gaunt black man hobbled out onto a desolate section of the superhighway, newly opened to traffic, in order to hitchhike. There was no exit close by, and by his breathless manner I could see it was some kind of an emergency for him. He must have been up in his seventies, and with a desperately obeisant gesture he doffed his floppy hat, waved it and held it out, almost blindly, as if asking alms from the gods in the sky. It was too stark and sudden for me, as naked as slavery. I had been dreaming the night before of several red foxes that were struggling in a steel trap, and me clubbing them, each fox that had been beaten dead reviving to struggle and be clubbed again. I was wondering about myself, and why it was that though the people I most cared about were women, the only people whom I really wrote about were men. I was whizzing by at eighty miles an hour, frantically lonely, singing in my loudest bathroom voice again that, "God is good, God is great!" and didn't have sufficient time to react with anything beyond astonishment to what to a white Southerner would have seemed only a very plain and homey gesture of beseechment.

Mushpan Man

He was real flesh and blood, not a folk construction like Paul Bunyan—and he plied the trade of an appleman for almost fifty years with inspired generosity, not ascending solely to a single day's public drama, like John Henry, the steel-driving hero of Big Bend Tunnel in West Virginia. Yet Johnny Appleseed, too, has survived simply as a folk figure of whom little is known, as a memory fuzzy in outline, mainly inscribed in children's literature and turn-of-the-century romances and poetry or Louis Bromfield novels.

Born John Chapman (1774–1845) in Leominster, Massachusetts, he proved to be a man with a mission along the frontier, which in those days included western Pennsylvania, Ohio, Indiana, and Illinois. If he had kept a diary, he might be compared with John James Audubon and George Catlin, who come down to us through their own words and pictures, although—more of a frontiersman than they were—he worked humbly and busily to facilitate that frontier's passing. In a way, his name is as durable as Andrew Jackson's, who died in the same year. But Johnny Appleseed has been remarkably neglected by the historians, probably because he conforms to none of the national stereotypes and illustrates nobody's theories.

We think of the swaggering, unscrupulous prototype frontiersman who bushwhacked Indians and scouted for the Long Knives, the mountainman who went into the bush with two horses and a squaw, and in order to live, ate his packhorse in January, his saddle horse in February, and his sad squaw in March. In the gaudy parade of liars, killers, pranksters, boasters, and boosters that fill up B. A. Botkin's *A Treasury of American Folklore*, Johnny Appleseed, along with Abe Lincoln and George Washington, occupies a tiny section entitled "Patron Saints." (John Henry and Paul Bunyan are "Miracle Men.") But, though a legendary walker, he is fabled as much for abusing his feet as for sporting tin pots on his head or cardboard headgear. In icy weather, at best he wore castoffs given to him—sometimes one shoe and one broken boot, tied on with varicolored string wound around his ankle, sometimes only one shoe, with which he broke trail through the snow for his bare foot. He preferred, if possible, nothing at all. There is the story of Johnny quietly confronting a pharisaical camp-meeting preacher who had demanded of the congregation, "Where now is the man like the primitive Christian who is traveling to Heaven barefooted and clad in coarse raiment?" Johnny, of course, walked forward in the upside-down coffee sack with holes for his head and arms that was his usual garb, and lifted his bruised bare feet, one by one, putting them right on the pulpit stump.

Nowadays we like heroes in *boots*, however. Saxophone players, clerical workers, hair stylists, "antiheroes," women dressed for the office, partially disrobed ladies, vacationers fussily dashing into an airport taxi, all are likely to wear cowboy boots, jackboots, ski boots, sandhog boots, desert boots, with kinky belt buckles that broadcast a physical vigor and spiritual sadism the wearer doesn't really even aspire to feel. Our great West, our old westering impulse, has become a costume jewel.

Anomalous, unassimilable, Johnny Appleseed was a frontiersman who would not eat meat, who wished not to kill so much as a rattlesnake, who pitied the very mosquitoes that flew into the smoke of his campfire. He liked to hear the wolves howl around him at night and was unafraid of bears, yet reportedly slept without shelter one snowy night rather than roust out of hibernation a mother bear and her cubs who had crept into a hollow tree that he had intended using. Although he would sometimes buy a worn-out horse to save it from mistreatment, boarding it with one of his friends for the winter, and would scour the woods in the fall for lame horses that the pioneers, packing their way through the country, had abandoned, apparently he believed that riding the beasts was discourteous to them. He only employed a horse to carry his bags of seeds or, late in his life, to drag an old wagon.

Though in a sense he was the nation's paramount nineteenth-century orchardist, Johnny Appleseed denounced as wickedness the practices of grafting and pruning, by which all commercial fruit is produced, because of the torture he thought such a knifing must inflict on the tree. He was shy in a crowd but a regular sermonizer among people he felt at home with—probably a bit of a bore at times, but no simpleton. In Steubenville, Cincinnati, and Urbana, Ohio, he knew the leading New Church Swedenborgians, and between his arrival in central and northern Ohio and the time of his death, Swedenborgian societies sprang up in at least twelve of the counties there, many individuals testifying that it was Chapman, the colporteur of Christian literature, who had first "planted the seed."

As a religious enthusiast, he was more on the Franciscan model than the harsh zealots, from Puritan to Mormon, whom American social historians are accustomed to writing about. And as an entrepreneur with considerable foresight about the eventual patterns of settlement, he allowed himself to be utterly clipped and gypped in matters of real estate through much of his life. When somebody jumped one of his land claims, his main concern seemed to be whether they would still let him take care of his apple trees. When he sold apple seedlings, he liked to be paid with an I.O.U., scarcely having any use for money except to give it away to needy families, and left to God and the debtor's own conscience the question of whether he was finally paid off. Instead, he bartered for potatoes, cornmeal, salt, and flour, and peddled cranberries—a fruit that the pioneers combined into stews or dried with suet for a midwinter treat. Often he shucked corn, split rails, and girdled trees for his keep. He ate nuts and wild plums in the woods on his trips, and cooked his corn mush, roasted his potatoes, and probably carried Indian-style "journey bread," which was made by boiling green corn till it was half done, drying it again in the sun, then browning it in hot ashes when ready to eat, pounding it fine, and possibly stirring in birch or maple syrup or summer berries or honey (though Johnny always left enough of that in the comb for the bees to live on). If many people never paid him for the seedlings he distributed so diligently, others returned his kindness by their hospitality to him as he passed back and forth. The belt of territory he worked in gradually shifted westward during the course of his life, but he wintered in the easternmost towns—after his strenuous summers at the borders of settlement—and so would migrate between several homesites, several circles of friends.

He gave little gifts of tea when he had money, but probably didn't drink it himself, preferring a Biblical drink of milk or milk and honey. He did use snuff, however, and would sip a dram of hard liquor to warm up in cold weather—if one can generalize fairly about his conduct from isolated instances of testimony about five decades of such intense and fervent activity. He was wiry in build, short by our standards but average for then, with peculiarly piercing blue eyes, good teeth, a scanty dark beard that later turned gray, and uncut dark hair, parted down the middle and tucked behind his ears. When not in a coffee sack, he dressed in a collarless tow-linen smock or straight-sleeved coat that hung down to his heels, over a shirt and burr-studded pants that had been traded to him for his apple seeds.

He was quick-talking and restlessly energetic as a visitor, but wind-beaten, hollow-cheeked, and gaunt-looking from eating so little and walking so far. Yet somehow, despite his eccentric demeanor, he was remarkably effective in the impression he made, "some rare force of gentle goodness dwelling in his looks and breathing in his words," as W. D. Haley wrote in *Harper's New Monthly Magazine* for November 1871, in the first biographical sketch that brought Johnny Appleseed to national attention. Not even small boys made fun of him, knowing his boldness at bearing pain—besides walking barefoot in the snow, he would poke needles into himself without flinching, for the children's edification. He had a string of good stories of Indians and wolves for them, and presents of ribbon and whatnot that he carried with him to give to their sisters.

He felt comfortable with children, and probably wistful, particularly with girls. Holding a six-year-old child on his lap, he would speak of someday having a "pure wife in Heaven." He seems to have imagined that it might be possible to adopt an orphan of about that age and raise her up to be just such a wife, even on earth. There are indications that at least once he tried, but that in adolescence the girl, like other girls, began to flirt with other men. Another time he announced that two female spirits had shown themselves to him and told him they would be his wives in the afterlife, bidding him abstain until then. He took an untheatrical view of the hereafter, however—a place he didn't think would be all that different in geography or its earthly occupations from the world he lived in. Resurrection was the simple continuation of the spiritual being without its corporeal, or "natural," adjuncts, and the indifference to physical discomfort which he cultivated can no doubt be partly ascribed to his impatience to see that process speeded, says Robert Price, his principal biographer. But he liked to joke that Hades at its worst wouldn't be worse than "smoky houses and scolding women" or "Newark," a raunchy Ohio border settlement.

Despite his small roach of a beard, unkemptly clipped, and his dark horny feet and deliberately apostolic costume, he kept himself clean, and "in his most desolate rags" was "never repulsive," his acquaintances reported. Arriving at a house where he was known, he happily stretched out on his back on the floor near the door, with his head on his knapsack and his feet tilted up against the log wall. Removing his discolored Bible and Swedenborgian tracts from the pouch he created for them inside his smock by tying his belt tightly, he would ask with exuberance, "Will you have some fresh news right from Heaven?" While the men smoked or fleshed a fox skin and the women cooked or quilted, he read and extemporized, his voice now roaring scriptural denunciations of evil, now soft and soothing. By middle age, he didn't hesitate to introduce himself to strangers as "Johnny Appleseed," enjoying his notoriety, but before accepting hospitality he would make sure that there was plenty of food in the house for the children.

In good weather he slept outside; otherwise he would lie down on the floor close to the door of the cabin, as he "did not expect to sleep in a bed in the next world." But one can picture the suppers of applesauce, apple pie, apple strudel, apple dumplings, apple turnovers, apple cider, apple butter, and apple brown betty he was served by farm wives who had settled in the vicinity of his nurseries. One also can imagine the kidding he endured for bringing hard cider and applejack into the country (which already had "white lightning"—corn liquor). After the article in *Harper's* by W. D. Haley, twenty-six years after his death, there was a sudden revival of interest in Johnny Appleseed, with people writing their recollections or hearsay memories of him to small-town newspapers throughout the Midwest. He was compared to John the Baptist, a voice in the wilderness heralding a new religion, and professors said he had personified the spirit of democracy—one for all—in the New World. In more saccharine accounts, professional romancers reported that apple blossoms tapped at his window when he was born and strewed themselves over his grave when he died. "His mush-pan slapped on his windy head, his torn shirt flapping, his eyes alight, an American ghost," wrote Frances Frost.

"In his earthly life," Ophia D. Smith noted in a centennial tribute by Swedenborgians in 1945, "Johnny Appleseed was a one-man circulating library, a one-man humane society, a one-man [medical] clinic, a one-man missionary band, and a one-man emigrant-aid society." But because of the distance that separates us, and as a result of the void in scholarship until Robert Price's biography in 1954—the fact that for many years historians simply ignored him as a character fit only for children's stories—we can't make a good estimate of the quality of his mind. We do know he corresponded with a distinguished coreligionist in Philadelphia, William Schlatter, who was also his supplier of evangelical tracts, though, unfortunately, none of Chapman's letters have survived. We know, too, that he planted medicinal herbs wherever he went, plants such as mullein, pennyroyal, catnip, horehound, rattlesnake root, wintergreen, and dandelion (a native of Europe), instructing the settlers in their use. His favorite was the two-foot-high, bad-smelling mayweed, or "dogfennel," another alien, which spoiled the taste of milk when cows ate it and for a while was called "johnnyweed," with the idea that he might have been planting it everywhere as a practical joke. On the contrary, he seems to have really believed that its noxious smell in every Ohio dooryard would ward off outbreaks of malaria.

We know that he stayed out of fights in the rowdiest communities, even when provoked, according to his adage of living by the law of love although fearing no man. But we don't know how consistently he refused to eat animal flesh, or how constantly cheerful he was, or whether his habits of self-punishment—which smack of the perverse to our modern temperament—discomposed his neighbors, who were an infinitely hardier lot and more inclined to defer to the example of the self-mortifying earlier Christian martyrs. Though he must have brewed gentler poultices for other people's wounds, his method of healing his own was to sear the offending location with a hot piece of iron—as the Indians did—and then treat the burn. Such fortitude won the Indians' respect, and he planted some trees in the Indian villages as well as in white towns. For his stoicism, his knowledge of herbal medicine, and his selflessness, which they recognized as a manifestation of godliness, they seem to have revered him. More important, he respected and sympathized with them at a time when many white woodsmen shot them on sight like vermin, to clear the woods, or else humiliated them by catching their horses and tying sticks in their mouths and clapboards to their tails and letting the horses run home with the clapboards on fire. Swedenborg himself had said, "All things in the world exist from a Divine Origin . . . clothed with such forms in nature as enable them to exist here and perform their use and thus correspond to higher things." So the Swedenborgian spirit-world of souls and angels coexistent with a natural world, in which the true order of Creation had been diverted by man's misapplication of his free will from the love of God to his own ego, quite corresponded, as far as it went, with the Indians' view. To his credit, Chapman, who seems to have been friendly with the Quakers of Ohio, too, was able to recognize this.

He was born in poor circumstances in Leominster, in a cabin overlooking the Nashua River. His father, Nathaniel Chapman, was a farmer, carpenter, and wheelwright descended from Edward Chapman, who had arrived in Boston from Shropshire in 1639. Scarcely a year after the birth of John, Nathaniel's second child, the father left to fight in the Revolution as one of the original minutemen, first at Bunker Hill in 1775, then with George Washington's army in New York the next year, wintering at Valley Forge in 1777–78. John's mother had died, meanwhile. In 1780, following his discharge as a captain, Nathaniel Chapman married again, a Miss Lucy Cooley of Longmeadow, near Springfield, Massachusetts, and fathered ten more children by her. Though we have no proof that "Johnny Appleseed" was brought from his grandparents' house in Leominster to grow up here, he probably did spend his later boyhood in Longmeadow on the Connecticut River, learning to handle a raft and pirogue, learning about wildlife, with this new brood.

Longmeadow was on the Connecticut Path, walked by settlers going west toward the upper Susquehanna River, two hundred miles away. It's thought that John Chapman, around 1792, at the age of eighteen, set out with his half brother Nathaniel, who was seven years younger, for this frontier. They paused in the Wilkes-Barre region for a year or two, then may have ventured south to the Potomac in eastern Virginia and dawdled along from there toward Fort Cumberland, and then, via Braddock's Road, to the Monongahela, and on by 1797 to Pittsburgh, during what was now John Adams's presidency. According to one story, they traveled up the Allegheny that fall to Olean, New York, in search of an uncle who was supposed to have built a cabin there, only to discover that he had pushed on west. With scant provisions, they took over his abandoned home, and nearly starved. What saved them, it's said, is that while John hiked out to earn money for food, some passing Indians luckily dropped in on his brother and provisioned him and taught him to hunt. (We don't know if John was already a vegetarian—which would have been a terrible disadvantage for both of them in enduring such a winter.)

In any case, the experience may have estranged the two. With the warm weather, they separated—Nathaniel, in his late teens, being old enough to strike off independently and to settle on Duck Creek near Marietta in southern Ohio on the Ohio River eventually, where by 1805 Nathaniel, Sr., the former minuteman, also moved with his family. The older Chapman, though a captain in time of war, had been an indifferent provider, and died in 1807. One of his daughters, named Persis, and nineteen years younger than Johnny Appleseed, later was to play an important and softening role in Johnny's life; but there is little evidence that John and Nathaniel ever troubled to see much of each other again, until 1842. That was fifty years after they had sauntered out from Longmeadow together, and John, famous and cranky and old, with a "thick bark of queerness on him," as Robert Price expresses it, and only three years short of his death, trudged east from Fort Wayne,

Indiana, where he was living with Persis and her family, to Marietta, for a final reunion.

Mr. Price—who devoted, he says, the better part of twenty-five years to sifting the provable from unprovable legends about Johnny Appleseed—does not believe that the Chapman boys ever went from Wilkes-Barre to Virginia. Indeed, with the affectionate overfamiliarity of an expert who has perhaps overmastered a subject, he slightly belittles the legends he does believe. But he ascribes adventures aplenty to them in the area of the upper Allegheny near Warren, in northwestern Pennsylvania, where he has found evidence that they had moved in 1797. In the spring of 1798, along Big Brokenstraw Creek, Johnny may have planted his first apple seeds. Only four other settlers were in residence on the creek, but they were busy fellows who within ten years would be rafting pine logs clear to New Orleans. Johnny probably lost his patches of orchard land to a more aggressive citizen. The next season—his brother gone by now—he had moved fifty miles, to French Creek, another tributary of the Allegheny. He was exceedingly vigorous, doubtless a whiz at wielding an ax (one posthumous legend has him competing with Paul Bunyan). This was a time of felling great oaks and stupendous pines, of big snowstorms, when reportedly he toughed out one winter holed up on an island on French Creek, subsisting on butternuts alone. That spring, or another, he was so impatient to get an early start downriver that he set his canoe on a block of ice on the Allegheny, where it would not be crushed in the jams, and fell asleep and floated a hundred miles or so before he bothered to wake up.

It was an element in the myth of Johnny Appleseed that he could doze off in the most dangerous circumstances—so calm he was. Once, in Seneca territory, he was being chased by a war party, before he had made his name favorably known to the tribe, and as the story goes, he slipped into a swampy reedbed and lay with just his mouth above water, napping until the warriors gave up hunting him. In Ohio the Indians he knew were Delawares, Mohicans, and Wyandots, who were soon driven out of the state in the aftermath of the attacks they mounted (or allegedly hoped to mount) with British encouragement during the War of 1812. That summer and fall, with his woodcraft and marathon endurance, John Chapman fulfilled a hero's role, once racing thirty miles from Mansfield to Mount Vernon, Ohio, to summon reinforcements and arouse the white settlers to the peril posed by General William Hull's surrender to British forces at Detroit. He spouted Biblical language, according to at least one witness, and inevitably there were some false alarms: "The spirit of the Lord is upon me, and he hath anointed me to blow the trumpet in the wilderness, and sound an alarm in the forest; for behold, the tribes of the heathen are round about your doors, and a devouring flame followeth after them." This is the self-dramatist in him that made Casey Jones, John Henry, and Davy Crockett heroes also.

Casey Jones died from driving his locomotive faster than he ought to have. But Mr. Price reminds us that Chapman lived out his three score and ten years, and that the error of folklore is to simplify. The young buck strenuously logging, snowshoeing, existing on butternuts in the French Creek period, must have been quite a different figure from "Johnny Appleseed" practicing his kindnesses and charities during the two and a half decades when he lived in Ohio and brought apples to Ashland, Bucyrus, Cohocton, Findlay, New Haven, Van Wert, and many another town on giveaway terms. Odd as he was—with the gossip that trailed him hinting that earlier in life he may have been kicked in the head by a horse—he almost seems to have passed for a solid citizen here. People didn't mind him dandling their babies. He even suffered (we may infer) the very insignia of solid citizenship, a "midlife crisis," somewhere during the years from 1809 to 1824, when he would have been between thirty-five and fifty years old.

That is, he had been a mystic before, and he ended his days in Indiana as a kind of landmark, with the "thick bark of queerness" still on him, thoroughly a mystic again. But for a few years in central Ohio, apparently he tried to become a practical man. He speculated in a couple of town lots in Mount Vernon, one of which he sold after nineteen years for a profit of five dollars. By 1815 he had leased four quarter sections of land of a hundred and sixty acres each for ninety-nine years at nineteen dollars a year apiece—a Mrs. Jane Cunningham his partner. But a recession occurred in 1819, tightening the money supply miserably. As a man accustomed to selling his goods for I.O.U.s, he saw his principal holdings forfeited for want of money. His biographer makes the point that toward the close of his life, perhaps under Persis's influence, he bought another two hundred acres, around Fort Wayne. Altogether, a documented total of twenty-two properties, amounting to twelve hundred acres, can be totted up that he leased or owned for a time. But it would be a good guess to say that he accepted the 1819 recession as a lesson that he was intended to be an appleman, not a speculator, and an instrument of the bounty of God.

He had arrived on the Licking River in Ohio from the Allegheny in 1801, aged twenty-six. Only three families lived in what has become Licking County, but Ohio was just two years short of statehood by then. Ebenezer Zane was blazing Zane's Trace from

Wheeling, on the Ohio River, through Zanesville and Chillicothe, capital of the Northwest Territory, toward Maysville, Kentucky. Farther north, there was an access path from Pittsburgh for a hundred and sixty miles to the Black Fork of the Mohican River, and from Pittsburgh by an old Indian trail to Fort Sandusky and on toward Detroit.

He seems to have come this first time on foot with a horseload of seeds. More than three hundred thousand apple seeds will fit in a single bushel, so he had his work cut out for him. He may have been wearing his fabled mushpan on his head (if he ever did), with plenty of plantings in Pennsylvania behind him, and his vision of the figure he wanted to cut for the rest of his life in his mind. But we don't know if Johnny preferred winter to summer apples, or sharp flavors to sweet. We don't really know how hard he worked, because, set against this picture of a religious zealot, for whom apple trees in their flowering were a living sermon from God, is the carefree master of woodcraft who supposedly strung his hammock between treetops and lazed away the pleasant days.

He came back in succeeding summers to his nurseries to tend them—back to these patent and bounty lands "homesteaded," in a later phrase, or deeded to Revolutionary soldiers, or to the Refugee Tract, which was reserved for Canadians who had been persecuted by the British, or the Firelands, granted to Connecticut citizens in recompense for damage inflicted during the war. Straight land sales on settled portions of the Ohio River at this time involved terms of two dollars an acre, with fifty cents down.

In 1806—and perhaps the prettiest of all of the memories of John Chapman that have survived—he was noticed by a settler in Jefferson County, on the Ohio, drifting past in two canoes lashed together and heaped with cider-press seeds, both craft being daubed with mud and draped with moss to keep the load moist. He stopped to establish a planting a couple of miles below town, and probably another at the mouth of the Muskingum, at Marietta, near where his father had settled the year before. Ascending the Muskingum, past Zanesville, where the Licking River comes in, to a tributary called Walhonding, or White Woman's Creek, he poled up to the Mohican River and finally to the Black Fork of the Mohican, where he already may have had a nursery growing, because central Ohio by now was not unfamiliar country to him. His earlier seedlings would have been ready to sell if five years had passed.

With this canoe trip, apparently, his fame began. He had been a local character, but there were other applemen who made a business of selling trees, mostly as a sideline to farming. (Five pennies per sapling was the price at the time.) Furthermore, a hundred years before John Chapman ever arrived, the French had brought apple seeds to the Great Lakes and the Mississippi, so that some of the Indian towns along the old trails already had orchards, from which the settlers could trade or pilfer as the Indians were gradually driven away. Where Johnny differed was that he alone had set himself the task of anticipating the patterns of settlement, as a public mission, across what had become the State of Ohio by 1803. He moved along coincident with or a step ahead of the first flying parties of settlers, to have apple trees of transplantable age ready for them when they got their land cleared. Apple vinegar was the basic preservative for pickling vegetables such as beans, cucumbers, and beets; apple butter was a principal pleasure of winter meals; and apple brandy was one of the first cash exports that could be floated downriver to New Orleans. So he began to be recognized as something of a public servant as he went about.

He planted on loamy, grassy ground, usually at riverside, constructing a fence of the brush and trees that he had cut down, and girdling any bigger trees that stood near enough to cast their shade over the soil. He would clear a patch and plant and fence it, sometimes sleeping in his hammock—looking startlingly serene, swinging there, to travelers who were full of frightening tales of the woods. Or he might strip slabs of bark from a giant elm, and lay them against it for a lean-to, or toss together a quick Indian hut of poles and bark, stretching out on a bed of leaves inside. And then he drifted on, grubbed more ground clear, constructed another barrier fence. Some of these little gardens he never bothered to hunt up again, confident that the settlers would discover them. Others he hurried back to, hearing that a herd of cattle had broken in. Hogs ranged through these oak, hickory, and beech forests, as well as cattle, and there were great flocks of passenger pigeons, and wolves, which the more brutal pioneers skinned alive and turned loose to scare the rest of the pack. On the Whetstone River, near the Clear Fork of the Mohican, the Vandorn boys helped him to build a fourteen-by-sixteen-foot cabin for wintering over, impressed at how fearlessly he slept on top of a windfall as the wolves and owls howled.

He liked to plant on quarter sections set aside for the support of the first schools, or he might do so on an existing farm if the owner agreed to share what grew. Once a few years had passed, he wouldn't need to make such long trips for seeds and, if he was then working thirty miles away, might deputize a farmer who lived close to an orchard to honor the notes he wrote out for people who wished to purchase trees.

By 1816 Persis had moved with her family from Marietta to Perrysville, Ohio, on the Mohican's Black Fork. Mansfield lay between the Clear and Black forks, and Mount Vernon was on the Kokosing, which wasn't far off. So, with some of his kin in the area (his brother-in-law worked for him), and with the goodwill that his exploits in the War of 1812 had engendered, and the investments in land that he was attempting to pay for, the region around Perrysville became his home. During his forties he traveled less, but even after he had lost most of his land and had renewed his vows of poverty—moving west again with horseloads of apple seeds to the Miami and Tiffin rivers—he came back to Perrysville to winter with his family and friends.

His fifties seem to have been severely austere, like his twenties and thirties. He planted on the Sandusky; had fifteen thousand trees at Milan on the Huron; started a nursery in Defiance in northwest Ohio when that village was six years old, and other nurseries along the proposed route of the Miami and Erie Canal. From Toledo he traveled west up the Maumee River toward Indiana, working the banks of its tributaries—the Blanchard, the Auglaize, the St. Mary's—the population of Ohio, meanwhile, having vaulted from forty-five thousand in 1800 to five hundred and eighty thousand in 1820.

In 1822 he may have gone to Detroit to sightsee, and, around 1826, to Urbana and Cincinnati. In 1830, just after the future city of Fort Wayne had been platted, he is said to have landed on the waterside from the Maumee in a hollow log filled with seeds. Thereafter he labored in Indiana, boarding with Allen County families like the Hills and Worths for a dollar or two per week, but still going back to Perrysville to spend each winter, until 1834, when Persis and her husband moved out to join him.

Various myths have him continuing on to the Ozarks, to Minnesota, to the foothills of the Rockies. He did not, but undoubtedly he gave seeds to pioneers who ventured much farther west. He may have seen Illinois and the Mississippi River and crossed into Iowa. But Allen County lies at the watershed separating the Wabash, flowing to the Mississippi, from the Maumee, flowing toward Lake Erie and eventually the St. Lawrence River, so it is appropriate that Johnny stopped here. Like the plainsmen and mountainmen, he was a man still "with the bark on," but apples were his particular witness to God, and apples do not grow well on the Great Plains. "I, John Chapman (by occupation a gatherer and planter of apple seeds)," begins a deed from the Fort Wayne days. He was an appleman first of all. Maybe he didn't even long to participate in the drama of the Great West ahead.

He was a legend by now—a bluebird to the bluejay figure of the raftsman Mike Fink, who had poled the Ohio River nearby at about the same time. Mike Fink, a very rough guy who gouged out eyes in fights, and died twenty years earlier than Johnny on a trip to the Rockies, once set his common-law wife on fire in a pyre of leaves when she winked at another man. Fink is more typical of the frontiersmen we remember. What would a conventional movie-maker do with a vegetarian frontiersman like Johnny who did not believe in horseback riding and wore no furs; who planted fruit trees in praise of a Protestant God, and gave much of his money away to impoverished families he met; who would "punish" one foot that had stepped on an angleworm by walking with it bare over stony ground; who would douse his campfire when mosquitoes fell into it, and regretted for years killing a rattlesnake that had bitten him in the grass?

Near Persis's home in Fort Wayne, he had a log cabin and eleven cleared acres and timber cut for a barn when he died in 1845. He died not there but at the home of the Worth family on the St. Joseph River not far off, presumably of pneumonia contracted during a fifteen-mile trudge in mid-March, leading his black ox, to repair an orchard fence that cattle had trampled down. At his death—so the Worths said—he had on a coffee sack, as well as the waist sections of four pairs of old pants, cut off and slit so that they lapped "like shingles" around his hips, under an antiquated pair of pantaloons. His life had extended from the battle of Bunker Hill to the inauguration of James K. Polk as president; and the last person who claimed to have seen Johnny Appleseed with his own eyes didn't die until just before World War II.

As that 1871 issue of *Harper's* expressed it, he was a frontier hero "of endurance that was voluntary, and of action that was creative and not sanguinary." Perhaps it is inevitable that our memory of history should become oversimplified, but lately the distortion always seems to err on the side of violence. Anyone who examines the pioneering period will find that there were a good many selfless, gentle characters who belie the violent-entrepreneurial caricatures. Historians, by neglecting individuals of such munificent spirit as Johnny, and leaving us with only the braggarts and killers, underestimate the breadth of frontier experience, and leave us poorer.

Bears,
Bears,
Bears

Bears, which stopped being primarily predatory some time ago, though they still have a predator's sharp wits and mouth, appeal to a side of us that is lumbering, churlish and individual. We are touched by their anatomy because it resembles ours, by their piggishness and sleepiness and unsociability with each other, by their very aversion to having anything to do with us except for eating our garbage. Where big tracts of forest remain, black bears can still do fairly well. The grizzly's prickly ego is absent in them; they are unostentatious woodland animals that stay under cover and do not expect to have everything go their way.

Grizzlies never did inhabit the forested East. They lived on the Great Plains and in the Rockies and Sierras, much of it open or arid country; apparently they are more tolerant than black bears of hot, direct sun. In such surroundings no trees were at hand for the cubs to flee to and the adults developed their propensity for charging an intruder. For their own safety too, the best defense was an assault, and until we brought our rifles into play they didn't trouble to make much distinction between us and other predators. They still are guyed in by instinct to an "attack distance," as the biologists call it, within which their likely first reaction is to charge, whereas if they perceive a man approaching from farther off, they will melt away if they can.

Bears have a direct, simple vegetarian diet supplemented by insects and carrion or fish, so they need less operating space than a wolf, which weighs only about one-fourth what a black bear weighs but must obtain a classy meat meal for itself. Nevertheless, according to several studies, black bears require from one to five square miles apiece just to gather their food, and units of at least fifty square miles of wilderness for their wanderings and social relations. In this day and age such a chunk has other uses too. Loggers will be cutting on parts of it, and Boy Scouts holding encampments, canoeists paddling the rivers, and hikers and hunters traipsing across. Black bears were originally found in every state but Hawaii, and still manage to survive in about thirty, if only in remnant numbers, so that they seem able to coexist. They are coated for living up on the windy ridges or down in the swamps and hollows, where even the snowmobilers can't get to them during the winter because they are under the snow, and they give promise of being with us for a long while.

Probably the most ardent investigator of black bears right now is Lynn Rogers, a graduate student at the University of Minnesota. He's thirty-four, red-bearded, crew-cut, with a wife who used to teach English and two children, and he is another one of David Mech's protégés. He works in Isabelle (once called Hurry Up, until a leading citizen renamed it after his daughter), which is a logging village, a tiny crossroads with more bars than grocery stores, settled by "Finlanders," as they are called, in the Arrowhead region of northern Minnesota, now the Superior National Forest. The logging is fading as aspen grows up in place of the old stands of big pine, but the Forest Service plants red or white pine where it can (there is more jack pine, however), and the swamps are forested with black spruce. The lakeshores are pretty, with birch, cedar, red maple, fir and white spruce, and the whole place is bursting with bears. On a seven-mile stretch of highway near Rogers's headquarters thirty were shot in one year. This was before the townspeople became interested in his work; now they let the bears live.

Rogers is a two-hundred-pounder with a rangy build and a small-looking head, no more bearish than Mech's is wolfish. Though there are scientists who come to resemble the animals they study, more often they look like athletic coaches, animals being in some sense our behind-hand brothers and these the fellows who watch out for them. Rogers could well be a coach, except for the streak in him that makes him extraordinary. In the woods he moves at a silent trot, as only the rarest woodsmen do. His thoughts, insofar as they could be elicited in the week I lived with him, seemed almost exclusively concerned with bears—catching them, amassing more data on them. He seldom reads a newspaper or watches television, and likes to kid his wife about the "fairy tales" of literature which she taught in school. When he takes a day off, it's to snap pictures of beaver or to wait half the day in a tree for an osprey to return to its nest. He's lived only in Minnesota and Michigan—grew up in Grand Rapids—but once he did stop off in Chicago, when driving between the two states, to go to the natural history museum. If you ask what he'd like to do when his achievements are properly recognized, he says he'd want to stay in Isabella and study lynx or else fisher.

As he sits in a brooding posture at the kitchen table, his body doesn't move for long periods and he thinks aloud, not so much in actual words as with a slow series of ums and ahs that seem to convey the pacing of his thoughts. But he lectures nicely, full of his subject, and in the woods whatever is lummoxy drops away in that quickness, the dozen errands he's running at once—searching for a plant whose leaves will match the unknown leaves he has been finding in a given bear's scats, examining a local bear-rubbing tree for hairs left on the bark since his last check. If he's lost in his jeep in the tangle of old logging roads, he gets a fix on the closest radio-collared bear and from that figures out where he is. If he's near one of them and wants a glimpse, he lifts a handful of duff from the ground and lets it stream lightly down to test the wind before beginning his stalk. When he's radio-tracking from the plane that he rents, he watches his bears hunt frogs, or sees one surprise a wolf and pounce at it. If a bear in a thicket hasn't moved since his previous fix and is close to a road or a house, he may ask the pilot to land, if they can, to see whether it has been shot. Then, on the ground again, suddenly he'll climb an oak tree to taste the acorns on top, spurting up the branchless trunk without any spikes, his hands on one side pulling against his feet on the other. Lost in the yellow fall colors, munching bear food, he shouts happily from the tree, "What a job this is, huh?"

Wildlife biology as a profession interests me. Like the law, my father's vocation, it's one I follow. It's a stepchild among the sciences, however—badly paid, not quite respected, still rather scattered in its thrust and mediocre in its standards, and still accessible to the layman, as the most fundamental, fascinating breakthroughs alternate with confirmation of what has always been common knowledge—akin to that stage of medical research that told us that cigarettes were, yes, "coffin nails," and that frying foods in fat was bad for you. Partly because of its romantic bias, as a science wildlife biology has a tragic twist, since the beasts that have attracted the most attention so far are not the possums and armadillos that are thriving but the same ones whose heads hunters like to post on the wall: gaudy giraffes and gorillas, or mermaid-manatees, or "same-size predators," in the phrase ethologists use to explain why a grizzly bear regards a man thornily. It's not that the researchers have hurried to study the animals which are disappearing in order to glean what they can, but that the passion that activates the research in the first place is the passion which has helped hound these creatures off the face of the earth. Such men are hunters *manqué.*

Game wardens are also that way, but have the fun of stalking, ambushing, and capturing poachers, while so often the biologist sees his snow leopards, his orangutans, his wild swans and cranes, vanishing through change of habitat right while his study progresses—wondering whether his findings, like other last findings, invulnerable to correction though they soon will be, are all that accurate. Anthropology can be as sad a science when limited to living evidence and a primitive tribe, but the difference is that woodcraft itself is guttering out as a gift, and apart from the rarity now of observers who can get close to a wilderness animal which has not already been hemmed into a reserve, there is the painful mismatch of skills involved in first actually obtaining the data and then communicating it. Scientific writing need only be telegraphic to reach a professional audience, but again and again one runs into experts who have terrible difficulties in setting down even a small proportion of what they have learned. Eagerly, yet with chagrin and suspicion of anybody with the power to do the one thing they wish they could do (suspicion of city folk is also a factor), they welcome television and magazine reporters and interrogators like me, sometimes in order to see their own stories told, but sometimes to try to help save the animals dear to them—as if our weak words might really succeed.

But we observers have a piece missing too; maybe we put on our hiking boots looking for it. Like some of the wildlife experts— or like Lady Chatterley's gamekeeper, who was in retreat when he went into the woods—we don't entirely know why we are there. Not that an infatuation with wild beasts and wild places does us any harm or excludes the more conventional passions like religion or love, but if I were to drive by a thicket of palmettos and chicken trees way down South and you told me that a drove of wild razorback hogs lived back in there, I'd want to stop, get out, walk about, and whether or not the place was scenic, I'd carry the memory with me all day. It's said of a wilderness or an animal buff that he "likes animals better than people," but this is seldom true. Like certain pet owners, some do press their beasties to themselves as compresses to stanch a wound, but others are rosy, sturdy individuals. More bothersome to me is the canard that *when I was a man I put away childish things,* and I can be thrown into a tizzy if a friend begins teasing me along these lines. (A sportswriter I know has gone so far as to consult a psychiatrist to find out why a grown man like him is still so consumed by baseball.) Rooting around on riverbanks and mountain slopes, we may be looking for that missing piece, or love, religion and the rest of it—whatever is missing in us—just as so often we are doing in the digging and rooting of sex. Anyway, failure as a subject seems more germane than success at the moment, when failure is piled atop failure nearly everywhere, and the study of wildlife is saturated with failure, both our own and that of the creatures themselves.

Rogers is a man surpassingly suited to what he is doing. Like me— it linked us immediately—he stuttered and suffered from asthma when he was a child, and he's still so thin-skinned that he will talk about suing a TV station because it has edited his comments before airing them. But with these thick-skinned bears—pigs-of-the-woods—he is in his element. Just as it was for me while I stayed with him, each day's busy glimpses and face-offs fulfilled his dream as a boy twenty or twenty-five years ago: to track and sneak close to, capture, and fondle a noisy, goofy, gassy, hairy, dirty, monstrous, hot, stout, incontrovertible bear.

For their part, the bears have been engineered to survive. Whereas wolves have their fabulous legs to carry them many miles between kills, and a pack organization so resilient that a trapped wolf released with an injured paw will be looked after by the others until it is able to hunt again, a bear's central solution to the riddle of how to endure is to den. Denning does away with the harsh months of the year and concentrates the period when a bear needs to eat a lot in the harvest months when food is at hand. Although its breathing and heart rate slow by one half, and its metabolism subsides so that it loses only about five percent of its weight a month (half the rate at which it would shed weight during ordinary sleep), its temperature doesn't fall much while it is in the den. This distinguishes bears from bona-fide hibernators like bats and woodchucks, and means that they can give birth in the security of the den and can defend themselves if attacked. The bear's sense of danger is reduced, so that the carefully surreptitious visits Rogers makes in midwinter go off with a minimum of fuss, but in its easily defended hole it can even deal with a pack of wolves.

Males sleep alone, but a sow has the company of her cubs— generally two or three. They are born around the end of January and den with her again the following winter; then in June, when they are a year and a half old, she permits a brawly big male, often several in sequence, to disrupt the close-knit life that she and the cubs have enjoyed since they were born. He or she drive them off and roam a bit together for a week or two, but by the device of delayed implantation of the ova her new cubs are not born till the middle of winter, which gives her a respite. The cubs are exceedingly little when they do arrive, weighing just over half a pound apiece—half what an infant porcupine weighs. The porcupine possesses quills, open eyes, and other faculties to meet the world, whereas a bear cub has a great deal of developing to do in the dark den. Its eyes won't open for forty days, and small as it is, it isn't a drain on its fasting mother when suckling. Like a baby ape, it has a long interlude ahead of intimate association with her, an intimacy that will help make it far more intelligent than most animals.

Bears scrape out a depression for themselves under a pile of logs, a ledge or fallen tree, usually pulling in a layer of dead grass and leaves for insulation (paying a high price in heat and weight loss if they don't—one of the facets of denning that Rogers is studying). Some woodsmen claim that bears will position the entrance to face north in order to postpone the moment in the spring when meltwater chills them and forces them outside, before the snow is gone and much food has become available. Emerging in mid-April, the adults look in fine shape; with their winter fur they even appear fat, though they shrivel rapidly during those first weeks as they tramp about trying to find something to eat—as if the fat cells are already empty and simply collapse. In Minnesota they break a path to the nearest aspen stand and climb or ride down the young trees to bite off the catkins at the tips of the limbs. They sniff out rotten logs under the snow and bash them apart, licking up the insects that have been hibernating there. A mother will take her cubs to a tall tree, such as a pine, and install them on the warm mound of earth at its base in a resting spot which she scrapes on the south side, nursing them and sending them scurrying up the trunk whenever she goes off in search of a meal. Then when the horsetails and spring grasses sprout, the family begins to thrive.

The coating of fat that bears wear most of the year—and which was the frontiersman's favorite shortening—is of indirect use to them if they are shot, blocking the flow of blood, making them difficult to trail. Their flat feet, too, leave less of a track than the sharp feet of other game. Altogether they are excellently equipped, and if they don't insulate their dens or choose a sensible location for themselves, they'll probably come through the winter all right anyhow; the snow, melting to ice from the heat of their bodies, freezes into an igloo around them, complete with a breathing hole. If the complicated physiology by which they are supposed to fatten at an accelerated rate in the fall doesn't take hold (sometimes a mother gives so much milk that she stays thin), they muddle through even so, just as orphaned cubs do if they must winter alone without any denning instruction. The only dead bear Rogers has ever found in a den was a nineteen-year-old female, which despite this exceptionally advanced age, had given birth to two cubs. They had milk in their stomachs but apparently had been killed during her death throes.

In the past four years Rogers has visited a hundred and six dens, first observing the bears' autumn rituals and later crawling inside. He has an advantage over his friend Mech simply because bears do den; he can head right for any bear wearing a functioning radio—in 1972 there were twenty-seven of them—and, after tranquilizing it, attach new batteries, which with luck are good till the following winter. He can outfit the yearlings with radios before they leave their mothers, and the habit of denning makes bears of any age easier to trap. His traps consist of two fifty-five-gallon barrels welded together and baited with meat; far from finding the contraptions claustrophobic, the bears crawl comfortably in. Occasionally, when an animal is too bulky for the trap—as happened last summer when Rogers was trying to recapture a 455-pound bear whose collar had been torn off in a mating-season imbroglio—he sets foot snares at its favorite dump. This involves choreographing where the bear should place its feet by putting tin cans and other junk and branches close about the snare's ring in its regular path. The snares are an unerring type developed in Washington State, where for some unfathomed reason (they seldom do it elsewhere) bears tear apart young trees to eat the cambium lining the inner bark, and the timber companies have declared war on them.

By comparison, Mech's wolves are will-o'-the-wisps. From an airplane a frustrated Mech may see one of them wearing a collar whose radio went dead years ago. Even Maurice Hornocker, the mountain-lion man, who works in Idaho, has a simpler time of it, because his subjects, while they would be just as hard as a wolf to catch with an ordinary steel trap, obligingly leap into a tree in the winter, when snowed into a valley and pursued by hounds, where he shoots them with a tranquilizing dart and, climbing up, lowers them gently on the end of a rope as the drug takes effect. The best that can be said for wolves in this respect is that at least they do howl morning and evening in certain seasons, and are sociable souls, so that to keep tabs on one is to know the activities of five or ten others.

A heat scientist who is collaborating with Rogers in studying the biology of denning hopes to insert a scale underneath a wild bear so that a continuous record can be obtained of the rate at which it loses weight, to be collated with the winter's weather—weight loss being heat loss in this case, since the bear neither eats nor excretes. Another scientist in Minneapolis, a blood chemist, is creating from the unprecedentedly wide sampling of bears' blood that Rogers has sent him a profile of its composition, by season and in relation to sex, age, body temperature, sickness or behavioral peculiarities. In concert, they are particularly studying the break-neck conversion of food to fat during the late summer, and a nu-tritionist will analyze the many foods the bears eat. Rogers has charted their diet through the year, drawing on the evidence of scats, his walks and sightings from the air and their radioed loca-tions. The scats he sifts in a pan of water. Leaves, wasp heads, and carrion hair float to the top; seeds, tinfoil, and twigs sink to the bottom. He's also investigating the fine points of telling an ani-mal's age by counting the rings in a cross section cut from a tooth. Like the rings in a tree, a dark annulus is deposited in the cemen-tum every winter while the bear sleeps and a light one during the bright part of the year. The live-bear biologists pull out a lower premolar and the dead-bear biologists take a canine, but there are also false annuli to confuse the count.

Wildlife biology used to be rather hit-or-miss. Rogers's prede-cessors would hogtie a trapped bear once in a while and clap an ether cone on it, then proceed to take weights and measurements. From dead bears they catalogued parasites, and looked for placen-tal scars on the uterus. Sometimes a bear was caught and tagged to see where it would travel before a hunter shot it, or it might be color-marked so that it could be recognized at a distance, and trans-ported and released somewhere else to see whether it "homed." To maintain sovereignty, every state's game department insisted on going over much the same ground with these prankish experi-ments. More seriously, a study of bear depredations on livestock, if any, would be made, because the stereotype of bears as menacing varmints had to be discredited before the legislature could be per-suaded to remove the bounty on them, forbid killing them in their dens, and give them the spring and summer protection that ani-mals regarded as game receive. In state after state it would be pointed out that back in 1943 California had declared the grizzly its "state animal," but by then twenty years had already elapsed since the last grizzly had vanished from the state. Arkansas and Louisiana set out to right the violence of the past by importing several hundred Minnesota black bears at a cost of up to six hun-dred dollars apiece. A few have sneaked into neighboring states to delight the outdoorsmen and give the pig farmers the willies (for it's no legend that bears relish pigs), and so Mississippians have had cause to wonder and whoop at the sight of bear prints in the mud for the first time since back in the era when Faulkner wrote his masterpiece *The Bear*.

In the late 1950s tranquilizers began to be employed, then radio collars. A woodchuck in Maryland bore the first such device; now even turtles and fish are saddled with transmitting equipment, and there is talk of substituting a microphone for the beep signal in the case of certain outspoken creatures like wolves, to record their life histories vocally. Some experts distrust such tools, suspecting that the hallucinogen in the tranquilizer, the obtrusive handling of the animal while it is immobilized, and having to wear an awkward collar may alter its personality and fate. But Rogers is a believer. In Minnesota he has captured a hundred and eighty-three different bears, some many times—one a day during the peak of the summer. Earlier, in Michigan, he had assisted in catching about a hundred and twenty-five. Flying four hundred hours in 1972, as much as his budget allowed, he totted up more than three thousand fixes on his bears. Of the thirty-seven he had put radios on during the previous winter, he could still monitor eighteen in late September and locate nine others whenever he wished to pay his pilot extra for a longer search. One of the travelers, a three-year-old male he had first tagged in its mother's den, went clear to Wisconsin, nearly a hundred and fifty miles, before it was shot.

To place all this in perspective, the State of New Hampshire, for instance, until recently had only one bear trap, a converted highway culvert that was trundled out three or four times a year. The game wardens got so excited when it was used that two of them would sleep overnight in a station wagon parked close by so as to be there when the door clanged. Before Rogers's program began, the most sophisticated telemetric figures on black-bear territoriality had been drawn from the State of Washington, where seventeen bears had been radio-located four hundred and eighteen times from the ground.

At Rogers's cottage the phone rings with reports of sightings, friends recognizing his ear tags and collars; everybody keeps an eye out the window in the evening for bears crossing the fields around Isabella. He likes these neighbors and talks endlessly—bears, bears, bears—and his wife Sue loyally wears shirts with big bear tracks painted on them. She's witty, slightly conspiratorial, and a great help to him, pushing him as she might urge on a student of hers who was talented but disorganized. The data keeps pouring in because he has such a network of methods set up to collect it, and he's out gathering more every day besides. One has the feeling that without her the study might strangle in congestion. He mentions an expert he knew in Michigan who in the course of a decade had collected more information on bears than any other man there, but who, as the years went on, could never write down what he'd learned and get credit for it. Finally, to cushion his disappointment, his chief transferred him to the task of collecting a whole new raft of raw data on deer.

Rogers has received a modicum of funding from the state's Department of Natural Resources, the federal Forest Service, the National Rifle Association, and other disparate groups. Mostly, though, it is some Minneapolis magnates who call themselves the Big Game Club who have backed him, and particularly a poker-faced department-store owner named Wally Dayton, who will drive up, go along on a tour with the enthusiastic Rogers, see a few bears, and head back toward the Twin Cities without a hint of his own reactions, except that shortly thereafter the university will get a contribution earmarked for his work. At first, in my time with him, it had seemed sadly chancy to me that he had been afforded so little official support for a project I knew to be first-rate. But soon such a sense evaporated. Rather, how lucky it was that this late-blooming man, who creeps through the brush so consummately that he can eavesdrop on the grunting of bears as they breed, had discovered at last, after seven long years as a letter carrier in his hometown, what it was that he wanted to do! In his blue wool cap, with Santa Claus wrinkles around his eyes because of the polar weather he's known, shambling, blundering, abstracted at times, he is an affecting figure, a big Viking first mate proud of the fact that he can heft a 240-pound bear alone. He kisses his wife as he starts out, one pocket full of his luncheon sandwiches, the other with hay-scented packets of scats he forgot to remove after yesterday's trip (they smell pleasant enough, and he likes carrying them as boys like carrying snakes).

In grammar school, with his breathing problems, he couldn't roughhouse and was kept indoors—the teacher would give him a chance to tell the rest of the class what birds he had spotted out the window while they had been playing. As his asthma improved, he and a friend named Butch used to jump from tree to tree or swing on long ropes like Tarzan, until Rogers took a bad fall and was hospitalized. They swam in the summer, plunging into deep ponds and kicking their way underwater along the turtle runways on the bottom to go after snappers, whose meat they sold in Grand Rapids for a dollar a pound. They would never leave off exploring any pond where the fishermen told them there was an oversized fish until they'd determined whether or not it was a great six-foot pike. He still laughs remembering the times when it turned out to be nothing more than a carp.

In adolescence his stutter was the difficulty and he took extended solitary fishing trips. Boyish, he once went through an entire winter in Michigan without wearing an overcoat to see whether he could tough it out, having read of a man who went into the woods stark naked one fall to find out if he could clothe himself with skins and prevail. He was a colorful postman not only because of stunts like this but because hordes of dogs congregated about him on his rounds, following him for hours; in the afternoon sometimes he carried the little ones home in his pouch. He did some judo and boxing in gyms and got into street fisticuffs; he still likes to step into a fight where the odds are three or four against one and knock out all the bullies. Even after he had returned to college and met his wife and started studying bears, Rogers almost lost a finger when some bear feces got into a cut and he refused to go to a doctor at first. Only recently he inflicted what he is afraid may have been a permanent strain on his heart by racing through a swamp after an athletic bear scientist who makes it a point to always keep up with his hounds.

One might speculate that like Jack on the Beanstalk, he *has* to be boyish to be so indefatigable at sneaking up next to these furry ogres. He speaks proudly of his two plane crashes while out spotting bears; his one mishap when a bear chewed him occurred when he was working in front of a high school class with an under-dosed bear that climbed to its feet and staggered off, and he was so embarrassed that he tried to wrestle it down. Like a denizen of the woods, he seems full of anomalies to an outsider. He was a Vietnam hawk and hippie-hater during the war, but was glad not to serve in the army himself when his asthma offered him a chance to stay out. He's a member of Zero Population Growth and is thinking of getting a vasectomy, yet kept asking me what it was like to live in New York; didn't the girls smoke an awful lot and wear too much makeup? Though he is working on his doctoral thesis, only lately has he entered what he calls a transitional stage away from his parents' fundamentalist beliefs. He went to a Baptist parochial school and junior college, and not till he went to Michigan State, after the mail-carrying years, did he encounter a serious argument against the theory of life propounded in Genesis. Taught Darwinism for the first time, he had to learn to stop raising his arm in astonishment in biology class and quoting the Bible. The teacher was nonplussed and would suggest "See me afterwards," but then would avoid the meeting, and the students naturally thought he was funny. Offended, Lynn also postponed matching up his parents' ideas with the rest of the world's. He was superb at bear-catching, after all, and felt he was working at real biology, not bookish stuff, and because he was keeping his thoughts to himself, when he did argue about evolution it was usually just as a doubting Thomas with a more convinced fundamentalist, not with a scientist who might have had it out with him. He still seems to be waiting for the rejoinders which never came when they should have, to explain things for him.

"Darwin is full of holes too, you know," he said to me in the jeep, looking to see whether I'd answer, but I smiled and shrugged. For years he and his friend Butch, swimming, leaping from tree to tree, had lived with the dream of Tarzan in their minds, but it was just Butch who had been allowed to go to the movies. He would come back after the show and tell Lynn about Tarzan's feats.

On one of our mornings together, a caller notified Lynn that a bunch of grouse hunters had pumped enough birdshot into a bear caught in one of his foot snares to kill it, so he went out to do an autopsy. It was a mother with milk in her udders and two surviving cubs which had run away. She was brownish compared to an Eastern black bear but blacker than many Western bears. Her feet were cut from stepping on broken glass while garbage-picking, and years before her right ear had been torn off. While he worked, the hunters who had shot her showed up, hoping to claim the skin. They were rough, heavyset customers, one a battered-looking Indian, and the witnesses to the killing, who were also grouse hunters and were standing around in hopes that *they* might get the skin, were too scared to speak up until after the culprits had left—which they did just as soon as they heard Rogers talking about getting the law after them. Then when the witnesses, two St. Paul men, after he'd helped tie the gutted bear onto their car, felt safe enough to enlighten him, Rogers could scarcely believe his ears, that people were so chicken-hearted. He hollered at them, threatening to take the bear back, went to a phone, and called all the game wardens around.

We drove to several other dumps—perhaps a desolate sight to most people, but not to him. Gazing up at the white gulls and black ravens wheeling above, he imitated how his bears weave their heads, looking up at the birds. He told cheery stories, wretched stories. Somebody in Isabella had gutshot a bear with a .22, and the beast took five months to die, at last going from den to den in the middle of winter, in too much pain to be able to sleep. It died in the open snow, its belly bloated with partly digested blood, having shrunk down to ninety pounds.

That afternoon David Mech's crew from Ely delivered one of his radioed bears, #433, which had been caught in one of their wolf traps. They'd already tranquilized it, and he treated its banged paw; "Poor 433, poor 433." He marked down the latest data on it and drove it back to its home territory. Sometimes he howls to a pack of Mech's wolves for the fun of it until they answer him, and has caught about twenty wolves in bear snares, enjoying his own mystic moments with them. He uses a choker on the end of a stick while he tapes their jaws and wraps a weighing rope around their feet, careful not to let them feel actually in danger of strangling, however, or they go mad. Crouched over them, he achieves an effect similar to that of a dominant wolf; the thrashing animal gives up and lies quietly. Sometimes a possumlike catatonia slips over it and it loses consciousness for a while.

The next day, because one of the newly orphaned cubs had been caught in a snare, he had a chance to tag it in order to keep track of its fortunes. Thanks to the marvelous alimentary system bears have, young orphans tend to stay fat, and they hang together through their first winter, but with no mother to defend a territory for them, many questions remain about how they eventually fit into the pecking order of the area. All summer he had been in radio contact with two cubs a poacher had orphaned in June, when they were not long out of their mother's den. They'd been keeping body and soul together, traveling cross-country in a haphazard fashion, presumably scuttling up a tree if a wolf or another bear materialized, until a Duluth, Missabe and Iron Range Railway train killed them. They had begun by eating their mother; maybe could not have survived otherwise, since they were unweaned. One can imagine them at first simply scratching at her udder in order to reach the milk curdling inside.

In a barrel trap Rogers had caught a three-year-old male, blowing like an elephant because of the resonance of the barrels. Bears really can huff and puff enough to blow the house down. While it chuffed at him through one vent he injected the drugs Sernylan and Sparine into its shoulder through another, then lifted the door and rubbed the bear's head as it went under, boyishly showing me that he could. This was unfortunate because the bear's last waking image was of that dreaded hand. Licking its nose and blinking and nodding while the shot took effect, it kept its head up, straining, sniffing as though it were drowning, or like a torture victim struggling for air. Once Rogers live-trapped seven bears in a single day, and once in the winter he handled five bears in one den—four yearlings and their mama. He says that in his experience all really large bears are males, though a hunter sometimes thinks he has shot a "big sow" because the males' testicles retreat into their bodies after the breeding season.

Later he shot a grouse for his supper, and showed me a few

empty dens, of the ninety-four he has located so far. We drove to a bleak little hamlet called Finland to check on bear #320, a sow he had already pinpointed more than two hundred times in his studies of territoriality. She goes there every fall to eat acorns, staying till the snow is thick before hurrying twenty-odd miles back to her home stamping ground to dig her den. "What a job!" he said again, exuberantly showing me balm of Gilead, climbing an oak tree or two, pointing out a dozen different kinds of birds, and halting by the road to jump up on the roof of the jeep and do a sweep with his antenna to see whether another bear was anywhere near.

In a typical day he will jounce along abandoned logging trails for as much as six hours, then go up with his pilot for another four hours, the plane standing on one wing most of the time in tight circles over a succession of bears. Cautious pilots cost the project money, but he has found a young man who is paying for his plane with bear-study money and is daring enough. Wearing a headset, homing in according to the strength of the beeps entering each ear, Rogers directs him by hand signals. Sometimes the beeps sound like radar chirps, sometimes like the *pop-pop-pop* of a fish-tank aerator. On the ground they are still more accurate, to the point where he can distinguish not only a bear's movements across humpy terrain but its restlessness during a thunderstorm, its activity pawing for ants, or digging its den.

These bears produce more cubs than the mothers of Michigan, which ought to signify that they eat better; yet the cubs seem to grow slower. Rogers tabulates the temperatures for each week of the summer, believing that the weather may be as important a factor as the availability of food. At the end of a hot summer with plenty of blueberries, the first-year cubs he was in touch with weighed only an average of thirty-two pounds, but another year, when there were practically no blueberries but the temperature was cooler, another group had managed to fatten to an average of forty-seven pounds. An older bear once expanded from eighty-nine to two hundred and fifty-five pounds in a year, and another gained ninety-five pounds in forty-two days, ending up at three hundred and eighty, and nevertheless crawled into a barrel trap, getting so stuck that Rogers had to stand the barrels on end and lift them off to free the poor fatty.

Despite these gourmand triumphs and the fact that his bears face little hunting, Rogers finds that the average age of the population is only about four and a half—just about the same as biologists calculate for much more severely hunted places like Vermont, where almost a quarter of the bears are shot every fall. Even without the attrition from hunting, the mortality among cubs, and more especially among yearlings and two-year-olds, is high. Nobody has quite figured out what happens to them. G. A. Kemp, a researcher at Cold Lake, Alberta, has theorized that the population is regulated mainly by the adult boars, which kill the subadults if there is a surplus. The Craigheads, working with the grizzlies of Yellowstone, have suggested that dominant bears—grizzlies that occupy themselves principally with being king of the hill around a dump or other gathering point, rather than with eating—seem to lose the will to live when defeat comes, and fade from the scene.

Bears don't mature sexually until they are four, which, combined with the circumstance that the sows only breed every other year, and plenty of eligible sows not even then, gives them one of the lowest reproductive capabilities of any animal. Now that his research has extended through several years, however, bears that Rogers handled as infants, then watched play on their mothers' backs, are themselves giving birth. Occasionally he tracks them for a full twenty-four hours, using student assistants, discovering when they travel and how far and fast. In this wild region, they do most of their sleeping in the dark of the night, from midnight to five.

From his plane in the fall he photographs the terrain in color so as to delineate the zones of vegetation, mapping these to compare with his radio-marked bear ranges for the same area. Keying the bears to the vegetation indicates the feed and habitat they prefer, and also which logging practices of the past have benefited them. Logging, like a forest fire or a tornado, brings in new growth, and even in the primitive section of the national forest, where cutting is not allowed, bears haunt the openings where vetch and pea vine have had an opportunity to sprout and where the windfallen trees are dry from the sun and teem with bugs. On the other hand, clear-cutting does them no good because, like other game animals, they are uncomfortable without hideouts nearby. Sometimes the Forest Service, adding insult to injury, sprays on a herbicide to kill the young aspens and birch—the trees here which are most palatable to wildlife; Rogers is on the watch for any birth defects in his new cubs that may result.

In the spring and early summer the bears' diet is salady—early greens in shady places, and clover, grass, plantains, pea vine and vetch. They dig out grubs, chipmunks and burrowing hornets, clean up wolf kills, eat dandelions, strawberries (the first of the berries), juneberries, bilberries, thimbleberries, chokeberries, chokecherries, rose hips, haw apples, wild plums, hazelnuts and osier dogwood. Raspberries, although abundant, are not eaten in the quantities one might imagine, perhaps because they grow singly on the cane, but bears do feast on blueberries in midsummer, pausing only for a week or two to give closer attention to the berries of the wild sarsaparilla plant. In Michigan and New England they stay above ground into November, munching nuts in the hardwood forests and apples in derelict orchards, but in Rogers's wilderness the last crop eaten is the fruit of the mountain ash—red, berrylike clusters. By October most of the bears have chosen their dens and are puttering around—they excavate less than grizzlies—sleeping more and more, gradually letting their bodies wind down, except for a few savvy males which journey to Lake Superior to visit the dumps at the resorts there, eating until the snow covers their food before making tracks back. The Craigheads, indeed, think that grizzlies may possess an instinct to enter their pre-dug dens during a storm, when the snow will cover their tracks. When a bear stops eating and its intestines are empty, a seal of licked fur, pine needles, and congealed digestive juices forms across the anus, putting a period to the year.

Usually they are tucked in their dens before the first harsh cold snap. The cold itself doesn't affect them except to put hair on their chests, but once the food supply is blanketed over, their interests are best served by going to sleep. During the winter their tapeworms starve to death and their cubs have maximum protection, and, for the rest of the year, they generally give every evidence of invulnerability to natural disaster because of the array of foods that suit them. In 1972, for example, when a June frost had ruined both the blueberry and mountain-ash crops, the Isabella bears needed to improvise an unsugary diet of salads right into the fall, then ran out of fodder entirely a month earlier than usual; yet when they denned they wore the same good belting of fat.

Disease, too, like malnutrition, is uncommon among bears; their preference for solitude helps ensure that. One of the mysteries that have intrigued biologists, therefore, is how predators or quasi-predators, especially such redoubtable beasts as bears and wolves, regulate their own numbers. Most prey animals are kept within bounds by being hunted—if not, they pop like popcorn until an epidemic combs through them—but what natural force rides herd on the hunters? Among bears, the burly males unquestionably pluck out and kill a proportion of the wandering young if an area becomes thick with them—as will a sow with cubs of her own kill other cubs—and the device of delayed implantation of the ova probably offers a kind of hormonal "fail-safe," by which some of the bred mothers simply do not wind up pregnant by autumn, if conditions are bad during the summer. The complexities of fertility and sterility operate as a balance wheel for wolves and mountain lions also. Several studies on these other animals are coming to fruition now, and more and more evidence points to sterility in conjunction with territoriality as the answer. To compare the findings is fascinating.

Mountain lions are geared for a life alone, and each inclines so sedulously to solitude that they rarely fight one another. The toms, in particular, according to Maurice Hornocker, don't overlap in their ranges. The females are slightly more tolerant; besides accepting some overlap among neighbors, they make adjustments of range from year to year so that those with big yearling cubs to provide for and train occupy more space than does a mother with newly born kittens. In the snowy country of central Idaho the females each have a winter range of from five to twenty square miles, and a male will encompass the home territories of two or three females, like smaller geometric figures within his own bailiwick, though he steers clear of actual contact with them except to consort briefly to breed. Mountain lions neither cooperate nor directly compete in hunting, and their scent-marking, which seems to be done mostly by the toms and which takes the form of periodically scratching with the hind feet a shovel-shaped scrape in the soil or in needles and leaves under a tree, compares with the punctilious, gossipy sort of urination male wolves indulge in and the regular round of rubbing-trees boar bears maintain. The lion is different, though, in that he doesn't pursue a rival to punish him if he is trespassing. Instead, his territoriality has been likened by Hornocker to a system of "railway signals," which, merely by notifying one cat of the presence of another, effectively "closes" that track to him. Since male mountain lions will sometimes kill kittens they come across, as boar bears kill cubs, it makes ethological sense for the species to insist upon a territoriality that is exclusive—only one dangerous male is regularly in the vicinity. On the other hand, the females, upon whom falls the responsibility of feeding the young, benefit by being willing to allow some overlap in their ranges; they can follow the game as it drifts about.

A newly grown lion setting out in its third summer from its mother's abode rambles along in an easy fashion with, in effect, a safe conduct through the territories of older lions but no desire to settle in and try to rub shoulders with them, until eventually it locates a vacant corner of the world to call its own. This impulse to clear off, which is present in young wolves and young boar bears as well, discourages inbreeding and helps to ensure that a lion lost from the population anywhere is likely to be replaced, that no plausible lion habitat goes undiscovered for long. The reclusive temperament of mountain lions befits their solitary techniques in hunting—based on the ambush, the stalk—and the way that they hunt, in turn, dovetails naturally with the abrupt, broken country they are partial to—terrain not so suited to the convivial, gang-up manner of pursuit which wolves, living usually at a lower, flatter elevation, prefer. But as is true of wolves, lions feel the urge to breed only after they have managed to establish a territory; or to put it the other way around, they do not take up permanent residence, even if they find an empty niche, until they locate scent signs and symbols around indicating that here they will be able to breed.

Despite Mech's discovery that lone wolves, dispensing with territoriality, roam more widely and often eat better than wolves in a pack, those in the prime of life do pair up and live in packs within a territorial discipline if they can, They put up an outright fighting defense once they have plumped upon ground of their own. Perhaps the fact that they fraternize so freely contributes to their readiness to fight; being sociable, they want company, but place a strict limit on how much they want. Hornocker speculates that such gregarious predators can afford the luxury of an occasional test of strength (though their howling and scent posts allay much of the need), whereas a solitary cat cannot. A mountain lion, depending wholly upon itself, must keep fit, and so as an economy measure the race has evolved a gentlefolk's way of spacing its populace about.

Individually too, bears have no other creature to lean on except themselves, but grazing the forest meadows as they do, they can nurse an injury along when necessary, and aggressiveness toward their own kind has a biological function for them. The bullying of the weak by the strong first puts good virile genes in the cubs, then weeds out the dullards among the yearlings and two-year-olds. The ladder of dominance in a wolf pack is a matter of still greater importance, because in the relatively level country wolves frequent, where game is easier to find than in a lion's convoluted topography and where there is more of it to go around, they must have no last-minute doubts as to who is boss; they must all streak after the same beast, swarm upon it, dodge its front hooves and bring it down. The bickering and the spurting of pee on each other's piss that they like to do is not just boundary-marking, but reaffirms which one—to judge by that tangy thermostat deep inside the body (and even a dog can distinguish one unit of urine in sixty million parts of water)—will lead the charge.

Wolves and bears are fastidious in their sexual clocking, breeding only so that the bear cubs will be delivered during the denning period and the wolf puppies into the lap of the spring. If a female lion loses her kittens, however, she may come into estrus again almost immediately. She has the onerous task of killing food for the litter, as sow bears do not and a bitch wolf need not, and is more likely to lose some of them, and so is equipped for another try. But like the bear, once her young are developing, she does not breed again until the second year, because no pack structure surrounds them to nurture them in the meantime. (The bitch wolf can go right at it the next February.)

Both bear and wolf scientists remark on how many of the females they study are barren in years when, to judge by the calendar, they ought to give birth. When an animal requires several square miles to stretch its legs and its psyche and to forage for food, inhibition assumes an importance. The creature must not simply be physiologically ready for offspring; it must have a great spread of land at its disposal, a competence, a self-confidence, and a wolf pack is wonderfully elastic in regulating this sort of thing. The strongest youngsters, with the wherewithal of nerve, fan out at the age of two to colonize new territory, but the old pack—parents, pups of the spring and yearlings of the year before, and sometimes older shrinking violets who haven't yet made the transition to independence, or an adopted senior widowed wolf—continues to hold the fort.

If the hunting is good in the winter, it's very good, with deer floundering in deep bogs of snow, but if it's bad, there are no summer beaver moseying about to be ripped up and no baby animals for hors d'oeuvres. When faced with starvation, a pack will evaporate rapidly from eight or ten or twelve to the single primary pair, as the others, barred from eating the sparse kills, head away in desperation to try their luck elsewhere. Then, from the odds and ends of packs that have disintegrated, a new apportioning of the countryside occurs. Sometimes a big pack will coalesce for a season if two former littermates, each leader of a family on ranges that adjoin, meet affectionately again, maybe after weeks of howling to each other, and throw in their lot together. In a pack, although several females may be nubile, only one of them conceives, as a rule. The lid is on unless the dominant animals are put out of commission, whereupon all sorts of pairings become possible.

Like other recent studies (Jonkel and Cowan's in Montana, for instance), Lynn Rogers's investigations suggest an almost equally ingenious instinctual realpolitik for bears. No pack exists—though grizzlies occasionally are prone to live in a loose sort of pack arrangement—but the boar black bears of Minnesota each roam over a chunk of geography averaging more than sixty square miles during the June–July breeding season. This is about the same freehold that a small wolf pack would use, but since the bear does not need even remotely as much land for food, he merely bestirs himself to be certain that no other male is around where he is at the same time. Males overlap, in other words, and Rogers thinks that two miles is about the buffer they insist upon, scratching, rubbing against so-called bear trees for the purpose of warning lesser males to beware. In his experience, sows seldom make use of these signposts, but do, by contrast, appear to enforce a severe territoriality upon each other, driving other sows, including large ones, beyond distinct boundaries that they lay out. Although Rogers hasn't figured out the method of marking that they employ, because the area involved is usually less than ten square miles, it is easier for them to exclude a trespasser than it would be for a boar to try to do the same. The boar is excellently situated, since six or eight or more sows live within his stamping grounds. Though each will be receptive to him for only a few weeks every couple of years, he doesn't have to depend on the mood and good health of any one of them in order to breed. They don't wait upon his welfare either, because each lives within the roaming range of several boars—the smaller specimens giving way before the fearsome bruisers, but skulking back. Boar bears are more likely to come to grief than sows because of their wandering disposition, yet whenever one is killed, others are on the scene—the whole uncanny setup being just the reverse of how mountain lions live.

June is an ideal month for bears to breed. They have had about three months to flesh out and recover their aplomb after the winter's sleep and plenty of opportunity remains for serious fattening before they slip below ground again. Wolves court and breed in the most grueling month instead—February, just when they should need to save their energy—because they must do so in order to give birth in April; but their love life goes on year-round and culminates extravagantly on the midwinter hunt. That's a time when all prudent bears are hoarding their fat and their newborn young under the ice and snow. The cubs grow from half a pound to five pounds before they even see the sun.

Bears hoard, wolves spend. Under the circumstances it's no wonder that scarcely half of the bitch wolves conceive, that though a wolf gives birth to at least twice as many pups as the sow does cubs, half of them probably won't survive for a year. Even the five or ten square miles the sow defends against other females would be more land than she needs for herself, if she weren't also defending nourishment for her cubs and for those of previous years. The winter of their first birthday, they den with her, then in the following summer are driven off as she keeps company with her paramours, but they are not driven outside her actual territory; they are still welcome there. They split up and den separately from her that fall, weighing maybe eighty pounds. In their third summer the mother appears with a new brace of cubs, and now they must keep severely clear of her. The males, not yet sexually capable, are full of urges and strike off on free-lance jaunts, as wolves and mountain lions of the same age do, each trying to light upon an empty space among the crazy quilt of bear bailiwicks that intersect throughout the forest. One young bear may travel thirty miles and set up shop, only to have a close shave with a resident bear, after which he will dash straight back to his mother's domain to recuperate for a little while before sallying forth on a different tack. Because he's slower to mature than a wolf or mountain lion, when he does find a neighborhood that suits him he has a couple of years to explore the district before committing himself. By scent he makes the acquaintance of the various sows he will pursue and the boars he must rival, eventually reaching at sexual maturity a weight of perhaps two hundred and twenty-five pounds when fat in the fall or a hundred and seventy-five pounds in the hungry spring.

Young males are the pioneers when bears resettle an area such as grown-over farmland. But they must cool their heels until a food shortage or some more arcane pressure pushes the sows toward them. Their sister cubs tend to linger in the mother's realm, living in isolation but protected from molestation by other sows because of the territorial right which they retain. One obvious effect of this procedure is that whenever a new sow does breed, her partner will probably have originated in another region, but as long as her mother remains sexually active, it appears that she will not do so. She lives there in reserve—in limbo, as it were, like an unhatched egg—in a section of her mother's territory as small as a single square mile, against the day when the elder sow meets with a disaster, whereupon the range will pass to her. Then her turf may shrink a bit, as the sows on the borders challenge her boundaries, but sooner or later she blossoms to the task of defending it.

When Rogers was starting his study, he almost ran out of funds in August when the bears he was tracking left their haunts after the agitations of the mating season, and went for trips he hadn't expected—vacations, the impulse might be called. The males sometimes travel substantial distances and mingle festively without much quarreling, and he was paying his pilot to chase them. The sows don't wander so far, but may go ten or twenty miles, as if to eat new plums and cherries, or merely ramble into an unfamiliar loop of land adjacent to their regular duchy, which for the time being they stop patrolling. This custom is another means by which bears discover gaps left by mishaps and exploit them so as to keep the countryside producing bears at full capacity. It is also a kind of relaxation which wolves could not afford because the territoriality of a wolf pack is based on the exigencies of hunting.

These are exciting discoveries, and of the several authorities engaged in zeroing in on the details, I didn't doubt that Rogers was the best. I liked his rushing way of driving and hiking and his enormous hunger for data. I liked his enthusiasm for the unfashionable black bear (many more scientists are studying the wolf), and as we toured, enjoyed being in the shadow of a man larger and more vivid than myself—though with his bigness, as with the bigness of big women, went an affecting vulnerability. His ums and ahs annoyed me, yet I was saying um and ah myself by now. We kept remarking how we had each spent hours after school alone, daydreaming of seeing wild animals in the woods and searching out their hideouts and handling them—not imagining that such good fortune might ever really be ours. Here we were, he said, in woods that many people drive a thousand miles to camp in, people who felt that if they could happen upon a bear it might make their whole summer excursion—and we could see one anytime.

Rogers has put radios on seventy-two over the years, and when he's trying to enlist somebody's support or testing a student who wants to help him, he generally goes to a den. The kids (or me, or Wally Dayton) crouch down on their hands and knees, peering into the troll-like crevice where mushrooms grow. Whether or not the smell of the bear actually persists inside, it *seems* to, and one is reminded of humble caves that a boy might run away to, and of digging to China, and of bottomless cracks in the earth. In the fall, after the bear has gone to sleep in its new hole, Rogers will tie a thread across the mouth so that on his next visit he will know whether it has woken up and scrambled outside for an interlude.

Whenever he gets near a bear in the flesh, as in mixing with them in their dens, he comes into his own—decisive, direct. Where other biologists explode the tranquilizer into an animal with a dart gun, leaving a wound, perhaps knocking the bear out of a tree so that it is killed, he does almost all his injecting by hand. The sows stand chuffing at him, slamming their paws on the ground to scare him, but he runs at them, stamping *his* feet, and stampedes both sow and cubs into separate trees. Then he climbs up and sticks the needle into their round rear ends, before lowering them one by one on a rope as the drug takes effect. Approaching a bear denned under the snow, he slips off his parka so it won't squeak as he crawls. Wriggling forward underground, he carries a flashlight in one hand and the syringe in the other, fastened to the end of a stick. If the bear is awake and panics and begins to come out, he rolls quietly to one side of the entrance and hunches there, poking it with the drug as it lumbers past; it can't get far. Sometimes bears make a blowing sound, like a man loudly cooling soup, which he listens to, not taking the warning to heart unless it is accompanied by a lifted upper lip—this being a true giveaway of belligerence. "It's like driving in town. You've got a traffic light to tell you when to stop." Usually, though, the bears stay becalmed, resting in their nests, merely sniffing the syringe when it is presented to them, making no more objection to the prick than they would to an insect's bite. He takes his time; the air inside the den is dead and hardly carries his scent.

Weather causes worse problems. Some days Rogers has to break trail on snowshoes for miles for his snowmobile, and must put the needles and vials of drugs in his mouth to warm them; the tubes of blood that he collects go in his shirt. For his blood-tapping and temperature-taking he must haul the bear outside, and if there are cubs he deals with them, squeezing into the furthest recesses but finding them unresisting once the mother has been subdued. Newborns have blue eyes and pink noses, and the smell left by his hands does not make the mother abandon them. He listens to their hearts, measures the length of their fur, and wraps them in his parka until he is finished examining the mother. Even knocked out, the bears are all right in the cold, although in the summer they sometimes need to be bathed in cool water after panting in a metal trap; he washes off the matted mud if they've been struggling in a snare. After he's through, he replaces the family just as it was—wriggling inside the den, dragging the cubs and mother in after him, adjusting her posture and limbs so that she'll wake up feeling natural.

On September 22 we spent a red-letter day together, starting at a dump where gulls and ravens whirled above us and Rogers scanned the line of trees for any fat rear end that might be beating a retreat. He flew for four hours, locating all the bears whose radios were functioning; then back on the ground, as a check on his methods he went to three of the fixes to confirm that the bears were where he'd marked them. He inspected seven denning places, showing me how he discovers the hole itself by the raking that bears do as they collect insulation. This is while the ground is clear of snow, so he memorizes how to find it later on by lining up the nearby trees. Number 414's chamber last winter was under a clump of boulders, fifteen feet back through a passage. Number 320's was under a bulldozed pile of birch that the loggers had left. A few miles away we watched a female preparing a small basket-shaped sanctum under the upturned roots of a white pine, from which she sneaked, like a hurrying, portly child, circling downwind to identify us before clearing out. Another bear, a hundred-pound male, was hollowing a den under a crosshatch of windfalls just above a patch of swamp. He too scrambled silently away downwind ahead of us like a gentleman disturbed in a spot where he's afraid perhaps he shouldn't be.

In a pea-vine clearing Rogers photographed three bears eating and obtained some scats. He tasted bear delicacies as he walked, spitting out prickly or bitter leaves. In one of his traps was a young male, chopping its teeth, clicking its tongue, with a strong ursine smell of urine. Rogers answered with the same sounds, and when he let the bear loose it bounded toward the woods like the beast of a children's fairy tale—a big rolling derrière, a big tongue for eating, and pounding feet, its body bending like a boomerang.

We ate rock tripe off the rocks, saw moose tracks, wolf scats, two red-tailed hawks, three deer, and a painted turtle. The dogwood was turning purple now, the aspens golden, the plum bushes red, the pin cherries brown, and the birches and hazel and thimbleberries yellow. There was pearly everlasting, and blue large-leafed aster still blooming in the woods, and sweet fern that we crushed in our hands to smell. Alders had grown up higher than the jeep on some of the roads we followed. "Doesn't have too much traffic," said Rogers.

There is sometimes a sadness to David Mech's work, when he knows in advance from the blood tests he does which of his wolf pups is going to die. But Rogers's cubs are hardier, the winter holds no terrors for them, and when they do disappear it is not due to the sort of anemia which an investigator can foresee. I thought very highly of him—this admirable animal-catcher, this student of wild foods and smells, this scholar of garbage dumps. Because his bears like dumps, so does he.

Hailing the
Elusory
Mountain Lion

The swan song sounded by the wilderness
grows fainter, ever more constricted, until only sharp ears can
catch it at all. It fades to a nearly inaudible level, and yet there
never is going to be any one time when we can say right *now* it is
gone. Wolves meet their maker in wholesale lots, but coyotes in-
filtrate eastward, northward, southeastward. Woodland caribou and
bighorn sheep are vanishing fast, but moose have expanded their
range in some areas.

Mountain lions used to have practically the run of the Western Hemisphere, and they still do occur from Cape Horn to the
Big Muddy River at the boundary of the Yukon and on the coasts
of both oceans, so that they are the most versatile land mammal in
the New World, probably taking in more latitudes than any other
four-footed wild creature anywhere. There are perhaps only four
to six thousand left in the United States, though there is no place
that they didn't once go, eating deer, elk, pikas, porcupines, grasshoppers, and dead fish on the beach. They were called mountain
lions in the Rockies, pumas (originally an Incan word) in the
Southwestern states, cougars (a naturalist's corruption of an Ama-
zonian Indian word) in the Northwest, panthers in the tradition-
ist East—"painters" in dialect-proud New England—or catamounts.
The Dutchmen of New Netherland called them tigers, red tigers,
deer tigers, and the Spaniards *leones* or *leopardos*. They liked to
eat horses—wolves preferred beef and black bears favored pork—
but as adversaries of mankind they were overshadowed at first because bears appeared more formidable and wolves in their howling
packs were more flamboyant and more damaging financially. Yet
this panoply of names is itself quite a tribute, and somehow the
legends about "panthers" have lingered longer than bear or wolf

tales, helped by the animal's own limber, far-traveling stealth and as a carryover from the immense mythic force of the great cats of the Old World. Though only Florida among the Eastern states is known for certain to have any left, no wild knot of mountains or swamp is without rumors of panthers; nowadays people delight in these, keeping their eyes peeled. It's wishful, and the wandering, secretive nature of the beast ensures that even Eastern panthers will not soon be certifiably extinct. An informal census among experts in 1963 indicated that an island of twenty-five or more may have survived in the New Brunswick–Maine–Quebec region, and Louisiana may still have a handful, and perhaps eight live isolated in the Black Hills of South Dakota, and the Oklahoma panhandle may have a small colony—all outside the established range in Florida, Texas, and the Far West. As with the blue whale, who will be able to say when they have been eliminated?

"Mexican lion" is another name for mountain lions in the border states—a name that might imply a meager second-best rating there yet ties to the majestic African beasts. Lions are at least twice as big as mountain lions, measuring by weight, though they are nearly the same in length because of the mountain lion's superb long tail. Both animals sometimes pair up affectionately with mates and hunt in tandem, but mountain lions go winding through life in ones or twos, whereas the lion is a harem-keeper, harem-dweller, the males eventually becoming stay-at-homes, heavy figureheads. Lions enjoy the grassy flatlands, forested along the streams, and they stay put, engrossed in communal events—roaring, grunting, growling with a racket like the noise of gears being stripped—unless the game moves on. They sun themselves, preside over the numerous kibbutz young, sneeze from the dust, and bask in dreams, occasionally waking up to issue reverberating, guttural pronouncements which serve notice that they are now awake.

Mountain lions spirit themselves away in saw-toothed canyons and on escarpments instead, and when conversing with their mates they coo like pigeons, sob like women, emit a flat slight shriek, a popping bubbling growl, or mew, or yowl. They growl and suddenly caterwaul into falsetto—the famous scarifying, metallic scream functioning as a kind of hunting cry close up, to terrorize and start the game. They ramble as much as twenty-five miles in a night, maintaining a large loop of territory which they cover every week or two. It's a solitary, busy life, involving a survey of several valleys, many deer herds. Like tigers and leopards, mountain lions are not sociably inclined and don't converse at length with the whole waiting world, but they are even less noisy; they seem to speak most eloquently with their feet. Where a tiger would roar, a mountain lion screams like a castrato. Where a mountain lion hisses, a leopard would snarl like a truck stuck in snow. Leopards are the best counterpart to mountain lions in physique and in the tenor of their lives. Supple, fierce creatures, skilled at concealment but with great self-assurance and drive, leopards are bolder when facing human beings than the American cats. Basically they are hot-land beasts and not such remarkable travelers individually, though as a race they once inhabited the broad Eurasian landmass all the way from Great Britain to Malaysia, as well as Africa. As late as the 1960s, a few were said to be still holding out on the shore of the Mediterranean at Mount Mycale, Turkey. (During a forest fire twenty years ago a yearling swam the narrow straits to the Greek island Samos and holed up in a cave, where he was duly killed—perhaps the last leopard ever to set foot in Europe on his own.) Leopards are thicker and shorter than adult mountain lions and seem to lead an athlete's indolent, incurious life much of the time, testing their perfected bodies by clawing tree trunks, chewing on old skulls, executing acrobatic leaps, and then rousing themselves to the semiweekly antelope kill. Built with supreme hardness and economy, they make little allowance for man—they don't see him as different. They relish the flesh of his dogs, and they run up a tree when hunted and then sometimes spring down, as heavy as a chunk of iron wrapped in a flag. With stunning, gorgeous coats, their tight, dervish faces carved in a snarl, they head for the hereafter as if it were just one more extra-emphatic leap—as impersonal in death as the crack of the rifle was.

The American leopard, the jaguar, is a powerfully built, serious fellow, who, before white men arrived, wandered as far north as the Carolinas, but his best home is the humid basin of the Amazon. Mountain lions penetrate these ultimate jungles too, but rather thinly, thriving better in the cooler, drier climate of the untenanted pampas and on the mountain slopes. They are blessed with a pleasant but undazzling coat, tan except for a white belly, mouth and throat, and some black behind the ears, on the tip of the tail and at the sides of the nose, and so they are hunted as symbols, not for their fur. The cubs are spotted, leopardlike, much as lion cubs are. If all of the big cats developed from a common ancestry, the mountain lions' specialization has been unpresumptuous—away from bulk and savagery to traveling light. Toward deer, their prey, they may be as ferocious as leopards, but not toward chance acquaintances such as man. They sometimes break their necks, their jaws, their teeth, springing against the necks of quarry they have crept close to—a fate resulting in part from the circumstance that they can't ferret out the weaker individuals in a herd

by the device of a long chase, the way wolves do; they have to take
the luck of the draw. None of the cats possess enough lung capacity for grueling runs. They depend upon shock tactics, bursts of
speed, sledge-hammer leaps, strong collarbones for hitting power,
and shearing dentition, whereas wolves employ all the advantages
of time in killing their quarry, as well as the numbers and gaiety
of the pack, biting the beast's nose and rump—the technique of a
thousand cuts—lapping the bloody snow. Wolves sometimes even
have a cheering section of flapping ravens accompanying them,
eager to scavenge after the brawl.

It's a risky business for the mountain lion, staking the strength
and impact of his neck against the strength of the prey animal's
neck. Necessarily, he is concentrated and fierce; yet legends exist that mountain lions have irritably defended men and women
lost in the wilderness against marauding jaguars, who are no
friends of theirs, and (with a good deal more supporting evidence)
that they are susceptible to an odd kind of fascination with human
beings. Sometimes they will tentatively seek an association, hanging about a campground or following a hiker out of curiosity,
perhaps, circling around and bounding up on a ledge above to
watch him pass. This mild modesty has helped preserve them
from extinction. If they have been unable to make any adjustments to the advent of man, they haven't suicidally opposed him
either, as the buffalo wolves and grizzlies did. In fact, at close
quarters they seem bewildered. When treed, they don't breathe a
hundred-proof ferocity but puzzle over what to do. They're too
light-bodied to bear down on the hunter and kill him easily, even
if they should attack—a course they seem to have no inclination
for. In this century in the United States only one person, a child
of thirteen, has been killed by a mountain lion; that was in 1924.
And they're informal animals. Lolling in an irregular sprawl on a
high limb, they can't seem to summon any Enobarbus-like front of
resistance for long. Daring men occasionally climb up and toss las-
sos about a cat and haul him down, strangling him by pulling from
two directions, while the lion, mortified, appalled, never does muster his fighting aplomb. Although he could fight off a pack of
wolves, he hasn't worked out a posture to assume toward man and
his dogs. Impotently, he stiffens, as the dinosaurs must have when
the atmosphere grew cold.

Someday hunting big game may come to be regarded as a
form of vandalism, and the remaining big creatures of the wilderness will skulk through restricted reserves wearing radio transmit-
ters and numbered collars, or bearing stripes of dye, as many elephants already do, to aid the busy biologists who track them from

the air. Like a vanishing race of trolls, more report and memory than a reality, they will inhabit children's books and nostalgic articles, a special glamour attaching to those, like mountain lions, that are geographically incalculable and may still be sighted away from the preserves. Already we've become enthusiasts. We want game about us—at least at a summer house; it's part of privileged living. There is a precious privacy about seeing wildlife, too. Like meeting a fantastically dressed mute on the road, the fact that no words are exchanged and that *he's* not going to give an account makes the experience light-hearted; it's wholly ours. Besides, if anything out of the ordinary happens, we know we can't expect to be believed, and since it's rather fun to be disbelieved—fishermen know this—the privacy is even more complete. Deer, otter, foxes are messengers from another condition of life, another mentality, and bring us tidings of places we don't go.

Ten years ago at Vavenby, a sawmill town on the North Thompson River in British Columbia, a frolicsome mountain lion used to appear at dusk every ten days or so in a bluegrass field alongside the river. Deer congregated there, the river was silky and swift, cooling the summer air, and it was a festive spot for a lion to be. She was thought to be a female, and reputedly left tracks around an enormous territory to the north and west—Raft Mountain, Battle Mountain, the Trophy Range, the Murtle River, and Mahood Lake—territory on an upended, pelagic scale, much of it scarcely accessible to a man by trail, where the tiger lilies grew four feet tall. She would materialize in this field among the deer five minutes before dark, as if checking in again, a habit that may have resulted in her death eventually, though for the present the farmer who observed her visits was keeping his mouth shut about it. This was pioneer country; there were people alive who could remember the time when poisoning the carcass of a cow would net a man a pile of dead predators—a family of mountain lions to bounty, maybe half a dozen wolves, and both black bears and grizzlies. The Indians considered lion meat a delicacy, but they had clans which drew their origins at the Creation from ancestral mountain lions, or wolves or bears, so these massacres amazed them. They thought the outright bounty hunters were crazy men.

Even before Columbus, mountain lions were probably not distributed in saturation numbers anywhere, as wolves may have been. Except for the family unit—a female with her half-grown cubs—each lion seems to occupy its own spread of territory, not as a result of fights with intruders but because the young transients share the same instinct for solitude and soon sheer off to find vacant mountains and valleys. A mature lion kills only one deer every week or two, according to a study by Maurice Hornocker in Idaho, and therefore is not really a notable factor in controlling the numbers of the local deer. Rather, it keeps watch contentedly as their population grows, sometimes benefitting the herds by scaring them onto new wintering grounds that are not overbrowsed, and by its very presence warding off other lions.

This thin distribution, coupled with the mountain lion's taciturn habits, make sighting one a matter of luck, even for game officials located in likely country. One warden in Colorado I talked to had indeed seen a pair of them fraternizing during the breeding season. He was driving a jeep over an abandoned mining road, and he passed two brown animals sitting peaceably in the snow, their heads close together. For a moment he thought they were coyotes and kept driving, when all of a sudden the picture registered that they were *cougars!* He braked and backed up, but of course they were gone. He was an old-timer, a man who had crawled inside bear dens to pull out the cubs, and knew where to find clusters of buffalo skulls in the recesses of the Rockies where the last bands had hidden; yet this cryptic instant when he was turning his jeep round a curve was the only glimpse—unprovable—that he ever got of a mountain lion.

Such glimpses usually are cryptic. During a summer I spent in Wyoming in my boyhood, I managed to see two coyotes, but both occasions were so fleeting that it required an act of faith on my part afterward to feel sure I had seen them. One of the animals vanished between rolls of ground; the other, in rougher, stonier, wooded country, cast his startled gray face in my direction and simply was gone. Hunching, he swerved for cover, and the brush closed over him. I used to climb to a vantage point above a high basin at twilight and watch the mule deer steal into the meadows to feed. The grass grew higher than their stomachs, the steep forest was close at hand, and they were as small and fragile-looking as filaments at that distance, quite human in coloring, gait and form. It was possible to visualize them as a naked Indian hunting party a hundred years before—or not to believe in their existence at all, either as Indians or deer. Minute, aphid-sized, they stepped so carefully in emerging, hundreds of feet below, that, straining my eyes, I needed to tell myself constantly that they were deer; my imagination, left to its own devices with the dusk settling down, would have made of them a dozen other creatures.

Recently, walking at night on the woods road that passes my house in Vermont, I heard footsteps in the leaves and windfalls. I waited, listening—they sounded too heavy to be anything less than a man, a large deer or a bear. A man wouldn't have been in the woods so late, my dog stood respectfully silent and still, and they did seem to shuffle portentously. Sure enough, after pausing at the edge of the road, a fully grown bear appeared, visible only in dimmest outline, staring in my direction for four or five seconds. The darkness lent a faintly red tinge to his coat; he was well built. Then, turning, he ambled off, almost immediately lost to view, though I heard the noise of his passage, interrupted by several pauses. It was all as concise as a vision, and since I had wanted to see a bear close to my own house, being a person who likes to live in a melting pot, whether in the city or country, and since it was too dark to pick out his tracks, I was grateful when the dog inquisitively urinated along the bear's path, thereby confirming that at least I had witnessed *something*. The dog seemed unsurprised, however, as if the scent were not all that remarkable, and, sure enough, the next week in the car I encountered a yearling bear in daylight two miles downhill, and a cub a month later. My farmer neighbors were politely skeptical of my accounts, having themselves caught sight of only perhaps a couple of bears in all their lives.

So it's with sympathy as well as an awareness of the tricks that enthusiasm and nightfall may play that I have been going to nearby towns seeking out people who have claimed at one time or another to have seen a mountain lion. The experts of the state—game wardens, taxidermists, the most accomplished hunters—emphatically discount the claims, but the believers are unshaken. They include some summer people who were enjoying a drink on the back terrace when the apparition of a great-tailed cat moved out along the fringe of the woods on a deer path; a boy who was hunting with his .22 years ago near the village dump and saw the animal across a gully and fired blindly, then ran away and brought back a search party, which found a tuft of toast-colored fur; and a state forestry employee, a sober woodsman, who caught the cat in his headlights while driving through Victory Bog in the wildest corner of the Northeast Kingdom. Gordon Hickok, who works for a furniture factory and has shot one or two mountain lions on hunting trips in the West, saw one cross U.S. 5 at a place called Auger Hole near Mount Hor. He tracked it with dogs a short distance, finding a fawn with its head gnawed off. A high school English teacher reported seeing a mountain lion cross another road, near Runaway Pond, but the hunters who quickly went out decided that the prints were those of a big bobcat, splayed impressively in the mud and snow. Fifteen years ago a watchman in the fire tower on top of Bald Mountain had left grain scattered in the grooves of a flat rock under the tower to feed several deer. One night, looking down just as the dusk turned murky, he saw two slim long-tailed lions creep out of the scrubby border of spruce and inspect the rock, sniffing deer droppings and dried deer saliva. The next night, when he was in his cabin, the dog barked and, looking out the window, again he saw the vague shape of a lion just vanishing.

A dozen loggers and woodsmen told me such stories. In the Adirondacks I've also heard some persuasive avowals—one by an old dog-sled driver and trapper, a French Canadian; another by the owner of a tourist zoo, who was exhibiting a Western cougar. In Vermont perhaps the most eager rumor buffs are some of the farmers. After all, now that packaged semen has replaced the awesome farm bull and so many procedures have been mechanized, who wants to lose *all* the adventure of farming? Until recently the last mountain lion known to have been killed in the Northeast was recorded in 1881 in Barnard, Vermont. However, it has been learned that probably another one was shot from a tree in 1931 in Mundleville, New Brunswick, and still another trapped seven years later in Somerset County in Maine. Bruce S. Wright, director of the Northeastern Wildlife Station (which is operated at the University of New Brunswick with international funding), is convinced that though they are exceedingly rare, mountain lions are still part of the fauna of the region; in fact, he has plaster casts of tracks to prove it, as well as a compilation of hundreds of reported sightings. Some people may have mistaken a golden retriever for a lion, or may have intended to foment a hoax, but all in all the evidence does seem promising. Indeed, after almost twenty years of search and study, Wright himself finally saw one.

The way these sightings crop up in groups has often been pooh-poohed as greenhorn fare or as a sympathetic hysteria among neighbors, but it is just as easily explained by the habit mountain lions have of establishing a territory that they scout through at intervals, visiting an auspicious deer-ridden swamp or remote ledgy mountain. Even at such a site a successful hunt could not be mounted without trained dogs, and if the population of the big cats was extremely sparse, requiring of them long journeys during the mating season, and yet with plenty of deer all over, they might not stay for long. One or two hundred miles is no obstacle to a Western cougar. The cat might inhabit a mountain ridge one year, and then never again.

Fifteen years ago, Francis Perry, who is an ebullient muffin of a man, a farmer all his life in Brownington, Vermont, saw a mountain lion "larger and taller than a collie, and grayish yellow" (he had seen them in circuses). Having set a trap for a woodchuck, he was on his way to visit the spot when he came over a rise and, at a distance of fifty yards, saw the beast engaged in eating the dead woodchuck. It bounded off, but Perry set four light fox traps for it around the woodchuck. Apparently, a night or two later the cat returned and got caught in three of these, but they couldn't hold it; it pulled free, leaving the marks of a struggle. Noel Perry, his brother, remembers how scared Francis looked when he came home from the first episode. Noel himself saw the cat (which may have meant that Brownington Swamp was one of its haunts that summer), once when it crossed a cow pasture on another farm the brothers owned, and once when it fled past his rabbit dogs through underbrush while he was training them—he thought for a second that its big streaking form was one of the dogs. A neighbor, Robert Chase, also saw the animal that year. Then again last summer, for the first time in fifteen years, Noel Perry saw a track as big as a bear's but round like a mountain lion's, and Robert's brother, Larry Chase, saw the actual cat several times one summer evening, playing a chummy hide-and-seek with him in the fields.

Elmer and Elizabeth Ambler are in their forties, populists politically, and have bought a farm in Glover to live the good life, though he is a truck driver in Massachusetts on weekdays and must drive hard in order to be home when he can. He's bald, with large eyebrows, handsome teeth, and a low forehead, but altogether a strong-looking, clear, humane face. He is an informational kind of man who will give you the history of various breeds of cattle or a talk about taxation in a slow and musical voice, and both he and his wife, a purposeful, self-sufficient redhead, are fascinated by the possibility that they live in the wilderness. Beavers inhabit the river that flows past their house. The Amblers say that on Black Mountain nearby hunters "disappear" from time to time, and bears frequent the berry patches in their back field—they see them, their visitors see them, people on the road see them, their German shepherds meet them and run back drooling with fright. They've stocked their farm with horned Herefords instead of the polled variety so that the creatures can "defend themselves." Ambler is intrigued by the thought that apart from the danger of bears, someday "a cat" might prey on one of his cows. Last year, looking out the back window, his wife saw through binoculars an animal with a flowing tail and "a cat's gallop" following a line of trees where the deer go, several hundred yards uphill behind the house. Later, Ambler went up on showshoes and found tracks as big as their shepherds'; the dogs obligingly ran alongside. He saw walking tracks, leaping tracks, and deer tracks marked with blood going toward higher ground. He wonders whether the cat will ever attack him. There are plenty of bobcats around, but they both say they know the difference. The splendid, nervous *tail* is what people must have identified in order to claim they have seen a mountain lion.

I, too, cherish the notion that I may have seen a lion. Mine was crouched on an overlook above a grass-grown, steeply pitched wash in the Alberta Rockies—a much more likely setting than anywhere in New England. It was late afternoon on my last day at Maligne Lake, where I had been staying with my father at a national-park chalet. I was twenty; I could walk forever or could climb endlessly in a sanguine scramble, going out every day as far as my legs carried me, swinging around for home before the sun went down. Earlier, in the valley of the Athabasca, I had found several winter-starved or wolf-killed deer, well picked and scattered, and an area with many elk antlers strewn on the ground where the herds had wintered safely, dropping their antlers but not their bones. Here, much higher up, in the bright plenitude of the summer, I had watched two wolves and a stately bull moose in one mountain basin, and had been up on the caribou barrens on the ridge west of the lake and brought back the talons of a hawk I'd found dead on the ground. Whenever I was watching game, a sort of stopwatch in me started running. These were moments of intense importance and intimacy, of new intimations and aptitudes. Time had a jam-packed character, as it does during a mile run.

I was good at moving quietly through the woods and at spotting game, and was appropriately exuberant. The finest, longest day of my stay was the last. Going east, climbing through a luxuriant terrain of up-and-down boulders, brief brilliant glades, sudden potholes fifty feet deep—a forest of moss-hung lodgepole pines and fir and spare, gaunt spruce with the black lower branches broken off—I came upon the remains of a young bear, which had been torn up and shredded. Perhaps wolves had cornered it during some imprudent excursion in the early spring. (Bears often wake up while the snow is still deep, dig themselves out and rummage around in the neighborhood sleepily for a day or two before bedding down again under a fallen tree.) I took the skull along so that I could extract the teeth when I got hold of some tools. Discoveries like this represent a superfluity of wildlife and show how many beasts there are scouting about.

I went higher. The marmots whistled familially; the tall trees wilted to stubs of themselves. A pretty stream led down a defile from a series of openings in front of the ultimate barrier of a vast mountain wall which I had been looking at from a distance each day on my outings. It wasn't too steep to be climbed, but it was a barrier because my energies were not sufficient to scale it and bring me back the same night. Besides, it stretched so majestically, surflike above the lesser ridges, that I liked to think of it as the Continental Divide.

On my left as I went up this wash was an abrupt, grassy slope that enjoyed a southern exposure and was sunny and windblown all winter, which kept it fairly free of snow. The ranger at the lake had told me it served as a wintering ground for a few bighorn sheep and for a band of mountain goats, three of which were in sight. As I approached laboriously, these white, pointy-horned fellows drifted up over a rise, managing to combine their retreat with some nippy good grazing as they went, not to give any pursuer the impression that they had been pushed into flight. I took my time too, climbing to locate the spring in a precipitous cleft of rock where the band did most of its drinking, and finding the shallow, high-ceilinged cave where the goats had sheltered from storms, presumably for generations. The floor was layered with rubbery droppings, trampled down and sprinkled with tufts of shed fur, and the back wall was checkered with footholds where the goats liked to clamber and perch. Here and there was a horn lying loose—a memento for me to add to my collection from an old individual that had died a natural death, secure in the band's winter stronghold. A bold, thriving family of pack rats emerged to observe me. They lived mainly on the nutritives in the droppings, and were used to the goats' tolerance; they seemed astonished when I tossed a stone.

I kept scrabbling along the side of the slope to a section of outcroppings where the going was harder. After perhaps half an hour, crawling around a corner, I found myself faced with a bighorn ram who was taking his ease on several square yards of bare earth between large rocks, a little above the level of my head. Just as surprised as I, he stood up. He must have construed the sounds of my advance to be those of another sheep or goat. His horns had made a complete curl and then some; they were thick, massive and bunched together like a high Roman helmet, and he himself was muscly and military, with a grave-looking nose. A squared-off, middle-aged, trophy-type ram, full of imposing professionalism, he was at the stage of life when rams sometimes stop herding and live as rogues.

He turned and tried a couple of possible exits from the pocket where I had found him, but the ground was badly pitched and would require a reeling gait and loss of dignity. Since we were within a national park and obviously I was unarmed, he simply was not inclined to put himself to so much trouble. He stood fifteen or twenty feet above me, pushing his tongue out through his teeth, shaking his head slightly and dipping it into charging position as I moved closer by a step or two, raising my hand slowly toward him in what I proposed as a friendly greeting. The day had been a banner one since the beginning, so while I recognized immediately that this meeting would be a valued memory, I felt as natural in his company as if he were a friend of mine reincarnated in a shag suit. I saw also that he was going to knock me for a loop, head over heels down the slope, if I sidled nearer, because he did not by any means feel as expansive and exuberant at our encounter as I did. That was the chief difference between us. I was talking to him with easy gladness, and beaming; he was not. He was unsettled and on his mettle, waiting for me to move along, the way a bighorn sheep waits for a predator to move on in wildlife movies when each would be evenly matched in a contest of strength and position. Although his warlike nose and high bone helmet, blocky and beautiful as weaponry, kept me from giving in to my sense that we were brothers, I knew I could stand there for a long while. His coat was a down-to-earth brown, edgy with muscle, his head was that of an unsmiling veteran standing to arms, and despite my reluctance to treat him as some sort of boxed-in prize, I might have stayed on for half the afternoon if I hadn't realized that I had other sights to see. It was not a day to dawdle.

I trudged up the wash and continued until, past tree line, the terrain widened and flattened in front of a preliminary ridge that formed an obstacle before the great, roaring, silent, surflike mountain wall that I liked to think of as the Continental Divide, although it wasn't. A cirque separated the preliminary ridge from the ultimate divide, which I still hoped to climb and look over. The opening into this was roomy enough, except for being littered with enormous boulders, and I began trying to make my way across them. Each was boat-sized and rested upon underboulders; it was like running in place. After tussling with this landscape for an hour or two, I was limp and sweating, pinching my cramped legs. The sun had gone so low that I knew I would be finding my way home by moonlight in any case, and I could see into the cirque, which was big and symmetrical and presented a view of sheer barbarism; everywhere were these cruel boat-sized boulders.

Giving up and descending to the goats' draw again, I had a drink from the stream and bathed before climbing farther downward. The grass was green, sweet-smelling, and I felt safely close to life after that sea of dead boulders. I knew I would never be physically younger or in finer country; even then the wilderness was singing its swan song. I had no other challenges in mind, and though very tired, I liked looking up at the routes where I'd climbed. The trio of goats had not returned, but I could see their wintering cave and the cleft in the rocks where the spring was. Curiously, the bighorn ram had not left; he had only withdrawn upward, shifting away from the outcroppings to an open sweep of space where every avenue of escape was available. He was lying on a carpet of grass and, lonely pirate that he was, had his head turned in my direction.

It was from this same wash that looking up, I spotted the animal I took to be a mountain lion. He was skulking along some outcroppings at a point lower on the mountainside than the ledges where the ram originally had been. A pair of hawks or eagles were swooping at him by turns, as if he were close to a nest. The slant between us was steep, but the light of evening was still more than sufficient. I did not really see the wonderful tail—that special medallion—nor was he particularly big for a lion. He was gloriously catlike and slinky, however, and so indifferent to the swooping birds as to seem oblivious of them. There are plenty of creatures he wasn't: he wasn't a marmot, a goat or other grass-eater, a badger, a wolf or coyote or fisher. He *may* have been a big bobcat or a wolverine, although he looked ideally lion-colored. He had a cat's strong collarbone structure for hitting, powerful haunches for vaulting, and the almost mystically small head mountain lions possess, with the gooseberry eyes. Anyway, I believed him to be a mountain lion, and standing quietly I watched him as he inspected in leisurely fashion the ledge that he was on and the one under him savory with every trace of goat—frosty-colored with the white hairs they'd shed. The sight was so dramatic that it seemed to be happening close to me, though in fact he and the hawks or eagles, whatever they were, were miniaturized by distance.

If I'd kept motionless, eventually I could have seen whether he had the proper tail, but such scientific questions had no weight next to my need to essay some kind of communication with him. It had been exactly the same when I'd watched the two wolves playing together a couple of days before. They were above me, absorbed in their game of noses-and-paws. I had recognized that I might never witness such a scene again, yet I couldn't hold myself in. Instead of talking and raising my arm to them, as I had with the ram, I'd shuffled forward impetuously as if to say *Here I am!* Now, with the lion, I tried hard to dampen my impulse and restrained myself as long as I could. Then I stepped toward him, just barely squelching a cry in my throat but lifting my hand—as clumsy as anyone is who is trying to attract attention.

At that, of course, he swerved aside instantly and was gone. Even the two birds vanished. Foolish, triumphant and disappointed, I hiked on down into the lower forests, gargantuanly tangled, another life zone—not one which would exclude a lion but one where he would not be seen. I'd got my second wind and walked lightly and softly, letting the silvery darkness settle around me. The blowdowns were as black as whales; my feet sank in the moss. Clearly this was as crowded a day as I would ever have, and I knew my real problem would not be to make myself believed but rather to make myself understood at all, simply in reporting the story, and that I must at least keep the memory straight for myself. I was so happy that I was unerring in distinguishing the deer trails going my way. The forest's night beauty was supreme in its promise, and I didn't hurry.

The Moose
on the Wall

Since it is likely that the last wild animals of large size and dignity that people will see will be stuffed ones, I paid a visit to my neighborhood taxidermist in northern Vermont to learn how he does his work, and what precisely it is: by what means these few crick-necked and powdery phantoms of the great game confluxes of the past will be preserved. The area where I live still has a smattering of black bear, and plenty of deer, some bobcats, and an occasional coyote migrating in from westerly parts. The beaver are beginning to come back, now that nobody much traps them, and the groundhogs and skunks and porcupines are flourishing as the farms become summer places, where they aren't shot as varmints. The cougars, wolves, and wolverines are long gone, but the humbler animals, meek, elusive, adaptable, are doing all right for the moment—in fact, my friend the taxidermist says that when he was a boy and this was farm country, people would travel for miles just to set eyes on a bear's track, if one was reported. The wildlife left will probably continue to prosper until the seasonal owners break up their properties into smaller and smaller tracts as land values rise.

My friend is a likable man with white hair, a quiet, spacious, mild face well used by his sixty years, a farmer's suspenders, a carpenter's arms, and an acumen in the woods, or a love for the woods, that no doubt exceeds my own, though my bias and his are opposed. We are allies nevertheless, because hunting and non-hunting naturalists when taken together are only a dot in the populace, at least when wildlife conservation is involved. Clean air and water, provision for beaches and lakes and parks—these causes draw a dependable measure of support from good men and women everywhere, but animals unseen, whose wish is to steer clear of mankind, get less attention. Hunters do fret about them, however, keeping tabs on the toll the winter snows take, and the relentless shrinkage of open land. Hunters miss the moose and mountain lions and pass along rumors that a handful still somehow survive here in the Northeast. Besides, hunters are folk who like to walk half a dozen miles before having lunch, to get their feet wet, pant up the ledges and draws, cook over a fire, and perhaps finally haul a load of meat home on their backs; and they take their ration of blood as they find it, in a natural fashion, not transmogrified onto the TV. Hunters are as attentive as the predator animals to the habits of what they are after; and some of them want visible proof on the wall of what they got for their trouble—the taxidermist does this for them. In some ways his work resembles an undertaker's, with the congenial difference that he needn't hurry or pretend to be sad.

In the window of his shop is an old display of two newborn bear cubs, bleached white by the sun, sitting in a tiny boat on a pond. The pond is represented by a sheet of plastic, with realistic-looking trout underneath. There are also some dusty pheasants and ducks, their colors dead now. But the splendor inside is undeniable—deep, virile black hides of bears seized at the prime, just before they would have dug in for a winter's sleep. These are stacked in piles, glossy, blue-black, and there are other mounds of orange and caribou-colored deer hides. Visiting, I was surprised at the number of tools along the workbench: fleshing and cartilage knives, saws and scalpels in rows, pliers, pincers, hammers and mallets, bone snippers and scrapers, curved sewing needles, forceps, punches, drills, picking tools, tweezers, stiff wires. The plywood tables are big enough for him to stretch out a nine-foot skin to dry after it has been soaked in the tanning tub and washed in fresh water. The soaking goes on for six weeks or so—he has sacks of alum, which is the main ingredient in the pickling acid. There is salt in quantity too, for drying the flesh side of the skins when they first arrive, and plaster of paris, and sacks of grainy roof-insulation material which is used to thicken the plaster of paris.

Ideally, the taxidermist is given the skull of the animal along with the hide, if a head job is wanted, not simply the flat tanned skin. After boiling the skull until all the meat has fallen away, he rebuilds the original shape of the head by thumbing plaster into the grooves and cavities on the skull so that the skin fits over it again as neatly as before. For deer, whose jaws and teeth are not to be emphasized, he doesn't need more than the skull's top plate, where the antlers attach, but a carnivore is most realistically mounted when the teeth that you see are the real teeth, not hoked up from wax in an oversized jaw. He restructures the underpart of a deer's face by whittling a small block of cedar or basswood, though of course he could buy entire preformed heads made of papier-mâché from the wholesalers—heads of moose, deer, or the numerous and various African antelopes. A ready-made jaguar's wax mouth and paper skull costs only about $12. A set of artificial porcelain teeth is $5.95 for a tiger and $1.95 for a coyote, because these are higher-quality than wax.

He could buy rubber noses by the gross as well, but usually he molds the animal's nose out of putty, attaching it to the snout that he shaped from wood or from plaster of paris and painting it black. Each ear is a piece of soft lead bent so that the skin slips onto it alertly. The eyes are glass; and he has a watchmaker's cabinet of compartments and drawers filled with fox eyes, owl eyes, loon eyes, lynx eyes, coon eyes, lion eyes, snake eyes. Some are veined or show lifelike white corners and carefully differentiate iris and pupil. The catalogue lists twenty-eight sizes, from a buffalo's down to a hummingbird's, and there are cheapjack economy grades, eight pairs for a dollar. He can buy rubber tongues, set into a roll like a wolf's tongue, but unless he is rushed he carves his from wood. He glues the tongue inside the skull, and the lips, gums, and roof of the mouth he forms out of wax and then paints them the correct color. Next, he sews and pins the eyelids and cheeks into an appropriate expression and whittles a frame for the neck. He likes to whittle—that basic craft—first using a drawknife, later a delicate spokeshaver, such as wagon wheels used to be carved with. When only wadding is needed, as for stuffing squirrels and birds, excelsior serves very well, or cotton batting. A bad craftsman would insert the filler as if he were stuffing a cushion, but it's best to wind it tightly first into a credible stance and tie it with thread for permanence. He polishes and lacquers the hooves of the deer and blows with a bellows at the game birds to clean their feathers. Songbirds are wired into a pert pose, wings outspread or beak pointed left; wires bore down through their legs to the varnished perch.

Many droll requests come from customers, surpassing the sort of ideas an undertaker encounters. Some people want blinking lights installed in the eyeholes of the lynx that they've shot. Or they'll put their house thermometer in a deer's leg; they'll want a fat mother porcupine stuffed conventionally but with the fetuses found inside her embalmed in a talcum-powder bottle like little rolled-up human babies. A local minister who had served as a missionary in Africa brought back the ears and a foot of an elephant he had shot, and a souvenir strip of leg skin like hard bark. Sometimes a hotel man will buy a pair of bear cubs a farmer has

killed and, under the general umbrella of humor, ask that they
be preserved in a standing position on their hind legs to hold
the ashtrays in the lobby. ("Oh, pardon me, little sir, may I use
you?")

Understand that I'm making a figurative investigation—the
animals native to Vermont which have survived so far are not in
danger of quick extinction. The end of subsistence farming has
worked to their advantage, and, paradoxically, before the farmers
appeared and cleared the land, the Indians of nearby Canada had
called this section of New England the Desert because the unfelled
timber grew so thick that game was scarce. Still, these modest
creatures—flittering does fleeing with a peahen's squawking cry,
a pony's hoofbeats, and a carousel motion; porcine black bears rooting for mushrooms, rooting for grubs; and all the parade of back-
field inhabitants, like the varying hares which explode through the
ferns and the fire cherry and in winter turn white and nibble iron-
wood nuts—represent the much bigger ghosts of creatures gone.

Taxidermy, or the notion of saving the scalp, horns, and teeth
of game, goes along with a fairly advanced stage of settlement.
The frontiersmen and homesteaders hunted for meat—it was labor to them, it was feeding the family; other than furs to dress
themselves in, they didn't often keep tokens. The Indians, having
evolved a game-oriented religion and culture, were more likely
to save an especially superb big skull, but they also killed for use
and didn't go in for tricking the animal up as a mannequin. The
practice of mounting heads to hang on the wall developed only
as the white towns became county seats, long after the first arti-
sans like blacksmiths and carpenters had arrived, when hunters
became "sportsmen." Earlier, a fellow might throw a phenomenal
skin embodying the memories of real risk and adventure up on
the cabin roof to freeze and dry; he might even salt it. By and by
the sun would convert the flesh side to a brown board, and it
would be tacked in the entryway—that was the taxidermy.

Once in the old gold town of Barkerville, British Columbia,
I was talking to a prospector and his wife, both over seventy-five.
Their serenity and good cheer were plain; wilderness gardening
had obviously agreed with them, so had the solitude, and there
was no counting the tonnage of creek sand that they must have
panned in a lifetime. But what brought the sense of their achievement home to me as they talked was suddenly to notice two ante-
diluvian grizzly hides hanging in the hallway just behind them:
from floor to ceiling, a plush chestnut brown with darker shades.
A basketball player could have enveloped himself in either one
with room to spare. Apparently both husband and wife had shot

other bears, but had happened to save these. They didn't mention them until I did, and as with every other keepsake they had, didn't stress or boast about the circumstances, just said that the bears had strayed within range on their creek in different years and had seemed to be taking up a settled abode. On a whole host of topics that we touched on, the skins completed what was unsaid.

I'm not against keeping trophies if they define or somehow enlarge the possessor, if they're taken seriously, and if they memorialize the animal world, besieged and warranted for an early death as it surely is. Old dirt farmers and mild-mannered old taxidermists are outdated too; they will go the way of the wildlife soon. (There is another taxidermist in town, a retired fellow with pouchy cheeks, an upright posture, and a face like a squirrel, who keeps his first-prize ribbons from the state fairs of 1911 and 1913 under glass.) This business of my friend's employs three generations. All day outdoorsmen, wearing red shirts or hip boots, drop in and talk, and he and his son and the young boy, scraping the flesh from a black wolf's legs, listen in. They throw sawdust on the floor and handle the beasts that arrive as farmers do their own butchered stock—it lives to live but it lives to be shot. The older man has hunted moose in northern Quebec that put all these little buck deer in the shade, so he's got photographs of the vanished big stuff. When he talks it's always of hunting and game: knolls and ledges to scale, ravines to bypass, and openings which open up as you reach them. Game is like vastly enlivened farm stock; you study it, wish it well, go for the prize.

Along the walls there are shelves of skulls, tagged for insertion into the bear skins which are being prepared. When the skins are tanned, repairs are made—holes sewn up, bald spots touched over with paint or patched with scraps from another skin. The claws are cleaned, the blemishes concealed, and the obligatory pained-looking snarl, which the animal seldom wore while it was alive, is inscribed on the face. Bear rugs cost the clientele 25 dollars per square foot nowadays, and in a year the shop gets up to seventy of them to work on, though last fall was an unlucky one for hunters because the mast crop was sparse and scattered and a heavy, early snowfall put all the bears in Vermont to bed ahead of time (an estimated thirty-five hundred live in the state). Also, by late November upwards of two hundred deer have been brought in, the floor is heaped high with salted skins, antlers are lying all over the place. Some people want the deer's feet mounted on a plaque under the head and set with an upward poke, to be utilized as a gun rack. The workroom has samples of this arrangement nailed to the walls, and big moose feet, and a great moose head is exhibited, with its pendulous bell, long-suffering ears, and primeval superstructure, bony, leaf-shaped. There's a lovely gray bobcat hanging head down, and a stuffed horned owl, a goshawk, some quail, some black ducks, a Canada goose, a pouter pigeon, two mink, a fox skin, beaver kits, the unfinished head of a coyote with its lips and eyes intricately pinned, and a yearling bear posed standing up, holding a pair of field glasses, as if to help it see better next time.

Snapshots of big men and downed bear, of deer sprawled on the ground and hunters squatting, are tacked on the wall. About fifteen thousand deer a year are killed in Vermont, almost two per square mile, although only one hunter in ten who buys a license is successful in making a kill. The out-of-state hunters do a little bit better statistically, strangely enough, maybe because they're at it full-time while they're here. Then during the winter perhaps just as many deer starve to death. The deer that we see in the north are still healthy-looking, though there are very few predators left who can prune the herds in a natural fashion, taking the weaker individuals so that the wintering areas are not overgrazed. Bobcats have become scarce because they are hunted year-round, and bobcats aren't really up to the task anyway. Eventually our deer are expected to shrink to the wizened proportions of some of their cousins in southern Vermont or southerly New England, where often the bucks can't even muster the strength to sprout antlers and the fawns that they father are comparably frail—most being shot within the first two or three years of life, in any case. What with the game diminishing in grandeur, the short hunting seasons, and complicated regulations, a talented old-fashioned hunter finds his style crimped. For want of any better game, he exercises himself by hunting coons or the few other small surviving predators. One fellow in town, who runs the school buses, a lanky, devoted, preeminent hunter who probably was born too late, goes after bobcats with dogs every weekend all winter, patrolling the snowy deer yards, believing that he is protecting the deer. Bobcats have diminutive chests; they can dash in a burst of speed but soon must get into a tree if the hounds are close, not being equipped for a distance race. A photo shows him with seventeen of the creatures hammered frozen to the side of his house, each with clenched paws and a grimace. He collected the ten-dollar bounty on each, cutting off the tails, and threw the bodies on the town dump.

There is a furred compendium on the tables, a dukedom in furs, not only raccoons and otter and bucks, but skins from the West—grizzly and cougar—as if the supply would never run out. All around

the top of the room dozens of black-and-white tails are fastened—
these the white-tail deer tails which they flip up to warn one another
when they have cause to bolt, and which they wag vigorously in the
fly season, just as a horse does. Almost every evening I watch deer in
my field, their coats as red as a red fox. They snort with the sharp
sound of a box dropped. Sometimes you only see their tall ears,
in a V, the late sunlight shining through pinkly. Originally, a
hundred or more years ago, only a moose trail and horse trail
wound past where I live. It is exceptionally moosey country,
with ponds, mountains, lakes and bogs—country that cries out for
moose, in fact. Moose love water. When hard pressed by wolves,
they will spend the whole winter knee-deep in a pond, standing
close to where a spring comes in and the water won't freeze; and
in the summer, browsing on the bottom, they wade out so far in
search of water plants that they finally get in over their heads
and push up the tips of their noses every few minutes. The huge
bulls, however, are a sight surpassing the vision one had of them,
transcending the mind's inventions. You would think that when
they caught sight of themselves reflected on the surface of a smooth
lake they would be frightened.

Even the bank in town has the head of a moose fixed to the
wall, as a remembrance of the old days. It looks like the head of
a horse or a cow poking through the half-door of a stable. And
looking at it, I get the benign sense of good existing in the world
that I have sometimes when I look at a cow—those big ears thrust
forward, and those big eyes, as if we all have at least two ways of
communicating with each other in this world: sound and sight. A
youngster came into the bank while I was there and stared for a
long time at the moose head. After a while he went to the door
and tried to go through to the other side so he could see the rest
of the animal. To begin with, they had to tell him it wasn't alive.

A Run
of Bad Luck

Bad ions in the air, bad stars, or bad luck: call it what you will—a run of bad luck, in fact. I was driving down the Thruway in Vermont to consult a doctor in New York, and hit a deer. Didn't see the deer till the impact, sharing its surprise. Deer, unlike domestic animals, are afraid of cars and leap as you pass, either into you or away. It lay in the deep grass, heaving like a creature stranded on the beach.

Sure enough, as befitted the omen, in New York City the doctor's news was bad. Then within a day or two, Pier 50, a huge ramshackle structure across the street from where I live, caught fire and burned hectically for seven hours, although surrounded by fireboats, as only an abandoned pier can. The neighborhood was layered in smoke for a couple of days—for me, acrid testimony to what the doctor had said. There were also a few of the usual New York hang-up phone calls, and then, as if to push me into a sump of depression, somebody—a vandal aroused by the fire, or someone who thought I had parked in his parking space—poured sugar into the gas tank of my car, not enough to destroy the engine but enough so that I returned to Vermont in relief.

In the meantime, my mother, in another city, had gone into the hospital for surgery, and one evening that week my daughter and I were out walking along a wooded road (I was carrying her on my shoulders), when a car passing another car bore down on us at high speed, its roar not easy to distinguish from that of the slower one; I barely heard it in time. This, in the context of the other incidents, particularly shook me because it seemed to bear a hint of malevolence; I felt very small. Then, within days, my next-door neighbor there, an old man as close as a relative to us, died of a stroke. Another good friend and country mentor went into the hospital after a heart attack. News came from New York as well that a friend in the city had killed herself. I marshaled a motley assortment of tranquilizers and sleeping pills left over from the past—divorce, career crisis, other bad occasions. I had that feeling of luck running out, that I must be *very careful*, although, on the contrary, I was becoming deadened, not alert. At such a time, the opposite of invulnerable, one must take care to move in a gingerly fashion and not get so rattled that an accident happens. I had considered myself a sort of a Sunday's child much of my life, but suddenly intimations of death and calamity were all about.

I remembered talking to a woman who had survived a snow-slide by swimming along on the surface while whooshing downhill for a hundred yards—as people caught in an undertow or even in quicksand save themselves by flattening out and floating if they can. Just so, I should ride the current until it turned. The best advice I have heard on bearing pain is to fix one's mind upon the idea that the pain is in one place—the other side of the room—and that you are in another; then, where you are, play cards or whatever. Cooking, fooling with my daughter, I realized more distinctly than at any time in years that although my life was not really at stake right now, I believed in some form of reincarnation or immortality—this a conviction, not a wish. I pray in airplanes during takeoff, but it is with a sense of praying *pro forma,* as if the location of my belief weren't really there, but were more generalized, in a bigger God. There are ideas central to society which we seldom question in order that society will hold together—as, for instance, the notion basic to medical care that everybody has a contribution to make, or "a right to life." But there are other conceptions, such as the idea of God, which we disparage and scarcely consider, until later, smiling sheepishly in our mind's eye as if we had disputed the fact that the moon moves in the sky, we admit to having been wrong, and to having known all along that we were wrong.

Once, highborn ladies would flee to a convent if some unnerving sequence of events overtook them, not necessarily taking orders, but resting, collecting their wits. And when they strolled in the cloister around a bubbling fountain, the walkway itself possessed a soothing, perpetual quality, with each right-angle turn leading straight to another. Walking for many hours, they looked at the lindenwood saints, the robust faces—at the Virgin's implacable verve, or else at a dolor portrayed with an equally saving exaggeration. Coincidentally, I went to New York's own Cloisters, and because the reality of each bad event had been dulled by the others, it was for me one of those queer times when people recognize how much they can adjust to—how quickly, for example, they could settle into the routine of life in a prison camp.

Of course I had my daughter to entertain, and in the country I walked in the woods, watching the aspens quake (said by legend to occur because Christ's cross was of aspen). I have an old army siren, hand-cranked, that I climbed with up on the mountain at twilight, to persuade a family of coyotes nearby to answer. I was relieved that the random incidents seemed to have ended. I thought of two friends in the city who had recently suffered crises—heart attacks at forty. One fellow, as the pain surged through him, found himself muttering stubbornly, "No groveling, Death!" When he was out of danger he wrote seventy-some letters to friends from his hospital bed, each with a numbered series of thoughts directed to the recipient. The other man is that rare case where one can put a finger exactly on the characteristics of which one is so fond. He married the same woman twice. Although it didn't work out either time, she was well worth marrying twice, and to my way of thinking this showed that he was at once a man of fervent, rash, abiding love, and yet a person of flexibility, ready to admit an error and to act to correct it.

Both my mother and country mentor were now on the mend, and my own doctor reported good news. Prospects began looking up. What I'd gained from the period, besides a flood of relief, was the memory of how certain I'd been that the intricacy and brilliance of life cannot simply fold up with one's death—that, as in the metaphor of a fountain, or the great paradigm of rain and the ocean, it sinks down but comes up, blooms up and sinks down again.

Heart's
Desire

Of all the poignant ways to earn a living, one that seems most affecting in this well-clothed age is when somebody undresses and tries to win fame and fortune by presenting to us his body. The "strong back," mocked by the brainy for centuries and now by the machine, is an endangered animal. As for prizefighting—two people bashing each other for our delectation—it's almost too barefaced to be believed. So is the whole carry-over, the outrageous labor relations, the predatory eating—three-pound sirloin steaks—the tax men crouching in the wings, and the stars floating in a balloon in the comic strips to signify a knockout—that not merely symbolic death, but a near approach, like sniffing too much glue.

In the American Dream one socks one's way to success, and here is a man who is doing just that, bloodying the loser, puffing up his face, leaving him for dead. Fight fans congregate in the arcades under the arena before entering, eyeing each other for sudden shifts of fortune (ups and downs are what fighting is all about), and watching the retired boxers, now rather chapfallen, and the columnists, the gamblers, the tanned well-heeled fellows with their women who like to rub shoulders with the fight crowd three or four times a year. Right alongside the fat ticket holders with rings on their pinkies who've made some sort of KO in the world are harried scalpers, who dodge among them, barely eluding arrest, and maybe part of the best of it for some of these prosperous guys in the good seats is knowing that, however much in earnest the victor is, the entire production is a joke on him. He's taken the injunction literally. He's too dumb to know that one can't actually *sock* one's way to success—that isn't how it's done—and so his shambling victory dance in the ring, when he thinks he is "champion of the world," is the dance of a dunce. Even during his moment of victory he's a loser as well; he's getting nowhere,

a champion only in Harlem. From the vantage point of the specta-
tor, it's heads I win and tails you lose.

But there are also plenty of likable boxing fans, especially,
as with other sports, those who resemble hobbyists. Hobbyists
are people who allow a few chinks in their city armor to show,
gathering together for the sake of their enthusiasm and revealing,
whether diffidently or in raucous tones, something of what they
really live for. One hears a combo of them blowing Dixieland
down in a cellar, sees them with cameras in Inwood Park, hears
about "frog and toad freaks" from a pet-store owner, reads news
of medallion collectors deep in the *Times,* and of the volunteers
who varnish each new acquisition at the South Street Seaport.
Some cycle, or sing hymns or just explore New York as a hobby—
knowing about the chocolate and coffee stores on Christopher
Street, the bums who fry slabs of pork over a blaze in a barrel on
Gansevoort after the wholesale butchers there close up.

Fifteen years ago boxing fans were like that. They'd go to
Stillman's Gym to watch Isaac Logart or Joey Giardello work out—
pay fifty cents, chat with the trainers, nod to the fighter himself.
These private excursions were necessary for a fan who wished
to go far with the sport because it was so corrupt that several of
the best fighters were never seen outside a gym—at least not till
their sharpness was gone and they wouldn't derail anybody the
smart money was in league with. Such wastage might be impossible today because there's less talent around, but the best
fighter I ever saw was a light heavyweight named Harold Johnson. Though he was finally permitted to try for the championship in 1961 and won, by then fifteen years had passed since he'd
started fighting, and seven years since he'd last fought someone
of championship caliber, and he was past his prime. I managed
to watch him during the middle 1950s by going to South Philadelphia and finding a certain empty flat over a vacant store in
a sunny slum square where this superb dynamo was sparring. He
was laughing because of his own speed and strength, even though
only three or four of us were witness to what a panther he was.
Archie Moore wouldn't fight Johnson for fear of losing the title;
the other contenders wouldn't sign with him lest he knock them
out of contention; the up-and-comers were avoiding him because
he would blight their careers—so that long years of waiting were
in the offing. Yet he was at such a peak that he couldn't help
laughing.

The gym was also the place to be in the case of dizzy youngsters who were being overmatched and trained up for slaughter.

Sugar Hart, another Philadelphia fighter, a welterweight as slim and vain as a girl, was such a one. Just as the isolation of Philadelphia may have helped to smother Johnson's career, so it favored building Hart up. Nobody saw him, but they heard that in Philly he was looking very good. He chalked up knockouts and got on TV, until everybody was willing to fight him—the comers because his name would look fine on a list of victories, and the better contenders because he represented a payday they needn't fear. So, very soon, overmatched, he got into some fast company, got smashed and smashed again, till the fanciness, the eagerness, the confidence and the vanity were crushed. But in the gym, among friends, this hadn't happened as yet. Here, for the interested fan, was talent and youth, assurance and innocence, quick feet, stylish hands.

Boxing is a waning sport, not turning silver-plated as so many sports have. There would be no dearth of fans if there were more excellence, but what hope can there be that in the America which we foresee people will trouble themselves to fight for money that can be had much more easily? Fewer fighters mean fewer gyms, and fewer fans in them. The best left in New York is the Gramercy Gym, "Home of Champions," on Fourteenth Street a few doors from Luchow's restaurant, among the diamond buyers and chow-mein places, next to a discount store called Straight from the Crate. Floyd Patterson trained here and later Jose Torres, during the years that their manager, Cus D'Amato, operated it. Yellow, black, and red posters paper the walls, announcing historical events starring such luminaries as Frankie Ryff, Sonny Liston, Buster Mathis—fights at the Roseland Ballroom in Taunton, Mass., the Jersey City Armory, the Alexandria Roller Rink, and Sunnyside and Madison Square Gardens.

The Gramercy Gym is two flights up some littered, lightless stairs that look like a muggers' paradise, though undoubtedly they are the safest stairs in New York. Inside, two dozen bodies are chopping up and down, self-clocked, each fellow cottoned in his dreams. Some are skipping rope, turbaned in towels, wrapped in robes in order to sweat. These are white-looking figures, whereas the men who are about to spar have on dark headguards that close grimly around the face like an executioner's hood. There are floor-length mirrors and mattresses for exercising and rubdowns, and two speedbags banging like drums, and three heavy bags swinging even between the rounds with the momentum of more than a decade of punches. The bell is loud, the fighters jerk like eating and walking birds, hissing through their teeth as they punch, their feet sneakering the floor with shuffly sounds. They wear red shoelaces in white shoes, and peanut-colored gloves, or if they're Irish the gloves are green. They are learning to move their feet to the left and right, to move in and out, punching over, then under an opponent's guard, and other repetitive skills without which a man in the ring becomes a man of straw. The speed bags teach head-punching, the heavy bags teach body work, and one bag pinned to the wall has both a head and torso diagrammed, complete with numbers, so that the trainer can shout out what punches his fighter should throw. "Bounce, bounce!" the trainers yell.

There are mongooses and poleaxes, men who hog the floor with an aggressive stance, men whose heavy arms flip out of a clinch like a thick tunafish. The room is L-shaped with a rickety ring set in the L, and so crowded that one might infer that the sport is thriving, though most of the young fighters speak Spanish now. Chu-Chu Malave, a promising welterweight of twenty-one with hard fists and a 15–3 record, has girl-length hair that he ties in a rubber band when he is fighting; and he trains in a shirt with Bach's head on it. He is an acting student, lives in the East Village, and seems touching and young. Another boy wears an "Alaska Hiway" shirt and lizard-green shoes. He sucks in a mouthful of water and spurts it out grandly. Everybody is trying to sock his way upwards through life, but they are divided between those who prefer to fight while moving forward and those who like to fight as they move back. Naturally, then, the arena matchmakers will try to pair a man from group A with one from group B.

In the ring the spittle flies when the punches connect and the real rumbles start. Gym fighters sometimes don't look quite as good under the kleig lights, and sometimes are never given much chance to fight anywhere else—the "animals" down in Philadelphia, who are left to rot in their gyms and fight their hearts out where nobody can see them, are still joked about—so everybody likes to look good at least here.

The king of the Gramercy Gym is Carlos Ortiz, a blocky lightweight who has been fighting professionally for seventeen years. He was the champ in 1962–65 and 1965–68, retiring the next year, but in 1971 began a comeback. He has fought four or five tune-up appearances in the same number of months, and the word is that although he may have lost his legs, he has not lost his punch. He sports a red headguard, baggy blue sweatpants, and an NMU shirt, has a nose that looks bobbed because of all the violence wreaked upon it, and fights as watchfully as a lathe operator bending to a machine. It is perhaps this attentiveness that's so overwhelming. But with the youngsters he is gentle, pulling every punch even as he shovels their resistance aside and swarms over them. (I thought of the legendary way wolf cubs took on their lupine form, licked into shape by the tongues of their mothers.) Then he leaves for the day with a gorgeous redhead with a million curls.

It's a career that's naked to the world—just the simple matter of wins versus losses, the vitality or lack of it observed exactly by a horde of thousands. And there is no disguising the cruelty of the losses; the crowd has watched the man nearly get killed, jeering and pitying him, shaking their heads with a chuckle. Only a series of savage beatings awaits the fighter as he approaches his middle years, the doctors sardonically stitching his eyelids. Maybe this is what makes these personalities so unassuming when you sit down with them. I was eavesdropping on the interviews done by Vic Ziegel, the *New York Post*'s boxing specialist, and watching the managers handle their fighters, wiping a hand across the face of a black man to find out how much he was sweating, then slapping him lightly like a horse if it seemed not enough. When this happened, the kids who hadn't yet proved themselves withdrew into a private smile, their dreams of glory someday, when they might cut a swath. Floyd Patterson's simon-pure teenaged face looked out from the wall above this inscription: "Congratulations to America's greatest boxing expert" (unnamed). "Your prediction of my success is a great encouragement to me. I shall try to keep your record perfect."

Walter Seeley is a roofer and a featherweight who commutes every day after work from Long Island to train. He has a victim's gutsy tired face, a bear-it grin, and has suffered only one loss in thirty fights. A career assessment of him would say that not only aren't the fans very much interested in his weight division (the featherweight limit is 126 pounds), but there are very few fighters competing in the same class outside the Far East.

Bobby Cassidy is a left-handed middleweight, a bar owner and marathon runner who also comes in all the way from Long Island. He's had fifty-four fights in eight years, losing just twelve, has had good management, and was ranked tenth in his class once. His nose, however, looks double-parked, his eyes are recessed, and he bleeds easily. Being left-handed probably helped him early in his career because other young fighters were baffled by that factor and he has good fists and good underneath shots, but is not much for strategy. He is black-haired, fun-loving, yet oddly quixotic, and impressed me as a lovely man riding along on a battered wide smile that might carry him through almost anything.

Dan McAloon has milk-white legs, an amused, mustached face, squaring into a beard, and teaches phys ed at a private school. Sometimes he brings his wife and baby to the gym to watch him train. By last year, at twenty-eight, he'd worked up a string of nice showings, including two at Madison Square Garden that earned him a bout with Emile Griffith. Griffith, who is the last of three marvelous Cuban fighters (he was Isaac Logart's protégé, as Logart was Kid Gavilan's), was welterweight champion for a number of years, and gave him a boxing lesson, beating him painfully. Then another former welter champ, Billy Backus, outpointed him badly and humblingly at Syracuse. But he has offers from Italy and the West Coast.

Benny Huertas has been an up-and-down fighter since 1964. Recently he'd accumulated a string of wins, then was knocked out in the first round. Shook up by that, he lost twice more and is only now springing back, fighting well in France. He is another heedful lightweight, weaving, protecting his face like a purse.

Tom Kocan is a dishwasher, a heavyweight with a thin face but an unsettling right hand. Lonely-looking in a lonely sport, he fights best late in a bout when exhausted and loose.

Smoky Roy Edmonds at twenty-four is soft-spoken, hopeful, endearing. He runs on the horse path in Central Park every morning, fueled by his aspirations. He was sidetracked by two automobile accidents last year but is waiting now for his manager, who is a guard at Sing Sing, to finally arrange for him to appear in Madison Square Garden in a preliminary for the first time.

The gym is a period piece, as authentic as rope, and these people bring it alive. For their pains, their long months of training, they are paid $150 for fighting four rounds at the Garden, and $50 or $75 at the lesser showplaces where most bouts take place. For a six-rounder the fee jumps to $500—$100 or $150 elsewhere— an increase due more to the punishing competition accompanying the jump than the number of rounds. At Sunnyside Garden in Queens, a famous old club where all boxers fight eventually, the men in the main event get about $1,000 apiece, as an advance against 10 percent of the gate. The manager takes one-third, and since even wrestling outdraws boxing today, the prices have not changed in twenty years. One night I went to see Bobby Cassidy battle an awkward, stubby rock of a barroom brawler named Gil Diaz, whose middle-aged legs soon gave out and who even before then hadn't dared take the chance of sitting down between rounds.

Eight hundred and ninety-five people had paid $4,950 at the Sunnyside box office. The promoter barely broke even.

Beforehand, Vic Ziegel and I ate supper with Cassidy's manager, Paddy Flood, and his previous manager too, an antique dealer named Al Braverman, both of them enthusiasts and former fighters. A scout from Madison Square Garden was there, and the *Daily News* man was expected as well. As the sport sinks, these hands gather around and retell the myths, the bad-guy stories: how the best time to pay off your fighter after a fight is as you walk away from the arena in the dark of the night. You count his share of the money into his hand, and exhausted, cut, beaten up anyway, and what with the bad light, he doesn't know what he is getting. They all seemed like decent men, however, exhilarated like kids as fight time approached—this stuff was for the sake of the mystique. Braverman talked about "the chills" he'd gotten during the great sequences of a fight last week, though he's been watching prizefights for forty years. Paddy Flood, Ziegel, and I had driven out from Manhattan with an off-duty cop, a friend of Flood's who beat the stoplights and drove up on the sidewalk and made U-turns and used every other trick to twist through the usual jams. On First Avenue we saw a man with a chimpanzee in his car and hooted at him. We saw Johnny Carson, ferret-like in a red sweater, dodging on foot between stalled cars. The cop began telling celebrity stories, and we yelled out the window at Carson, "Hey, Johnny. Hey, Johnny," until he turned. Then, happy as clams, we hollered at him, "FUCK YOU, JOHNNY CARSON!"

Cassidy won by a technical knockout in the fourth round. I got the impression that the other fighter had been accepted as a match for him on the assumption that Cassidy would be able to dispose of him around this midpoint. Cassidy sat panting, smiling and toweling his face in the dressing room while we questioned him, adhering to the tradition that newsmen seldom speak to the loser. Smoky Roy Edmonds had won his preliminary bout by a knockout too, and he and the fellow he'd beaten were placed knee to knee in another dingy, narrow room as we listened to him softly voice his heart's desire about where he wanted to go from here. It wasn't so different from casually congratulating any man who has had some success, except that the smiles directed by the spectators to the loser are rather as if a good joke had been played on him, instead of his just having died in effigy.

That's it, I suppose. Lose in boxing and you are a joke; win and sooner or later you are a joke also. It's a kind of extravagant burlesque of the course of anybody's career, even of life itself. The fighter who fights too long looks into the mirror one day and realizes that his face has gradually been transformed by the pounding into a skull.

The Lapping,
Itchy Edge
of Love

We're to have a baby soon. I can feel him
bang my wife's stomach, and already, even before he is born, we're
losing sleep and discombobulated. During the night M. shifts in
discomfort from the bed to the sofa and back, although her face is
at a pitch of beauty much of the time, and occasionally we're
seized with momentary panic that the event is now. Since we have
not been married long, the pregnancy has brought us into an instant intimacy. We're hanging pictures and buying the furniture
we hadn't bothered with earlier; a dozen times a day I nuzzle her—
"Into the lion's mouth!" I say. Sometimes her belly seems very
large, and that's a little alarming, but sometimes it seems to grow
smaller and that's depressing. M. wears loose sweaters so that she
can pull the neck open and look directly down her front, talking
to him. I claim that he's a frog jumping under a towel, but she says
his movements are like oatmeal slowly, irregularly bubbling—a
cooking sensation—unless he stands painfully on her spleen. A
woman in the prenatal class at the hospital startled the group by
confessing she couldn't tell the difference between her baby's stirrings and gas. The instructor ignored this and returned to the subject of pushing: "Think vagina." Putting on diaperlike pads, the
women lay on their backs, opened their legs, and practiced the exercise: push, push and blow; push, push and blow. "Push, Mrs.
Winograd. You're not pushing."

Alone, we make babies of one another in preparation for the
baby, or M. will poke her stomach sharply and stare intently at it,
as if she can see through to inside. She pushes her stomach against
me or lies on the couch wiggling her feet, but I tell her that she's too
fat to kiss; I tell her the only reason she's still beautiful and hasn't

turned from beauty into beast is that I've kissed her so much in the past.

This is my first baby, but not my first marriage. Both marriages began in neurotic confusion and a sense of impasse, though they were honest in the fact that love quickly grew. Usually people love because they want to; we love when we're ready to love, which, as often as not, is when we think we have reached a dead end. There is also that agitating wait for the chance meeting—the meeting some people wait for their whole lives long—but unless we're ready to marry we're not likely to, no matter whom we manage to meet. As we climb in and out of bedrooms and run to parties, we're partly ransacking ourselves for the potential to tarry awhile and not lose hope or lose our temper or our trust.

Since, at first, love includes such a dose of the urgencies, in the weeks before the wedding ceremony one comes back and comes back to see that this really *is* the right person and that the marriage isn't simply being jumped into because each of you feels boxed in. M.'s mother, a widow for many years, married again shortly before we did, so she and her mother were mirroring one another's emotions. For my part, I'd thought ever since my divorce that I'd thrown my first marriage away carelessly, arrogantly, ignorantly, and so I'd been eagerly awaiting my chance to try again. That had been the blundering marriage of one's twenties; this was the marriage of which much is hoped.

On our wedding morning we spoke over the phone on tiptoe, not wanting to upset anything. Then the happiness, the confidence, the chatter afterwards—*at last*—and the exuberance of the word "wife." I knew I was giving myself more wholeheartedly than before, with less wariness and self-distrust. I'd had four years of bachelorhood between marriages and was sick of it: I realized again how sick when I went on a business trip for several weeks, returning unexpectedly, and found the apartment a mess: earrings on the floor, dust in puffs, tumbled clothes. I'm a neatness bug, but this disorder just seemed like delicious complexity.

We had a short, auspicious honeymoon, with Edwardian meals, champagne, flowers, and strolls in the park, where I talked through the bars to the Bengal tigers in their own language by way of indicating my competence as a bridegroom. Now we own a wine-red Parego baby carriage and wait for the sea change which is under way. It's a peculiarly vulnerable juncture, like the month before one goes into the army, when every hearty soul who has preceded you is an authority on what you ought to expect. The natural-childbirth people speak of the penultimate pleasure which their program of yoga builds up to, while in the opposite camp are the jumpy women who confide to M. that labor is brutal beyond describing. Most people do neither; they simply say by the light in their faces that the childbearing years are about as gay as any they can remember. We're told, incidentally, that our Jeremy (as we think of him) is going to be a girl, because the heartbeat is strong and steady and the outline of M.'s stomach is generally round, not humpy, although as big as a pumpkin.

For the time being the preludes of sex bore me—the whole repetitive preoccupation with the next pair of bobbledeboobs. It's probably part of the conditioning for fatherhood, but it should enable me to set down some erotica without wetting the page. Of course everything is fluids—kissing is fluids, babies are fluids, having a baby is fluids. Thank God a shapeless being is going to emerge instead of somebody already formed—a little loan shark or a beauty queen. In the pudginess is a new beginning. One woman I know has relegated sex to oblivion by another means. She is in residence at a famous group-therapy center on the West Coast where hugging is the path to the godhead, and she pays her way by giving massages, herself naked. I can see her among her customers, all of them male, because she's a peachy-cheeked, moist-lipped person, tall, big-figured and energetic, always a searcher, always in earnest, and rather chaste. The week her divorce became final she cut her hair off, but she may have grown it out again. I see her struggling with the bodily cholers of the man of the hour, who now over-, now under-reacts. At this center the patient is encouraged to holler. It hurts him a bit, but the obstructive ego is gradually dislodged.

As a boy I too was taught to try to cut down on being self-centered, though the method was merely for me to try to quit using the pronoun "I." When writing home from camp, I would scan my letter, notice how often "I" occurred, and cross it out wherever I could, changing the sentence structure or implying the word. We're all told to be less selfish, that we must love as well as be loved, but I was slow. After a late entry into the world of sex, it was my satisfaction during my twenties to see a brief succession of women fall into involvements with me. I watched and did my best to help it happen and then, like a kindly pasha, would try to make it easy for them. Only after the fact did the sensations of love or despair or scrupulous empathy penetrate me.

Madness is the main fear we have nowadays, and even ahead of the immediacies of love, my relations with women have been full of apprehension on this score: fear that my mother was going crazy, fear of derangement in my first wife, and in my second, although less so. If I've not cared for a woman, I've still managed to wonder once in a while whether she was going nuts; I just haven't been as rattled by the possibility. None of my dire premonitions has ever come true, and, needless to say, I've doubted my own mind as well; but the sterility of being engrossed this way makes my thirty-some years seem years of skimming—a bumbling, problematical passage which, while it has taken a long time to live, sometimes appears more like a rehearsal for life than a life actually being lived. Even sexually it seems to me I am inexperienced, because there is a deadly sameness to my history: accepting love as soon as it's offered, growing very exacting and bossy, but later in a curious turnabout becoming submissive and boylike, a sort of "mother's helper," as one girl put it, until the affair reached its indifferent end, whereupon I could exercise my talent for tender regret.

I think that most people feel inexperienced in love and sex. Either they've loved only one woman and wistfully envy the mustachioed philanderer, or else they've philandered themselves and wish that they'd been deep and true. How the world admires the staunch old fellow who has seen his wife through thick and thin, raised his family, and never once looked to the side. But how it cherishes the old reprobate too—the rake of seventy-three who still has a gleam in his eye, who loved 'em up and wet his wick and left 'em high and dry! Most of us can admit that we started off pretty well, with a doting father and hovering mother, but we fouled up that nest in short order; it wasn't fitting that we just love them; we had to defy them and shake them off. Then, having been standoffish in one set of circumstances, it's not so easy to stop. So you look and see yourself, a suggestible, quite consistent figure of fun, through the succession of old neighborhoods and changing cities and combinations and pairings of friends and various institutional arrangements and tie-ins, and it's as if all along you had been expecting the chance for a second run-through—as if you've been rehearsing. In the resignation that masquerades as cynicism, perhaps, or in a sense of confident, fortified quietude, you can recognize the distinctions between now and when you were "young." Nevertheless, you still do feel young and blundering. The figure you've cut remains about the same as far back as you can remember: piling minor mistake upon minor mistake, in fairly good faith, never eminent, never in jail, but leading, however adventurously, a quite uneventful life.

All three proposals of marriage I've made were prompted, not volunteered: once when the girl was already spoken for, once by an impatient brother-in-law, and once by the fact of conception. Pregnancy is not a bad reason for getting married, it seems to me, since there are other options, in any case, and the period provides a quick testing in loyalty and cooperation. We quarreled in order to pull on the ties binding us, and then from the same intuitive, compelling affinity which had drawn us into the fix, we decided gaily to go ahead. More than gaily; we decided the fix was the jackpot. The wedding was followed by a month of baby-talk. You can't quarrel in baby-talk, and of course by now we didn't want to quarrel. On the one hand, it was too late, and on the other it was too early. Quarreling only suits an established marriage. Both of us had marinated in bachelorhood long enough; an established marriage was what we wanted. In courtship you worry and wriggle towards the edge of love, and we knew we had reached the edge.

Our first child will arrive a few months before my fourth book is published, since I am tardy in these matters. I was a virgin when the first came out; indeed, I hoped that being published would help me with girls. It didn't, but a gathering aura of neediness did. I'd been afraid I was homosexual, though I'd done nothing overt since the ninth grade, when a friend and I made lip-smacking noises in the dark at a party after our more advanced friends, who had brought girls, turned out the lights at 11:00 P.M. We sat awkwardly on each other's laps; and for years afterwards I did now and then feel the impulse to embrace a man, until the hubbub of heterosexual sex submerged it. For one thing, I liked breasts too much to become a homosexual. I wanted the breast so much that I couldn't believe that a woman might want me to have it too. The word "modesty," which was the word I heard used, should have given the secret away, since you are often modest about what you are rather proud of.

Already in grammar school a white blouse was exciting when worn by a black-haired girl. I couldn't make the first move, but when I got home from school the baby-sitter who looked after my sister would tell me to stretch out on the couch with my head in her lap. Even this invitation embarrassed me, and usually I'd eat a big bowl of cornflakes instead and turn on *Jack Armstrong*.

When I was fourteen I got to know the town veterinarian because of his interest in falconry. He was no great shakes as a vet, so I had steered clear of him with my dogs, but he trapped duck hawks every spring on the flyway which passed over Oenoke Ridge, and starved them in hoods and trained them and sneaked out stealthily at night to the spacious brown barns at Hoyt's Nurseries to catch the wild pigeons which roosted there and were an acceptable meal. His wife was a French war bride with a white startled face. They stayed late in bed in the morning, and when he appeared he was always yawning. The yawn is what I remember about him, more than the shed full of hawks. Without really knowing what it meant, I imitated him, and on some subterranean level I still seem to like the picture of myself yawning.

Then there were the maids we had, a series of black and old Polish ladies. As a small boy I was fascinated by their poverty and poor education but not until later did I realize that they were as female as anyone else. They didn't figure in my daydreams; the dream girls were blondies who lived in the forest and needed an outlaw protector like me. I masturbated oddly anyway. As a Boy Scout trainee, I had read the Manual about "Conservation," which equated strewing one's spunk on the bedsheets with burning down woods and polluting streams, so I used to keep the stuff in, pressing my finger on the duct until the contractions stopped. Later on, like everyone else, when I let it out, I would pull back the covers to see how far up the bed it had shot, proud if it hit my chin.

While one is a youngster watching others make out, bachelorhood is not the inert sort of interval that it becomes. The shoeleather I beat to death! I walked and walked, looking at lights across the Hudson, the Allegheny, and the Mississippi. Every lonely lighted window in the distance seemed to mark where a woman sat by herself, though the excitement of seeing the wide world was sufficient for me without pushing my luck and trying to meet somebody. I hung around the burlesque halls, astonished whenever the dancers spoke from the stage, endowing their public bodies with the squeaky voice of a piglet squeezed. In several experiences with prostitutes I was impotent. They were my neighbors in the hotels where I was staying, so we were friendly later, but in Chicago I went to a roaring six-story whorehouse with a special exit into a dogleg alley, everyone blacker than I was used to, and I was scared. The woman's room was equipped like a midwife's except that it was painted red; she was fortyish and had a pup underneath the bed which at first I imagined was a mugger; the building echoed like a pocket Algiers. My chums in Times Square had asked me whether their being black was what hung me up, but this woman didn't; she just said to go ahead and do anything to her I could think of. When I couldn't think of anything, she pushed a walletlike breast out of her brassiere in exactly the spirit I had expected a woman would evince if I let her know how much I coveted her breasts: oh, if *that's* what you want.

The first girl I really went out with had a better-shaped back than front, as a matter of fact; it was a marvelously graceful back. My feet smelled terrible that year—it's an ailment the nervous suffer from—they smelled like a forest fire. Her father would ask if a tire was burning somewhere in the house, and I'd go upstairs and run the tub or sit with my feet on the windowsill or suggest going out for a walk. It seems as though all we ever did was walk. Finally I did lose my cherry, and discovered, among other revelations, that I could talk to women with less difficulty than I had with men. At college when I'd walked about Cambridge with a mountain climber named Pamela I'd been unable to muster a single comment except that the houses were "strange," or such and such a professor was "strange," because "strange" was the only word I could get out. We lay at the foot of the Bunker Hill Monument, so that it loomed like a giddy cliff over us, the spotlight on it, and hitchhiked chastely across Massachusetts, always like mutes, never exchanging a word. But now the magical greasing powers of sex and of touch had unblocked my mouth, and I held forth with all of the eloquence of a prisoner released. Of course it did me no harm with my new friend that I continued to stutter badly with everyone else, because she assumed that this was explicit proof of love. I suppose for a minute or two sometimes it was. A hasty trotting period followed, spent in basement apartments that smelled of cats. I went on ersatz honeymoons in New Hampshire with heavy German girls and women writers, their short stories waiting unread at the *Partisan Review* going on ten months. At this point also I fell for the future wife of a close friend; there was a guilty chest-beating to-do on my part about that. Apparently she thinks that my infatuation was permanent, and there aren't many irritations to match the condescension which a woman metes out to a man who she believes has loved her vainly for the past umpteen years.

My first wife was a mathematician who was living in the Bronx in half of a subway motorman's house. Van Cortlandt Park was close, and Sugar Ray Robinson lived nearby. I was writing a prizefight book, so I watched his house, which was equipped with blinking tree lights and broken pugilists who served as houseboys. I had a motor scooter and combat boots, and when my first wife heard their crunch along the sidewalk she knew that it was either me or a murderer. Mr. Clean, the detergent man, with a ring in one ear and a shaved head, was another neighborhood celebrity. In retrospect the whole courtship has a poignancy because of her earnestness and because of details of this sort, just the kind that old-marrieds recite. She is somebody I'll never meet in anyone else's skin, and when we last talked on the phone I twisted and throbbed and couldn't speak, though I was capricious and domineering as a husband, faithful only in a literal sense. We lived in howling cold tenements because if anybody was living that way in the pomp of New York we wanted to too; I was the radical and she was the idealist. But for half our time together we traveled to Sicily and Spain, needing to lean on each other wherever we went because of being strangers, and hence procrastinating on our central problems. Oddly enough, timid as I was, I was a father in that marriage instead of a son, and while I made some redeeming gestures, my memories of my behavior are mostly of the obstinacies, petty and large. In particular, I wouldn't let her have a child, which is a sore thought in this present gleeful interlude because it bewildered her and made her wretched. It was the sticking point; it was what I withheld. Later I offered her the child, under whatever circumstances, and turned on the waterworks. She was the strong one then, though while we were married it didn't seem that she was going to be. To try to describe her—her voice, her dresses, her squirrel's-nest hair, the way she walked and wore her high collars—is fruitless and painful. Later I cried, later I loved, when it was too late. There were reunions and pinpoint depictions of the whole-cake, whole-spirited love that in our clearest moments we had hoped to achieve. Finally we got the divorce, printed in Spanish, which rests in my safe deposit box—that dreary receptacle—along with a yellowing christening certificate, my father's will, and several repudiated contracts and unlucky investments. Young as we were, constituted as we were, and given the jazzy climate of divorce of the period, we did what we did, smashing what we smashed. Although my new marriage casts a wider net and is serene by comparison, this early one remains like a rip in my life.

We begin, way back, with our mothers, and if a marriage breaks up we find to our astonishment that they are still there. Mine, when she heard a divorce had been decided upon, felt for a minute or two undivided delight: I was going to be hers. Instead, I put more distance between us. I was like the fellow I saw yesterday on the Gansevoort Pier sitting by the water on a copy of the *Sunday Times*. He had grown a fluff of hair on his lip to hide his fretting, he was balding, and he appeared miserable, though well under control, as a man old enough to be balding generally is. Rightly or not, I had the sense that he was depending on the bulky *Times* to hold him in place; at least reading it would kill a few hours. I was more fortunate: I went to Europe and began the wild-oats bachelorhood we are all eager for at one point or another.

All five women from that year in Europe have turned up in New York recently: among them, the movie press agent's secretary who misused me slightly in Rome, the lanky Norwegian girl whom I rather misused, and the British girl whom I lived with in marital amity for a number of months. The two of us took up residence on

Samos, and every evening we walked to the harbor to watch the caiques bob in the dusk, eat slices of octopus with a toothpick, and drink ouzo. We climbed to Zoodochos Pighi, a high monastery in the pine trees which is like a stone castle facing the Turkish mountain of Mycale. In France I knew a tough, rich American girl who loved to fight, whose eyes used to snap, as the saying goes, who tore into a fight with real relish, a marvelously brassy sexpot without the slightest socialist guilt about being so rich—she just liked the freedom and the purchasing power. We were appreciative of each other's bodies, and she was of the type who are writers' girls, who like raunching about with writers. At one time she had been married to a novelist who drank as the novelists of legend do and waved a pistol when he fought with her.

The first of the five to return was a frizzy-haired young redhead who had thought she loved me over there, but quickly realized she didn't when she got back to Manhattan. Though she was a persistent virgin, she used to let me take her into my bedroom and feel her bosom—which amounted to practically a third of her body because she was so skinny—while she watched my antics quietly, smiling a little. Then after a few minutes she'd leave (having interrupted a taxi ride, perhaps, in order to do this), with a show of affection on both sides but no reference to when we might see each other for longer. I suppose in her fundamentalist's way she was watching and waiting to see if I wouldn't fall for her head over heels, until she realized that she didn't care if I did. Her intensity was her greatest appeal—those blazing cheeks and half-shut eyes—but like a country girl come to the fair, she stood on her guard against malarkey.

I was a glutton for fannies, large mouths, and the other staples. Short-haired girls are sexy because their hair is short and long-haired girls are sexy because they're long-haired. The running around isn't really the same as onanism, because it's celebrative as onanism never is; but it surely is brusque. For one skittery long-haired research assistant, sexual intercourse was the "center" of every day; she thought she needed it that often. I didn't, but I got tired of the attempt before the idea. Her voice was like a bicycle horn and she thought my views on any subject were ridiculous; yet she had a soft spot for me and let me indulge my passion for her, which was carnal and virtually irremediable. I was always ringing her street-doorbell, and she'd come out and kiss me, even if she had other company. Occasionally she may have hoped we would wind up married; she'd bring out slipcover fabrics for me to pass judgment upon. We watched television in bed, heaped round domestically with blankets because it was a drafty Village apartment with warped floorboards. Her closets were stuffed with clothes I didn't like, but we went in for nudity a good deal. Her bathroom was painted blue and red and heavily scented; a whole wall of the apartment was hung with beads and belts. Because she got up early to go to work, I lay alone in the bed an extra hour, drinking in the smells, and feeling kept. When she was dressed she looked elfin, but she wasn't elfin undressed: I ate my way around her, and called and called and called, getting her infernal answering service or letting the phone ring thirty-five times. Sometimes I started out for her apartment if there was no answer so that I could at least anticipate arriving and trying the door. She had areolae the color of reddish acorns, a puffy stiff muff, a funny pad of fat just above her buttocks, and hair I trembled to take down when she asked in a beeping voice, "Would you undo my hair?"

As I say, the memory is of a twitchy frenzy, a zaftig, olive-country body one size larger than small, and lots of trekking back and forth between my house and hers. My balls felt like a bushel basket, and though she would have made my life a misery if we had married, a penis is like Steinbeck's Lenny—he doesn't know what's going on.

Let's see . . . these anecdotes are not about love, only about the itching.

On the East Side I knew a splendid neurotic blonde who owned more books than a bookstore and kept a cupboard full of hors d'oeuvres fixings and draped tapestries across her walls. She had a father problem and used to try to murder me with her big boobs— a flirt with death, as it were. "Don't smother; don't smother," she'd whisper, bearing down, stopping up my mouth and flattening my nose. She was another writers' girl; numerous colleagues of mine had borrowed money from her and disported themselves. She was breezy, friendly company, good for the eyes, and always danced away from commitment with a throaty chuckle. Now she's on the razor's edge of spinsterhood, while an understanding of her difficulties has begun to dawn on her; I suppose it's a race against time.

I knew a girl from Queens who lived in Brooklyn and was a barmaid in Manhattan. Later a Negro moved in with her, so that I couldn't talk to her when I phoned, but for a while she'd told me the adventures that came her way each night: men offering twenty dollars just for a surreptitious squeeze. Ginny, my one youngster, a Wellesley senior, was another girl whose bosom was a cross she had to bear (her words). It wasn't so much for her bosom that I liked her, though, as for her sunny nature, her intelligence, her sturdy bottom, and her fine-textured yellow hair. She was a round-faced, classy beauty, plump, smooth-skinned, brown-eyed, and all the other things we love. Not to leave her as perfection, she had an asthmatic's pigeon-ridge marring her chest, and she had father troubles too, the fellow having allowed his boss to assault her in exchange for a promotion, so that when she came near a high window, she would muse about ending it all. But she was born to thrive, it seemed to me; she was joyful, and I enjoyed the tutor's role, showing her that she had gifts to give, that she could put a man to sleep when no pill could—that she was practically all gifts, indeed. She had fun experimenting with me in such activities as quarreling and letter-writing, until she graduated from college and went to Bonn to work for a newsmagazine.

There are the girls you hold your breath for because their breath is bad; there are the stringbean spirited girls who entwine you in every move they make because they squirm so much; there are the generous-hearted, squared-off girls—daughters of butchers' union organizers, who served time in the WACs, perhaps—who are around to talk to. My address book still has a currency because the phone numbers are up-to-date, and a married man without such a recent acquaintance with the bleaker winds of bachelorhood might feel that he was missing out somehow, reading about the new morality, the lurid teenie-boppers. As a heterosexual, half the world is potentially his lover; half the world seems to be bending its energies to attract him, and sometimes it must be a little painful when he walks in the evening streets.

Dealing with people is a question of finding out what is important to them, yet we seldom bothered to. The anonymity, the sexual state of war, the rush, the risks, the tantalizing, the pounding uptown and down: these made the prize seem like a prize. Once every year or two I was meeting a woman I might have married with a fair prospect for success, and we would pretend that it was coming true, that we each had somebody to live with, to bring our bruises to. Actually it was the brink of love, but I would make the simulation do, quite content to pretend that we were married or soon to be so. When the liaison fell through I'd change apartments or take some time out for despair. Once I sent some of my friends an invitation to my own funeral: which is the craziest thing I've done.

So finally with M. the vigilance relaxed, the canniness. Like an exhausted manatee, I sighed and sank down, letting myself cross the brink. So did she, for that matter, whose history in these proceedings had been similar to mine, when you boil it down. We got ourselves pregnant more by inner design than by coincidence, and now she wanders around the apartment in the middle of the night, eating figs and Mallomars, while we wait for this hollering orange to make an appearance, this Molly-Jeremy. We already have enough love to extend to the baby, but no baby as yet, so we play endless naming games, and M. pokes me exploratively with her thumb. You can't fall out of loving a baby; you can't divorce a baby. And we look backwards at our parents. M.'s father, an articulate, turbulent man, used to enter the room where she was doing her homework and lift her glasses off, clean them for her, and give them back, going out again without a word. Although, in company with one-third of American men, I thought my mother's love verged on a passion, when she phones now it is mainly because she is alone, is a widow, and must face the empty house. She's a graceful, likable woman, Western and tall, and I must shake off my habit of shaking her off.

The Problem
of the
Golden Rule

Like a good many New Yorkers, I've often wondered whether I was going to be mugged. I've lived in a number of neighborhoods, and being a night walker, have many times changed my course or speeded my stride, eying a formidable-looking figure as he approached. But it's never happened, and I imagine that if it finally does there may actually be a kind of relief, even a species of exhilaration, as I pick myself up—assuming that I am not badly hurt—because a danger anticipated for a long time may come to seem worse than the reality. People who come home and encounter a robber in their apartment who flees are likely to be less shaken up than the householder is who simply steps into a shambles of ransacked bureaus and upended beds: they've seen the fellow; they know he's human. A friend of mine wrestled a burglar for several minutes around the floor of his living room, both of them using the trips and hip throws that they remembered from their teens, until by the time my friend won and phoned the police they were old acquaintances.

I know, too, that to describe the few incidents of violence I've met with in the past makes them sound more grisly than they were in fact. In the army, my platoon was put in the charge of a peculiar sergeant who, mostly for reasons of his own, had us do squat jumps one noontime until we could no longer walk or stand up. Then he strolled among us kicking us to make sure that we weren't faking. It was a hot drill field strewn with packs and stacked rifles and other movie props, and yet the experience was not nearly as bad as one would anticipate if he were told at breakfast what to expect that day. We just followed orders until we couldn't get up and then we lay where we were on the ground until the sergeant was satisfied that we had done what was humanly possible. Even in a true atrocity situation that's all that is ever done: what is humanly possible. Afterwards one becomes unresponsive and fatalistic; terror is no longer a factor unless torture is added.

Next day the sergeant wanted to have it both ways, so he set us into formation and told us what he was going to make us do, and thereupon went off to the latrine to give us a chance to stand at attention and think and stew. Another sergeant promptly walked up and dismissed us, however. We hobbled away in every direction as fast as possible, while the two sergeants met to discuss the issue in the barracks door. They met person-to-person, and we had been punished person-to-person, and the facelessness of the mugger whom one anticipates meeting on Little West Twelfth Street was never a part of it. This, like our doing whatever was humanly possible, made the experience supportable.

I visualize Armageddon not as a steel-muzzled affair of push-botton silos under the earth but as a rusty freighter, flying the Liberian flag, perhaps, which sails inconspicuously up the Hudson past my apartment and goes off. Beyond that I don't see any details—though, as a non sequitur, I expect the tunnels and bridges would fill up with hikers leaving the city before it was too late. A woman I know says she sees Armageddon as getting under the bed. What we do with the insupportable is to turn it to terms we can file and forget. Unfortunately we are able to deal almost as handily with the nuclear bombs that have already gone off as we are with the ones that haven't. If as individual fighting men we had razed Hiroshima, then the horror of its destruction would persist as a legend to our great-grandchildren because it would have been witnessed and done on the spot—also because of the somber old notion that residing in every man is a spark of divinity, whether the man is an enemy or a friend. This putative spark is central to most religious belief; and right at the root of Western ethics is what is called, under one of its names, the Golden Rule. But spark or no spark, since in practice we cannot react to others with unabashed fellow feeling, we usually reduce the Golden Rule to a sort of silver rule, doing to them just about what we think they would do to us if they had the opportunity. And this works—has been working—though the new impersonalized technology is challenging its workability, along with another behemoth among changes, which is that today there are too many people. Where there are too many people, we get tired of following even the silver rule, tired of paying that much attention, of noticing whom we are with and who is who. For the agnostic as well, basing his reverence for life on its variety and on a Jeffersonian fascination with the glimmerings of talent in every person, the glut is discouraging. Although we don't ridicule these old ideas, the sentiments that people have for one another in a traffic jam are becoming our sentiments more and more. A groan goes up in any suburb when it's announced that a new complex of housing for two thousand souls is going to be built on Lone Tree Hill. And the vast sigh of impatience which greeted Pope Paul's traditionalist statement of faith in the sanctity of the seed germs of life points to the tone to come. *Life for the living,* people will say: body counts in war and baby counts in peace. We grant each union man his $10,500 a year, and then the hell with him. He, for his part, doesn't care if our garbage cans fester with rats when the union goes after $10,900.

Never have people dealt so briskly with strangers as now. Many of us have ceased to see strangers at all; our eyes simply don't register them except as verticals on the sidewalk, and when we must parley with them we find out quickly what they are asking from us, do it—maybe—and that's that. When I was a child I remember how my astonishment evolved as I realized that people often would not do the smallest thing to convenience another person or make him feel easier for the moment. Of course I'd known that *kids* wouldn't, but I had thought that was because they were kids. It was my first comprehension of the deadness of life. Everyone has discovered at some particular point life's deadness, but the galloping sense of deadness which alarms so many people lately, and especially the young, goes way beyond such individual discoveries to dimensions and contexts that have brought revolution to the U.S. Even in the arts the ancient austerities have been deemed insufficient, and we have actors who jump into the audience and do their acting there. When acting seems to fail, they improvise, and finally improvisation isn't enough either, and instead of having an actor play the drug addict, the addict himself must appear onstage and play himself—like the toothpaste tube blown up and hanging on the museum wall: "Look, if nothing else, I'm real." This is the era when students are so busy trying to teach their teachers that they are hard to teach, and when the chip on the shoulder of the man in the street is his "personality"—personality is quarrelsomeness. The revolution, in any case, is overdue, but maybe our best hope is that we remain at least idiosyncratic creatures, absorbed close to home. Dog owners, when they walk their dogs, show nearly as exact an interest in their pets' defecations as they would in their own. The same communing silence steals over their faces, the look of musing solemnity that usually only the bathroom mirror gets a glimpse of.

The worst public tragedy I've witnessed was in Boston, when from a distance I saw a brick wall fall on a company of firemen.

Some, with a great shout, got away, but even the leap that they made while the rest crumpled is blurred as a memory compared to the images of two old men whom I knew very slightly at the time. Mr. Kate wrote cookbooks in the winter and hired out as a cook on a private yacht during the warm months. His other love, besides cooking, was opera, and he lived in a room shaped like a shoebox that cost him eight dollars a week. He served himself candlelit meals on a folding table and concocted all of his recipes on a hotplate set in the sink. By contrast, Mr. Hurth, although a somewhat less cultivated man, was an alumnus of Brown University and lived in a large ground-floor room in the same house. He had ruined himself in a scandal in St. Louis, where he had been a businessman, but that was all I learned. What he'd done next was to come to Boston and throw himself on the old-fashioned, private or "Christian" charity, as it used to be called, of a roommate from college, though thirty years had passed. He was a pleasant subdued man ordinarily, swinging from sweet to vaguely hangdog, but he was a drinker, and so this benefactor no longer asked him to Newton Centre for Thanksgiving because he was likely to break the furniture. When he did, he'd leave his glasses behind by mistake so that he'd have to go back out again for a whole second festival of apologies. Through charitable intercession, Mr. Hurth was on the payroll of the John Hancock Insurance Company, being listed on the books as a claims investigator, though actually (charity compounding charity) his single duty was to work for the United Fund once a year on a loan basis. The campaign was a brief one, but he was a bitter, floundering functionary, faced with his fate if his drinking should snap off his last sticks of presence and respectability.

As I say, next to the memory of two nodding acquaintances the death of some distant firemen is small potatoes. I was reminded of that catastrophe the other night for the first time in years while watching a fire on Third Avenue. Here in the bigger city one is witness to such a cataract of appalling happenings that they pass remembering. I saw a man who had just been burned out of his apartment turned away from a hotel in the neighborhood because he had a little blacking on him, although the shock and fear stood in his eyes. "Sure, there was a fire there, all right," the manager told me with a laugh. "I never take them in, those victims. They're dirty and they're scared to death. They're not worth the nuisance."

He was a modern, casual villain, however, impartial, just the kind who is not memorable. I came upon a much less gratuitous drama a few days afterwards. A child of two or three had been stuck inside one of those all-glass phone booths with a spring door which cannot be opened except by a grown person because of where the handle is placed. The world was passing—this was on the open street—but he was feeling his way around the glass in gathering panic, trying to find an escape route, reaching up and reaching down. Every few seconds he let out a thin, fluting scream so pure in pitch that it was hardly human; it was *pre*-human. You could see him thinking, learning, recording discoveries. He reached for the phone, but that was too high up; he thumped each pane of glass, searching for the door, and pounded on the metal frame, and screamed to find out whether screaming would work. He was boxed into his terror, and you could see him grow older by leaps and bounds. I'm just this month a new father, so I was as transfixed as if he were my child. His governess or baby-sitter, baby-walker, or whatever she was, a short shadowy woman such as you might see manning a subway change booth, was standing right next to the glass, apparently feasting her eyes. Whether it was supposed to be a "punishment" or merely a pleasure fest, the child was too frightened by now to notice her.

Maybe our cruelty will save us. At least the cruel do pay attention, and the woman would probably have let him out before the crowd got around to hearing him. She had moved to the door, looking down at him intently as he pushed on the glass. I was seething, partly because I found that some of the woman's sexual excitement had communicated itself to me, which was intolerable, and partly because my cowardice in not interfering was equally outrageous. We've all become reluctant to stop and stick our noses in—a man is run over by a Breakstone cream-cheese truck and we pass quickly by. But cowardice was what it was in this particular event, since even under happy circumstances I stutter and it requires an enormous gearing up of nerve for me to step into a public fracas on the street. I strangle; I can't speak at all and must either use my hands on the stranger or gag and quaver, unable to put two words together. The seams of human nature frighten me in this regard, and the whole confrontation ethic of the sixties, much as I have entered into it on occasion, gives me nightmare visions because I have no conventional means of battling. I see myself as unable to protest in words to the person whose behavior has angered me and so using my hands on him; then just as unable to explain myself to the crowd that gathers, but only shuddering and stuttering; and then in court again enforcedly silent, dependent on the empathy or telepathic capacities of the people who are there to convey my side of the controversy.

Weaving like a nauseous moose, I was working my way toward her, when the woman, with a glance at me, pushed the door of the booth open, reached inside, and pulled the boy to her and walked away. In effect, I was let off, because only an exceptional well-doer would have tracked the woman down from that point on and questioned her about her psyche.

But there are times when one isn't let off, when one's very humanity hangs at issue and perhaps my specific problems with my stutter are an epitome of what each of us meets. Once in northern New England when I was snowshoeing, a hunter started shooting at me, really only to scare me, pinging with his .22 in my immediate vicinity. I was on an open hillside which I'd already realized was too slippery to climb, but as long as I kept scrabbling there in silence on the ice, like an animal in trouble, he was going to keep on pinging. Because a stutterer's every impulse is to stutter softly, unobtrusively, it's twice as hard to shout one's way through a stutter as to wedge through in quiet tones; but from the sheer imperatives of survival I shouted, "I CAN SEE YOU!" I shouted it several times again, although I couldn't see him; he was in the woods. I was insisting and reiterating that I was a human being: if I could get that message across to him he would stop shooting at me. It was even worse than my conception of a courtroom trial because this was one of those rare emergencies when we can't trust all our faculties to operate together for us— the movements of our hands, our youth or age, our manner and expression—some compensating for the inadequacies of the others. I had to go to bat with my speaking abilities and nothing else. So I shouted to him that I could see him, by which I meant I was a man, and he stopped shooting.

More recently, I was on a tiny Danish island off the coast of Sweden, wandering around some seventeenth-century fortifications and the walled town, now a huddled fishing village. I had sat on the sea wall to watch the cloud action but was distracted by the spectacle below me of a boy mistreating a wild duck. Oddly enough, many times an incident where a person, rather than an animal, is being mauled and manhandled is easier to shrug off. The fact that he's a person complicates the case. As an onlooker you can see, for example, that he has gotten himself drunk and let his guard down, lost his dignity, talked out of turn. But the duck, with its wings clipped, presumably, was only trying to run away. The boy would catch it, pummel it and grip it tightly, trundling it about. Finally I got off my bench and went over and told him falteringly to cut that out. Many Danes speak English, but he was twelve or so and he may not have understood me. Like a mirror of myself, he stared at me without trying to say a word. Then he squeezed the duck again hard in both hands. My bugaboo about trying to explain myself to strangers rose in me, along with my indignation. Instead of looking for a local fellow to translate and take over, I lifted the duck from his arms, and with the sense of right and doom that I have dreaded in foreseeing a confrontation on the street, carried it down the stairs of the sea wall and released it on the beach. The boy ran for help; the duck paddled into the waves; I climbed to the promenade and started walking as deliberately as I could toward the small boat which had brought me to the island.

Uncannily soon, before I'd gone a dozen yards, practically the whole male populace was on the scene. "Hey! Turn around!" they yelled. I took another couple of steps away and then did so. They told me very plainly in English that they were going to throw me over the seawall. They said the duck had been rescued by the boys of the island—their sons—after it had swum through an oil slick and almost drowned. Now, because of what I'd done, it really *was* about to drown, and when it went under, they would toss me over. This was not spoken in joking tones, and I could see the duck getting heavier in the water; its feathers, though as tidy to the eye as a healthy duck's feathers, had no buoyancy. Meanwhile, I'd fallen into something like what a prizefighter would call a clinch by refusing to acknowledge by any sign that I understood what was being said to me. It is a psychological necessity that when you punish somebody he understand the reason why. Even if he doesn't accept the guilty finding, you must explain to him why you are punishing him or you can't do it. So while they could scarcely contain their frustration, my face displayed bewilderment; I kept pretending to grope to understand. I was doing this instinctively, of course, and as their first impetus to violence passed, I found myself acting out with vehemence how I had seen the boy mistreat the duck. The men, who wanted at the least to take a poke at me, watched doubtfully, but there was a Coast Guardsman, an off-islander, who seemed to be arguing in Danish on my behalf. Another man went down to where the duck was swimming and reached out; the duck perceiving itself to be sinking, had moved cautiously closer to shore. And when the duck was saved I was saved; I only had the island's boys waiting for me in the embrasures of the wall.

Yet this quite comic misadventure, when every dread came real—I couldn't say a single word to save my life—was just as numbing as those ninety-five squat jumps at Fort Dix. Only later was it terrifying. And in a way it makes up for the memories I have as a teenager of watching flocks of bats murdered with brooms and frogs tormented—moments when I didn't interfere, but giggled ruefully to keep my popularity and stifle my outcries.

Sociology progresses, and the infant mortality rate goes down. Nevertheless we know that if the announcement were made that there was going to be a public hanging in Central Park, Sheep Meadow would be crowded with spectators, like Tyburn mall. Sometimes at night my standing lamp shapes itself into an observant phantom figure which takes a position next to my bed. It doesn't threaten me directly, and I stretch out to clutch its throat with careful anger. My final grab bumps the lamp over. This electric phantom is a holdover from my vivid night demons when I was eight or ten. I never saw them outright, thank the Lord, but for years I fell asleep facing the wall to avoid beholding my destruction. I'd "whisper," as I called it, when I went to bed, telling myself an installment of a round-robin story, and when the installment was over I'd wait for the demons, until I fell asleep. Later, just as invariably, I faced the outer room so I could see them come and have warning to fight. Such archaisms in our minds are not an unmixed evil, however, because they link us to humanity and to our history as human beings. My wife says every man she's been familiar with would smell his socks at night before he went to bed: just a whiff—each sock, not only one. I do this too, although the smell has been of no intrinsic interest to me for twenty years. The smell of each sock checks precisely with the other one and smells as vital as pigs do. Maybe it reassures us that we're among the living still. We need to know. In the fifties I also liked the smell of air pollution. I didn't think of it as air pollution then—nobody did—but as the smell of industry and the highways I hitchhiked on, the big-shouldered America I loved.

In 1943 George Orwell said the problem of the times was the decay in the belief in personal immortality. Several French novelists had turned existentialist and several English novelists Catholic (possibly the same reaction), while he himself, like many of the more likable writers, had adopted a hardy humanist's masculine skepticism. Twenty-odd years later, the problem appears only to have grown more piercing, though it is not put into the same terms. You can't have as many people walking around as there are now and still simply see them as chips off the divine lodestone. Nor is the future *1984:* that's too succinct. At first the new nuclear bullying, the new technocracy, made mere survival more the point, because we wanted to be sure of surviving here on earth before we worried about heaven. Lately, instead the talk has been about overpopulation, and city people have started venturing to the outback, buying acreage with all the premonitory fervor of Noah sawing logs. Everyone wants space to breathe; the character of city life has drastically deteriorated, and there's no questioning the statistics, just as there used to be no questioning the odds that eventually a nuclear war was going to penetrate our precautions through that old fontanel of existence: human mix-up.

When we say that enough is enough, that we have enough people on hand now for any good purpose, we mean that the divine spark has become something of a conflagration, besides an embarrassment of riches. We're trying to make a start at sorting the riches, buying Edwardian clothes but also Volkswagens, and settling down to the process of zoning the little land there is. As we also begin to cogitate on how the quality of life can be improved, we may be in for a religious revival, too. It's a natural beginning, and faddism will probably swing that way, and after all, we *are* extraordinary—we're so extraordinary we're everywhere. Next to the new mysticisms, old-fashioned, run-of-the-mill religion is not so hard to swallow. The difficulty will be how we regard individual people, a question which involves not only whether we think we're immortal but whether we think they are. The crowded impatience of suburb-city living doesn't often evoke intimations of other people's immortality, and neither do the hodgepodge leveling procedures of a modern democracy. So much of the vigor of the Victorian church, for instance, grew out of the contrast between its members and the raw, destitute brown masses who covered the rest of the globe. Among an elite, self-congratulatory minority even the greatest of attributes—immortality—seemed plausible.

But maybe I'm being overly sour. We have wiped tigers off the earth and yet our children hear as much about the symbolism of tigers as children did in the old days. And next to the subway station I use there is a newsdealer who was blinded in Orwell's war, the Spanish War, in the mountains behind Motril. He wears the aura of a revolutionary volunteer. He dresses bulkily, as if for weather at the front, and rigs canvas around his hut as neatly as a soldier's tent. Not one of your meek blind men, he's on his feet most of the day, especially in tough weather, pacing, marching, standing tall. He's gray and grim, hard and spare, and doubtless lives surrounded by the companions that he had in the Sierra Nevada. But he's too bluff and energetic to be a museum piece. If you help him cross the street you get the rough edge of his tongue. He searches for the lamppost with his cane like a tennis player swinging backhand, and if he loses his bearings and bumps against something, he jerks abruptly back like a cavalier insulted, looking gaunt and fierce. I pity him, but I take note of him; he counts himself among the living. I buy a paper and go home to my newborn baby, who is as intense and focused (to my eye) as a flight of angels dancing on a pinhead.

I don't believe in a god you can pray to, but I do find I believe in God—I do more than I don't. I believe in glee and in the exuberance I feel with friends and animals and in the fields, and in other emotions besides that. Anyway, as we know, it really isn't necessary to see sparks of a grand divinity in someone else to feel with the old immediacy that he is kin; we can evolve a more sophisticated Golden Rule than that. We will be trying to refine and revivify the qualities of life, and the chief stumbling block is that we must somehow reduce the density of people in our own comings and goings without doing it as we do now, which is by simply not seeing them, by registering them as shadows to dodge by on the street. Without degenerating into callousness, we must develop our ability to switch on and off—something analogous to what we do already with body temperature in a harsh world. Generally we'd button up if we were out walking, but when the Breakstone cream-cheese truck ran over an old man, this would be a time when our ancient instinct for cherishing a stranger would spring to being.

I live in a high-rise apartment and keep a pair of field glasses next to the window to use whenever somebody emerges on one of the rooftops nearby. There are ten or fifteen regulars—old people hanging wash, high school kids who have come up into the open to talk where they can be alone. All of them are neighbors to me now, though on the street I probably would turn away from them— even the bathing beauties would not be beauties there. Admittedly I am a bit of a voyeur, as who isn't, but the population density on the rooftops seems about right. In fact, I roused myself not long ago to drive some robbers off a roof across the street by gesticulating sternly. They waved back as they went down the fire escape like people who've escaped a fall.

Bragging
for Humanity

Henry David Thoreau, who never earned much of a living or sustained a relationship with any woman that wasn't brotherly—who lived mostly under his parents' roof (and is buried simply as "Henry" in his father's graveyard plot), who advocated one day's work and six days "off" as the weekly round and was considered a bit of a fool in his hometown, sometimes even having to endure the nickname "Dolittle"—is probably the American writer who tells us best how to live comfortably with our most constant companion, ourselves. We find ourselves brought to life in Thoreau's books if we too want to simplify our roster of obligations and clutter of habits and possessions, to be independent of wage-slave constrictions and social obiter dicta, and if we know that common sense and honesty do not always coincide with prevailing tastes and majority opinion. His masterpiece, *Walden,* is controversial because it goes against the grain of conventional social arrangements and go-getterism and established religion. But when he went traveling he became a more convivial man of letters, and particularly in the Maine woods, "far from mankind and election day," he discovered so little to displease him that there's no hint of churlishness or reclusiveness in his buoyant account, even on the eve of the Civil War, whose roiling approach profoundly disturbed him.

Born in 1817, Thoreau died of tuberculosis in 1862 in his middle forties, having kept a voluminous journal from the age of twenty but having published only a smattering of magazine articles and poems and two books, the first of them at his own expense. *A Week on the Concord and Merrimack Rivers* appeared in 1849 and sold only 219 copies in four years. Its failure commercially delayed for five years the scheduled publication of *Walden* (1854), which then took five years to sell out a printing of two thousand copies, priced at a dollar apiece. His fame—and two more marvelous books, *The Maine Woods* (1864) and *Cape Cod* (1865), edited by his sister Sophia and his friend Ellery Channing from manuscript versions and magazine pieces—was posthumous. Nevertheless, it's easy to exaggerate Thoreau's obscurity at the time of his death, which in no way equaled Herman Melville's parched solitude, for instance, in the four decades after *Moby-Dick* came out in 1851. These two great American romantics were almost exact contemporaries, like their masterpieces, and neither's achievement was recognized for the better part of a century. But Thoreau had had the good luck to be born in Concord, Massachusetts, where he was thrown into contact with many of the literary figures of the day, notably Ralph Waldo Emerson, who became his mentor and champion, and Bronson Alcott, Margaret Fuller, Nathaniel Hawthorne, James Russell Lowell, Orestes Brownson, and, on a wider scene, with such personages as John Brown, Walt Whitman, and Horace Greeley, the editor of the *New York Tribune,* who frequently tried to further his interests. Thoreau was an uningratiating, prickly man who quarreled with the most powerful magazine editors he dealt with, and whose ideas then seemed overly simple or prosaic and unfashionably straightforward. Lowell, Whitman, Henry James, Sr., and William Dean Howells, among others, were not impressed with him. But despite the small, fitful notice his work had received, his friends saw to it that Concord's children were released from school to attend his funeral, two Boston newspapers ran admiring obituaries, and Emerson, perhaps the most influential intellectual in the country, eulogized him in *The Atlantic Monthly.*

As a young man at rather loose ends, Thoreau had lived for three years in Emerson's house; and it was Emerson who bought and loaned him the land on the shore of Walden Pond where he built a ten-by-fifteen-foot cabin and wrote the bulk of his first two books. During those busy twenty-six months (1845–47), he also made his first trip to the Maine woods, and spent a night in Concord's jail, protesting paying taxes for the Mexican War, which was unpopular among educated New Englanders as being waged in the furtherance of slavery—an experience that produced his classic essay "Civil Disobedience." Emerson's kindnesses and patronage and advocacy were of crucial importance to Thoreau's career, and Thoreau made no substantial departure from Emerson's Transcendental ideas as enunciated in the older man's earlier, already famous essays like "Nature," "Self-Reliance," and "The Over-Soul." It was not in the ideas but in the expression of them that he surpassed his friend, with aphorisms such as "We are constantly invited to be what we are"; or "The mass of men lead lives of quiet desperation"; or "I have traveled a good deal in Concord"; or "The

sun is but a morning star." One might argue with each of these state-
ments, but each is so succinct as to sum up an ordinary essay, and
the manner in which he lived was succinct enough to reinforce every epigram he wrote. Planting beans next to his pondside cabin
("seven miles" of bean rows: he meant to be self-sufficient in beans,
to make "the earth say beans instead of grass"), he can be reduced
to the ineradicable simplicity of Johnny Appleseed or Paul Bunyan,
Daniel Boone or Nathan Hale, Babe Ruth or Paul Revere, as a
national archetype.

Transcendentalism was the liveliest intellectual movement of
nineteenth-century America. It presupposed the immanent presence of God within both man and nature, more recognizable by
intuition than by one's powers of reasoning, and it epitomized the
overall emphasis upon nature with which American authors forced
themselves onto the world stage—a raw new continent insisting
that nature here was not a closed issue and might even be where
God lived. Transcendentalism paralleled the work of such English
romantic writers as Wordsworth, Coleridge, and Thomas Carlyle.
It drew from German metaphysical philosophers like Immanuel
Kant, as well as from Eastern religious teachings, but imbibed a
special confidence from the vast, dramatic fact of the wilderness
behind it, and was sanguine in a way the two great nature-oriented
novels of that century in America, *Moby-Dick* and *Huckleberry
Finn*, are not. It was much more specifically an American expression than Wordsworth and Kant were "English" or "German." Indeed, Transcendentalism originated among its New England in-
ventors partly in reaction to the severe orthodoxies of Calvinism
and the overrationalism of Unitarianism. Nevertheless, because
Emerson, for example, had never sailed the ocean on a whaling
ship or trapped beavers for a season in the Rockies, his declama-
tions and revelations could seem a bit bookish or otherworldly to
people who had done so, as if they were imagined, not experienced. Transcendentalism needed a Thoreau who actually undertook to live by its ideals, trying them out winter and summer in
the woods, getting wet, getting cold, closely examining nature on
the ground, from flowers to ice, woodchucks to moose, as Emerson—a man of the world, man of affairs, editor, and cynosure—
did not.

During this extraordinary half decade—Whitman's initial version of *Leaves of Grass* came out in 1855, a year after *Walden,* and
Hawthorne's *Scarlet Letter* in 1850, one year before *Moby-Dick*—
nature was much celebrated with a New World imprint, and Thoreau was the most exuberant participant. "The light which puts
out our eyes is darkness to us. Only that day dawns to which we

are awake. There is more day to dawn," is his exhortation, in closing *Walden*. That the ideas he was espousing had not started with him made his task easier, because in literature, unlike science, what matters is not who's first but who has said it best, and he could tinker with, elucidate, illustrate, reformulate, and perfect them. Here, for example, is Emerson's earlier statement of Thoreau's pithy dictum, "I have traveled a good deal in Concord": "I am not much an advocate for traveling," said Emerson, "and I observe that men run away to other countries because they are not good in their own, and run back to their own because they pass for nothing in the new places. For the most part, only the light characters travel. Who are you that have no task to keep you at home?"

Emerson did not lack boldness. On slavery, he was "an abolitionist of the most absolute abolition," he said, and he also addressed the 1855 Women's Rights Convention in Boston. For being a religious nonconformist, he was exiled from Harvard University's speakers' platforms for twenty-nine years after uttering what was described by one shocked adversary as "the latest form of infidelity." Though he had abandoned the Unitarian ministry by the time he was thirty-five, he gave as many as eighty free-lance speeches a year and soon became an internationalist who had met everybody from Ivan Turgenev, Max Muller, John Ruskin, and Hippolyte Taine in Europe to the Californians Bret Harte and John Muir. His friendship was crucial to Thoreau's development, but Emerson was a mover and shaker who befriended many young writers, a kind of intellectual father-to-his-country who could inspire disciples locally and yet discourse between the continents as Benjamin Franklin and Thomas Jefferson had done, with a countenance that would befit currency or postage stamps, like theirs.

Thoreau, though far from being the first "nature writer"—none has ever surpassed the great dithyramb to the animal kingdom in God's answer to Job in the Book of Job, *Behold now Behemoth*—has come to stand for the whole genre. He does seem typical in that he was a social conservative but a political radical. Such authors don't welcome industrial or technological change, which only serves to remove mankind still farther from nature, and they are often furious at human-scale inequity and wars of imperial conquest, which tend to strike them as outgrowths of that change. Slavery and the Mexican War of the 1840s outraged Thoreau and Emerson much in the way that the civil-rights struggles and the Vietnam War engaged the passions of nature lovers in the 1960s. It is no accident that Thoreau, and not some other classic writer, pioneered the notion of civil disobedience—affecting Tolstoy, inspiring Gandhi—and that he delivered orations on behalf of the fiery revolutionist John Brown. "The greater part of what my neighbors call good I believe in my soul to be bad, and if I repent of anything, it is very likely to be my good behavior. What demon possessed me that I behaved so well?" he wrote in *Walden*. To Emerson's mild dismay, he was himself a revolutionary.

But what has made him more imperishable was a deeper radicalism, nearly as pervasive as his love of nature. He was writing *Walden* during the height of the California gold rush and of the larger westering fever of hope and excitement, when the existence of the Oregon Trail seemed an elixir of wealth and youth. But he merely dismissed the premise of trying to pile up money or of changing the scene of one's efforts. It was exploring oneself that mattered, and witnessing each day at home. (The continent might scarcely have been settled if Thoreau's priorities had held sway.) As one of a line of writers going back to Rousseau, he said, "I should not talk so much about myself if there were anybody else whom I knew so well," and like Walt Whitman, he devoted his life to presenting his enthusiasms, assuming that they had universal application. Neither a hermit nor a mystic of one of the stripes that have arisen in the extremism of our own day, he loved Homer and Chaucer, could translate French and Greek, invented a better lead for pencils, was a student of weather and water, and was an excellent land surveyor. It was originality, not faddishness, that led him to take to the woods, grow his own food, read about Eastern religions, wax vehement against slavery and help in the Underground Railway, advocate conscientious objection as a political weapon, explore the lore and character of Indians, and criticize the common man as well as political parties and establishment figures. Though born only two and a half years after the end of the War of 1812, he was a modernist in believing that the cost of a thing is "the amount of what I will call life which is required to be exchanged for it." In an age of worldwide exploration, he readily belittled adventurer-explorers because he believed they were not properly mystified or exalted by conundrums closer to home. He was more of an ecologist than a taxonomist in an era when science was mostly confined to taxonomy, and at a time when the frontier was being gutted, he went into the woods, he said, as "chaplain to the hunters."

In school he had occasionally been called "the Judge," yet one of the appealing paradoxes about Thoreau is how seldom this offish individualist and "solitary" lived or even traveled alone, how close he was to his family and chatty with his neighbors, how repeatedly and obstreperously he involved himself in public controversy. *A Week on the Concord and Merrimack Rivers* is about a lark of a trip he enjoyed with his brother John, floating and ruminating in a fifteen-foot dory, when Henry was twenty-two. *Cape Cod*, although rather more somber, recounts his impressions while walking the beach and the scrublands on three brief, almost impromptu jaunts to the Cape ten or fifteen years later, twice in the company of Ellery Channing, when he was much concerned, in any case, with the plentiful anecdotes that he gleaned from the inhabitants.

His journeys to Maine, in 1846, 1853, and 1857, bracketed his walks on the Cape and were planned more ambitiously, as if carrying a heavier significance. They were strenuous warm-weather paddles and hikes made always with a paid guide and at least one additional companion—on the first trip, altogether a party of six. Thoreau, as we read him, seems like a personable, vigorous Harvard graduate who, after trying to teach school and then a stint in his father's pencil-manufacturing business, had realized that his only wish was to become a writer and had set out to do so. As on the Cape, his professional purpose was to write thoughtful, descriptive essays for such magazines as *The Atlantic Monthly* and *Putnam's Monthly*, not a seamlessly coherent effort like *Walden*.

This is our most commonsensical Thoreau, and his guides respected his aptitudes, utilized him in the rapids, on the carries, and at trail-blazing, camping affably and volunteering as well as trading information with him. Thoreau, sleeping less and working harder than most of his companions, not only gathered a short glossary of Abnaki Indian words and compiled a list of birds and vegetation seen, but persuaded Joe Polis (the Indian that the sympathetic Emerson later said he "deserved") to tell him numerous stories and bits of folklore, such as that the first moose was a whale that crawled up on the land with jellyfish for bowels. He even got Polis to sing. Cedar beer, hemlock tea, moose lips (a dish), wolf howls, cougar tracks, houses sixty miles apart, salmon eaten off a birchbark plate with a fork whittled from an alder twig: these were some of his delights.

Logging was the industry, but Maine was so roomy that the Abnakis had not been annihilated or seriously embittered. The rivers saw log drives instead of flotillas of trippers, and "God's own horses"—moose—were still abundant. Thoreau met two métis hunters who had shot twenty-two for the skin trade. A guide was really needed in those days, and this is a rare episode in Thoreau's work when we see him as an employer, paymaster (though he must have supervised employees at his family's pencil factory too), and bourgeois Bostonian on vacation. He seems wholly natural in the role, but exults at one point that he is seventy-five miles from a road, and at another that there are still places where one "might live and die and never hear of the United States, which make such a noise in the world—never hear of America, so called from the name of a European gentleman." Joe Polis asks after a brother who has not shown up at home for a year or so after going off hunting—not worried that he is dead so much as wondering where in a woods so big he is contentedly wandering. In the virgin timber the loggers like to have a yoke of oxen mount each giant stump, "as if that were what the pine had grown for, to become a footstool of oxen," Thoreau observes. More happily, he lies listening to Polis talking in his own language to a St. Francis Indian they encounter, trying to guess their subject matter by their gestures.

"Generally speaking, a howling wilderness does not howl," Thoreau says, but revels in the campfires ten feet long and four feet high, with snowberry and checkerberry tea, trout and moose-meat, and talk of snapping-turtle-and-beaver meals with men who write to one another on the sides of trees. The fish in the streams below Mount Katahdin are as colorful as flowers, and bite wildly. Indeed, theirs is only the fifth party of white people to have climbed it, he says—a mile high and known as *Kette-Adene,* "greatest mountain," to the Indians. And although Thoreau wasn't an exceptional woodsman—only an exceptional writer—his ebullience brimmed so high he climbed way ahead of his guides and friends on the day they reached the foot of the mountain, got himself close to the top, then came back and led the rest of them partway up the next morning, till, when they tired once again, he left them and scrambled clear to the summit by himself. Awesome with boulders the size of the cabin he had recently built at Walden Pond (as the route that he took still is, if you climb it alone on a day of mixed sunshine and fog), the steep pitch and bleak tundra on top reminded him of "a cloud-factory," and of the earth at its beginnings, made of "Chaos and ancient Night." Mountain peaks are among the unfinished parts of the globe, he says, and imagines Nature speaking to him: "Why came ye here before your time? . . . I have never made this soil for thy feet, this air for thy breathing. . . . Shouldst thou freeze or starve, or shudder thy life away, here is no shrine, nor altar, nor any access to my ear."

It's high-flown, but not a preposterous-sounding apostrophe for any reader who has hiked on barren, fog-swept terrain, and of a piece with his frequent arpeggios to Indians, "the red face of man," who eat "no hot bread and sweet cake," but muskrat, moose-meat, and the fat of bears. Though happy and enthusiastic in the wilderness (he hails the heroism of the first white settler's dog on Chamberlain Lake, whose nose must take the porcupine quills for the rest of his race), he is not sentimental, but quite cool in his judgments—a freethinker first and a chum second—and pays the Abnakis the compliment of his close interest, seeming to scribble notes almost nonstop, noting even the piles of moose hair they have scraped at campsites to lighten the weight of their loads. "Here, then," he had said, explaining part of why he'd entered these wild woods, "one could no longer accuse institutions and society, but must front the true source of evil."

He was not a man who looked for evil, however—only for foolishness. He was primarily a fact-seeker and a rhapsodist, and relished announcing incongruities when no revelation was at hand. He was capable of sadness and pity as well as fanfares, but did not really believe in evil. Disappointed on his first trip to Maine by the failure of two Penobscot Indians to show up because of "a drunken frolic," he comments matter-of-factly on their resemblance to "the sinister and slouching fellows whom you meet picking up strings and paper in the streets of a city. . . . The one is no more a child of nature than the other." But Joe Polis's intelligent assistance during the third trip made him wax transcendental in a letter to his friend Harrison Blake: "I flatter myself that the world appears in some respects a little larger and not as usual smaller and shallower for having extended my range. . . . The Indian . . . begins where we leave off," he adds, and as a result seems "so much the more divine; and anything that fairly excites our admiration expands us."

His book on Cape Cod is somewhat gloomier and more jittery. The sea is not a light subject; and he begins with the sight of dead people washed ashore from the wreck of an immigrants' ship and mourners arriving from Boston to collect the bodies. But generally, except for those few hours atop Katahdin or at the Cape, Thoreau never knew a Nature that he couldn't trust. Nevertheless he celebrated the idea that we "hardly know where the rivers come from which float our navy"—as did Melville, just as rapt, often as jubilant. For both, nature was the central contingency, the core question or moral event of human existence. "From the Passamaquoddy to the Sabine" (Maine to Texas), the continent is still "No-Man's Land," Thoreau exclaimed. At the Redwood Agency in Minnesota, at the end of his life, he even met the Sioux war chief Little Crow, who a year later was to lead an uprising in which eight hundred white pioneers were killed. But for Melville, nature encompassed the constant possibility of drowning, or of a Little Crow turning murderous, or a dose of solitude that was so strong and deep that it inflicted a madness like poor Pip's in *Moby-Dick* upon the sufferer.

Thoreau had no interest in the pathology of solitude and didn't engage in marathons of living alone; malignancy of any kind did not intrigue him. And gaily competent as he was when savoring a trip to the wilderness, he never thought of *staying* in Maine. Quite a sociable man, he was mostly concerned with far more domesticated expressions of nature, and he was offering himself as an exemplar of how anybody could live in leisurely allegiance to it even on the outskirts of a settled community. There was some gallantry to the experiment because so many people ridiculed it. Of course, the conventional thing for a man with a taste for the woods to do was to go West; and when *Walden* failed to be appropriately understood beyond the circle of his friends (*Knickerbocker* magazine reviewed it together with P. T. Barnum's autobiography as "humbug"), he seems to have lost heart, or at any rate, the impetus of confidence. His most radical views had always been concerned with how people should live, not the idea of preserving wild places at the expense of profit and development. His ire was more aroused as he watched people hiring away their lives piecemeal than by clearcut logging, and more by what went on inside New England's textile mills than by the smoke they spouted. Except for slaves and the newest immigrants, people then still seemed a precious commodity to everybody—neighbors noticed daily and personally. How decently they lived their lives was a matter of lifelong observation.

Thoreau's was stripped down to few entanglements apart from those he had been born with, and he devoted it mainly to keeping his six-thousand-page journal based on his long afternoon walks when he went out in search of new premonitions as well as in order to spot the phenomena of natural history in which he rooted his essays. His biography is barebones: he visited New York City twice, Staten Island, Fire Island, walked in the Catskills and Berkshires. He never married, didn't go to church, never voted, never drank alcohol, and smoked nothing "more noxious than dried lily stems," said Emerson. "He had no temptations to fight against—no appetites, no passions, no taste for elegant trifles. A fine house, dress, the manners and talk of highly cultivated people were all thrown away on him. . . . When asked at table what dish he preferred, he answered, 'The nearest.' . . . There was somewhat military in his nature not to be subdued, always manly and able, but rarely tender, as if he did not feel himself except in opposition. He wanted a fallacy to expose, a blunder to pillory. . . . It cost him nothing to say No; indeed, he found it much easier than to say Yes. . . . 'I love Henry,' said one of his friends, 'but I cannot like him; and as for taking his arm, I should as soon think of taking the arm of an elm tree.' " He was a born protestant, Emerson added in the funeral oration which remains the best summary of his qualities ever written; yet "no truer American existed." And though the circumstances of his life appear remarkably uncomplicated, he made so bold as to comment upon everybody else's.

Emerson, speaking affectionately of Thoreau's "endless walks and miscellaneous studies," mentions that the pond lily was his favorite flower and his favorite tree a certain basswood that bloomed in July, whose scent was "oracular" and yet earthy. The grate of gravel under his feet disturbed his delicacy so much that he avoided the highroad when he could for a path through the woods. Thank God they could not cut down the clouds, Henry had said of the axmen then infesting New England. But Emerson believed that "great men are more distinguished by range and extent than by originality" (in an essay on Shakespeare). "The hero is in the press of knights and the thick of events." So it was inevitable that Emerson didn't entirely apprehend Thoreau's achievement. With his energy and practical ability, he had seemed "born for great enterprise and for command, and I so much regret the loss of his rare powers of action that I cannot help counting it a fault in him that he had no ambition. Wanting this, instead of engineering for all America, he was the captain of a huckleberry party," Emerson wrote, in hyperbole. "Pounding beans is good to the end of pounding empires one of these days; but if, at the end of years, it is still only beans!"

America was pounding its way to prominence as a world power and mightily engrossed in inventorying its resources. We can see from reading *The Maine Woods* that Thoreau was indeed a brisk organizer. Emerson perhaps conceived that he had the wherewithal to be a sort of John Wesley Powell, the Civil War hero who, though left with one arm, explored the thousand-mile sequence of canyons of the Green and Colorado rivers seven years after Thoreau's death as head of a small daredevil expedition, and wrote a superb book about it; then went on to become not only director of the U. S. Geological Survey but also the first director of the U. S. Bureau of Ethnology. The vigor, pleasure, and breadth of curiosity Thoreau exhibited in Maine give at least a hint of how successfully he might have pursued such a dashingly nineteenth-century type of career if he had wanted to. Frederick Law Olmsted, the landscape architect who designed Central Park and many other parks from the late 1850s on and who probably contributed more pleasure to the public than any other American artist has, is another example of uncloistered intellectuality. So are John James Audubon, who died in 1851 after writing a vivid journal of his travels as well as painting an encyclopedia of Creation, and George Catlin (1796–1872), who wrote about the vanishing Indian tribes almost as brilliantly as he painted them. John Muir (1838–1914) walked about as far as any American except the original mountainmen and virtually founded the conservation movement here. Francis Parkman graduated seven years behind Thoreau at Harvard, went west to live among the Sioux, published a sprightly account of his adventures in *The Oregon Trail,* and immediately plunged into his life's work, a seven-volume history of *France and England in North America,* which for scholarship and stylistic and dramatic panache remains a benchmark in American historical writing.

But Emerson, in complaining of Thoreau's lack of vocation, was partly addressing his own dilemma. America since Jefferson hasn't had a national intellectual, and like the skeptic Henry Adams, Emerson often wondered what he himself was—what he should do. He was as rapturous a writer as Thoreau, although possessed of a more comprehensive versatility and more temperance in his passions. He wrote an insightful, delightful book on *English Traits* and others on *Representative Men* and *The Conduct of Life,* and the titles of his many essays bespeak his aspirations: "Love," "Friendship," "Heroism," "Prudence," "Intellect," "Art," "Experience," "Character," "Politics," "The American Scholar." However, Thoreau tended to address a number of themes simultaneously. Thoreau's method was to write in such a way that topics blended with each other indirectly, which because life itself makes no neat demarcations is one key to his mastery. But after *Walden,* his emphasis gradually changed from individual reform to social reform and from Transcendentalism to a more modest fascination with nature as natural history, probably influenced by the coming tragedy of the Civil War as well as by his failure to win much recognition.

"I brag for humanity," he had written in *Walden;* and his bold irreverence, self-assurance, and certainty that nature was the central theater of life carried it off. Without Emerson, fourteen years older, to encourage and champion him, his life would have been far more problematical and threadbare. When one reads the chronology of his life, with its edgy penury and fits and starts, what seems remarkable is not how little but how much he wrote. His famous, cocksure pronouncement that "the mass of men lead lives of quiet desperation" is a dubious proposition—yet wasn't his? Well, no, it wasn't. He had set as his principle that what he thought—not just how he lived, but what he *thought*—mattered surpassingly, and that one man operating alone with no resources except his eyes and ears, his powers of logic, intuition, association, and language, could be pivotal in the meritocracy of the mind. He'd been a wall plasterer, chimney builder, appletree grafter, had paid his dues as a walker and canoeist, had slept sometimes in huts or on the ground, and made no fuss about his college credentials. ("Let each sheep wear his own skin," he said, when asked whether he wanted a sheepskin diploma.) And what still makes him uncannily appealing is not just his eerie contemporaneity of spirit as he writes about Maine, Cape Cod, or Walden Pond, but his assumption that all speculation is open to him, that no prevailing opinion can stand against plain common sense.

Transcendentalism was eclipsed by a century's worth of literary realism in the aftermath of the Civil War; but not Thoreau. Most freewheeling essay-writing in America on any subject derives from him, and that's because he was exact, tactile, and practical in what he said, despite being a romantic. The twentieth century's horrific wars didn't crush the force of his sensibility for readers either, though one can argue with his aphorisms. Indeed, we're "constantly invited to be what we are," as he said. Yet for the rest of us the choice may embrace contradictory impulses: true-blue husband and yet romancer of women; indefatigable mother and yet a workaholic lawyer; lover of the city but lover of the ocean. Thoreau never appears to have considered that anybody he was writing for might be any different from him—might want children, for instance, or might love sumptuous food and sensual alliances and volleys of conversation as well as piney woods and loons calling. "Fire is the most tolerable third party," he wrote (though his tiny cabin at Walden did contain three chairs). The rich salt crackling of hemlock needles was "like mustard to the ear."

The death of his brother from lockjaw in 1842 had propelled Henry into a nervous collapse with psychosomatic symptoms, and the execution of John Brown seventeen years later afflicted him similarly; so he was clearly a vulnerable man, not impervious to ordinary emotions. But he had few complicating cross-loyalties and gave no hostages to fortune. He believed that life was for exulting and for self-invention; and walking out of doors about four hours a day (buttering his boots to waterproof them), using his "Realometer" on what he observed, or inspecting the beautiful patterns of fern leaves and of the rainbow tints of clam shells in the dark mud of rivers, while smelling the "raspberry air," he lived enviably. One reads Thoreau for his foxy grace and crystalline precision, his joyful inventories and resilient spirits. Like any good naturalist, he believed that human nature is part of nature, not set aside from it, and his attention did not intensify when he was looking at human behavior instead of at wind riffling a lake. He had consummate faith that integrity and direct speaking would carry the day—that if he spoke his mind it would turn out to be something fresh and forever. And nature repaid his faith by making that true.

Dogs
and the
Tug of Life

It used to be that you could tell just about
how poor a family was by how many dogs they had. If they had
one, they were probably doing all right. It was only American to
keep a dog to represent the family's interests in the intrigues of the
back alley; not to have a dog at all would be like not acknowledg-
ing one's poor relations. Two dogs meant that the couple were dog
lovers, with growing children, but still might be members of the
middle class. But if a citizen kept three, you could begin to suspect
he didn't own much else. Four or five irrefutably marked the
household as poor folk, whose yard was also full of broken cars
cannibalized for parts. The father worked not much, fancied himself a hunter; the mother's teeth were black. And an old bachelor
living in a shack might possibly have even more, but you knew
that if one of them, chasing a moth, didn't upset his oil lamp some
night and burn him up, he'd fetch up in the poorhouse soon, with
the dogs shot. Nobody got poor feeding a bunch of dogs, needless
to say, because the more dogs a man had, the less he fed them.
Foraging as a pack, they led an existence of their own, but served
as evidence that life was awfully lonesome for him and getting out
of hand. If a dog really becomes a man's best friend his situation is
desperate.

That dogs, low-comedy confederates of small children and
ragged bachelors, should have turned into an emblem of having
made it to the middle class—like the hibachi, like golf clubs and a
second car—seems at the very least incongruous. Puppies which in
the country you would have to carry in a box to the church fair to
give away are bringing seventy-five dollars apiece in some of the
pet stores, although in fact dogs are in such oversupply that one

hundred and fifty thousand are running wild in New York City alone.

There is another line of tradition about dogs, however. Show dogs, toy dogs, foxhounds for formal hunts, Doberman guard dogs, bulldogs as ugly as a queen's dwarf. An aristocratic Spanish lady once informed me that when she visits her Andalusian estate each fall the mastiffs rush out and fawn about her but would tear to pieces any of the servants who have accompanied her from Madrid. In Mississippi it was illegal for a slave owner to permit his slaves to have a dog, just as it was to teach them how to read. A "Negro dog" was a hound trained by a bounty hunter to ignore the possums, raccoons, hogs, and deer in the woods that other dogs were supposed to chase, and trail and tree a runaway. The planters themselves, for whom hunting was a principal recreation, whooped it up when a man unexpectedly became their quarry. They caught each other's slaves and would often sit back and let the dogs do the punishing. Bennet H. Barrow of West Feliciana Parish in Louisiana, a rather moderate and representative plantation owner, recounted in his diary of the 1840s, among several similar incidents, this for November 11, 1845: In "5 minutes had him up & a going, And never in my life did I ever see as excited beings as R & myself, ran ½ miles & caught him dogs soon tore him naked, took him Home Before the other negro[es] at dark & made the dogs give him another over hauling." Only recently in Louisiana I heard what happened to two Negroes who happened to be fishing in a bayou off the Blind River, where four white men with a shotgun felt like fishing alone. One was forced to pretend to be a scampering coon and shinny up a telephone pole and hang there till he fell, while the other impersonated a baying, bounding hound.

Such memories are not easy to shed, particularly since childhood, the time when people can best acquire a comradeship with animals, is also when they are likely to pick up their parents' fears. A friend of mine hunts quail by jeep in Texas with a millionaire who brings along forty bird dogs, which he deploys in eight platoons that spell each other off. Another friend, though, will grow apprehensive at a dinner party if the host lets a dog loose in the room. The toothy, mysterious creature lies dreaming on the carpet, its paws pulsing, its eyelids open, the nictitating membranes twitching; how can he be certain it won't suddenly jump up and attack his legs under the table? Among Eastern European Jews, possession of a dog was associated with the hard-drinking *goyishe* peasantry, traditional antagonists, or else with the gentry, and many carried this dislike to the New World. An immigrant fleeing a potato famine or the hunger of Calabria might be no more equipped with the familiar British-German partiality to dogs—a failing which a few rugged decades in a great city's slums would not necessarily mend. The city had urbanized plenty of native farmers' sons as well, and so it came about that what to rural America had been the humblest, most natural amenity—friendship with a dog—has been transmogrified into a piece of the jigsaw of moving to the suburbs: there to cook outdoors, another bit of absurdity to the old countryman, whose toilet was outdoors but who was pleased to be able to cook and eat his meals inside the house.

There are an estimated forty million dogs in the United States (nearly two for every cat). Thirty-seven thousand of them are being destroyed in humane institutions every day, a figure which indicates that many more are in trouble. Dogs are hierarchal beasts, with several million years of submission to the structure of a wolf pack in their breeding. This explains why the Spanish lady's mastiffs can distinguish immediately between the mistress and her retainers, and why it is about as likely that one of the other guests at the dinner party will attack my friend's legs under the table as that the host's dog will, once it has accepted his presence in the room as proper. Dogs need leadership, however; they seek it, and when it's not forthcoming quickly fall into difficulties in a world where they can no longer provide their own.

"Dog" is "God" spelled backwards—one might say, way backwards. There's "a dog's life," "dog days," "dog-sick," "dog-tired," "dog-cheap," "dog-eared," "doghouse," and "dogs" meaning villains or feet. Whereas a wolf's stamina was measured in part by how long he could go without water, a dog's is becoming a matter of how long he can *hold* his water. He retrieves a rubber ball instead of coursing deer, chases a broom instead of hunting marmots. His is the lowest form of citizenship: that tug of life at the end of the leash is like the tug at the end of a fishing pole, and then one doesn't have to kill it. On stubby, amputated-looking feet he leads his life, which if we glance at it attentively is a kind of cutout of our own, all the more so for being riskier and shorter. Bam! A member of the family is dead on the highway, as we expected he would be, and we just cart him to the dump and look for a new pup.

Simply the notion that he lives on four legs instead of two has come to seem astonishing—like a goat or cow wearing horns on its head. And of course to keep a dog is a way of attempting to bring nature back. The primitive hunter's intimacy or telepathy with the animals he sought, surprising them at their meals and in their beds, then stripping them of their warm coats to expose a frame so like our own, is all but lost. Sport hunters, especially the older ones, retain a little of it still; and naturalists who have made up their minds not to kill wild animals nevertheless appear to empathize primarily with the predators at first, as a look at the tigers, bears, wolves, mountain lions on the project list of an organization such as the World Wildlife Fund will show. This is as it should be, these creatures having suffered from our brotherly envy before. But in order to really enjoy a dog, one doesn't merely try to train him to be semihuman. The point of it is to open oneself to the possibility of becoming partly a dog (after all, there are plenty of sub- or semi-human beings around whom we don't wish to adopt). One wants to rediscover the commonality of animal and man—to see an animal eat and sleep that hasn't forgotten how to enjoy doing such things—and the directness of its loyalty.

The trouble with the current emphasis on preserving "endangered species" is that, however beneficial to wildlife the campaign works out to be, it makes all animals seem like museum pieces, worth saving for sentimental considerations and as figures of speech (to "shoot a sitting duck"), but as a practical matter already dead and gone. On the contrary, some animals are flourishing. In 1910 half a million deer lived in the United States, in 1960 seven million, in 1970 sixteen million. What has happened is that now that we don't eat them we have lost that close interest.

Wolf behavior prepared dogs remarkably for life with human beings. So complete and complicated was the potential that it was only a logical next step for them to quit their packs in favor of the heady, hopeless task of trying to keep pace with our own community development. The contortions of fawning and obeisance which render group adjustment possible among such otherwise forceful fighters—sometimes humping the inferior members into the shape of hyenas—are what squeezes them past our tantrums, too. Though battling within the pack is mostly accomplished with body checks that do no damage, a subordinate wolf bitch is likely to remain so in awe of the leader that she will cringe and sit on her tail in response to his amorous advances, until his female coequal has had a chance to notice and dash over and redirect his attention. Altogether, he is kept so busy asserting his dominance that this top-ranked female may not be bred by him, finally, but by the male which occupies the second rung. Being breadwinners, dominant wolves feed first and best, just as we do, so that to eat our scraps and leavings strikes a dog as normal procedure. Nevertheless, a wolf puppy up to eight months old is favored at a kill, and when smaller can extract a meal from any pack member—uncles and aunts as well as parents—by nosing the lips of the adult until it regurgitates a share of what it's had. The care of the litter is so much a communal endeavor that the benign sort of role we expect dogs to play within our own families toward children not biologically theirs comes naturally to them.

For dogs and wolves the tail serves as a semaphore of mood and social code, but dogs carry their tails higher than wolves do, as a rule, which is appropriate, since the excess spirits that used to go into lengthy hunts now have no other outlet than backyard negotiating. In addition to an epistolary anal gland, whose message-carrying function has not yet been defined, the anus itself, or stool when sniffed, conveys how well the animal has been eating—in effect, its income bracket—although most dog foods are sorrily monotonous compared to the hundreds of tastes a wolf encounters, perhaps dozens within a single carcass. We can speculate on a dog's powers of taste because its olfactory area is proportionately fourteen times larger than a man's, its sense of smell at least a hundred times as keen.

The way in which a dog presents his anus and genitals for inspection indicates the hierarchal position that he aspires to, and other dogs who sniff his genitals are apprised of his sexual condition. From his urine they can undoubtedly distinguish age, build, state of sexual activity, and general health, even hours after he's passed by. Male dogs dislike running out of urine, as though an element of potency were involved, and try to save a little; they prefer not to use a scent post again until another dog has urinated there, the first delight and duty of the ritual being to stake out a territory, so that when they are walked hurriedly in the city it is a disappointment to them. The search is also sexual, because bitches in heat post notices about. In the woods a dog will mark his drinking places, and watermark a rabbit's trail after chasing it, as if to notify the next predator that happens by exactly who it was that put such a whiff of fear into the rabbit's scent. Similarly, he squirts the tracks of bobcats and of skunks with an aloof air unlike his brisk and cheery manner of branding another dog's or fox's trail, and if he is in a position to do so, will defecate excitedly on a bear run, leaving behind his best effort, which no doubt he hopes will strike the bear as a bombshell.

The chief complaint people lodge against dogs is their extraordinary stress upon lifting the leg and moving the bowels. Scatology did take up some of the slack for them when they left behind the entertainments of the forest. The forms of territoriality replaced the substance. But apart from that, a special zest for life is characteristic of dogs and wolves—in hunting, eating, relieving themselves, in punctiliously maintaining a home territory, a pecking order and a love life, and educating the resulting pups. They grin and grimace and scrawl graffiti with their piss. A lot of inherent strategy goes into these activities: the way wolves spell each other off, both when hunting and in their governess duties around the den, and often "consult" as a pack with noses together and tails wagging before flying in to make a kill. (Tigers, leopards, house cats base their social relations instead upon what ethologists call "mutual avoidance.") The nose is a dog's main instrument of discovery, corresponding to our eyes, and so it is that he is seldom offended by organic smells, such as putrefaction, and sniffs intently for the details of illness, gum bleeding, and diet in his master and his own fellows, and for the story told by scats, not closing off the avenue for any reason—just as we rarely shut our eyes against new information, even the tragic or unpleasant kind.

Though dogs don't see as sharply as they smell, trainers usually rely on hand signals to instruct them, and most firsthand communication in a wolf pack also seems to be visual—by the expressions of the face, by body English and the cant of the tail. A dominant wolf squares his mouth, stares at and "rides up" on an inferior, standing with his front legs on its back, or will pretend to stalk it, creeping along, taking its muzzle in his mouth, and performing nearly all of the other discriminatory pranks and practices familiar to anybody who has a dog. In fact, what's funny is to watch a homely mutt as tiny as a shoebox spin through the rigmarole which a whole series of observers in the wilderness have gone to great pains to document for wolves.

Dogs proffer their rear ends to each other in an intimidating fashion, but when they examine the region of the head it is a friendlier gesture, a snuffling between pals. One of them may come across a telltale bone fragment caught in the other's fur, together with a bit of mud to give away the location of bigger bones. On the same impulse, wolves and free-running dogs will sniff a wanderer's toes to find out where he has been roaming. They fondle and propitiate with their mouths also, and lovers groom each other's fur with tongues and teeth adept as hands. A bitch wolf's period in heat includes a week of preliminary behavior and maybe two weeks of receptivity—among animals, exceptionally long. Each actual copulative tie lasts twenty minutes or half an hour, which again may help to instill affection. Wolves sometimes begin choosing a mate as early as the age of one, almost a year before they are ready to breed. Dogs mature sexually a good deal earlier, and arrive in heat twice a year instead of once—at any season instead of only in midwinter, like a wolf, whose pups' arrival must be scheduled unfailingly for spring. Dogs have not retained much responsi-

bility for raising their young, and the summertime is just as perilous as winter for them because, apart from the whimsy of their
owners, who put so many of them "to sleep," their nemesis is the
automobile. Like scatology, sex helps fill the gulf of what is gone.

The scientist David Mech has pointed out how like the posture of a wolf with a nosehold on a moose (as other wolves attack
its hams) are the antics of a puppy playing tug-of-war at the end of
a towel. Anybody watching a dog's exuberance as he samples bites
of long grass beside a brook, or pounds into a meadow bristling
with the odors of woodchucks, snowshoe rabbits, grouse, a doe and
buck, field mice up on the seedheads of the weeds, kangaroo mice
jumping, chipmunks whistling, weasels and shrews on the hunt, a
plunging fox and a porcupine couched in a tree, perhaps can begin
to imagine the variety of excitements under the sky that his ancestors relinquished in order to move indoors with us. He'll lie down
with a lamb to please us, but as he sniffs its haunches, surely he must
remember atavistically that this is where he'd start to munch.

There is poignancy in the predicament of a great many animals: as in the simple observation which students of the California
condor have made that this huge, most endangered bird prefers
the carrion meat of its old standby, the deer, to all the dead cows,
sheep, horses, and other substitutes it sees from above, sprawled
about. Animals are stylized characters in a kind of old saga—stylized
because even the most acute of them have little leeway as they play
out their parts. (*Rabbits,* for example, I find terribly affecting, imprisoned in their hop.) And as we drift away from any cognizance
of them, we sacrifice some of the intricacy and grandeur of life.
Having already lost so much, we are hardly aware of what remains,
but to a primitive snatched forward from an earlier existence it
might seem as if we had surrendered a richness comparable to all
the tapestries of childhood. Since this is a matter of the imagination as well as of animal demographics, no Noah projects, no bio-
nomic discoveries on the few sanctuaries that have been established
are going to reverse the swing. The very specialists in the forefront
of finding out how animals behave, when one meets them, appear
to be no more intrigued than any ordinary Indian was.

But we continue to need—as aborigines did, as children do—a
parade of morality tales which are more concise than those that
politics, for instance, later provides. So we've had Aesop's and medieval and modern fables about the grasshopper and the ant, the
tiger and Little Black Sambo, the wolf and the three pigs, Br'er
Rabbit and Br'er Bear, Goldilocks and her three bears, or Little Red
Ridinghood, Pooh Bear, Babar and the rhinos, Walt Disney's animals, and assorted humbler scary bats, fat hippos, funny frogs, and

eager beavers. Children have a passion for clean, universal defini-
tions, and so it is that animals have gone with children's literature
as Latin has with religion. Through them they first encountered
death, birth, their own maternal feelings, the gap between beauty
and cleverness, or speed and good intentions. The animal kingdom
boasted the powerful lion, the mothering goose, the watchful owl,
the tardy tortoise, Chicken Little, real-life dogs that treasure bones,
and mink that grow posh pelts from eating crawfish and mussels.

In the cartoons of two or three decades ago, Mouse doesn't get
along with Cat because Cat must catch Mouse or miss his supper.
Dog, on the other hand, detests Cat for no such rational reason,
only the capricious fact that dogs don't dote on cats. Animal stories
are bounded, yet enhanced, by each creature's familiar lineaments,
just as a parable about a prince and peasant, a duchess and a milkmaid, a blacksmith and a fisherman, would be. Typecasting, like
the roll of a metered ode, adds resonance and dignity, summoning
up all of the walruses and hedgehogs that went before: the shrewd
hillbilly image of Br'er Rabbit to assist his suburban relative Bugs
Bunny behind the scenes. But now, in order to present a tale about
the contest between two thieving crows and a scarecrow, the story-
teller would need to start by explaining that once upon a time
crows used to eat a farmer's corn if he didn't defend it with a mock
man pinned together from old clothes. Crows are having a hard go
of it and may eventually receive game-bird protection.

One way childhood is changing, therefore, is that the nonhu-
man figures—"Wild Things" or puppet monsters—constructed by
the best of the new artificers, like Maurice Sendak or the *Sesame
Street* writers, are distinctly humanoid, ballooned out of faces and
torsos met on the subway. The televised character Big Bird does
not resemble a bird the way Bugs Bunny remained a rabbit—
though already he was less so than Br'er or Peter Rabbit. Big
Bird's personality, even her confusion, haven't the faintest connection to an ostrich's. Lest she be confused with an ostrich, her voice
has been slotted unmistakably toward the prosaic. Dr. Seuss did
transitional composites of worldwide fauna, but these new shapes—
a beanbag like the *Sesame Street* Grouch or Cookie Monster or
Herry Monster, and the floral sorts of creations in books—have
been conceived practically from scratch by the artist ("in the night
kitchen," to use a Sendak phrase), and not transferred from the existing caricatures of nature. In their conversational conflicts they offer him a fresh start, which may be a valuable commodity, whereas
if he were dealing with an alligator, it would, while giving him an
old-fashioned boost in the traditional manner, at the same time box
him in. A chap called Alligator, with that fat snout and tail, can-

not squirm free of the solidity of actual alligators. Either it must stay a heavyweight or else play on the sternness of reality by swinging over to impersonate a cream puff and a Ferdinand.

Though animal programs on television are popular, what with the wave of nostalgia and "ecology" in the country, we can generally say about the animal kingdom, "The King is dead, long live the King." Certainly the talent has moved elsewhere. Those bulbous Wild Things and slant-mouthed beanbag puppets derived from the denizens of Broadway—an argumentative night news vendor, a lady on a traffic island—have grasped their own destinies, as characters on the make are likely to. It was inevitable they would. There may be a shakedown to remove the elements that would be too bookish for children's literature in other hands, and another shakedown because these first innovators have been more city-oriented than suburban. New authors will shift the character sources away from Broadway and the subway and the ghetto, but the basic switch has already been accomplished—from the ancient juxtaposition of people, animals, and dreams blending the two, to people and monsters that grow solely out of people by way of dreams.

Which leaves us in the suburbs, with dogs as a last link. Cats are too independent to care, but dogs are in an unenviable position, they hang so much upon our good opinion. We are coming to *have* no opinion; we don't pay enough attention to form an opinion. Though they admire us, are thrilled by us, heroize us, we regard them as a hobby or a status symbol, like a tennis racquet, and substitute leash laws for leadership—expect them not simply to learn English but to grow hands, because their beastly paws seem stranger to us every year. If they try to fondle us with their handyjack mouths, we read it as a bite; and like used cars, they are disposed of in the scurry of divorce or when the family relocates or changes what it's "into." The first reason people kept a dog was to acquire an ally on the hunt, a friend at night. Then it was to maintain an avenue to animality, as our own nearness began to recede. But as we lose our awareness of all animals, dogs are becoming a bridge to nowhere. We can only pity their fate.

Other Lives

There often seems to be a playfulness to wise people, as if either their equanimity has as its source this playfulness or the playfulness flows from the equanimity; and they can persuade other people who are in a state of agitation to calm down and manage a smile. If they believe in God and an afterlife, then the parts of life we are not responsible for are naturally rather a game. If they don't believe, they find that generally it is more sensible to be amused than miserable. But what used to surprise me and make me a good deal less critical of everybody was to realize how vulnerable nearly anyone is, including these grown-up types. Unless he craves to straddle the world, there may be just a kernel of basic reassurance that each person needs. He needs some friends, some modest success in love or love life, a reasonable sense of accomplishment in the work that he does, and a home. Yet these benefits, in competition, are not so easily obtained. If our needs seem relatively simple, the psyches with which and the circumstances from which we must win satisfaction are not, and we live a long while, besides, seldom able to rest on our laurels.

So one discovers that everybody's equilibrium is surprisingly shaky, that you can't with impunity criticize someone, and that if you do criticize him you may rattle him more than you had intended. More to the point, though, I began to grasp that snap judgments are incomplete, unjust, that the complex of emotion and difficulty in which another man or woman lives cannot be quickly ascertained. Of course, the glory and luck of it is that running counter to all that shakiness is a resilience: you can't shake up the person for long. Most of us have a way of riding out assaults or disappointments of even the toughest variety, an animal salubrity that somehow takes over and that we trust in, that makes us begin to grin a little again after a night's sleep, a long walk in the sunshine, a good meal or two.

The great leveler nowadays is divorce; almost everybody thinks about it, whether because we expect to be happy all the time— daily, weekly—or because we want the smell of brimstone in lives made too affluent and easy. Maybe some of us will end up back with the same wives and husbands again at the end of our lives (we sometimes hope so), but in the meantime it's as if marriage had become a chancy, grim, modern experiment instead of an ancient institution. *We have other lives to lead,* we say to ourselves, casting about for more freedom or erotic sizzle, more simplicity, leisure, "integrity" at work, or money, or whatever. Physiologically men reach their sexual peak at nineteen, an appropriate age for their original life span of thirty years, but now they have forty more years to go, and the expectation is that every year should be terribly straightforward or terribly crowded in every respect. To be original is to be lonely, we've always been told, and for that reason, too, we may feel the need for some form of hazard to enter our lives, especially if it was not in our diet when we were young. Many divorces are not really the result of irreparable injury but involve, instead, a desire on the part of the man or woman to shatter the setup, start out from scratch alone, and make life work for them all over again. They want the risk of disaster, want to touch bottom, see where bottom is, and, coming up, to breathe the air with relief and relish again.

It's not easy. The public effort to look harmonious may help hold some couples together. After sitting in silence going to a party, they will hold hands in the taxi when they come home; they make love rarely, but do so with pleasure if they have company staying over. Moreover, some of their differences are disconcertingly homely ones. She wants to sell the house, he wants to keep it, and they disagree about the children's school. He resents the fact that she got herself pregnant "accidentally" for each of the children, but she is sick and tired of battling his timidity, which, among other things, would have meant that he'd never have had any children at all if she hadn't taken matters in hand. He resents almost as a betrayal her quick abandonment of most of the sex games—what she calls "Krafft-Ebbing" now—that so pleased him during their courtship and drew him on, but she is tired of holding him to a maturity that should befit the head of a household; it doesn't seem to come naturally to him. Bachelors fall into two types, as she sees them—the "glassies," who reflect back what they encounter, and the thickset, blocked, sad fellows, to whom passivity is a pain and a blight—and he probably would have been one of the latter if she hadn't turned up, had their first child, and settled down into family life, exchanging her rakish black boots for shoes. She wants to go to Europe this summer, whereas he wants to bask at the beach. She thinks he treats his mother and father badly and that his behavior in their own fights is a continuation of hangups

he has with them, but he makes no bones about his contention
that her affection for *her* parents is livelier than what she feels for
him, that even her preoccupation with motherhood is partly an
attempt to give to the world her mother all over again.

They're at swords' points; grotesqueries come to the fore. He
carries a portable radio everywhere, even to the dinner table, the
bathroom, and she constantly plays with the dog. He's sick of the
hack of her nervous cough and she of his scratching his ass. In bed,
when they argue late into the night or lie rigid, unable to speak,
she crosses her arms on her chest and he holds his balls as if to keep
them intact for life later on. Apprehension and exhaustion make
them postpone separating, but they take to fighting via notes left
in prominent spots about the house, bulletins to be read in silence
and answered by the same method, which cuts down the talk. Yet
neither really wants this disaster; their nerves and their stomachs
beg them to have a care.

For a poor boy, just earning a lot of money used to be plenty.
Now moneymaking is seldom sufficient—*we have other lives to lead.*
On the contrary, the higher the wages, the more wildcat strikes
there are; a malaise afflicts the assembly lines. It's their time off
that people are concerned with. Hitchhiking has had a new vogue
for its dramatization of rootlessness, and a good many young men
and women brought up comfortably in the suburbs have plunged
into bucolic living, the men immediately confronting the extraordinary question of whether or not they could build a house for
themselves. To do so seemed essential to them, and a surprising
proportion did manage somehow. As one visits among the communes, one finds the woods full of houses—sheepherders' cabins,
Japanese hutches, alpine chalets, airy, belvedered, summery bow-
ers—that often are empty. The fellow, hastily beginning the job,
worrying about that formidable scatter of sawmill lumber—the
footing and sills and studs and siding—forgot to think about locating water, or built uphill from his spring. Or maybe the site is
so woodsy-lovely that his girlfriend finds it frightening at night;
they're sleeping instead in a Volkswagen van parked next to
the central farmhouse. Isolated shacks dispersed about may have
come to seem in conflict with the overall experiment in living.
Or perhaps the builders merely moved on, leaving these homes
like dated bomb shelters.

Some communes are for homesteading, others are rest homes
or pleasure domes. Some are loose neighborly arrangements not
unlike pioneer settlements where the people pitched in to help
one another; others have a religiosity about them, though it may
rather smack of the Children's Crusade. In Vermont, close by

the subsistence existence that with some difficulty can still be achieved—outhouse, staked pig—is the fact of Boston or New York a few hours away. Even though the choice of living this way has been deliberate, a communard would have to be unusual to shut himself up on a mountain slope as if the contemporary world didn't exist at all. So these people make trips out, dipping into the maelstrom of the city every few months, working locally in town if they need cash, a rhythm that can be precise. Movies, restaurants, traffic, then home to a brook they can drink from: silence, noise, silence and noise.

Because it's a bad time for ideology, the communes are fading in favor of families who live private lives on a separate but cooperative basis. The problem remains that a place where land is cheap enough for the simple life is also a depressed area, where even the natives don't find much work, and so the women tend to do better than the men as the months become years. Not feeling obliged to come up with the mortgage money, the women set about doing what they might do anywhere—taking care of the kids, being ameliorative, homemaking. Particularly if they are the earth-mother sort to begin with, they thrive, while the men are dishwashers during the tourist season or carpenters or mechanics or set up a bakery, do leatherwork, carve salad bowls, drive a truck, until the limitations to earning a living in such a parched economy may come to seem not worth the candle.

I don't believe this rural activity is only a footnote to the divisiveness of the Vietnam War. People are going to keep choosing a manner of living to suit themselves, and there are going to be different ways: we forget what miracles we are. On summer holidays some of the long-haired couples and communes in my town in Vermont get together for a big softball game, everybody contributing food for the meal that follows. The lush grass is high except where they've knocked it down, the outfield is full of extra fielders, and each team tries to run up the score. Watching the playing, the smiles people wear as they swing, I think it must be as gleeful a time as any, these late twenties that most of them are in. Sometimes I feel as though I'm looking at snapshots taken today of one or another of them, young, happy, at a kind of peak, on the best afternoon of their twenty-eighth summer. It's so American a scene that nearly everyone must be represented here, the lank hair only a disguise. I wonder where they will be, what will have happened to them, what changes their faces will show in twenty-eight more. Smiling in the sun, a girl takes a strong swing, and I feel perhaps some of the same painful tenderness she herself would feel years from now, holding pictures from today in her hands, pictures such as old men and women will show you to indicate that they too were graceful once and had happy times.

Afterwards, when the crowd is gone, my friend who owns the ballfield calls in his herd of goats for milking. "Goatee! Goatee!" The goats with their bland farmer faces run in a bevy of white bobbing heads, mild-looking. The unfinished new barn is a competent crosshatch of joists and roof beams, taller than it will seem when it is completed. We are friends because recently we walked forty-five miles together, cooking over wispy fires, eating from the same pot, hunching under a canvas fly in the rain. He is so well settled here after eight years that it took me almost the whole hike to see him in the other guise that I always look for: what he would have been if he hadn't left New York City. Finally, in the rain when he was tired, I did recognize the New York face he would have worn, and it was darkly confused and sad. Often behind the communard's veil of hair one sees a man who is just marking time, sliding past forks in the road that he should take, but here was my friend, with his fields and his garden and goats, in the midst of life.

During the Black Power period of the late 1960s in New York City, one baby-sitter who came to our apartment looked at our baby's blond head, and when she thought that they were alone, said to her, "How would you like to be thrown out the window?" But another baby-sitter caught my hand when I paid her and tried to kiss it and lay it against her cheek, while her knees bent as if she were going to kneel—this not "camp," you understand; her boyfriend was a white policeman, and it was actually what she most wished to do. There is no accounting for individuality. Hairdressers at the same time were costuming themselves as if for service under the Jolly Roger, with hanging the penalty if they were caught. Their savage mustaches would have fit them to ride with a bandit band in the massifs of Afghanistan.

In New York if I go out my door and turn left I'm at the federal holding penitentiary almost immediately. Loudspeakers, guards with carbines, men in fetters taking a last look at the street before being led inside. There are attorneys, and the rigmarole of bread deliveries, and visiting wives, mothers and babies—"ten years!" in the snatches of conversation. It's said not to be a harsh place and probably would not have the facilities to handle much trouble, in any case. The guards who do look like ugly customers are the out-of-staters from prisons like Lewisburg who have driven in vans to transport the sentenced prisoners for a longer stay. They play with their chains as they wait—long waist and leg chains.

Turning right on the street, I'm soon at a drug peddlers' location, a slithy spot at midnight, where two dozen trucks are kept closely parked in a narrow lot and the very moonlight is blocked off by railroad tracks running above. Over by a single bulb at the far corner a mechanic, as a cover, is leaning into an engine, making some repairs, while the sellers, several of them, pace in and out between the tight trucks, quickly disappearing in the darkness to reappear at another spot. A series of Dickensian starvelings scutter up, each one palavering furtively and then moving off, while other addicts await their turn in the gloomy doorways down the block. They are mostly so thin that they remind me of the poverty of another continent, casting desolate-looking faces backward as they come, to see whether anybody is following them. But some drive up and park; and there's a courier service for wholesale deals, because every few minutes an off-duty taxi swings slowly past to make a pickup—if the cabbie is scared he keeps going around the block until one of the peddlers whistles at him. It's a perfect maze, and if all the people transacting business in an evening were scooped up, they would fill the federal detention headquarters. Some will find themselves there rapidly enough anyway. For them it is only a step from being free to being nabbed. They've already largely been nabbed.

The foghorns of this stretch of the waterfront, carried through the window, cause a slippage of resolve in me, just as they must work to demoralize the prisoners and peddlers and addicts nearby—we have other lives to lead. I'm not so sure I know what is permanent any more, although as recently as a year or two ago I thought that I did. The stars, the flowers, and so on—genes, mountains, and even the sore points of love. Picking at the heaps of raspberries growing up from the ruins of an old barn—sweet from the manuring of twenty years—I'd find a quietude in that. And our choreography, too, outlives us. A porcupine pushes its head around the corner of the house, and with weak bulging eyes cautiously sits up on its hindquarters before venturing onto the lawn. Porcupines chew holes in houses, so I slide inside for my gun. When my dog sees me loading he thinks his time may have come. He knows there is no escape, if so, having seen other men shoot other dogs, and he cringes as our eyes meet. The porcupine, which had retreated alongside the house, heads for the woods when I reappear, its waddle suddenly transformed into a flight for life. It is a primitive animal that when wounded still only waddles, cannot limp, but die it does, holding its wound with one hand and bracing itself with the other, sighing as a person would. Yet during this sad episode I've felt larger, quicker, hardly myself, augmented as though by the fact that each of us has moved along tracks older than our own time and place.

Most people enjoy some sense of permanence, even rather approving of the circumstance that old people eventually die (part of the permanence), until they themselves grow old. Children represent immortality, supposedly, and, to look at their scooting energy, they probably do. Their shouts are sufficient proof of that—shouts as harsh as a crow's cry that the next generation picks up at the age of five. Our image of ourselves throughout later life remains that of a person in his early twenties, old people say, and this may be part of the meaning of the vivid, monotonous schoolyard shouts. But much of my own feeling of permanence has been grounded in the wildness of the natural world. Wildness is permanence because it is what is unaltered, an infinity of particulars which are changing only very slowly without special reference to man. That the sun shines just as brightly on somebody who is dying of thirst in the desert is our good luck, because if he could turn out the sun for himself it would go out for us as well. Now, however, "wildness," instead of being infinity and superabundance, has a different reference: often simply the sniper gone haywire up in the bell tower. The glass panel in a taxicab that used to be there to protect the toffs from the unblanched opinions of the cabdriver is now intended to shield him from the violence of the toffs.

We don't know enough about what has been destroyed of the natural world even to take inventory; and though there should be other reasons besides what we call nature to believe in the permanence of the world, if nature in health and wealth and variety is to be permitted to exist only for its recreational value to man, then we must base our convictions about the world's permanence in the meanwhile, on the permanence of him. That wouldn't be so hard to do, when one considers people to be more good than bad, except for the exceptional power at hand nowadays in those brutal moments, even just to the local vandal. Ten years of good intentions can't match one night of cruelty; what we watch is the dangerously balanced duality. Where the Indians were spellbound by the succession of thunderheads in their sky—which was so much bigger than ours—we eye ourselves; or when we do turn our attention away from our own psyches, we watch our leaders, who have become bigger than the sky.

Looking at clergymen in the street, I notice the same inward stitching of worry in their faces that was characteristic of the profession when I went to church as a boy. It's like the face of a man at a sickbed when the patient has turned aside to his basin. The profession is in eclipse, almost in disrepute. First the civil-rights people wanted to know where the clergy had been for the past century or more; then the environmentalists wondered whether the clergy's sense of continuity extended only as far back as Christ's time. But clergymen have never claimed to be particularly prescient. They knew they weren't visionaries, but conventional fellows—good men at a sickbed—who tried to practice what everybody else preached, and who sorrowed about the same things a little bit more. They had not been much concerned with the lot of Negroes or the carnage in Vietnam until a larger constituency was; so, with the vulnerability of individuals who are both conventional and conscientious, they are quite rattled and feel blameworthy now.

The people with the fewest qualms are the evolutionists—those who remain evolutionists. Against most of the evidence of instability and disorientation, they proffer the same serviceable idea: that we have other lives to lead. Which is just what we always wished. To be married, yet take a vacation from marriage; to work and to loaf; to be kind and yet tough, rich yet idealistic; to live and to die.

We have our freedom and miraculous variance, and lately I've tried to discover which is the wildest mountain left in Vermont, from scouting as well as map-reading and talking to people. I think that I have. A jeep could bump to within a mile or two of the east or west base, but nobody happens to climb it. The mountains round about are encountered first, and it's an intricate, broad-topped, low little mountain, a confusion of starfish ridges and high swamps thick with windfalls. Nothing spectacular, no cliffs, waterfalls, or fifty-mile views, just lots of forest. Its only distinction is its wildness, and moose, bear, lynx, and coyotes make their homes there. I'm drawn to it and frequently wind toward it in walks, tasting the creeks that run off its sides, getting to know the valleys below, spending the night on mountains nearby so as to look at its contours at dusk and at dawn. Old logskidding trails go halfway up, and I soft-foot up some of these, watching for animal prints, but though it seems like a low little mountain, hiding its higher complexities, eventually I turn back, postponing climbing clear to the top. Such an important event should not be rushed. If this indeed is the most remote mountain in Vermont, I hope to explore it gradually for many summers and never really climb it. Wildness is indifference, wildness exists without any knowledge of whether or not it will be destroyed. Its survival on this last mountain matters not to the mountain, nor to the attributes that define wildness, but only to me.

Half the battle is knowing what matters, and if we are prepared to make up our minds, an almost unlimited number of choices exists; in a way, the world is less crowded than it used to be. Alongside the closeness and safeness and sameness of modern living is a frightening roominess—cheap instant travel, swift risk and misery, old-fashioned loneliness and poverty, wars marbled with primeval terror, yet scholarship leading straight toward the roots of life, and so many experiments in pleasure in progress that it takes only a minimal gift for adventure for somebody to live several lives in the space of one. What is scandalous or impermissible now? Kicking a child in the street; maybe a few other odd taboos. So, what is happening is that we come to face the decision: do we want to explore ourselves in several marriages or in only one? Do we want one life to lead, or more? And how much does our own ambivalence really interest us? Is our self-concern the best focus in life? No doubt there aren't single answers; nor will our private answers necessarily have much to do with how we behave. Instead, as always, we trust that when we make a mistake we will land on our feet. What we know, as social sea changes come roaring at us, is that human beings are extraordinarily adaptive.

I stand on a pier near my house, looking at the river and south toward the larger harbor. If I were feeling glum it might seem an escape route, but I'm simply watching the sunlight jiggle on the wide currents, which are refreshingly broader than the yardsticks of distance that one is used to in the city. The water's jiggling and skittering establishes a parallel lightness in me, and though the weather happens to be cold, the sun's warm sheen brings out from within me, besides my good spirits, the lizards, snakes, turtles that I sprang from—all the creatures that merged to make me and that loved the sunlight, depending upon it so much that even if I no longer need it as imperatively myself, I can't feel it on my skin without slowing my thoughts and my feet, stopping and closing my eyes for a moment to *bask*.

So the day is lovely: there's sunshine that I turn my throat to slowly, the water hopping and sparkling, and many moiling dogs. Out of doors, the dogs too arouse a level of existence that is usually sleeping in me. It's as if I had grown from them and my feet were still linked to them, as if I were dangling my legs in the spaciousness of them. Fortunately for my own safety, however, I'm neither lizard nor dog, because this is the center of the city and two or three hundred people besides me are taking their ease on the pier. An inventory of what they look like could encompass the history of the world, which, needless to say, I'm not up to; but I'm at home with them. Without sparing much attention from the boats and the children, the lovers and girls and old people whose stories I'd like to hear, I can pretty well spot people in trouble or those who spell trouble, and can get a handle on anybody who ambles near. Schizophrenia, diabetic collapse, belt-between-the-teeth for epilepsy—subway things. There are encroach-ers and trapped people and people here before they go home to dress for a party. One can place them in their apartments and with their friends.

Hundreds of people, and a freighter steaming grandly by, and barges, tugboats, police boats, sightseers' launches. The West Side Highway provides constant engine static; and two private planes are crossing overhead, and now a 707, big, flat, gray as the newest invented metal, on a descent pattern, sweeping around to-ward La Guardia Airport. A helicopter, too, is sliding downtown, very low and arrested-looking above us, with another angling in from New Jersey. From every direction aircraft are converging, it seems—I suddenly notice a third helicopter—and the trucks on West Street, and the roar of the cars on the highway over them, and some stunting guy in a powerboat making waves down where we are, and these crowds of wrought-up people here to relax for an hour. Lizard though I am, dog that I am, I am able to absorb it all. Somehow the more the merrier. I'm grinning. It's like swim-ming in the ocean, and suddenly Lake Superior is dumped in, then the Danube and Nile, then the Caspian Sea. One bobs above them. Whether one will always bob above them is a question. But, grin-ning, one finds that somehow each increment is adjusted for; one rides above it. It can all be absorbed.

The Midnight Freight
to Portland

Railroads provided the big bones of American industry and of much of the country's mythology, too, until the current containerized epoch of trucks and the small-world era of planes. Children rushed out and waved and their fathers stood alert when a train steamed through town, sometimes crossing at street level, bringing all traffic to a halt, and maybe stopping to let passengers off or maybe not, though they would look out of the windows ironically, in any case. Part of the privilege of being downtown was to see them and to watch the train, boiling with noise and momentum, the crew ten feet above the ground, detached-looking and farsighted even as they loafed. Their travels lasted nights and days—even the gandy dancers were legends—and no writer who seriously pursued the chimera of the great American novel could neglect to learn some of the lore of railroading.

Recently I rode a freight train from Island Pond in northeastern Vermont to Portland, Maine, to see how the trains run; there has been no passenger service on the line, or anywhere else in Vermont, for years. This is the last hundred and fifty miles of the famous Grand Trunk international rail route from Montreal to the ice-free saltwater harbor in Casco Bay, something that the Canadians needed in 1853, when the last spikes were driven with a good deal of fanfare and acclaim. Later, when icebreakers were making more headway in the St. Lawrence, Portland still possessed a thriving year-round port where enormous amounts of Western grain arrived by rail to be shipped abroad. Twenty-six train crews were based in Island Pond to handle the activity; now there are only six. Island Pond is a railroad and sawmill town which does not hide the fact that it has come down in the world, although it's got some dairying going on where the woods aren't too thick and a little tourism. The station is a frowning sooty brick pile with a plaza-sized area left vacant all around. Many of the other local buildings look like old railroad stations too.

Since the 1920s the Grand Trunk's trackage and perquisites have belonged to the Canadian National Railways. Not wanting to go as a hobo, I'd written to the office in Montreal and was received royally. The station agent put me under the wing of Claude Seguin, his brother, the head-end brakeman on the train I rode. Seguin is a loose-cheeked, modest, drawling man with a farmer's emotive hands, an outdoorsman up early for long walks on his days off, who had been helping a neighbor clapboard his house. Like many railroad men, he collects timepieces as a hobby, even buying large restaurant clocks at auctions, cleaning off the grease, and putting them up around the house. I asked if he'd seen any hoboes lately. He said not for four or five years, although the crews used to let them ride if they looked decent. "We're just glorified hoboes ourselves, you know."

The engineer was Eddy Boylan, a quick gray active man well past the years when he may or may not have made some mistakes. The seniority system works excellently in railroading, ensuring that nobody who is still trying to prove something will be risking other people's lives. All these men were hefty veterans over fifty years old, with austere, snowy minds and furry, neutral-sounding voices: Joe Vautour, the fireman; Joe Cargill, the rear-end brakeman; and Donald MacDonald, a judgely, stern, but witty man who rides in the caboose ("buggy") and keeps the waybills straight.

I was eager to talk, but when the train pulled in we left immediately, as soon as the Montreal crew stepped off. It was dusk, and a full harvest moon—white, not red, in this cold border country—stood low in the sky toward Portland. The leaves were turning but not yet falling, and we entered fir forests, with low deserted mountains and tamarack bogs and bushy round wild islands posted in a series of lakes. The streams were black and shining; the clouds spread into herringbone patterns. I rode alone in the second of three engines, and Seguin or the fireman paid me visits. The engineer drives from the right-hand side of the front locomotive, controlling the other locomotives from there. The fireman, who nowadays, in the post-steam era, functions as a sort of copilot, sits at the left-hand window, looking out at crossings which the engineer can't see. He's there if the engineer gets sick or wishes to eat, in time of hazard, or if the walkie-talkies that the brakemen carry fail and they are dependent upon hand signals. Since he is basically a featherbedder, though, the fireman is mainly supposed to be good company, and Vautour, who has a world-worn face, a furrowed forehead, a buffeted nose, bushy eyebrows, and a voice like William Bendix's, fills the bill.

The two brakemen sit watching for sparks, smoke, or hot-boxes as the train rolls along, one seated facing backwards in the first engine, the other located in the monitor, which is the double-decker compartment on top of the caboose. We were hauling only fifty-two freight cars, considered a light load, because, as it happened, a rail strike was threatened for midnight. I had assumed the president would sign a cooling-off order, but in a pressure play, he was delaying doing that, and since even this spur which angled down from Canada might be affected, the railroad was stripping for trouble.

We ran alongside the Connecticut River for a while after crossing into New Hampshire. At North Stratford the crew "set off" ten cars. Delicately waving his light in signal patterns, Seguin hopped off and on and off to turn the switches and uncouple. Between Groveton and Berlin we skirted the Upper Ammonoosuc River through an expanse of national forest. A deer paused dazzled on the track as we rushed toward it, and Boylan turned off the headlight and tooted. Under the moon, the White Mountains showed themselves in rotund grays and navy blues; lots of empty land, a sense of calmness. Every station had a telegraph operator, usually wearing an eyeshade and a checked shirt, who stepped outside to wave. In Berlin we hitched onto a switching engine that the railroad wanted hauled out of harm's way to Portland, in case there was a strike. Berlin has a big stone station and a round-the-clock paper plant pluming steam and smoke. The crew was quite worked up about the possibility of the strike and how far they should take the train if one was called, whether they shouldn't just leave it standing somewhere on a siding as soon after midnight as they heard. Apparently they assumed that the railroad would then have the responsibility of hiring a taxi to take them home to Island Pond.

The shaking and the roar, the rumbling wheels, the amalgam of jolts, hisses, and shivers, the rocking and big-bopping over the rails were all as intimately familiar to me as my childhood itself. Though I've never been a railroad fan the way some people are, I sometimes rode at the front window of subways and Toonerville Trolleys as a boy, and admired the figure cut by the engineers on bigger trains as they swept by. Even the track-walker hiking through town on his own lonely schedule intrigued me. Just as a man who has wished to be wealthy and watched rich men for years is not bewildered about how to behave or what to do when his windfall finally does come, so to be up in that engine myself did not seem novel or astonishing. It was about as I'd expected: the majestic height at which we rode, the swath that the headlight illuminated in front, the rich diesel fumes, the tilty file of telephone poles, the murky train winding behind. The horn's tattoo was properly pristine. In the moonlight the spruces bulged. There was a breezy, box-shaped chemical toilet perched in among the turbines, a water cooler to drink from, and panels of gauges, gears, and levers, with stenciled advisory warnings and small red lights. A pull-rope was attached to the whistle, which Boylan jokingly told me I should pull if I had a question. We sat on upholstered jump seats, not so comfortable that you could fall asleep.

Three hours out, we were in Maine, a land of redolent sawmills, clusters of cozy houses with lights in the bedrooms, and a night fog that was gathering across the fields. Chill air, crisp moonlight, gunmetal-colored lakes, and tumultuous trees—rollicking, big-topped hardwoods against the sky. At South Paris, a hundred miles from Island Pond, we left off another seven cars, Seguin hopping along the catwalks and the cowcatcher area under the engine's nose. The locomotives revved with the whorling, encompassing sound of a ship's engine—electrical, oil-burning sounds. South Paris is a tranquil little county seat, but it has a shoe-manufacturing plant, a tannery, linoleum and sled-and-ski factories, and a berry cannery. Bouncing along catch-as-catch-can, flying a freight train's white flag on our front, we passed on through Mechanic Falls to Lewiston Junction, and set off two cars which contained cereals and one refrigerator car carrying meat. Because of the projected strike, Boylan and the crew detoured two miles with the meat and placed it at the wholesaler's door, where it could be unloaded promptly. Lewiston has a feed mill, a Formica and plastics plant, a factory producing bridge girders, and a General Electric facility.

At Yarmouth Junction we disposed of three more cars, which were to be transferred to the Maine Central, then highballed swiftly towards Portland, brazenly blaring our horn, through dozens of deserted crossings with flailing signals. The extra work and the fact that we had stopped to inquire about strike news at almost every station had made us very late; it was three in the morning. Crossing a drawbridge outside Portland, we ran alongside an arm of the bay. Since we had just emerged from the North Woods, the smell of the salt water stung our lungs. It was a marvelous arrival, a rank, spacious, open harbor. In the yards next to the water, Boylan simply parked the train, and, each man with his overnight kit, we walked away, leaving it right where it was, to be dealt with later.

We slept in a bunkhouse over the terminal offices, a remnant of Portland's heyday as a port. When I woke up the view was like a Channel town in France, with smudged seacoast weather and Frenchy frame houses spotted on sandy hills. Mewing white gulls had collected on the piers in crowds. Low-rent industry—ironmongeries, beer warehouses, and fender shops—was casually clumped about. The groceries featured olive oil. On East India Street a plaque announced that this had been the site of Fort Loyal, built by the English settlers in 1680 and destroyed ten years later by Indians and French. Through the rain I saw an orange-and-black freighter, a lighter, and some coastal boats.

Here on the seacoast the crew looked like men out of the woods, slow-speaking, their faces delineated and chunky. They let me look at their noble gold watches, which the railroad inspects every November and May. We breakfasted in a bar where four or five wet prostitutes were having coffee, "too wet to climb on," the trainmen said. Spread over the wall was a picture of Bobby Orr horizontal in the air after scoring a winning goal, and the talk, perhaps because of me, was mostly of the heroic era of steam, prior to 1955. The brakemen kidded around, saying they had told the janitor at the terminal that I was a reporter for *Time* and that he was cleaning up like mad, scrubbing cupboards that nobody had even looked into since before the era of steam. MacDonald, the conductor, was trying to think of stories I could use. There used to be contests between the engineers and firemen, he said. If they couldn't manage to get along and the engineer demanded more steam, the fireman *gave* him more steam, until he had more than he wanted, maybe, so that the safety valves were popping, and the fireman would make him figure out how to use it. Putting in more water cooled the boiler, but then the pressure died, or the fire itself might die if there was slate mixed with the coal.

As it turned out, the president had never needed to act, because at the last moment the union limited the strike to three breadbasket railroads in the Midwest, whereupon a federal judge issued an injunction. We left belatedly at 2:10 P.M., pulling twenty-six empty cars that were going to Moncton, New Brunswick, to haul the turnip crop and two that were full of canned goods for Minneapolis and Denver. For a while I was with MacDonald. His desk is the main article of furniture in the caboose, though there are also fold-up beds, a wooden bench, kerosene lamps, and an oil stove. Each freight car is in its logical order in the train, and its waybill must give a description explicit enough to help the customs men, who hold the train for an hour after it passes Island Pond. MacDonald says he doubts that any of the crews indulge in smuggling now, but back during Prohibition and afterwards, when some of the crews were younger, the Mounties used to hide behind a boxcar in the Montreal rail yards and suddenly jump out and mount the moving engine and search everybody. Luckily there was steam then; they had a firebox where they could throw the contraband.

MacDonald drinks tea from a thermos and carries Preparation H because of the hard benches he sits on and a miniature screwdriver for tightening his glasses. He has a clean, cutting smile that breaks through this methodical exterior, however. His principal avocation seems to be women, or remembering them. The handsome, slicing smile gives him away, paring ten years off his age. Just as caïque captains on the Ionian Sea flash mirrors at the widows who live on the islands they sail past, so does MacDonald wave and give a high sign to some of the lonely ladies of Maine.

At the Maine Central Railroad's yards at Yarmouth Junction we picked up thirty cars—1,750 tons. Several of these were empty grain hoppers which had carried soybean meal; others had brought asbestos and were going back out West for more. The carloads were either potatoes or else wood pulp or rolled newsprint manufactured to the north in towns like Madawaska; the waybills were from the Bangor and Aroostook and the Belfast and Moosehead Lake Railroad. At Danville, we added on eleven more cars and at Mechanic Falls another one—now we were hauling seventy. Because of the tangled schedule, our caboose brakeman had been replaced by a fairly young man who had worked fifteen years for the railroad, all of them right in the Portland yards. This was to be his first trip up the line—indeed, the first time he had ever left the state of Maine. Yet he was worrying whether we would reach Island Pond on time so that he could catch the return train and not have to stay over.

The coastal drizzle had preceded us inland, and when the wheels slipped on the track, lights on the panel flashed. I was in the second locomotive again as we began to climb out of the Maine flatlands into the mountains before entering New Hampshire. Westbound, the so-called deciding grade of this particular route is at Bryant Pond, close to the state border. Though each of our engines could pull 2,300 tons on the level ground, their limit for this slope (and therefore for the trip) was calculated at

1,865 tons. Besides being high and steep, it was magnificent abandoned country with forests stretching away for miles, with ducks and herons in all the ponds and lots of creeks—lovely back country, of which we got a view uncluttered by motels.

We acquired nine more cars in Berlin, Seguin adroit and cautious as he moved between them, signaling. A "run-off" is a derailment; a "head-on" is a wreck. The "tell-tales," as he said they were called, used to fascinate me; they are the long strings which hang overhead wherever the tracks near an underpass and slap a man who is on top of a freight car to warn him before he is decapitated. It is the nature of railroading that even a minor goof by somebody means that he has to take a long walk, at the least, maybe the length of a hundred cars.

Because of the rain, night settled down around us much faster. The windshield wipers and heater hissed with enough decibels to have alarmed an ear doctor, quite apart from the roar of the diesels themselves, but I found sitting there in the eye of the roar so soothing that I would have been content for another dozen hours. Railroads are the one great exception among our huge machines in that we've finally assimilated them.

Sometimes a hard rain will clean the tracks nicely, but this was a light greasy drizzle. The ponderous train climbed up into Vermont from the trench of the Connecticut River with difficulty, whining around double-reverse curves at five miles per hour, Boylan using his sand judiciously. (Each drive wheel of a locomotive is serviced by a pipe from a sand reservoir.) The roar had become a lugubrious groan, alternating between two notes like a Parisian police car; it's not the number of cars so much as the load in them, and not the load so much as whether the wheels can grip the tracks. All torments end, however. We followed the Nulhegan River up and out, hooting the horn, regaining speed. White cedars, red spruces, and firs and tamaracks—wild north country. Of course the whole experience was definitive. One wouldn't say that riding a night freight is like driving all night in a mufflerless car across the Texas panhandle, but one might say that driving a mufflerless car across the Texas panhandle all night is somewhat like riding a night freight train. At last, at nine-fifteen in the evening, after seven hours, we pulled into Island Pond again. The Montreal crew took over.

Fred King
on the Allagash

One of the arguments used by the logging industry in opposing proposals that a few wilderness areas be set aside is that there is no real wilderness left in the Northeast, anyway, or east of the Mississippi, or in any mountain range in the West that may be discussed—no tract of forest that hasn't already been logged, no river drainage that hasn't been dammed. It's all gone now, say the lumbermen complacently. But it's all that we have, the conservationists insist, and so the battle is joined.

On the Allagash watershed in northern Maine, woods that have been logged over three or four times, a compromise was struck. The lumbermen gave up very little of their land, and yet the first of the nation's officially "wild" rivers was brought under state control—conveyed, in effect, to the canoeists. Because of where it is and because the acreage involved is small (twenty-four thousand acres in government hands, versus 1.1 million, for example, in the Boundary Waters Canoe Area of Minnesota), the Allagash Wilderness Waterway has quickly come under recreational pressure, perhaps representing the managerial dilemmas other areas will soon face. I wanted to see what it was like, and—most unfashionably in this democratic age—hired a guide so that I could use my paddle as a writing table part of the time and, being a novice, not bother with questions of navigation.

Fred King was talking about bush pilots in the motel at Shin Pond, where we met. He said there were old pilots and bold pilots, but he knew of one who was both old and bold. This man would fly out a sick fisherman at night in a little plane with no instruments, by moonlight alone. Fred King keeps track of these things. He's fifty-eight, looks forty-five, has short hair which is bluish gray, round glasses, a boyish doggy grin, a face deeply cut by grinning and a mouth big enough to grin with. It's a pleasing face; his body is straight and quick like a chipmunk's and he has an immediate laugh, provocatively loud, and likes to stop still when on the move and sound off on the matter at hand, then impulsively move forward again, seeming never to walk if he can run. At home in Augusta he keeps a jug of Allagash water to mix with his drinks, and doesn't much like December because of the short days; "I'd sell December awfully cheap." Until he became too controversial for the local talk show, he would go on TV in December, in his red guide's shirt, and kill the long evenings that way.

It's only been in the past ten years that Fred has canoed. His father died when he was young, and though he had started in college with the idea of graduating as an engineer, he quit and went off for two years to the woods, wintering in a cabin he built for himself six days distant by team and wagon from the community of Ashland, Maine. He was trying to trap—this was in the middle of the Depression—but went about it wrong. The right-headed way to learn how to trap would have been to pair up with an older fellow and learn from him, he says. Instead he had a full-time job just surviving, and during the first winter had to reinforce his roof with material hauled on a toboggan from an abandoned shanty several miles away.

He still likes to be by himself. His ideas sound as if they had been worked out in isolation in the woods and perhaps spoken first in a loud voice all alone. He has a tight shipshape cabin on Chemquassabamticook Lake where he goes in midwinter and works on improvements, hauling now with a snowmobile. He's got to break trail for the snowmobile on snowshoes—it's not like the ads—but he loves the rigor of the winter woods, cooks for himself, and sleeps fitfully, listening to the radio and waiting for his mouse trap to snap. The mice he feeds to the gorbies—Canada jays—outside.

Fred worked on highway crews and during World War II was a shipyard pipe fitter in Portland, but has been self-employed ever since. He would buy a piece of land and build a house on it, doing all the work, then "find somebody fool enough to buy." By fifty he tired of that, not so much because it was strenuous as because he wanted to go back to his original vision of himself. Though not an exceptional woodsman, he's taken the trouble to learn some of the historical lore, and particularly to latch on to a few of the vanishing old rivermen and listen and learn from them, trying modestly to carry on some of the traditions in their name. He also has a kind of guffawing admiration of wealth: more successful men who have blasted a steadier ascent in the world he calls "roosters." "Quite a rooster," he'll say of a fellow who wears nifty clothes nowadays, and will boisterously recite a ditty he learned in school:

> *Dear Lord, in the battle that goes on through life,*
> *I ask but a field that is fair . . .*
> *A chance that is equal to all in the strife,*
> *And the courage to do and to dare.*
> *And if I should win, let it be by the code,*
> *With my faith and my honor held high,*
> *And if I should lose, let me stand by the road*
> > *and cheer as the winner goes by.*

Another old chestnut of his is "So late we get smart, so soon we get old."

The Allagash flows north for ninety-some miles. Its headwaters connect several lakes, and were tampered with in the 1840s by loggers who were competing to float the logs south to the Penobscot and down to Bangor instead of north on the Allagash to Canada by way of the St. John River. The tampering has since been set straight, and now a parking lot has been laid out beside the Great Northern Paper Company's bridge at Chamberlain Lake, a two-and-a-half-hour drive from the nearest town. Fifty-four hundred people were waterborne on the Allagash in 1970, a number that's rising 15 percent a year and is concentrated in the two warmest months, so that the state authorities know that soon they will have to institute a system of advance reservations. The campgrounds, however, are tactfully dispersed, and though logging is going on within four hundred feet of the water, a screen of trees, deceptive but pristine-looking, has been left, like the false fronting of a movie-set street.

We put in at Chamberlain on July 17 in a brisk splashing wind, our old-fashioned cedar canoes contrasting with the light aluminum canoes more modernist types were using—the Sierra Club fellows with their families and dogs who fill up his stage set and offend Fred King's sense of what's wild. The vacationers who employ King like his big tents and good steaks on ice and the canned provisions and sauces he brings, though they're not sure they're roughing it properly. The chic way to travel requires carrying thin packets of freeze-dried food, and not much of it, and feather-light sleeping equipment such as backpacking mountaineers have more reason to want—a line that Fred doesn't swallow at all. In the first place, the men he admires, "Moosetowners" who are now in their eighties, used to earn their living poling thirty-foot bateaux up the Allagash loaded with tons of supplies. The

measure of manhood was not roughing it on dehydrated foods but
hefting a great big load on a portage and living well. Also, the
Maine woodsman usually respected the rich as people who had
won their spurs in another world, and did not expect them to
prove themselves in the woods with feats of do-it-yourself, but were
perfectly willing to cater to the "sports" a bit for good pay. Fred
says the Sierra Club characters (most of them "lefties"), with their
"tin," "bang-bang" canoes, look like internees as they stand in a
row waiting for reconstituted soup to be ladled into the tin bowls
they hold. Instead of enjoying a meal, they study their maps as if
they were eating them.

We sports in his party probably weren't up to the role. Sports
lately are "pilgrims," he says laughingly, "groping for something."
They believe, as he does too, that even in its protected status the
Allagash River is being altered irrevocably, and so they have
rushed to experience it before the herds finish it off. But his customers admire the conservationists and disdain the lumbermen
who controlled the region until now, while he admires the lumbermen and has little use for the Johnny-come-lately conservationists.
They think that a rainy day on a canoe trip is a disaster and therefore to be wet and uncomfortable on a rainy day is natural, whereas
he thinks that rain is natural and that to be wet and uncomfortable
on a rainy day is unnecessary and unnatural.

We had sun, the trees thrashed in the wind, and the surface
rippled in shark's-teeth patterns as we went up the lake, until we
turned close to the western shore. There were mud beaches every
quarter-mile. Chamberlain is an expansive lake, with salmon and
togue, and is potentially dangerous when the wind rises. As we
crossed toward Lock Dam the waves ruffled up to the gunwale.
King said that a canoeman's basic instrument was his pole, not his
paddle (referring again to the old-timers), so that this deep-water
stuff was an uneasy business for them. We were using an outboard
motor, however. I was a passenger in the bow, his other customers,
a Long Island couple, being towed in the second canoe.

The lock tender himself was a summer visitor, a white-haired
salesman with an ulcer whose wife wrote children's books. He gave
us a couple of minutes of lively water to get us started down the
two miles of river that flows into Eagle Lake. Its pitch for a moment looked steep, brimming around us, and we could see varicolored streaks, as lurid as tropical fish, on the rocks underneath
us where canoes had scraped. King gave a lesson in snubbing downstream with a pole, the bow being loaded heavily and the steering
done by holding the canoe's stern in position, letting the current
work on the bow. We saw a muskrat, a loon, and beaver-work in the

winding channels, and then emerged on Eagle, a wide, even prettier lake, the shoreline more indented than Chamberlain's, with moosier swards by the water and a hillier setting, with plenty of leafy hardwoods high up and behind. Terns, ducks, two loons, and an osprey flew over, and we had a fresh breeze at our tail. The loons whinnied in clarinet tones. At Pillsbury Island a boys' camp was in possession, with a great many canoes. We were using the motor all the way, intending to put twenty miles behind us, because in these public playgrounds one must travel out of phase with the particular contingent of enthusiasts who happened to start down the chute the same day, yet not catch up with the parties who set out previously.

We ran into waves tipped with whitecaps, the wind shifting into a headwind, and a navy-blue curtain lowered in front of us. The murky curtain turned purple, the water turned black and the wind hard and strong—the waves coming in gusts, the canoe shipping water—as we met the storm. It was a smothering front, and passing beyond it, we were soaked by a pellety rain, but found some protection in the lee of Farm Island, then in a narrows, where we tied up at Priest's Camp. In the drumbeating rain as, laughing, we threw up our tents, Fred pretended we'd almost drowned to make it more dramatic for us. He said that when he first began guiding he'd been scared he might do something wrong and had gone to an old-timer for advice: "Just take lots of eggs and jam, Fred."

We were sharing the site with a middle-aged Boston couple, the man equipped with muttonchops and a mustache like an English eccentric, and two local Maine fishermen who, trusting in the fact that it was mid-July, had neglected to bring a tent. Fred probably would have lent the Boston people some scraps of canvas, but he left the Maine men to sleep in discomfort under their canoe because they ought to have known better. My own companions were from Oyster Bay, the husband, Jim, once a Marine first lieutenant, now a market-research chieftain, well-heeled, revisiting his memories of sleeping on the ground in the Pacific theater thirty years ago, which he'd promised himself that he never would do again. He had four kids at home, a narrow head, a large jaw, and a pouchy face that looked as if he had laughed at his boss's jokes about five thousand times too often, a face that looked as if maybe he had been served up one of his kids at a business lunch once and had gone ahead and eaten it anyway. But he was smoothly bright and intelligent, what is called an omnivorous reader, slept lightly, and was skillful and pleasant and easy with people. His wife, Audrey, whom I liked better, wore a tously blond wig over long black hair that she thought was "too oily," had a touching squint, a good heart, and dental trouble. She was soft-natured, vaguely appealing, more loving than loved. A hard struggler, she loyally tramped after her husband in all his nerve-testing undertakings—climbing to fire towers, and so on—and was never allowed to be tired or scared. On Long Island, she said, she ran with him around the high school track every morning at six o'clock, although she hated it. After twenty-eight years of marriage the word "dear" sounded sad when he said it, but they'd brought along nine days' worth of mixed martinis in plastic bottles, as well as a dose of the anti-Semitism which is sometimes an ingredient of stories around the camp fire. Fred partook too.

Next morning we went to look at a relict tramway which had hauled saw logs in the first years of this century, and a railroad spur used for pulpwood later on, both constructed in order to get the logs from this lake into a different drainage that would carry them south. During the 1920s as many as five thousand men worked here. Beans were cooked all night in holes in the ground; the hogs that went on the table along with the beans were kept on Hog Island. Farm Island was for pasturing the oxen, but half of it was never cleared and is still black spruce. Black spruce and white, and sedges and cattails, cover this industrial blur where "Dynamite" Murphy, the dynamiter, and other famous figures once worked. Now a mother duck was running on the water with flapping wings, teaching her babies to fly. I'm such a child of the times that although half of my ancestors were lumbermen in the West, when talking to a proud lumberman of today I all but blush for him as he recounts his exploits, so King and I didn't always see eye to eye at the railroad site.

We circled the lake, slipping into each estuary and up Soper Brook, then up Snare Brook. Dozens of ducks; fish nests down through the water, scooped in the gravel. A great blue heron flew up. A dragonfly chased by a kingbird got away by dodging close to our bow. The brooks were silty but the wetland grasses were a tender light green. After a half mile or so the alder growth would close in and beaver cuttings would block the brook, and where we had to stop we'd see moose tracks. When we walked, Fred was quick, and with his small intelligent face looked like a professor afield, though his right arm is beginning to go bad on him—too much holding a chain saw. In the black-fly season he sometimes sews his socks to his pants to protect his ankles, and leaves them on for four or five days, he said.

We admired clusters of magnificent white pine left by the spruce and fir loggers of recent times. The original booty up here was pine. Some trees were a hundred and fifty feet high, seven feet thick at the butt, and wanted for naval masts. Before chopping such a whopper, the loggers would throw a nearby spruce against it, climb to the top of the spruce and so reach the climbable branches of the pine, from which they could see for ten miles across a great spread of spruce forest to other "veins" of pine.

We stayed at Priest's Camp a second evening, enjoying a rainbow. A boys' outing party arrived, and there was a special avidity in the way King and Jim and Audrey watched them set up their camp: *these* boys weren't smoking pot. Rain fell hard most of the night, until a clearing shower came just at dawn. Then trilling loons and King's cry, "Wake up, wake up, up with the buttercups!" I imagined him as the "cookee" around a logging camp in the old days whose light weight kept him from competing in physical feats with some of the men but who bubbled with jokes whenever they broke off work for a meal. He said, though, that he hadn't developed much interest in people until his late forties; having been concerned before then with excavations, machinery, and physics.

We always started earlier than anyone else, just as we seized the best campgrounds and pushed past the trippers at every point, but the advantage of this for observing game was lost, either because of the outboard motor or else King's loud anecdotes echoing on the water. At such times, before the sun rose, when for an hour we had the Allagash to ourselves, he exasperated me and I was sorry I'd come with a guide, but of course from his standpoint this silence-on-the-waters was more Sierra Club nonsense. The old-timers moved through frontier America hollering as loud as could be, unless they were hunting—cutting the silence with hoots, dispelling some of the loneliness of the woods and warning the panthers and bears away. To this day, in parts of Alaska where there are grizzlies a prospector will put a stone in a tin can inside his pack, so that he walks with a constant *clink-clank.*

In the passage from Eagle to Churchill Lake we saw mergansers, scaups, herons, gulls, and an osprey again. Baby ducks fled in front of us like fish flipping along the surface to dodge a deep shark, the mother among them flittering strongly to set the example. A logging bridge crossed above us; we saw an otter underneath. The shores displayed sleek and bristly "cat spruce" (white spruce), beaver houses, cedars, and drowned-looking alder-covered beaches leading to a fir point where the Indians used to camp to escape the flies. On Churchill, with the sun a silvery band on the water, we caught up with a swimming cow moose midway across. Her body was invisible; her head was like a blunt boat, the ears the housing, and her hairy neck hump nearly underwater. It was a groping blind-looking head, sightless as a whale's, a feeling and suffering-looking head, the nose so huge and vulnerable that other undiscovered senses might have been contained inside. Two terns were diving on her with creaky cries. Her ears lay back as her big pumping legs hurled her ashore, and she swerved to look at us, first over one shoulder, then over the other.

Churchill is a rangy lake, the shore opening and narrowing, with a mountain skyline. Heron Lake, formerly a holding pen for the logs, leads on to Churchill Depot dam. The ranger there, whose name is Clyde Speed, talked about the moose that he sees, and we toured the outdoor museum of log sleds, water sleds, old bateaux, Lombard tractors, Watson wagons, and looked into the boarding house, and engine and blacksmith shops, all defunct. Lombard steam log-haulers preceded the internal-combustion engine in the woods for a decade or two around World War I. Each of them could do the work of sixty horses, a blue flame issuing like a blowtorch from the exhaust pipe on a cold night. They were precursors of the tank and farm tractor because they ran on a caterpillar tread. In 1938 Fred King had walked to this spot to explore; he loved its tall tamaracks and big pines and gave us a chance to poke about. In places like this he always announced that he was only a "fake woodsman," and that although occasionally he spoke for some of the old fellows who couldn't go on TV themselves and spout off, if we wanted to meet the real thing we'd have to go farther afield.

The Chase Rips, the one risky spot in ninety-two miles, began here. Fred had been casual in speaking of it, once suggesting that Jim perhaps might want to practice a bit with his pole in Soper Brook, but now as we lugged our craft down below the dam (paying Clyde Speed to truck the duffels around) he began to hum nervously. We watched other voyagers as their canoes first entered the current like the little cars at a carnival being gripped by the cogs of a loop-the-loop.

I had an easy time in Fred's bow. Often he takes old people through these rapids who can give him no help, who are getting their final look at the outdoors. But Jim and Audrey, suddenly realizing they hadn't practiced enough in Soper Brook, were on their own, Jim cautiously trying to get the feel of the pole, hanging himself up against the bank several times. Fred, who had drifted almost too far ahead to shout, yelled at him to stand up and move more toward the middle of the canoe. "Stand up! You don't fight Joe Louis sitting down. Get on your hind legs!" Fred had stripped to the waist. A moosefly bit him, and he laughed and said, "They'll bite a chunk out of you and fly up on a branch and sit there right in front of you eating the chunk."

The river before us fell off, abrupt as the end of a table; all of a sudden it didn't appear to be there. Then, curling up like a hairdo, it fluffed around us, high at the prow, as we slid down into the rapids themselves. The noisy water was popping in points, peaks, and tufts, blotting out all other sights and sounds. We could have been surrounded by other canoes and not noticed them. This was the first pitch, full of rocks, several hundred yards long. The second was shorter but "downhilly," the many rips sticking up as if to chum with us, as the water curled and crabbed around. Riffles, bumps, a wild backdrop of trees. Jim was way back in the first pitch still but beginning to grab hold of the river's hand now. "Good boy!" King shouted to him, a regular educator, jittery on his behalf. "We'll make you an honorary Moosetowner. I ain't got the authority, but I can recommend you." Everywhere on the river there was midmorning light and a hiss as of thousands of snakes, the water backing up recalcitrantly into cowls. Jim's canoe came stumbling, angling along like a cub, edging to the bank, but he jumped out at every bad juncture to wade and push, as a canoeman should. We all took a breather together against some shore rocks to eat raisins and talk.

The third pitch was energetic with knobby rocks sticking up like bad luck itself, every one striped with canoebelly paint. King has broken canoes here—a rock square-on at forty-five degrees will do it, plunging through the bottom. A friend of his tried out a Plexiglas design here but gave his bowman heart failure, the rocks skinning by just an inch or two under his feet. A canoe should go where the water goes. "Where's the water?" a canoeman asks himself in the rapids when perplexed. Then, camping alone at supper, all the company he has is the bugs in his cup.

Poling is like snowshoeing and paddling like skiing, and we were able to paddle for a little while. We passed several parties who were "frogging" (walking) their way down the channel, leading their canoes, having become discouraged from tipping over so much. The river was gala with rocks, a hustling hubbub. King's craft snuggled in like an invited guest—but, no, a big jar. We skidded and sidled by the tough spots. Fred said not to try to signal to Jim or he'd misunderstand, and it would distract him. Soon he did tip and swamp, the canoe underwater. "Not too bad being in the river, just lots of water and rocks," Fred said, jumping in too to help hold and right their canoe and recover the gear that was floating downriver. Now that their string of conquests had broken, the two of them fell out again twice in quick succession, but learned to leap when they felt themselves going so that at least the canoe didn't sink. "Once they get wet they'll get wet again." Watching, Fred sang with tension.

After having covered a mile and a half (it semed much more), we stopped at a place called Big Eddy to dry out and have lunch underneath an old cedar, the water purling like Hiawatha's. When other people passed, we'd hear their piping shouts for a moment, but both the river and the dramatic forest—blue firs and black spruce—made them mirages.

We pushed on, the Allagash partying along, popping with rocks but forty yards wide, leaving plenty of current, till it tipped down steeply again and we slid at the edge of whole thievish mobs of rocks that nattered away, feeling their tug, zipping by Harrow Brook. There were scraps of canoes that had wrecked and washed down, becoming wedged in the rocks; some had been drawn up on the bank where they covered small piles of firewood, because a great many people had crawled ashore and spent time recuperating here. Jim and Audrey fell overboard twice more, though the river wasn't as severe. First he lost his balance; the next time she did. He was strong and uncomplaining but heavy and had lost his confidence, and Fred gradually formed the opinion that he was awkward and that overeducation had spoiled him. Fred stopped really rooting for him, though continuing to mutter encouragement— whether or not Jim and his wife were able to hear. Being as safe as a sack of peas in Fred's bow, I felt guilty for having it all so easy and knew that I would have looked worse.

We enjoyed peaceful minutes of drifting too, with brown mud on the bottom, just a few round white rocks dotted about, and the banks grassy, cedars leaning over the water, and white-collared birds darting close to our heads. Then for three hundred yards the river would turn feisty, roaring, tergiversating, as busy as rush hour, each rock having its say. We twisted through new rips and rapids, eluding sweepers, seeing the trout jump, and dragonflies in a mating clinch; jays called in the trees. The clouds were lovely, if we took time to glance upward. There were still-water sloughs, and gulls on the mud banks, and parakeet cries from the bear-jungle. Then a swift chute, dark choppy water, on into a wide, luxurious pool. Buzzing birds in the woods, occasional pines, more shaggy cedar, big pairs of spruce, a heron flying high with folded neck, a gangly flying loon, some green grassy islands. A winter wren sang. Then again the water crawled with ripples, with stream birds flying up, the water slanting alive with bubbles over a gravel bar.

After these last corrugations a wide boggy low-slung valley interrupted the forest, and there were red-winged blackbirds, bitterns, and other signs of slower water. We saw a speck of a bird diving on an eagle or osprey, harassing it for several minutes; hummingbirds and robins do this. The Allagash is thought to be visited by three or four eagles.

The bogs gave way to Umsaskis Lake, which after the rapids seemed placid and big, with bumpy timbered hills all around. We rested our backs, using the outboard. Fred said that in the years following the invention of outboards the Moosetowners kept trying them out and discovering that they could still pole upstream faster than a motor could go, so the older men never did bother adopting them.

We'd covered twenty miles, and camped on July 20 in the Thoroughfare leading from Umsaskis into Long Lake. The Oyster Bay couple were telling about their trip down the Colorado River and I was talking about other rivers I'd seen, when I realized that we were making poor Fred jealous; he wanted our attention fixed on the Allagash. They talked about their vacation in Japan too, where Jim wouldn't take his shoes off. "We beat the sons of bitches, so there's no reason why we should take our shoes off."

It was warm and the frogs on the Thoroughfare started croaking at 8:00 P.M. As I stood listening, the local ranger, making a last swing past, stopped to find out if everything was all right. He said that people in trouble generally just stand on the bank looking out, don't wave or shout. Sometimes he wonders how long they'd stand there if he didn't come over—two days, three days?—before they began to wave and yell.

Fred keeps a jeep at Umsaskis. The next day he drove us forty miles across International Paper Company roads to Chemquassabamticook Lake, where we boated to his cabin. The spot is close to Canada, and during Prohibition a good deal of booze was hauled to Fred's lake, where the canoemen took over and carried it via the waterways to Moosehead Lake and other resorts farther south. We passed some cabins of the era with double-split roofs: cedar shakes overlying a layer of earth, covering an inner roof composed of spruce poles.

Fred's maternal grandfather went to California for the Gold Rush, sold mining timbers there, and brought back fifty thousand dollars in gold. Gone now, Fred laughs, with a backward jerk of his head as if he were swinging an ax. His cabin is at what sixty years ago was One Eye Michaud's logging camp; and he's found the "greenhouse" (root cellar), the old beanhole, lined with rocks, with charcoal at the bottom, the outline of the bunkhouse, and that of a trapping cabin which must have predated Michaud. In his own cabin, built of peeled logs that he rolled up on skids to the height of the eaves, he has a hundred-year-old pair of caribou-hide snowshoes, and other antiques; even a scrap from a cedar tree where he cut some life-saving kindling one snowy night when he was caught on the lake by a bitter headwind and had to sit out the storm on the shore. He got under a spruce with the biggest fire he could scrape together and thought of all the things he'd done wrong in his life. Later he came back and cut that particular spruce for his new ridgepole, dragging it home on a sled made from two fenders.

His curtain rods are old setting poles; his clothesline is tied between saplings skinned by the beavers. He had a potato garden to tend, and we went out to see the stump of a virgin pine with the marks of the broad-ax that cut it still visible and a forty-year-old birch tree growing on top. We saw two barred owls calling each other, and a woodpecker drinking down ants on a stump, and moose and deer prints on the sandy beach, among the debris of mussel shells the gulls had dropped. In the winter it's so cold that the wings of the ravens flying overhead seem to squeak like an ungreased hinge. One Eye Michaud is said to have wanted to maintain his reputation as a hard man, and so, out here in winter weather, a four-day walk from the nearest town, he might fire somebody and then, leaning into the kitchen, announce, "Don't give this man any food!" It kept up appearances, and the fellow's knapsack was immediately filled.

Fred used to sneak up here years ago, even building himself a squatter's shack on a ridge of rock maple and yellow birch, since logged. The logging roads now extend everywhere, if one looks down from the air, like tributaries that join the main arteries leading to Canada and the pulp mills. We visited a fire warden named Leslie Caron with a round wrinkled face such as befits a man born in the puckerbrush, who as a boy had carried the mail by dogsled. He said the weather forecasters "must have read last year's almanac," and that he would retire and "be a free nigger" next year. Fred told about catching a six-pound lake trout and taking it up to the watchman in the fire tower on Ross Mountain as a present, assuming he'd catch another on the following day. He didn't, and as soon as the fellow climbed back to his tower, his dog got hold of the fish and ate it. Now the spotting is done by airplanes. Caron in a jeep chases out to where they are circling and tells them where he is in relation to them, because they can't see him through the cover of trees. Then they tell him where the fire is in relation to him.

In the morning the sunrise was golden through the thick trees.

A soupy mist covered the lake, which smoked like a hot spring. Two connubial loons floated side by side, then dived together. The water was as dark as blueberry jelly. We drove back to the Allagash and got under way toward Long Lake again. There we encountered some Explorer Scouts, the vanguard of a program which will scatter ten thousand boys every summer through northern Maine; also a private boys' camp, forty-four kids in twenty canoes.

Fred said there are three kinds of bears in Maine: black bears, maybe a few brown bears, and *Jalberts*. Sam Jalbert was born on a rock in the Allagash, and when he was three days old he fell off and has been in the river ever since. He poled upriver so much he grew arms as thick as his neck, and hands as wide as a shovel. He raised a family of ten kids and had to kill a lot of deer out of season to do it. Used to take sports down the Chase Rapids too. Once he stood on his hands in the stern and steered by tipping and balancing his body. The Jalberts helped dig the channels and build the dams, and this twenty miles we were doing today was Jalbert country, where they logged and had their landings. The logs couldn't simply be set on the river ice or they would be lost in the frenzy of spring breakup; they were kept at strategic points along the bank, then rolled in when the river began to relent but before it lowered.

Chemquassabamticook Stream came in from the west through a moosey flat—Fred has poled up there to his lake from the Allagash, taking all day. We saw a swimming beaver and three otter, two of which ran up on the bank like muddy rascals. Here at Harvey Pond is an old farm clearing, once a freight depot during the towboat era, before that a place where people stopped for vegetables as far back as 1820, along the so-called California Road, a wilderness path which headed west. The original Harvey was a squaw man with a long white beard and twelve kids who married and settled here, liking the warmth and bustle after a lonely life.

An osprey and some splendid ducks flew overhead. There was a last dam, with lilies and water weeds and fish jumping. A channel was maintained by the towboaters for the rest of the way to the St. John, and we sought this out where there were rapids. A couple of horses would drag upstream a boat sixty feet long and ten feet wide (One Eye tried one seventy-two feet long). Barrels of pork and beef weighing three hundred pounds were placed in the bow, barrels of flour behind them, and buckets of lard and blueberries alongside the tiny cabin in the stern. Coasting back, the horses got a free ride.

We passed bits of islands covered with driftpiles, saw a doe and a fawn, a sheldrake with seven ducklings, a squirrel swimming the river, its tail like a rudder. A heron flew up and stood for a minute atop a fir tree. The river curved gently in a stretch sweet as honey, softening its watery sounds so that we could hear the white-throated sparrows. After tilting with a few rocks again we entered a dead water which lasted for an hour's paddling, birds warbling all around, the water smooth, black and waxed. Tying the canoes together, we drifted as a raft, eating Fig Newtons, and hearing chain saws. Sweeney Brook, Whittaker Brook, and Jalbert Brook joined the current. Fred told the story of a guide on the St. John who used to drift along with a gallon of booze at his side. When he and his sports approached a serious rapids and they shouted across to him from their canoe over the roar of the water to ask how to deal with it, he would raise his tin cup and tell them, "I'll drink to that."

While Fred's "brain was in neutral" we hit some rocks, then met more brief rustling rips, rollicking through the Long Soo Rapids for a mile or so, through lovely still country. Only the water popped, a confabulation of rocks, with sandbars and other complexities and many dead elms and ashes that the ice had girdled in the crush of the spring. Fred sometimes picks fiddlehead ferns for his supper here. Entering Round Pond, we paddled to his favorite campground, and baked some bread, cut up chub for trout bait, and watched the ravens harassing the squirrels. Jim fished a springhole while I went to see Willard Jalbert, the Old Guide, as he likes to call himself, having become a bit of an institution. His description of fighting rearing bears with a double-bitt ax sounded as if he'd been looking at *Field & Stream* covers, but last fall at eighty-three he had shot a deer, and still could wend his way through the rapids with an outboard full-throttle, or hold his canoe where he wanted it with his pole while casting with his free hand. He once rode a log over the fourteen-foot drop of the Long Lake Dam, and used to play tricks on the ospreys, throwing out chub for them—a fish that is the butt of many river jokes—attached by a line to a log. "Everybody for himself and God for us all," he would call, going into the rips. But it has all somehow ossified now that the wilderness is gone.

At dusk we went for a joyride on the windy water. A thin-lipped bright sunset, a loon's giddy titter like a police whistle with water in it. Rain with thunder during the night.

From before sunrise, hard logging was going on at Round Pond, all by Canadian labor, the logs being trucked to St. Pamphile. The truth is the Yankee big-timber logger has been a myth for several decades, and old-timers like the Jalberts disguise their dismay at the fall-off in gumption among young Americans by grumbling that the hunting is tailing off because these Canadian woodsmen must be shooting the deer, tucking their carcasses among the logs and smuggling them out of the country.

We got started at 6:00 A.M., a sailing hawk peering down at us. A mist almost the color of snow lay between the lines of trees, so that although the weather was warm it was a wintry scene. In the Round Pond Rips a couple of ducks babbled in the thick of the fun, the water reverberating around them. Next, the Musquacook Rips and islands. King's echoing voice in the quietness irritated me exceedingly because this was not *my* sixtieth trip, but as he spoke of his "walking stick," which was his pole, and his "rain shirt," his poncho, exclaiming resoundingly, "Bubbles mean troubles," I had to remember that this was real history he was reliving, that he was a link with the boisterous rivermen whose intent was to knock down the forests and let the light in.

A buckskin-colored deer exploded with springy bounds. We saw a merganser family; a ridge scalped by a tornado. In a dead water we looked down and saw grasses growing on the bottom, while a whole populace of insects bounced in the air. The sun streamed through the morning vapors in warm yellow combinations on the west bank, but on the east the view was still snowy-looking. The black-growth forest humped into low hills. We floated past grassy islands, then sibilant stretches, the water combing through the rocks, turning the big ones yellow with reflected light and leaving a platter of calm downstream of each. There's a disastrous-sounding crunch when a canoe hits a rock and the floor lifts under one's feet, but the sound is worse than the results. We passed an old shack with a sod roof, now burgeoning with raspberries, and saw Savage Brook debouch through its delta, and Five Finger Brook. The water itself looked like running gravel, and we passed several old cabins that used to belong to characters like Sporty Jack (so called because of a birthmark he sported), and the Cunliffe Depot, the abandoned headquarters of a logging boss who rivaled Michaud. Michaud's hay farm was two miles below, now devoid of buildings but spacious after so many miles of woods. Then beaches and finally a slough called Finlay Bogan, where we saw kingfishers, fish jumping, islands foliaged with ice-scarred willows and silver maples. It became a still, rainy day with some occasional neighborly thunder. We ran by a few gentle rapids and shoals, seeing huge waterlogged stumps that were shaped like moose. The river here was a dream—rustling, windy, wild-looking and lush—chipper with birds, overhung with sweepers, dense with slow channels forking between the islands. It was beautiful and remote. The pioneers chose intervale land such as this whenever they could because the river had already partially cleared it for them and laid down topsoil in which the natural wild grasses had seeded, so that their stock could browse.

At the approach to Allagash Falls the water grew deep, the bottom rocky, and the forest black. Fred began to hum as we entered the rips that led to the lip, and we squeezed over to the east bank and camped in the crook of land where the portage begins. The water is churned butter-yellow as it goes over, and it spouts off the rocks below like the wake of a ship. I swam in the bombast below the falls, in deep potholes where the water was warm. It's a fat, plentiful falls, not notably high; once some daredevils went over in a bateau and survived. Looking down from above at the charade of destruction, I suddenly missed my wife. It was so lonely watching the water go over and smash that the mosquitoes began to seem friends. Fred, who was turning ornery now that the responsibilities of the trip were nearing an end, shouted from the supper fire, "Beavertail sandwiches" (Spam).

In scratchy places the channel generally stuck close to the outside bank. We'd try to go where the water went but not where it was making a fuss. Below the falls the Allagash achieved its maturity. It was plump, and the birds were dashes of white overhead, singing from every side. In a dead water, a large tributary, Big Brook, flowed in. Then McGargle Rocks, two short rapids with a pool between. We saw various map-eater parties in bang-bang canoes. Between McGargle and Twin Brooks is a nondescript stand of fifth-growth white birch and knobby pulpwood, not showing the logging industry at its best. As usual, Fred's voice scared off the moose in front of us; once we saw a stream of fresh pee on the gravel where one had fled.

The Twin Brooks enter the Allagash directly opposite each other in the midst of a rapids. There was a roar, and the channel was first on the left and then crossed over while we hopped about in the swells. " 'I'm lost!' the Cap'n shouted," Fred yelled in the fastest turbulence amid the rocks, before we slid into a pool where a seagull sat. We'd covered eight miles in two hours.

The water got moving again. The government-owned wild area ends at Twin Brooks, and soon we saw log trucks alongside the bank, and a ramshackle structure, the Allagash Inn, at Eliza Hole. The Allagash Inn was One Eye Michaud's jumping-off point on the river, where he kept his successive wives. Two were said to be mail-order floozies who decamped with his assets, but when he was old and pitifully sick and poor, the first of the four came back and nursed him.

One expects to arrive at some signs of civilization at the

mouth of a river. Ahead we could see the ridge carved by the St. John. The Allagash makes an S-turn to delay joining it, through Casey Rapids. We saw two last deer, smelled a skunk, an animal that prefers a civilized habitat, and heard new bird calls—field and song sparrows, bobolinks, meadowlarks. Crows had replaced the wilderness ravens.

Then the jukebox of the Allagash Pool Hall. Allagash proper is a sad shantytown, a sleeping shell of the Moosetowners' settlement, with everyone drawing food stamps now, but there are canoes on the lawns. It's ragged, not even quite right for potato country, backed smack up against New Brunswick. The old-timers, lame with arthritis after so many years of exposure to rain and cold, when they often slept in the snow next to a small fire, have become supersensitive to the cold. They find it torturing, tack up insulation everywhere, or pray for enough money to winter in Florida.

I had a butterscotch sundae and a strawberry milkshake. Fred King departed like a boy let out of school: no more entertaining or catering to us, no more wincing at the bumps delivered to his canoes. He would drive south until he got tired and sleep by the side of the road. Our vehicles had been brought around from Chamberlain Lake, but Jim and Audrey's new Chrysler had not weathered the trip well. The two of us left them changing a tire, putting gas into the empty tank from a one-gallon can, and reminding each other that no minor mishap should spoil such a fine trip.

Walking
the Dead Diamond
River

Lor many years the New Hampshire Fish
and Game Department has made a census of ruffed grouse along
nine habitat routes, each about forty miles long, representing
when taken together every variety of cover within the state. Lately
new highways and real-estate schemes in the southern counties
have forced the biologists to shift with some of these, and some of
the paths have been preempted by motorcyclists or Sunday walkers,
so that even if the grouse population in the area hasn't declined,
the annual count can't be tallied as scientifically as the censuses of
the past, which is discouraging to the men who do the counting.

But recently I had the fun of walking the wildest, northernmost
Grouse Survey Line, which crosses the headwaters of the Connecticut and Androscoggin rivers, country as remote and untarnished
as any in New Hampshire—owned by several lumber companies
and by Dartmouth College. It's country emptier than the much
better-known Presidential Range and the other mountains and
valleys of the White Mountain National Forest, lying to the south.
My companion was Karl Strong, who is the department's senior
biologist north of Concord.

This walk used to be made in midwinter on snowshoes, as well
as during the summer when the broods of new chicks can be
counted, but now that life is softer for everyone, it's done twice in
the summer instead. There are three cabins in the course of the
forty-two miles where Strong and his partner used to pack their
supplies and sleep over, but first they dispensed with their packs,
trucking their gear in ahead of time, and now they arrange to drive
home each night. In fact, it was lucky for Strong that we did it this
way because on one of the nights of our walk, August 24, a freak

killing frost developed that would have wiped out his vegetable garden if he hadn't been at home to hose down everything early in the morning. He raises about fifteen different vegetables, freezing or canning them so that his family can eat them all winter. Gardening is his passion, though one day in June when I talked to him he was on a schedule of waking up every three hours at night to feed an orphaned puppy. He's a reserved, lean, soft-spoken man, pale in complexion like a Scandinavian, not in any sense a softie in appearance but a cold-weather man, and the depth of his affection for living things does not show immediately. In talking to paper-company officials I found he is called "the missionary." When I mentioned this to him he laughed and said that his grandfather was a minister and that, like a minister, he puts in lots of work and accomplishes little.

He's a deer specialist; the grouse census is a job that he does for New Hampshire's bird biologist, who works with ducks and pheasants as well. He's uncannily attuned to deer and astonishes the paper-company foresters because he can actually smell a deer two hundred feet off. A gland in the deer's heel cords gives off a sex scent which Strong describes as resembling the smell of a certain fungus that is found in rotting birch stumps. He can smell porcupines too, but not bears, except for "dump" bears. This Grouse Survey Line is Strong's particular darling. He's walked it himself for fifteen years, watching his body gradually age when measured against its miles and seeing the trail and rivers change as logging and even sport fishing become modern industries. Logging may soon be done with laser beams or thin pressurized jets of water. Already the more technologically advanced companies cut pulpwood with monster-sized timber harvesters that can sheer a tract of forest right down to its roots, and then, right on the scene, the logs can be fed into chippers which dice them into papermaking fiber, chip-sized, to be trucked to the mill like freight. This is not done in New Hampshire yet, but there have been plenty of changes.

Though Strong's grouse path is mentioned in the Appalachian Mountain Club's *White Mountain Guide,* he hadn't been eager to have me accompany him because it is never hiked on, is purposely marked only very obscurely, and could be destroyed for useful game observation if the outdoor fraternity ever really discovered it. A path through splendid country that is traversed twice a year, not worn into ruts by a river of feet, is nowadays a great rarity and a precious one. He said I could come along if I could keep up with him and didn't get blisters, and if I recognized to begin with that any account of the New England wilds must be more of an elegy to pleasures now past than a current guide. We started at Second Connecticut Lake to go to Cornpopper Spring, which is under Magalloway Mountain. The sky drizzled intermittently, the temperature stayed around forty-five degrees with the first of the gusty cold front that killed several gardens that night, and we walked with clenched fists and "dishpan hands," as Strong put it. It was miserable enough, but the raindrops stippled the beech leaves beautifully and the firs in the rain looked as gray as steel. My hat was red, which looks black to a deer or a bear but which birds, with their sharp color sense, are alert to, so Strong planned to be extra alert himself.

Once out in the woods, he seemed younger immediately, lighter and gayer than back in town, remarking on the balsam smell in a soft voice that would be well suited to lovemaking—his wife packs notes into his lunch with the sandwiches—and reminiscing about a day in 1959 when he caught his limit of big fish in a beaver pond that we saw on Smith Brook, using only the naked hook itself, which he had twitched like a fly. We saw a kingfisher plopping from high up to catch a chub there, and a merganser diving. The forests around the Connecticut lakes are a baronial showpiece owned by the power companies that maintain the lakes as reservoirs, but we soon got into bushwhacking country where the tourists don't come. Strong says that by nature he should be a Democrat, believing the Democrats are closer to the Biblical injunction that we must be our brother's keeper, not dog-eat-dog as the Republicans are, but that the tourists are making him more conservative. He walks with quick quiet strides because the grouse try to steal away on the ground if they hear a man at a distance. When he thinks he has heard one of them call, creaky and peeping, he tramps noisily into the brush and claps his hands to scare up the covey so he can count it.

The low country was lush, with raspberry bushes in hoops and flowers head-high. We saw a broad-winged hawk, and saw beaver-work in the sandy-bottomed brook that we crossed and re-crossed—Strong said he thought the man who had laid out the trail must have been on snowshoes, unable to see the water. Strong himself made the mistake of blazing it recently with a paint called International Orange, which in some way sets the bears off; nearly every blaze was chewed. Up in the woods, the trail was cool and shadowy till we got into a logging area, where I learned from smelling the birch stumps that white birch is odorless (which is why it is used for Popsicle sticks), that black birch, a southward species, smells like wintergreen, Strong said, and is a flavor for chewing gum, and that yellow birch has a delicate, mellow, somewhat minty smell. The stumps of the latter were a wonderful yellow-orange inside. We saw one a hundred years old, just downed.

In the rain the skidders, which are a kind of modified, big-wheeled tractor most effective at hauling logs, had churned several hundred yards of poor Strong's trail into a comically gucky concrete-colored soup. The ruts, four feet deep, were running with rain. Slipping like a monkey on roller skates and balancing wildly with his arms, he insisted on walking the route anyway, laughing because laugh was all he could do.

We descended to Smith Brook again, finding a clearing where five bunkhouses and a horse hovel had once stood, near the remains of a log-driving dam and a tote road, trestled and corduroyed. We saw a doe and a fawn, purple trillium ("stinkin' Benjamin") with its wine-colored berries, Canadian dogwood with bright red bunchberries, and a grouse's scrape-hole in a dusty spot where the bird had bathed itself. We saw a brood of three (our count was eight for the thirteen miles that day). Up on Hedgehog Nubble we found the abundant turds of a moose that had wintered there. Moose winter high and deer winter low. New Hampshire has very few moose, but if they were anywhere, they would be here. At the turn of the century the last three caribou in the state were sighted and shot close by.

The clouds swelled gray and silver, settling on us. Sometimes the sun poked through, which hurt our eyes in a sky so dark. Strong smoked when we took a break, to let his liver "release its sugar," telling me that's why a smoker stays thin. We saw a waterfall, and moose and bear tracks, and more than one tucked-away valley with ferns, mosses, and snapdragons, usually the site of an old hunting cabin with the owner's army dog tags tacked on the door and some claw marks where a bear, hungry in the spring, had tried to break in. The resident hummingbirds flitted close to my red hat, sometimes half a dozen in the space of an hour, to investigate why it was the same color as their own throats. Up on Diamond Ridge at three thousand feet was a cold fir forest, very remote. Strong hunts from a cabin on Magalloway Mountain, using a muzzle-loader to make it a bit harder for himself. Last year he and his friends sighted in on a mama bear with her hackles up and three cubs, and there was lots of black smoke but no kill. He told me how tough it is to pull a three-hundred-pound bear out of the woods, or even one weighing two hundred pounds; they stretch when you pull but they don't move. Boy, he said, they seem smaller, though, when skinned out.

He has no laws to assist him when he advises the timber operators on behalf of the wildlife as to what they should do. (Nor do they seek his advice—he just goes around offering it.) He's always polite, the foresters say, and will come into the offices of the Brown Paper Company and simply tell them, "Well, we blew it," when a key stand of evergreens has been cut and some deer are going to die as a result. The whole forest is wildlife habitat, of course, but he restricts his marking activities to the 10 percent of the woods where the deer winter, or he wouldn't get anywhere. Even so, and being prudent, he cannot expect that more than about three-fourths of the trees he marks will be spared. Deer must shelter under mature softwood growth like fir or spruce in a snowy climate. The boughs block some of the wind and catch part of the snow, holding it up where it evaporates. Deer don't browse on trees of this sort unless they are starving; instead they look for young hardwood saplings like maple, poplar, and birch to gnaw on and peel, not trees of a size yet worth harvesting commercially. But before any other consideration they must have shelter. Rather than freeze in a zero wind or flounder about in deep snow where a dog could kill them, they will stay in a softwood grove and slowly starve.

In the north woods if there were no logging going on there would be few deer, the pickings would be so slim—just a frontier of big trees better suited to the life-style of caribou, which eat moss and lichen. But Strong's job is to intercede with the foresters so that a mix of clearings, glades, openings, and sizable timber for shelter is left. Although the personnel are getting brisker, more impersonal, the companies, feeling the pressure of the times, make a big stir about "multiple use"—land with game on it, land lovely for hiking—and he can appeal to that. The traditional cutting cycle used to be seventy or eighty years and the best foresters cut only about a seventh of the timber at hand in a decade, so that timber of every age was growing. Now in the rush for "fiber," younger and younger trees are cut, the cycle is down to forty years, and it's increasingly complicated to manage a forest so that the different requirements of dozens of creatures can be fitted in. Rabbits, for instance, thrive in an area five to fifteen years after the woods have been cut, and grouse fifteen to thirty-five years afterwards, but some of the furbearers and woodpeckers and other birds need much older timber.

The next day we were back at Cornpopper Spring, starting from there by 7:00 A.M., with the weather even a little colder but the sun a bit brighter, the wind having blown the rain away. We had ten and a half miles to go to Hell Gate on the Dead Diamond River, where the Fish and Game Department has a camp. Strong said he felt like putting his snowshoes on; the only way to get good and warm was to put on a pair of heavy snowshoes. His father came from the lumbering country of Patten, Maine, and he remembers pouring kerosene on a crosscut saw as a boy to make it go through a gummy pine. They hunted together. Then in 1944, while he was away as a navy medic, his father was shot in the woods for a deer (an average of five hunters a year are killed in New Hampshire).

The first mile of this section was a logging road now, and for a while farther on, alongside a glacial esker, a farmer had taken his tractor and plowed a track of his own so that his friends in their vehicles could reach a vacation cabin he'd leased. We met some loggers, who seemed like direct but limited men, a notch below the state-employed people I was meeting. We stood at the edge of a clearing watching three of them work without being detected by them. Strong's lip curled in amusement; what kind of woodsmen were they? He waited for them to notice us until he got tired and, like an Indian feeling benevolent today, simply walked peacefully away through the trees.

Since grouse usually run before they fly, a windy, disruptive day like this one was bad for hearing or spotting them. They were plentiful because June, when the chicks were new and likely to die of pneumonia if chilled, had been very dry—a June without storms is not good for the trees but is good for the grouse. Once grown, they are rugged birds and winter right on the scene, eating birch buds and diving deep into the snow to sleep, leaving no tracks on the crust for a fox to follow. Strong said that the foxes were beginning to build up again after a rabies epidemic in 1969. In the previous siege, in 1963, he'd had to take twenty rabies injections in the stomach as a precaution. It's best not to check for rabies in wildlife too often, the biologists say, because you'll find it so regularly that the fewer checks you make the fewer epidemics you discover. We saw both fox and bobcat scats. Fox dung is surprisingly dainty and small-bore, even considering the animal's whippet-thin body. Bobcats, and especially Canada lynx, look leggy, pathetic, and light as air, too, when their coats are skinned off. They are dumber than foxes if judged anthropomorphically by their IQ, but are so superbly cautious and stealthy, so hard to see and so wild, that by their own lights they are smart enough. In a lifetime Strong has sighted just three.

Raw deer-season weather. Strong blew his nose with his fingers, and pointed out where his nephew at seventeen had hit a bear with six shots, the bear dashing on till it finally dropped, nipping off strips of its own intestines as they fell out and trailed. (The nephew has never come hunting since.) We watched two hummingbirds feeding on jewelweed in a glade where Strong once saw twenty. We noticed a woodpecker hole high in a stub where two swifts were nesting. In the depths of the woods we came on a deer lick, with well-defined trails homing in like the spokes on a wheel; I heard one deer flee. The mud was white with minerals, and the roots of the trees had been exposed by the hooves. Strong used to lie here in a blind on moonlit nights to observe the goings-on— three or four deer at once pissing and shitting and drinking in the shallow pools, contributing nearly as many minerals back to the lick as they removed.

We picked hatfuls of hazelnuts for Strong's teenage daughters, and saw lots more neon-red bunchberry and bear-chewed blaze trees, but the trampled-looking grass that I would have assumed was another sign of game turned out to be just a casualty of the hard rains. We talked about how most naturalist writers rate poorly with full-time workers in the field, Thoreau, Fenimore Cooper, and Ernest Thompson Seton included. But I was wearing Strong's spare pair of rubber boots, and their good fit seemed to represent the friendship budding between us. Doctors, as another group which cultivates the outdoor life, also run into a lot of kidding from the professionals. Strong told me about two who had crashed in the Pemigewasset drainage while flying over the White Mountains one February and, with a surgical saw, tried to cut some green poplars next to their plane to make a fire. They died, which wasn't so funny, but if they had gone to a softwood grove a couple of hundred yards farther off, they could have broken off plenty of dry wood from the dead bottom branches just with their hands.

We were on the grassy banks of the East Branch of the Dead Diamond River, whose headwaters springs ten miles away we had seen the previous day. The day before it had taken me until the late evening to get the bones of my hands feeling warm again, yet now we were sweating already. The temperature was fifty-eight degrees (whenever Strong saw a grouse he took wind and temperature readings). We lunched partly on hazelnuts—a squash-seed taste—overlooking a thunderous sixteen-foot falls and its twisty catch-pool, a stretch where once in the 1950s Strong caught and threw back two hundred fish in a couple of hours. People had hiked in from what was then the closest road, in Maine, to catch four-pound brook trout, but now these holes were empty of fish.

We watched a bulldozer cracking down trees for a winter

haul road, which would need no gravel, only the natural mud architectured into shape on the night of the first freeze, whereupon for the next five months the log trucks would roar back and forth on the ice. However, this was a forest whose patterns Strong had helped to create, and even his management plans for the streams— that the skidders not silt up the spawning beds by operating along the banks—had been followed, so what we saw was not agitating to him. We followed the old tote road on the riverbank, used in log-driving ways. We'd crossed from the large township of Pittsburg (three hundred and twelve square miles) to the Atkinson and Gilmanton Academy Grant (fourteen square miles of woods, once sold by the aforesaid academy for four hundred dollars). Dartmouth, which owns the adjoining College Grant (forty-seven square miles) near Hell Gate, leases the recreational rights to this land at a dollar an acre annually so that its alumni and guests may feel free to spread out. Like most other state people, Strong resents the exclusion of the general public by these rich guys, bu : like me he had to admit to being glad that these woods would resemble a wilderness a little bit longer than unprotected forests. On the other hand, in the fall Dartmouth men kill only about seven deer for every ten square miles of land they have, whereas the public on ordinary timberland kills twice that many. This is not favorable news to a man like Strong who on his snowmobile tours finds twenty deer starved to death per square mile in the cramped wintering yards on even the public lands.

We argued about hunting—not that I could sensibly oppose hunting deer, but there are other beasts. I teased him as to whether this predatory "naturalness" he touted so highly wasn't downright dog-eat-dog Republicanism, but he wasn't to be hobbled by consistency, and pointed out again that too many tourists with city ideas were turning him in that direction anyway. Of course, the yearly symbolic deer he killed was like his assiduous gardening or the cabin he'd built for himself on Magalloway, as I understood. He said, though, that wildlife was public property, for all the people, and that therefore he resented anybody who posted his land against the free access of hunters. My answer was that, first of all, wild animals were perhaps the property of no one but themselves, a question I was willing to leave moot if he wished, and secondly that I resented any man's going on any land, public or private, and shooting some creature, dwindling in numbers, whose like I might have trouble ever seeing in a natural state, and then tacking its hide on his living-room wall—*that* concept of private property was offensive to me.

Strong said, Well, if his hunting something really means that you may never see its like again, I agree with you, he ought not to be hunting it, it should be a protected species; that's what biologists like myself are for. What I'd left out of the equation, however, he added, was the fact that many people who post their lands do not do so out of any beliefs corresponding to mine. Rather, they seem to think that in buying a piece of land they're buying the wildlife that lives on it too, along with the pines and the apple trees.

Okay, that infuriated me too; we were agreed. He'd started defining us as conservationist versus "preservationist," but I laughed and said, Look, if *you and I* name-call and can't get along, then what hope is there that the wilderness forces can ever combine? He smiled. I said, Bear in mind too that some of the people who object to hunting are not as ignorant about the woods as you think. What arouses them is not that a deer is shot which otherwise would eventually starve to death, but that the hunter gets such a kick out of killing it.

Do you see hunters butchering cows for kicks during the off-season? Strong asked. It's not the pain, it's the death, and it's not the death but the stalk and the woodsmanship and the gamey wild meat the fellow is after; the completeness of each of these complemented by the others. I understood what he meant, but to be one up I asked why, if the woodsmanship is the heart of the matter, there are so very few archers in the woods—archery requiring woodsmanship of such a high order that it does overshadow the kill. Strong said bow-hunting is just too hard to do for all but that handful of hunters. Success comes too hard, and most hunters are firearms buffs as much as they are woodsmen and enjoy the big bang and the bird-in-the-hand. Besides, he saw no reason why the kill ought to be overshadowed. The naturalness of the kill was akin to all of the other pleasures one felt in the woods, and in no sense skulky or inferior. It was his business to see that no animal was hunted into oblivion if he could help it, but to have a deer herd protected like the animals in a zoo, just to be looked at, never shaken up by a hunting season as by the whirlwind of natural predation—this was not woods or wilderness, he said angrily; this kind of situation would arrive soon enough as it was, as I should know.

We waded the East Branch just above where the Middle and West branches join, a black-looking shapely knoll in front of us and a high hardwood ridge beyond, all forest land everywhere, with bluish tall firs in the foreground that Strong had managed to save. The day before, I couldn't have believed today would bring prettier country, but it was like parkland in Colorado—forest and wild grasses interspersed. Though I was getting a charley horse, the marvelous ungrudging succession of Valhalla views, of black knolls, green grass and green trees, the forest unrolling, the sandy-banked river bending alongside—and long-legged Strong—put energy into my strides. As he talked, it became evident that this wasn't just Dartmouth country; it was also a private playground for a good many Fish and Game officers. They could get through the gates and camp and fish where no one else could.

Strong talked about his difficulties in the National Forest. There, too, the deer yards received last consideration, and the federal foresters fibbed to him, outmaneuvered him, or tried to treat him as some kind of hick in order to escape interference with their timber sales. In Canada, where he's gone as a consultant, the Crown Lands are sometimes overcut just as badly. A cord of softwood on the stump is worth six dollars, and if there are fifteen cords to the acre, on these vast tracts it begins to add up.

We saw a red-shouldered hawk, a meadow mouse, and bobcat droppings with a whole little mouse skull intact in one. There were the tracks of a raccoon that had been hunting tadpoles, two garter snakes, a goshawk's nest in a dead beech, and lots of deer prints. Two big red deer bounded off, showing each other the way with their fleecy tails. We were in the principal deer yard along the Dead Diamond now, country that Strong tours during the winter. He said the deer often die with their stomachs full of non-nutritive wood, having run off their fat during the hunting season and the season of rut, but if there are loggers working nearby they can survive off the sprouty tops of the fallen trees.

On a suspension footbridge we crossed to Hell Gate Camp, four grizzled huts in a breezy hayfield. We watched a party of Fish and Game recruits being taught how to disarm a hunter. They had been issued bird books and were learning how to identify ducks. As a biologist, Strong has no police duties. Most of the time he wears no uniform, and unlike the wardens who were instructing them, can drop in on a hunting or fishing camp in the guise of a hiker; even noticing a violation, he can move on if whatever is wrong strikes him as really not very important.

These hearties do not let you go without having coffee with them. The next morning we were delayed again while pleasantries were exchanged. I met no woodsmen among them but I did meet outdoorsmen who, feet up on the table, relished being here in this kingdom, with the white water hissing outside, instead of down at the office in Concord.

We waded the Little Dead Diamond, still steaming after the

frosts of the dawn. It's a noisy, energetic tributary stream, chiseling potholes and digging rock sculptures in rhythmic curves out of the limestone strata above Hell Gate. We followed it uphill. Six or seven years ago Strong used to catch his limit of ten trout here in an hour while he ate lunch, or feed crumbs to as many as twenty that were visible in the clear water. Now he's lucky if he catches three little ones. The spring freshet, loaded with rocks and ice, wipes them out of the fishing holes, and the stream is too precipitous to be repopulated from the main river below. Until recently a new population would always wash down from the gentler stretches—the stream heads at Mount Pisgah—but now these nursery pools too are being heavily fished by people who reach them in rough-terrain vehicles. No surplus exists.

My left leg was swollen tight with charley horses, yet this walk of eight miles through dense, choppy, unpretentious country which had never been settled or farmed seemed like the best scenery of the trip and a kind of climax. It was ambush country; you couldn't see far, but hidden away there were several quite glorious wilderness elms that Dutch elm disease hadn't found. We saw a splatter of tracks left by a sprinting bobcat alongside the stream. The stream popped and sparkled in the sun, pincering past obstructions, cutting a hundred cockscrew twists.

Leaving the Little Dead Diamond, we took its South Branch, ascending toward Crystal Mountain. Usnea moss ("old-man's-beard") hung from the dead limbs in the stands of young fir, a delicacy for the deer. The masses of moss covering the ground which Strong remembered from some of his early visits had disappeared since the last logging, replaced by raspberry thickets. We ate as we walked, and saw traces of every other creature that had been feasting also, every animal one might expect except for skunks, which stay nearer farmland. There was a new beaver dam, the drowning marsh trees turning red. There were spruce and alder—maybe good woodchuck country—as well as thick overgrowth scrub where the maple trees had been logged. We saw two broods of grouse, the first mother leading two chicks and the second five. It was a lovely high-ceilinged day, platter-blue, good weather for grouse to be out and about. (Our average count for the whole grouse survey was one bird for each mile and a half walked.)

We crossed into Dix's Grant from the Atkinson and Gilmanton Academy Grant, both owned by the Brown Paper Company. Parts of the bed of the South Branch had been preempted by their logging trucks, so it was badly messed up. Where it forked, we turned from the South Branch to Lost Valley Brook, climbing south through a concealed niche in the ridge, a little lost valley indeed, very isolated in spirit, where a decade ago Strong was marking thirty-inch birch, and hemlock and pine forty inches through. Now even the six- and eight-inch pulpwood is being removed. We found a dead shrew with fine-grained gray fur, and lots of deer sign. The skidders had cut ruts waist-deep, partly overgrown, no joke to fall into.

We talked about naturalness again. The Indians, Strong said, thought that one could no more own land than own the stars; that's why they "sold" to the whites so cheaply. We were drinking from the brook and I happened to remember how, in the Book of Judges, God told Gideon to choose an army to defeat the Midianites by taking his men to a stream and picking the ones who drank directly from the running water, lapping animal-like, not the more civilized ones who knelt and lifted the water to their lips. Strong liked that, but I said that maybe it just meant that the beastly fought better. He told me the latest promotional scheme involving his department was to transplant some ptarmigan from Colorado to Mount Washington's tundra and see if they lived. Unfortunately the question concerned not just the ptarmigan but New Hampshire's twelve fragile square miles of alpine ecology. Would the birds choose the rarest buds to eat, and what would the tramping feet of the hunters do?

At the source of Lost Valley Brook we entered a thick, dark, gloomy wilderness forest of pole-sized fir and paper birch that is one of the watersheds of the Dead Diamond and Swift Diamond rivers. The Swift joins the Dead fifteen miles or so below Hell Gate, and the waters of both go into the Magalloway River (where they meet the paved road), then into the Androscoggin, then the Kennebec, and finally into the ocean at Bath, Maine. Even up top here it was swampy, though, with many toad pollywogs enjoying the bogs; frogs, which start bigger, would be out of the tadpole stage by now, said Strong. We spotted some hawks—red-tailed and sharp-shinned—garter snakes, hummingbirds, bumblebees, high phloxlike flowers, red mushrooms, and false Solomon's-seal with red berries. Often the ground was cut every which way by beaver channels, like an obstacle course. Moss, muck and sucking mud, bank-beaver holes, wild grasses and sedges, poplars, cattails. The temperature, sixty degrees, up fifteen from when we had started, had me wet with sweat. Fourmile Brook, a portion of which was our destination, heads at a pond so remote that it is stocked with trout thrown out of an airplane.

This brook drops away down the ridge at such a steep pitch that the water sounds like a pistoning motor. We found an antique axhead, broad, rusty as ocher. The last go-through by the loggers had been recent, and so the growth was jungly and low, with plenty of the bugs and berries and wetness grouse like, but for some reason the hauling had been done with a bulldozer, not a skidder, and the ground had not been damaged too much. There was a heady honey smell everywhere from the flowers—purple, blue, yellow—and millions of bugs. Big-toothed poplar, willows and birch, moosewood and silver maples, alders, jewelweed, shadbush, small cedars. More deer sign, more pollywogs; a grouse brood of four, cheeping like chicks, trilling like mice.

Fourmile Brook is a good deal longer than the name indicates, with bad footing, and we spent much time on it before reaching Fourmile Camp. This is a tin-roofed government shack seventeen miles by woods road from the highway, in a clearing surrounded by hills. The wind from the south carried the smell of the pulp mill in Berlin, New Hampshire, a smell more fecal than what one encounters in the actual lavatories at the paper company. If I stepped off into the brush for a minute Strong said, "Is that you or Berlin?" It's a nagging, boiled-cabbage, boiled-egg smell at best, carried also on an opposite wind from the Canadian mills sixty miles north, or on an east wind from those of Oxford County in Maine. A wet light snowfall in the winter seems to sharpen it even more, which for a man with Strong's educated nose must be disturbing. We found a bear's droppings, and I remarked how queer it was that a man's would have affected us as more disgusting. He said the reason might be that compared with wild animals people overeat so enormously that they don't digest as much of the fermentable material. Not being a scientist, I suggested instead that maybe we're so egocentric we prefer to believe even the badness of some of our smells exceeds that of other creatures'.

A truck had been left for us at the camp. As we drove back toward town alongside the Swift Diamond River, we saw it had turned the color of mud from fresh logging that day. So had a stream called Clear Stream. Under New Hampshire's Clean Waters Act a fine of a thousand dollars a day can be levied for offenses like this, but it hasn't as yet been invoked.

Samuel Taylor Coleridge is said to have walked as far as forty miles in a day, and Carlyle once logged fifty-four in twenty-four hours on a walking tour. Wordsworth, the champion in this league, was calculated (by De Quincey) to have totted up 175,000 or 180,000 miles in a lifetime of peregrinations afoot. "I have two doctors," said Sir George Trevelyan of English-style walking, "my left leg and my right."

The American brand of walking of course has a different

mystique, almost forgotten lately, which dates back to the frontier and has little to do with the daily "constitutional" and therefore should be exercised in a setting so brawny and raw that the mileage can't even be guessed at. Since my own sports as a boy were running and walking, my image of athletic prowess has been a related one, but I was glad to get home to the soft bed and fortifying dinners of the Colebrook House Hotel each of these evenings. I'm lucky I wasn't born a few centuries ago. For the sake of the exultancy I feel in wild places I probably would have tried to get in on some of the exploration, and as I'm not that strong physically, I would have been one of the substantial number in almost every party who died. Even in balmy weather, when I've been alone on a true frontier, a hundred miles from the nearest dirt road, I've had crazy, incongruous sexual fantasies assault me, like a blanket pulled over my head, as if by them I sought to hide from more powerful fears—of grizzlies, illogical avalanches, of twisting my ankle or getting lost. Yet between these bouts with the fantastical, during which my eyes actually shut at times, I was all eyes, all elation and incredulousness, living three days in one.

Strong stretched his legs the next day on the last lap of eight miles. We both hoped we hadn't been chatting so much that we'd spooked any grouse, so he stayed in front of me, letting me see if I could keep up. We went from Fourmile Camp up a steep hardwood ridge which is part of Crystal Mountain, and down the other side. Many squirrel tracks at the rain pools, a red squirrel and chipmunk confronting each other on a short log (the chipmunk the one with the food in its paws), and a rapid goshawk. Goshawks will plunge right into a pile of brush after a grouse, like an osprey hitting the water chasing a fish. Strong said he saw his last peregrine falcon in 1954. In those days he would see up to fifty horses going home at night on their own along these trails from the logging sites.

Where we climbed, the ground was sometimes heaped with slash five feet high, wet from the night's rains, and the skidders had cut tank traps everywhere, making walking a sweaty struggle. The grouse we disturbed called to each other. The cocks live alone, each in his own territory, to which he tries to drum mates in the spring. The females nest on the bare ground, usually in some slight depression that they find at an elevated place near the base of a tree. They eat catkins, clover, foliage and fruits, but the chicks are not vegetarian; they eat beetles, ants, spiders, snails, flies and larvae, which are richer in protein and vitamins.

In a clearing we found the remnants of a loggers' supply

wagon. Spruce had been the climax forest and now that the big old second-growth hardwoods had been removed also, mostly fir was appearing, a short-lived, fast-growing species that buds early in the spring, risking the frosts but shooting up, its root system shallow and its limbs flimsy. Yet a fir woods, too, requires at least forty years to reach a commercially plausible size, and in modern business enterprise who's going to sit around for the next forty years with real estate like this, watching the dragonflies? Every management shakeup brings a change in plans, and Strong in his advocacy position with respect to the land is naturally on the firing line. Understand that a bear, for example, needs a minimum of about five square miles to forage in for his food supply. This is not counting the extra land he will roam through in the course of a year, which might comprise seventy-five square miles, or more than two hundred if he is hunted hard. The five square miles is an irreducible wilderness area that will grow his food, and although other bears may overlap with him, he will include their territory in his wanderings. A single deer's primary range for feeding is forty or fifty acres. A mink's, in a fertile marsh, may be only twenty, and a raccoon's ten, though, like the deer, they will each ramble a mile or more on occasion, utilizing the foodstuffs and crannies of a much larger acreage, and could not live in a wild state for long if really restricted to such a space. Yet if an acre is now to become worth a thousand dollars as recreational property, is that raccoon worth ten thousand dollars? Is a bear worth 3.2 million dollars? As in the suburbs, a raccoon can parcel together a home out of snips and pieces of people's backyards, but otter, bears, bobcats, and so on cannot. I had teased Strong about hunting, but I hoped he knew that the teasing had been a result of my friendship, that I understood that hunting by men like himself was never the villain in wildlife management. Rather, it was the summer people like me, who come crowding in, buying up, chopping up the land after the loggers have skinned off the trees.

A brook going downhill gave us a steady grade to the Swift Diamond River. The temperature rose to eighty in the afternoon, from forty-five. Squirrel and deer country, with lots of witch hobble—deer food. We met mosquitoes and saw a rabbit, an owl's striped feather in the leaf muck, and a woodchuck's tracks (a type darker than the reddish farm chuck inhabits these forests). Seeing a red squirrel chitting at us, bold in the certainty that we couldn't touch him, I had a sudden memory of the chattering exhilaration which as a boy I had felt just after a close brush with death in a car.

So must this squirrel feel at dusk when an owl swoops at him and he swerves round a tree trunk and escapes, feeling the wind of its wings. The Swift, like the Dead, was employed originally for freighting out the virgin softwoods, so that there was no need to build roads into this country at all until, scarcely ten years ago in the case of the Swift, the loggers came back again for the hardwood trees, which don't float as well. We followed the road alongside the Swift for half a mile, then waded it and struck up Nathan Pond Brook, through a narrow wild brushy defile under Cave Mountain, with yellow birch and soft and hard maples and cone-bearing alders ten feet high. The hummingbirds swarmed to my red hat again, and there were goldfinches, purple finches, and blueberry thickets where we stopped to feast, and shoulder-high joe-pye weed, fireweed, goldenrod, and beaver activity and engineered ponds.

Legally as well as perhaps geographically, it is no longer possible just to throw a pack on your back in the Northeast and hike cross-country for weeks, because casual camping has been prohibited. But here in this obscure little bypassed valley bursting with undergrowth the illusion of the old hiking freedoms persisted. Even the vivid fish in their pools didn't give me the feeling of claustrophobia and pity that I often get, looking at trout cramped into a brook. They had space and a churning current and complexity enough in their habitat to baffle a hunting mink.

The
Tugman's
Passage

Captain Artie Biagi, of the Moran Towing Company, broke into this organization of mainly Irish tugboatmen in New York harbor more than thirty years ago, when he was a young man job-hunting with a hangover. By a fluke, he fell into conversation with an individual in the adjoining booth of the men's room at Maritime Association headquarters near the Battery. He couldn't see the fellow, but—in that day more innocent than our own—after they had chatted awhile about his getting drunk the night before at the Red Men Lodge in West New York, New Jersey, and about his previous jobs in a tar yard and driving a laundry truck and as a deckhand on an army tug that had gone clear to Baffin Island, in Canada, he learned that his companion was a magnate of the shipping industry. Another tug captain of Italian ancestry—at that time a runaway from an orphanage, hanging about the docks on the Lower East Side—landed his first job when a paternal Irishman took pity on him and let him "ham" on his boat, working at first for just his meals.

Biagi's mother was German, and his father's mother was Scotch, so it's an accident of American sociology, he says, that he is called "Italian." Round-faced, soft-chinned, he is laconic on the bridge of a ship when giving directions for its docking, but then talkative when he gets back to the wheelhouse of his tug. Ten years ago, when I first went out on the water with him, he was servicing the S.S. *United States,* the English *Queens,* and the *Raffaello,* as well as the usual miscellany of tramp freighters and harbor barges, from a big 4,300-horsepower tug called the *Teresa.* Now, close to retirement, he has the 1,200-horsepower *Christine,* and a lighter schedule of two days on and two days off, and a crew—mate, engineer, cook, and deckhand—each man of which is full of memories.

Bobby Perlitz, the deckhand, is so gimpy after forty years of working on the waterfront that, to oblige him, Biagi uses a flimsy ladder Bobby can still manage to lift for the risky business of Biagi's climbing from the *Christine* to the decks of the ships he docks.

New York's port, when strike-free, is the busiest in the country, with more than seventy-five hundred arrivals in the course of a year. Opposite Sandy Hook, which curves into the sea from New Jersey to form the sheltering lip of the outer harbor, every ship picks up a pilot, who guides it up the channel, past Gravesend Bay, through the Narrows between Staten Island and Brooklyn, under the Verrazano Bridge, nearly seventeen miles altogether, to the Battery in Lower Manhattan—though most ships now will turn aside a little before that. They may tie up in the bleaker reaches of Brooklyn, or else head on around Staten Island, past Robbins Reef, Constable Hook, Sailors Snug Harbor, and Shooters Island in Kill Van Kull, up Newark Bay to the extensive new facilities for containerships in New Jersey, much more accessible to interstate truck traffic than the congested old streets of Manhattan's waterfront.

A tug or two will assist at tight passages and in the actual docking, before which Biagi or another tugboat captain will have boarded the vessel and assumed the responsibilities of the Sandy Hook pilot. The tugboat deckhands have heaved up their lines to the ship's seamen in the meantime. These seamen are a worldly, various assortment of Japanese, Indonesians, Germans, Slavs, and Danes, and they peer silently over the railing as the "monkey's fist"—the weight at the end of the rope—flies up to them. Fresh off the ocean, they look windblown, wet, and foreign, and they are tongue-tied with the tugmen, as the tugmen are with them, but as high as they are, they have a vigorous air, a forecastle fellowship with one another, yet also a sightseer's eagerness in new territory.

Biagi, spruce on the bridge, where there are always intimations of the nineteenth-century social order, radios instructions to Red Nordberg, his mate, in the *Christine*'s wheelhouse—"Come ahead slow," "Come ahead full," "Easy back"—which Nordberg, who is often out of sight of the ship's bridge under the flare of her bow, confirms by tooting on the tug's whistle. Within my own time on the water but before the era of walkie-talkies, this sort of communication was done from the bridge of the ship with a police whistle, and if there was a second tug, working at the stern, also the ship's whistle. Before radios were used in the harbor at all, a tug had to take a run past the company's office at the Battery after completing a job, and the dispatcher shouted the next assignment through the window with a megaphone. If the message was more complicated he waved a towel, and the tug captain tied up and went to a pay phone. Still further back, before there were such luxuries as offices and telephones, rival tugboats simply sailed out to Gravesend Bay at dawn and bargained against each other from ship to ship.

Both Biagi and Nordberg, whose brush-shaped red mustache swallows most of his smiles but who, even so, looks boyish, have won citations for bravery displayed in water emergencies. Over the years, they—like Richard Decker, the shy, fastidious engineer, who comes from a long line of Staten Island oystermen—have rescued people scalded in boiler explosions and sailors swimming between patches of blazing oil. They have seen people drown after being accidentally jostled off the Staten Island ferry, and many grayish, eel-gnawed bodies of suicides and murder victims. Once Biagi was bent over the bitt on a barge moored under the Brooklyn Bridge when there was a tremendous splash right next to the bow. He whipped around and noticed a white object rising underwater. It looked like some kind of ball, but he realized it was a bald head, instead. Mournfully the man's face bobbed out of the water. He was alive, still conscious. Their eyes met. "I want to die," he said, very calmly, because Biagi had started to kick off his workboots. Then the current caught him, in the sudden way it has in the East River—six knots strong—and gave him his wish.

Like most tugboatmen, all the *Christine*'s crew are family men, their children now grown up; that was why they never went to sea. Only the cook, Leo, has been divorced. Leo Catarina, born in the Philippines, is agile and thin, with a crouching posture that he has probably developed from stooping in so many galley hatches to peer out at the water and up the sides of big ships. He fills in as an extra deckhand occasionally, and though he wears a dashing, drooping mustache that makes him look younger than the others, and though he recently married a young Italian girl in Brooklyn who has given him a new baby who is the light of his life, outdoors he appears frail. His favorite stint, he says, was a period of years he spent cooking on a little tug on Lake Champlain, taking his son along sometimes for the trolling they did from the fantail as the boat pushed a barge. In the spring they might have a frost, and the tug would crunch through, breaking virgin ice—ice so clear and new it shattered like crystal a hundred yards ahead of them.

At lunch, Leo, serving chicken, liked to ask me, "Do you want white meat, dark meat, or Filipino meat?"—which I took to be the forestalling device of a man used to explaining his skin color.

Leo, and Bobby, from Rockaway, and Decker, too, calculated their exacta and box bets on the horses as they ate, the galley a clutter of *Doc's Daily Racing Selections, American Turf,* and *Racing Star.* Decker, who got his start on the water in 1933 as a messboy on a buoy tender, has impaired hearing—"boilermaker's ears"—from tending so many roaring diesels since then (tug engines being adaptations of railroad diesels originally, he said). Like other engineers I had encountered, he seemed slightly skittish, as if the deafening solitude of the engine room might accentuate the quirks and wariness that any person began with. Yet, hearing of his four children and seven grandchildren, whom he flies to visit on vacations, I realized that tugmen lead double lives. Most of them insist upon the point, and regale each other with tales of their soft berths at home.

Seamen, too, lead lives that are far-flung, sharply divided. But many tugboatmen go back and forth twice a week from the desolate, salt-stained piers of Red Hook to mow the lawn in some eminently domestic suburb of the city. Some keep a second, hideaway household in one of the five boroughs as well. Pulling hawsers half the night, backs aching—till they do it in their dreams for hours afterwards—and sleeping in the roar of the engine, in a dingy cabin, with a diesel galley stove, a firehose curled around the toilet in the john, they try to figure how to spend the extraordinary money some of them earn.

Biagi has seen to it that his son has also become a docking pilot (against the opposition of a few senior harbor Irishmen), and this has worked out well. Artie, Jr., in contrast to his father, is as edgy as a bullfighter. Tall, dark, gruff, and Latin, gravel-voiced, obsessed with his job, and pugnacious about it, he is a rising star in the rather nervous hierarchy of docking pilots, and Biagi, Sr., both enjoys his prominence and worries about his fits of perfectionist pique. It's not only a question of how the bosses respond to a temper tantrum, but the deckhands' reaction. Tug captains who fall off the ladder between ship and tug can be crushed or saved, according to whether the deckhand who was holding the ladder tries, in the split seconds available, to snatch the captain free of the churning water.

Artie, Jr., in a jump suit, with comb in hand, appears to be continually on show, at least to an audience of one, but he is not without humor. Dressed fussily in suede, he will stride onto an eight-hundred-foot tanker and tell the guard and the third mate, as he climbs the long staircase, that no, he's not the pilot; he is an investor who has just bought the ship and wants to inspect the bridge. In fact, it's traditional that top tugboat pilots dress spiffily—they wore dark suits, derby hats, and chesterfield coats in the old days, as Biagi, Sr., much impressed then, remembers—and that they also be contentious and jittery.

Each Biagi earned around seventy thousand dollars in 1978. After the purchase of a home in the exurbs and a fine car or two, what does one invest in? Other tugmen have sunk their funds into land development, a restaurant, stocks and bonds, a racehorse. The Sandy Hook pilots, who enjoy a similar monopoly in practicing their trade, make slightly less—a senator's salary. They may live all over, in Maine or Florida or the Carolinas, flying in and out of New York at biweekly intervals. In Artie Sr.'s case, he bought a twenty-seven-acre trailer park in the Poconos, expecting that his daughter and her husband would run it, but instead they got divorced. With the sort of energy he devoted to learning harbor charts many years ago, he has been taking flying lessons, there in Pennsylvania, living in a big empty house and studying the interesting points of instrument landing—wondering whether he might not have had a better time from the beginning if he had aimed to be an airline pilot.

Biagi has heart trouble, Nordberg is recuperating from an abdominal operation, Decker is sixty-three and fragile-looking. And so they all are full of life-and-death stories. Biagi remembers the smell of the nursing home where his poor mother, with sheepskin padding on her hips and elbows to prevent bedsores, finally died. On his index finger he bears a scar from when his daughter, as a baby, fell into convulsions and he stuck his finger in her mouth to try to clear her breathing. The doctor whose house they blundered into injected her, by mistake, with an adult's dosage of morphine; and yet she lived; she is in Texas now.

Being watermen, they have a special knowledge of tragedy and peril. The city's bodies end up bobbing in the tide, after having been mauled by the Hudson's ice all winter. And on the boats, although a hawser rarely actually snaps, if one only "jumps" off the bitt it can kill a deckhand. Or a bitt can break off, propelled like shrapnel. Not only the captain, climbing to a ship, can tumble into the rushing water between tug and ship. So can a deckhand, balanced on the rail or standing on a fender, as the tide throws ship and tug together with a hard bump. Or, if a tugboatman turns alcoholic, an oddly public drama may result. He sits on the pier under the giant Colgate clock in Jersey City, where the chandler's truck delivers grub to Moran's tugs and his old comrades are going to see him. When they swing ashore, they shake hands, give him sandwiches, maybe a coat. But he sells the coat. He's coughing. They stop again, talk to him, leave a sweater, pass a plate of food

to him. Sitting once again on the frigid bulkhead next December—
a figure who in better days had shared a thousand suppers in the
galley—he catches the captain's eye. He is slumped over. The captain touches him. He is dead.

More ships called at New York ten or twenty years ago, but they
were freighters—what are now called "break-bulk ships"—with a
forest of stubby cranes to reach into the several fore- and after-
holds, and they were smaller. Small shipping operators and the
nautical lines of the so-called developing countries still employ
these, but huge specialty ships, such as the twelve-deck car-carriers
that shuttle to America loaded with Toyotas, have become the
muscle of maritime commerce. There are vessels hollowed out to
carry nothing but grain or scrap metal, and innumerable containerships that carry not loose cargo loaded by means of slings and
pallets into holds but two or three thousand aluminum boxes that,
set onto flatbed tractor trailers, shoot off unopened to almost as
many destinations. With ships built for drive-on, drive-off convenience, a minimal crew can clear the harbor efficiently in a single
day if their arrival alongside the dock is timed to coincide with the
longshoremen's morning shape-up.

Containerships have a simplified profile, all of the housing being at the stern; and on the Jersey piers, jumbo black cranes like
dinosaurs lean over them to hasten the work. An American varia-
tion is the LASH (Lighter Alongside Ship), which transports perhaps ninety barges, instead of tractor-trailer bodies, and a five-
hundred-ton sliding derrick that rolls back and forth in order to
hoist them. Again, it isn't nearly as pretty a craft as an old-fashioned
freighter, but the harbor—a place of "grease," payoffs, pilferage,
"piecing" somebody off, where a man that you used to notice walking along in a lumberjack shirt ("Mr. Pier Eight") might have had
twenty thousand dollars in his pocket—is getting so automated that
soon only white-collar crime will be left.

In Buttermilk Channel, between Brooklyn and Governors Island, we intercepted a cargo ship, the *African Mercury*, which was
painted black, red, and white, with two sea horses on the bow. The
Diana Moran was also there, to help Biagi dock it. Because in the
current the ship would have turned like a weathervane if left to its
own devices, until finally the bow pointed into the "wind," or current, Biagi positioned the *Christine* and *Diana* at bow and stern to
counter this eventuality and keep it broadside as it entered the slip
at Brooklyn's Pier 11. A ship when broadside to the hop of the tide
is like a seesaw, with its fulcrum in the middle. But as the bow
slides inside the slip, escaping the current, the fulcrum naturally

shifts aft. As the *African Mercury*'s bow got "lighter" and the stern "heavier," Biagi adjusted the placement and thrust of his tugs accordingly. The whole process took three-quarters of an hour, until the ship's lines to the dock were fast.

We then sailed the *Hellenic Splendor* from Fifty-seventh Street, Brooklyn—a much quicker operation, the ship's own propeller backing her out. The *Christine* simply fastened to her bow and acted as the rudder. Next, we sailed a Japanese boat, *Blue Nagoya*, from Pier 36, north of the Manhattan Bridge on the East River; and then the LASH *Stonewall Jackson* from Brooklyn. After lunch we rendezvoused off Robbins Reef with a neat, white-and-green, Russian-built, Kuwaiti-owned vessel, *Al Mansouriah*, managed from Liverpool and headed for Port Newark. The captain, as Biagi mentioned afterward, was an Englishman born in Argentina named J. P. Kosidowski. Because of the jumble of origins and destinations, I thought of Józef Korzeniowski—Joseph Conrad.

We were so busy because three other Moran tugs were out of commission. The *Cynthia* had hit a ship with her wheelhouse in an awkward maneuver. "She tried to push the ship with her front window," as Biagi put it. The *Margot Moran*, towing a barge, had blundered into a piling, which did no damage in itself but stopped the *Margot* dead, so that the barge she was towing rode up over her stern and hit her capstan and rear housing. And the *Elizabeth* had thrown a bolt on her reduction gear.

Late this October afternoon, as we docked the ship *Mormacaltair* in Gowanus Canal, the seamen and two longshoremen who were hauling on a stern line got careless before the ship had come to a dead halt, and the rope tangled in the ship's screw. For half an hour they diddled with it while the ship's captain, by gently reversing engines, shook the rope, and the mate and pier boss radioed back and forth as to whether a diver ought to be called. The accident would turn serious if the propeller was torn askew. In New York the standard fee for cutting a line loose from a propeller is three hundred dollars, an honorarium that many times has been collected by a tugboatman swimming underwater with no gear but the cook's meat saw and a bandanna tied across his nose.

"Isn't that the way?" I said. "One man earns three hundred dollars for risking his life, and another just the same money for picking up the phone."

"It's come in handy, though," Biagi said.

In the evening at slack tide we helped a captain named Hugo van Slegtenhorst, from Hoagland, Holland, to steer his Shell Oil Co. tanker from a tank farm opposite Riker's Island in the Bronx to Ross Terminal in Kill Van Kull. She measured 748 feet long and 103 feet wide, and, lightened as she was, drew twenty-six feet of water. The controlling depth in the East River is only thirty-four feet, at Poor House Flats, opposite Twentieth Street in Manhattan, and so about a quarter of her load had had to be tapped off to barges before she had gone up the East River to the Bronx in the first place. On the other hand, if a ship's mast rides more than 126 feet high it will hit the Brooklyn Bridge (as happened recently with a tanker one of Biagi's friends was piloting), so not too much oil can be off-loaded before a trip in either direction.

Gliding south, we gazed at the storybook luxury of the Upper East Side of Manhattan almost as if we owned it. With the three-quarter moon, the cake-on-cliff buildings, beige and creamy, many lighted, some shadowy, were surpassingly beautiful. Houselights in Manhattan in their millions look glowingly yellow when seen from the river; skyscraper offices have white-lit windows; and the bridge lights are blue. The tanker, under its own steam and Biagi's guidance and with marvelous aplomb, slid the seven miles from Hell Gate to Lower Manhattan, whose intricacy of windows is even more crowded and jewellike and radiant—stunning when lit up because it is such a statement of power.

"Wall Street," we explained to a Dutchman who was new to New York, though by day the dense clutter of buildings does not loom as large. Jammed, hypertense, they do not really go together. Each was originally some architect's or tycoon's obsession—like a single impassioned shout—so that, looked at together, they add up to a cacophony. From a distance, however, out past the Statue of Liberty, they seem to sail on the water, narrow as a frigate.

Captain van Slegtenhorst had a crackerjack complement of officers and men on the bridge, and, in the competitive manner of captains, was glad that I, along with Biagi, could see it. I was underdressed for the bridge, and Artie had been prepared to apologize for me, but, on the contrary, the captain said that he assumed from the fact that I was underdressed and bore the good name of his hometown in Holland, I must be a millionaire.

We docked van Slegtenhorst at the Jersey tank farm where he would deliver the rest of his oil, and tied up with half a dozen other tugs at the Moran Company boatyard on Staten Island, which is across Kill Van Kull from New Jersey. I stayed several nights on the Christine, and sometimes Biagi had work to do as late as midnight or as early as five in the morning, so he is not a barfly. But I went across the street to visit Frank's and Ginger's, two tugmen's hangouts that still charge only thirty cents for a glass of beer. The barmaid at Frank's was a great, husky, slam-bang young lady who sang along with the jukebox for hours, but louder, and swung her body in the go-go style with such tireless pleasure that she made the place fun for everybody else, as well as for herself, and, in the wee hours, was inclined to treat the weary souls ranged in a row in front of her as a harem.

"My man from Moran," she would say, not meaning anybody in particular, though there were strays off the street, too, pleading with her. "I'm fifty-seven years old and still making a hundred forty-three dollars a week," said the man on the stool next to me very sadly, but she was so delighted with the music, her job, and the audience, she didn't linger for long to commiserate with him.

At dawn the water was milk-colored, red "nun" buoys clanged beside the channel back to Manhattan, and burnt-yellow ferryboats were crossing from St. George to the Battery. As we hurried to meet the Dole fruit boat *Bolivar* off Governor's Island, Biagi welcomed the new day in the noisy galley with his breakfast eggs—the yolks like breasts—"Good morning, dear!"

We docked the *Bolivar* at Pier 42, on the east side of Manhattan; then the coffee freighter *Ciudad de Cucuta* across the East River at Pier 3 in Brooklyn. We sailed the *Rio Amazonas* from Pier 5, Brooklyn, and the *Rio Teuco* from Pier 2, and soon afterwards, since we were working there, docked the *Asunción*, a slender little cargo ship, at Pier 8, and sailed the car-carrier *Höegh Target*, based in Oslo, from Pier 9. Before lunch, we went down the harbor to Thirty-ninth Street, Brooklyn, and sailed the *Delta American*, captained by a Southerner who said he had never been North before and was glad to be leaving.

Red Nordberg, who claimed that he was "not a moderate drinker—what I start I finish," talked about practical jokes he had played. Nailing a mate's shoes to the floor and waking him up for midnight watch, or putting cut-up rubber bands in his pipe and a lobster in his bunk, or pulling the tug's whistle by means of a rope from another tug, if they were all tied up for the night and he had brought his girlfriend to his cabin.

Tugmen never got much "grease" in the old days, and remain just spectators to the intrigue of drug smuggling that goes on lately. But Leo and Bobby Perlitz talked about the era when whole banana stalks would be handed to them after they had docked a fruit boat, and when the coal-barge companies gave out Christmas turkeys, and a Russian ship captain, happy at arriving in this mystical hive of a capitalist port, offered his docking pilot, besides the usual gift of fur gloves, vodka, and caviar, half an hour with the ship's whore. Some of the British boats had been crewed by Pakistanis, who kept live goats and chickens tethered on the poop deck and a stew pot cooking. You would see a couple of black women sneaking up the gangplank, first thing, as they docked, to service the crew. Nowadays, too, Bobby said, you might catch sight of a limber black woman going aboard with an amused expression, but she would be in uniform, working for Customs and Immigration.

We were directed by the dispatcher to go to the South Bronx for garbaging chores, and lunched on the river, our wake spreading like fish ribs behind us. Bobby called Leo "Chico" and "Pablo," to irritate him, and a new deckhand named Niels, whom we had picked up for garbage duty, "Johnny Bicycle," because he seemed so young, quick, and dippy. Niels had just quit a busboy's job at Studio 54, the nightclub for celebrities, and talked about all the celebs he could have snorted coke with. He talked about his first job on a tug, owned by another company, which he said had once been burned out and sunk in a naphtha explosion, so that its timbering was still warped from being underwater. The captain and mate had shouted at him constantly, and while he was coiling a rope on the stern a barge they were towing lurched right over the fantail and nearly cashed in his chips for him. Raw as he was, however, he was earning two hundred dollars a day from Moran, said Biagi, instead of two hundred dollars a week, as he would have on land.

Our stubby *Christine* chuffed up the East River past the United Nations building; the Shah of Iran, who was then hospitalized in New York Hospital; Mayor Ed Koch's 1801-vintage house; and South Brother Island, which is my favorite spot (or dot) in the harbor, an undisturbed minutia of wilderness with wide-spreading trees and underbrush, opposite Tiffany Street in the Bronx.

"G-man duty" pays "mud-scale" wages, higher than ordinary wages—"mud" being sewage, which, like the city's garbage, is hauled away by water. It is lazy, smelly, flyblown work, shifting empty barges into the waterside terminals where the sanitation trucks unload, and pulling them out again after three hours when they are full. Even though we also crossed Bowery Bay to perform the same service for the Borough of Queens, we had endless lounging time, or "government time," as Biagi called it.

I have heard other tugmen describe the wet scents of the garbage barges as reminding them of sex; and they get onto the subject of the ripening widows in their neighborhoods or apartment buildings, and want to look for a pay telephone, or will get up on the rail of the barge and look for skin magazines in the heap. But the smells are mostly a compendium of America's extraordinary sugar-rich diet, and the main action is provided by the sea gulls, which find here a sustenance substituting for the shellfish and spawning fish of primeval New Amsterdam, now so long gone.

Sparrows, starlings, and pigeons were crawling over the garbage, and one odd, humpy cattle egret, which looked cold, was feasting on insects. But it was the gulls' show. They settled themselves, vain of their wingspreads, with much kvetching, creaking and croaking, keeowing and *kuk-kuk-yucca-yucca*ing, on each fresh load, when we pulled a barge out of the shed. In what ethologists call "agonistic" behavior, they flexed their wings, pointed their heads straight up, and opened their bills before sidling over and pecking each other. Herring gulls, white with pinkish legs and black wingtips, were in the majority, and busiest at ripping open the plastic bags and grabbing the chitlings inside. Then perhaps they would perch on a burned mattress that protruded over the side of the barge while gobbling these tidbits down. But numbers of large all-white glaucous gulls and several huge black-backed gulls with white necks and heads, almost eagle-sized, dominated the mob. It was altogether a scene from the end of the world, and Biagi performed a species of jujitsu with the weighty barges, as the colliding currents of Long Island Sound and Hell Gate pried at them like a crowbar to wrest them out of his control.

While we were watching the gulls he spoke of a deckhand named "Holy John," now dead, who had believed that every sea gull was a dead seaman and had got terribly angry once when Biagi shot one. Biagi was a skeptical Catholic, and knocking his cup of coffee off the window ledge by accident—"That's my Italian accent"—he asked me what I believed about life after death. I said life was a borrowed gift; life, whether human or animal, might be as temporary as so many wavelets in the ocean that quietly fall back and can't be reconstructed again, after each rise. But the ocean they were part of was life. Life was as eternal as that.

"Now, that's worth all the trouble of having you along. All the trouble of explaining everything—just to hear one new idea like that!" Biagi exclaimed enthusiastically. "Whether it makes sense or not, that's what you don't hear on a job like this, a new idea." But I had been arguing that he had had more fun driving a tug for the last thirty years than he would have piloting airliners, so I suggested that there should be plenty of new ideas out here on the water.

It was dusk; cocktail hour. At the garbage terminal in Queens the sanitation men had hosed the barges till each one looked like a vast greenish condom. But a fancy, high-tailed, silvery jet came shrieking down just above our heads every minute and a half to hit the landing strip of La Guardia Airport, which was a few hundred yards away, lit like a Christmas tree. All the luxury of rushing by taxi to the midtown hotels was implied in the fanciness, luscious lights, and haste—but close by was a silent stretch of horizon where the city prison on Riker's Island is.

We were contemporaries, and Biagi was saying how at our present age he wouldn't dream of shooting a gull. He'd lost his taste, too, for the violent mood of strike time on the waterfront, when young tug-union members occasionally go touring by launch with a rifle in hand. Wouldn't it be crazy to shoot somebody over a matter of a couple of extra dollars in your paycheck? He said his wife said his check was getting too big for his own good now, anyway. People had gotten beaten up, sent to the hospital, for stepping into a phone booth to call home, when some dynamite-head on the picket line suddenly suspected that they might be finks who were calling the company.

Next morning we docked the *Hellenic Explorer,* a gray-and-white containership from Piraeus, at Thirty-third Street, Brooklyn. With a big, reassuring grin, the mate nodded at Biagi, grasping his elbows, and Biagi then entrusted his life to him for a second in swinging his body over the ship's railing, while a hard current bobbed the tug and ladder underneath him. Because I'd once lived for half a year on the Aegean, that generous Greek grin somehow struck home to me as a contrast to the softer, self-absorbed grins of landlubbers like myself whom I was seeing lately.

We also docked the *Hellenic Sky,* at Fifty-seventh Street, Brooklyn, and, in the afternoon, went up Newark Bay to sail the *Toyota Maru No. 8,* which was returning to Japan to fetch more Toyotas. While we were in Port Newark, we docked the *Covadonga,* a freighter from Barcelona, as planes took off and landed just across the fence, at Newark Airport.

In the twilight we sailed the *Export Freedom* from Howland Hook in Arthur Kill, and then, off Robbins Reef, threw a line to a Liberian scrap-metal ship and took it up Kill Van Kull, under Bayonne Bridge, around Bergen Point, and up Newark Bay to Pier 36, in Port Newark again. We sailed the *Atlantic Song,* a Swedish containership carrying backhoes and tractors, from Port Elizabeth, New Jersey, and docked the gray-and-white *Good Master,* a Greek freighter, in Brooklyn, an hour later—the Lower Manhattan skyscrapers taking on a cathedral shape in the distance in the meantime. We docked Dow Chemical's *Leland I. Doan* in Kill Van Kull, at flood tide, and the white, trim, high-riding 697-foot South African *Alphen,* in Brooklyn, and sailed the blue 425-foot *Stubbenhuk* from Bay Ridge, Brooklyn, heading for Hamburg.

Biagi said that except for purposes of calculation, he tries to ignore how lengthy some of his ships are, in order not to become intimidated, and that he blocks out of his mind past near collisions and lesser calamities, of which a considerable number are inevitable in a lifetime of harbor work. Like a dancing elephant, a ship being docked turns slowly but gracefully and importantly in the rush of the tide in front of a row of finger piers. It will swing left or right according to which way the water is running and whether the pilot means for it to enter the slip bow-first or stern-first. But the key decision the pilot must make is when he should start the turn. Then, by watching a single landmark on shore, he estimates, adjusts, and coordinates with his tugboats the ship's speed and position as it slides through what may be a ninety-degree shift. The new containerships come equipped with bow thrusters and stern thrusters—extra propellers that, in effect, enable them to move sideways at will. This invention, employed in concert with the ship's main screw, could even eliminate tugs from the docking process eventually, though they would still be needed for risky passages in a tight, intricate harbor like New York's.

We had one nervous moment. At night, in the confined area between Staten Island and New Jersey, Biagi, on the bridge of the *Leland I. Doan,* seemed to lose control for a spell. The *Doan,* a tanker loaded with God knows what combination of chemicals, yawed around in a four-knot tide as if to block the channel and drift down upon a containership waiting for clearance under a railroad bridge that crossed Kill Van Kull. The *Christine* alone was not strong enough to stop her, and Biagi had not asked for a backup tug to help. Finally, he saved the situation by first cutting and then after a moment starting the ship's own engines, while the captain of the *Doan,* standing beside him, clutched the edge of a table until his knuckles turned white.

Afterwards, in the *Christine*'s galley, Bobby, to relieve the tension, said a tug captain "must have big balls. That's half the job." He teased Decker, the engineer or "Chief," with Indian-chief jokes; said "How" to him. Decker, for his part, teased Biagi about being "only a pointer." The engine was the center of a boat, Decker said—even the old *Christine*'s had once made a trip clear to Vietnam—and the captain "only points where it should go."

Tugboatmen, although they have seamen's papers, quickly shrug off their allegiance to ships and the sea after each job. More than taxi drivers, they are really citizens of the city. They barge the sand the buildings are built of down the Hudson from Haverstraw, and get their water from Pier 36 in Brooklyn's Gowanus Bay. They can tie up anywhere, in any borough, for a catnap, and up the street there is a bar and a betting parlor. "Up the street" in waterside Brooklyn, Manhattan, Long Island City, Hoboken, and Weehawken was where all the nightlife was; and in such an enormous dukedom, if a tugman got into trouble in one neck of the harbor, he could do his drinking in another—or just cross the river. If he had a goon squad chasing him, he ran straight for the water, tiptoed down the stringpiece of the wharf, hopped onto his boat, and confidently threw the engine into full reverse—out into the sprawling harbor, simmering with lights at night.

Years ago, a tugman was likely to stay with the same boat until at last he was carried off feetfirst. And so, once somebody had learned the shapes of the different vessels in the Moran fleet and knew the patterns of their running lights, he could look around the Upper Bay and see where his friends were working, even at night.

A
Low-Water
Man

Leave the astronauts out of it, and the paratroop teams that free-fall for ten thousand feet or skate down by means of those flattish, maneuverable new parachutes. Leave out the six people who have survived the 220-foot fall from the Golden Gate Bridge, and the divers of Acapulco, who swan-dive 118 feet, clearing outcrops of twenty-one feet as they plunge past the sea cliff. Leave out even the ordinary high diver, who enters the pool rigid and pointed after a comely jackknife. Come down from such lofty characters to Henri LaMothe—who on his seventieth birthday last April dove from a forty-foot ladder into a play pool of water twelve inches deep.

The high diver in his development first increases his height, then crowds more gainers and twists into his drop, but LaMothe's progress in middle age and since has not involved ascending higher. Rather, he has provided himself with less and less water to land in: an ambition oddly private and untheatrical. Three feet, two feet, twenty inches, sixteen inches, fourteen inches. He strikes, not headfirst or feetfirst, which would be the finish of him, but on the arched ball of his belly. Inevitably, his endeavor over the years has been to manage somehow to jump into no water at all in the end. Since this is impossible, he is designing a break-away plastic pool whose sides will collapse as he hits, so that except for the puddles remaining on the pavement, he will at least experience the sensation of having done just exactly that.

It's as if LaMothe hasn't heard that during his lifetime man has learned to fly, or that he knows that the flying we do is not really flying. In the meantime his posture resembles a flying squirrel's. Apparently nobody else entertains similar ambitions, although one of the old-time carnival thrills was for a stunt man to jump feetfirst from a platform into a very considerably deeper hogshead of water, doing what divers describe as a tuck as he entered, then partly somersaulting and scooping madly. As the person dropped, he could steer just a bit by tilting his head—the head being the heaviest mass in the body—but like Henri's feat, this one was gilded with none of the nifty, concise aesthetics of fancy diving: no "points" to be scored, no springboard to bound from, no Hawaiian plunge after the midair contortions into a sumptuous, deep-blue, country-club pool, with a pretty crawl stroke afterwards to carry him out of the way of the next competitor. Such a performer lived on hot dogs and slept with the ticket seller and often received an involuntary enema through the two pairs of trunks that he wore; got sinus and mastoid infections and constant colds from the water forced into his nose.

LaMothe dives, however—doesn't jump—into water that scarcely reaches his calves as he stands up, his hands in a Hallelujah gesture. His sailor hat never leaves his head, his back stays dry unless the wash wets him, and yet so bizarre is the sight of a person emerging from water so shallow, that one's eye sees him standing there as if with his drawers fallen around his feet. As he plummets, his form is as ugly and poignant as the flop of a frog—nothing less ungainly would enable him to survive—and, watching, one feels witness to something more interesting than a stunt—a leap for life into a fire net, perhaps.

He wears a thin white-sleeved bodysuit that looks like a set of long johns (the crowd is likely to titter), and, up on his jointed ladder, huddles into a crouch, holding on to the shafts behind him. Like a man in the window of a burning building, he squats, stares down, hesitating, concentrating, seeming to quail, and finally letting go, puts out his arms in what seems a clumsy gesture, creeping into space between gusts of wind. He sneaks off the top of the ladder, spreading his fingers, reaching out, arching his back, bulging his stomach, cocking his head back, gritting his teeth, never glancing down, and hits in the granddaddy of all bellywhoppers, which flings water twenty feet out.

Though one's natural impulse when falling is to ball up to protect one's vitals, he survives precisely by thrusting his vitals *out*. He goes *splat*. And when a microphone is put to him—"How do you do it?"—Henri says, "Guts!" grinning at the pun. "Why do you do it?" asks the reporter. "I get a *bang* out of it!" sez LaMothe, sez that he is "a low-water man." In his long johns, white-haired, in that tremulous hunch forty feet up a guyed-out magnesium ladder that he folds up and wheels about for fees of a few hundred dollars, he's anything but an Evel Knievel. He's from vaudeville, a fire victim, his career a succession of happenstances.

In Chicago, growing up pint-sized with the nickname Frenchy —his father, a South Side carpenter, was from Montreal—he dove off coal tipples, bridges, and boxcars, swimming and swaggering at the Seventy-sixth Street Beach, doing the Four-Mile Swim off Navy Pier. In the winter he swam indoors with a gang that included Johnny Weissmuller, who was already swinging from the girders over the pool. But Henri's hands were too small, his build too slight for competitive swimming. To make a living he drove a cab and posed at the Chicago Art Institute, where he began to draw too. He stayed up late, speeding around town to neighborhood Charleston contests, four or five in a night—this being the Roaring Twenties—winning up to a hundred dollars an evening. He quit modeling in order to Charleston full-time, closing his act with handstands, back bends, and a belly-flop, sliding and rolling across the waxed floor. His girlfriend's specialty was the split; she'd kick him into his belly-flop, do the split over him, and "lift" him up with two fingers and dance on his stomach as he leaned over back-wards, balancing on his hands. They were local champions, and by and by he invented an Airplane Dance, his arm the propeller—"the Lucky Lindy," for Lindbergh—which he claims was adapted into the Lindy Hop. June Havoc and Gypsy Rose Lee's famously stingy stage mama took him to New York City as one of six "Newsboys" in their hoofer show, but he quit to dance in a musical called *Keep It Clean*. By 1928 he was dancing at the Paramount as "Hotfoot Henri" ("Hotpants" backstage), usually planted among the ushers or as a dummy sax player in the orchestra pit when the show be-gan. The clowning, pat repartee and belly-busters were right up his alley; on occasion he still will flop on his breadbasket into a puddle of beer at home to startle guests, or lie flat and lift his wife Birgit by the strength of his stomach muscles.

Although he'd been thankful to dancing for whisking him away from the Windy City and the life of a commercial artist drawing pots and pans for newspaper ads, after the 1929 crash he had to scratch for a job. He designed Chinese menus to pay for his meals, did flyer layouts for theaters and bands, and painted signs. He was art editor of the *Hobo News*, later the *Bowery News*, and tinkered, streamlining the stapler used everywhere nowadays, and inventing a "Bedroom Mood Meter" to post on the wall, like the ones sold in Times Square novelty shops. He got work drawing ad-vertising for a Long Island plastics company, and actually pros-pered; even flew his own plane. Mushing down for a landing, he would think of the pratfalls he had performed in the Charleston contests and his belly-flops back on Muscle Beach, clowning his way to popularity.

Clowning on the board at the swimming club for the executives, he heard the suggestion that he ought to do it professionally, and so after a stint in a shipyard during World War II he went swimming with Johnny Weissmuller's troupe in Peru. Then he went to Italy with his own water show, the Aquats, in partnership with two girls, one of whom, a Dane called Birgit Gjessing, became his wife. Birgit had been an actress in Germany during the war, a swimmer before that, and a puppeteer back home in Denmark, marking time after fleeing the collapse of the Reich. She's a lean lady of fifty-seven with a quick expressive face, a school counselor now, but she remembers playing chess in a wine cellar near Mainz during the worst of the bombing. At one point in 1944 she traded her winter coat for a bicycle, thinking to swim the Rhine while holding it over her head and then peddle on home.

Henri would emulate the dives the girls did and mess everything up, or get into a race and be towed through the water, roped to a car. He dressed as Sweet Pea or Baby Snooks with a curl painted on his forehead. Wheeled to the pool in a buggy by Birgit, dressed in a starchy costume, he would scramble up on the high diving board while his nurse underneath pleaded with him to climb down. She would fall in, and he would pancake on top of her, landing crisscross. He used break-off boards to make his dive doubly abrupt, or wore a pullover sweater fifteen feet long, which would still be unraveling as he stumbled backwards into his fall. In a beret, with his French mustache, he'd put on blue long johns with rolled-up newspapers over his biceps and a great cape and, calling himself Stupor Man, bend "iron" bars and launch himself on a mission of mercy from a high place, only to crash on his belly into the water. He would "drown" and need artificial respiration, but as the girls bent over him, would squirt water at them from his mouth. Then, running to apologize to Birgit, he would trip, belly-whop, and skid into her.

He wore low-necked bathing suits through which he could push his bay window, and sometimes to publicize the show would stand on his elbows on a building ledge, drinking coffee, eating a doughnut. Unfortunately it wasn't until both he and the century were into their fifties that his agent had sense enough to tip him off that the dive he was doing anyway as a water comedian would earn more money if done straight, so he speaks of those first twenty years of diving as "wasted." Then it was maybe another two thousand leaps before his seventieth birthday provided a gimmick to get him a *Daily News* centerfold and a spot on a David Frost show. For part of this long period he practiced commercial art in New York, but New Year's Eve would find him in Miami Beach dressed as the Baby New Year, poised in a third-floor hotel window as the clock tolled twelve, diving into "Lake Urine," the kiddie pool. He sprang out of trees, from flagpole yardarms and roofs—once from the ensign standard forty-seven feet up into two feet of water in the Westchester Country Club wading pool. Touring the country clubs, they "ate lentils," says Birgit. And always Henri looked a bit silly as he stood up, the water lapping at his shins: the less water the sillier.

Water shows are lumped with ice shows in the lower echelon of show business. The very term has a kiddie ring. Indeed, Birgit still shivers, remembering a week in Quebec when they had to perform in a hockey rink, paired with a skating follies, in water poured into a tank right on top of the ice. She wore a fish costume and executed finny undulations to "Basin Street Blues," but otherwise, as always, tried to get herself and the rest of the ballet swimmers out of the water at frequent intervals to remind the audience that they were really human in shape, not fishy. Ice skaters have no such identity problem. Water, on the other hand, elemental, deep, somber and healing as it is, imparts a nobility to swimming which no ice show can match. With the mysterious oceans behind it, stretching around the world, water can be a powerful ally.

But Henri, leaping into a thin film of water, has sacrificed the majesty of the ocean to the bravery of his frog dive. Landing as he does, on the paunch, the craw, the crop, he loses the pretensions to dignity of mankind as well. It's raw, realer than drama, and tremendously poignant; it's his masterpiece, he says, in a life of inventing, which, even when he's been shabbily treated on the show-business scene, nobody has been able to steal away from him. He talks now of diving from the Eiffel Tower or the Leaning Tower of Pisa, combining this with his dream of diving at last into no water at all.

He's a short, plump, pigeonlike man who rubs his stomach continually, bends his back and bulges his chest. His look is matter-of-fact, like a man calculating practicalities, yet self-preoccupied, like one who knows pain and catastrophe. Though he dives on an empty stomach with lungs half filled, he lives by the bulge of his stomach. Clapping his hands, he will demonstrate how his arched back is the key to surviving. If air is trapped between the hands the clap is loud, but if one hand is convex the impact is muted. Just so, he explains, an air pocket under his belly would "split me right open." His belly is holding up fine, but his back is decidedly less limber; his scrapbook of photographs testifies to what a bend he could bring to his work only a decade ago. Offstage he looked the daredevil then, and back in the fifties, his two lady partners would give him a rubdown after his feat. Now, because of the slackening that old age effects on the best of bodies, except for his stern mouth and nose he looks more like a health nut maintaining his youth.

He has a fluffy ring of white hair around his bald head, and likes being up on his ladder—says that he's happy up there. His beloved round pool glows like a globe below him, even seeming to expand. He says that a power goes out from him to intimidate the water. "That water is going to take the punishment, not me." Kids always ask whether it hurts. "Why do you care if it hurts?" he asks them. At the Hampton, Virginia, boat show, where I watched him leap, his dressing room was the aisle between the showers and toilets. Among other exercises he did his stretching drill holding on to a sink and swinging from the top of a toilet stall. "Coffee's working," he said, because emptying his bowels was part of the ritual so he would feel "clean," ready for the impact. He drank a cup half an hour before he climbed up the ladder, both as a laxative and to bring an alive feeling to his stomach. Women sometimes ask if he wears a jock strap, but "I just put my tail between my legs and go." After the evening act he celebrated with a swig of whiskey, rippling his stomach anatomy to help it down as he used to do to amuse the students at the Chicago Art Institute. For five or six hours afterwards in his room at the Holiday Inn he let his nerves unwind with the aid of beer, while concocting a vegetable-fruit mix in his blender and soup pot, the day's one big meal.

Once when he was a young man LaMothe swam the St. Lawrence River—something his father before him had done—fetching up at a convent, where the nuns hid their eyes. And once he was paid three thousand dollars for a week at the San Antonio Hemis-Fair, "banging my belly." Working shopping malls and sports shows, he carries his pool in a shopping bag; it's a filmsy low roll of fencing with a plastic liner which sways with the waves of the blow. (Again, Henri's agent had to wise him up to the hammy fact that the sides ought to be down as low as the water.) On his ladder, he lets all other sights and sounds except the bull's-eye blur out. He crouches, "hoping for" rather than aiming for it, and lets go, putting his froggy arms out as his body falls. A team of accident experts from General Motors has tested him and concluded that he hits with the force of gravity multiplied seventy times; or, with his weight, 10,500 pounds.

So he does what the bigger kids couldn't do, long after they have given up their own specialties. And since the death wish of a daredevil who is seventy years old must be fairly well under control, perhaps the best explanation for why he continues is that this is what he is good at. Humiliation is a very good school for clowns, and, watching him, as with certain other notable clowns, one is swept with a tenderness for him as he lands, God's Fool, safe and sound and alive once again. As with them, our fascination is enhanced because at the same time that he has sought our applause, he has seemed to try to obscure our appreciation, make the venture difficult for us to understand, and thereby escape our applause—a "low-water man."

Heaven
and
Nature

Afriend of mine, a peaceable soul who has been riding the New York subways for thirty years, finds himself stepping back from the tracks once in a while and closing his eyes as the train rolls in. This, he says, is not only to suppress an urge to throw himself in front of it but because every couple of weeks an impulse rises in him to push a stranger onto the tracks, any stranger, thus ending his own life too. He blames this partly on apartment living, "pigeon holes without being able to fly."

It is profoundly startling not to trust oneself after decades of doing so. I don't dare keep ammunition in my country house for a small rifle I bought secondhand two decades ago. The gun had sat in a cupboard in the back room with the original box of .22 bullets under the muzzle all that time, seldom fired except at a few apples hanging in a tree every fall to remind me of my army training near the era of the Korean War, when I'd been considered quite a marksman. When I bought the gun I didn't trust either my professional competence as a writer or my competence as a father as much as I came to, but certainly believed I could keep myself alive. I bought it for protection, and the idea that someday I might be afraid of shooting myself with the gun would have seemed inconceivable—laughable.

One's fifties can be giddy years, as anybody fifty knows. Chest pains, back pains, cancer scares, menopausal or prostate complications are not the least of it, and the fidelities of a lifetime, both personal and professional, may be called into question. Was it a mistake to have stuck so long with one's marriage, and to have stayed with a lackluster well-paying job? (Or *not* to have stayed and stuck?) People not only lose faith in their talents and their dreams or values; some simply tire of them. Grow tired, too, of the smell of fried-chicken grease, once such a delight, and the cold glutinosity of ice cream, the boredom of beer, the stop-go of travel, the hiccups of laughter, and of two rush hours a day, then the languor of weekends, of athletes as well as accountants, and even the frantic birdsong of spring—red-eyed vireos that have been clocked singing twenty-two thousand times in a day. Life is a matter of cultivating the six senses, and an equilibrium with nature and what I think of as its subdivision, human nature, trusting no one completely but almost everyone at least a little; but this is easier said than done.

More than thirty thousand Americans took their own lives last year, men mostly, with the highest rate being among those older than sixty-five. When I asked a friend why three times as many men kill themselves as members of her own sex, she replied with sudden anger, "I'm not going to go into the self-indulgence of men." They won't bend to failure, she said, and want to make themselves memorable. Suicide is an exasperating act as often as it is pitiable. "Committing" suicide is in bad odor in our culture even among those who don't believe that to cash in your chips ahead of time and hand back to God his gifts to you is a blasphemous sin. We the living, in any case, are likely to feel accused by this person who "voted with his feet." It appears to cast a subversive judgment upon the social polity as a whole that what was supposed to work in life— religion, family, friendship, commerce, and industry—did not, and furthermore it "frightens the horses in the street," as Shaw's friend Mrs. Patrick Campbell once defined wrongful behavior.

Many suicides inflict outrageous trauma, burning permanent injuries into the minds of their children, though they may have joked beforehand only of "taking a dive." And sometimes the gesture has a peevish or cowardly aspect, or seems to have been senselessly shortsighted as far as an outside observer can tell. There are desperate suicides and crafty suicides, people who do it to cause others trouble and people who do it to save others trouble, deranged exhibitionists who yell from a building ledge and closemouthed, secretive souls who swim out into the ocean's anonymity. Suicide may in fact be an attempt to escape death, shortcut the dreadful deteriorating processes, abort one's natural trajectory, elude "the ruffian on the stairs," in A. E. Housman's phrase for a cruelly painful, anarchic death—make it neat and not messy. The deed can be grandiose or self-abnegating, vindictive or drably mousy, rationally plotted or plainly insane. People sidle toward death, intent upon outwitting their own bodies' defenses, or they may dramatize the chance to make one last, unambiguous, irrevocable decision, like a captain scuttling his ship—death before dishonor—leaping toward oblivion through a curtain of pain, like a frog going down the throat of a snake. One man I knew hosted a quietly affectionate evening with several unknowing friends on the night before he swallowed too many pills. Another waved an apologetic goodbye to a bystander on a bridge. Seldom shy ordinarily, and rarely considerate, he turned shy and apologetic in the last moment of life. Never physically inclined, he made a great vault toward the ice on the Mississippi.

In the army, we wore dogtags with a notch at one end by which these numbered pieces of metal could be jammed between our teeth, if we lay dead and nameless on a battlefield, for later sorting. As "servicemen" our job would be to kill people who were pointed out to us as enemies, or make "the supreme sacrifice" for a higher good than enjoying the rest of our lives. Life was very much a possession, in other words—not only God's, but the soldier's own to dispose of. Working in an army hospital, I frequently did handle dead bodies, but this never made me feel I would refuse to kill another man whose uniform was pointed out to me as being inimical, or value my life more tremulously and vigilantly. The notion of dying for my country never appealed to me as much as dying free-lance for my ideas (in the unlikely event that I *could* do that), but I was ready. People were taught during the 1940s and 1950s that one should be ready to die for one's beliefs. Heroes were revered because they had deliberately chosen to give up their lives. Life would not be worth living under the tyranny of an invader, and Nathan Hale apparently hadn't paused to wonder whether God might not have other uses for him besides being hung. Nor did the pilot Colin Kelly hesitate before plunging his plane into a Japanese battleship, becoming America's first well-publicized hero in World War II.

I've sometimes wondered why people who know that they are terminally ill, or who are headed for suicide, so very seldom have paused to take a bad guy along with them. It is lawless to consider an act of assassination, yet hardly more so, really, than suicide is regarded in some quarters (or death itself, in others). Government bureaucracies, including our own, in their majesty and as the executors of laws, regularly weigh the pros and cons of murdering foreign antagonists. Of course the answer is that most individuals are fortunately more timid as well as humbler in their judgment than government officialdom, but beyond that, when dying or suicidal, they no longer care enough to devote their final energies to doing good works of any kind—Hitler himself in their gunsights they would have passed up. Some suicides become so crushed and despairing that they can't recognize the consequences of anything they do and it's not primarily vindictiveness that wreaks such havoc upon their survivors but their derangement from ordinary life.

Courting the idea is different from the real impulse. "When he begged for help, we took him and locked him up," another friend of mine says, speaking of her husband. "Not till then. Wishing to be out of the situation you are in—feeling helpless and unable to cope—is not the same as wishing to be dead. If I actually wished to be dead, even my children's welfare would have no meaning."

You might think the ready option of divorce available lately would have cut suicide rates, offering an escape to battered wives, lovelorn husbands, and other people in despair. But it doesn't work that way. When the number of choices people have increases, an entire range of possibilities opens up. Suicide among teenagers has almost quadrupled since 1950, although the standard of comfort that their families enjoy is up. Black Americans, less affluent than white Americans, have had less of a rise in suicides, and the rate among them remains about half of that for whites.

Still, if a fiftyish fellow with fine teeth and a foolproof pension plan, a cottage at the beach and the Fourth of July weekend coming up, kills himself, it seems truculent. We would look at him baffledly if he told us he no longer likes the Sturm und Drang of banging fireworks.

Then stay at your hideaway! we'd argue with him.

"Big mouths eat little mouths. Nature isn't 'timeless.' Whole lives are squeezed into three months or three days."

What about your marriage?

"She's become more mannish than me. I loved women. I don't believe in marriage between men."

Remarry, then!

"I've gone impotent, and besides, when I see somebody young and pretty I guess I feel like dandling her on my knee."

Marriage is friendship. You can find someone your own age.

"I'm tired of it."

But how about your company?—a widows'-and-orphans' stock that's on the cutting edge of the silicon frontier? That's interesting.

"I know what wins. It's less and less appetizing."

You're not scared of death anymore?

"It interests me less than it did."

What are you so sick of? The rest of us keep going.

"I'm tired of weathermen and sportscasters on the screen. Of being patient and also of impatience. I'm tired of the president, whoever the president happens to be, and sleeping badly, with forty-eight half-hours in the day—of breaking two eggs every morning and putting sugar on something. I'm tired of the drone of my own voice, but also of us jabbering like parrots at each other—of all our stumpy ways of doing everything."

You're bored with yourself?

"That's an understatement. I'm maybe the least interesting person I know."

But to kill yourself?

"You know, it's a tradition, too," he remarks quietly, not making so bold as to suggest that the tradition is an honorable one, though his tone of voice might be imagined to imply this. "I guess I've always been a latent maverick."

Except in circumstances which are themselves a matter of life and death, I'm reluctant to agree with the idea that suicide is not the result of mental illness. No matter how reasonably the person appears to have examined his options, it goes against the grain of nature for him to destroy himself. And any illness that threatens his life changes a person. Suicidal thinking, if serious, can be a kind of death scare, comparable to suffering a heart attack or undergoing a cancer operation. One survives such a phase both warier and chastened. When—two years ago—I emerged from a bad dip into suicidal speculation, I felt utterly exhausted and yet quite fearless of ordinary dangers, vastly afraid of myself but much less scared of extraneous eventualities. The fact of death may not be tragic; many people die with a bit of a smile that captures their mouths at the last instant, and most people who are revived after a deadly accident are reluctant to be brought to life, resisting resuscitation, and carrying back confusing, beamish, or ecstatic memories. But the same impetuosity that made him throw himself out of a window might have enabled the person to love life all the more if he'd been calibrated somewhat differently at the time of the emergency. Death's edge is so abrupt and near that many people who expect a short and momentary dive may be astounded to find that it is bottomless and change their minds and start to scream when they are only halfway down.

Although my fright at my mind's anarchy superseded my fear of death in the conventional guise of automobile or airplane crashes, heart seizures, and so on, nightmares are more primitive and in my dreams I continued to be scared of a death not sought after—dying from driving too fast and losing control of the car, breaking through thin ice while skating and drowning in the cold, or falling off a cliff. When I am tense and sleeping raggedly, my worst nightmare isn't drawn from anxious prep-school memories or my stint in the army or the bad spells of my marriages or any other of adulthood's vicissitudes. Nothing else from the past half century has the staying power in my mind of the elevated-train rides that my father and I used to take down Third Avenue to the Battery in New York City on Sunday afternoon when I was three or four or five so I could see the fish at the Aquarium. We were probably pretty good companions in those years, but the wooden platforms forty feet up shook terribly as trains from both directions pulled in and out. To me they seemed worse than rickety—ready to topple. And the roar was fearful, and the railings left large gaps for a child to fall through, after the steep climb up the slat-sided, windy, shaking stairway from street level. It's a rare dream, but several times a year I still find myself on such a perch, without his company or anybody else's, on a boyish or a grown-up's mission, when the elevated platform begins to rattle desperately, seesaw, heel over, and finally come apart, disintegrate, while I cling to struts and trusses.

My father, as he lay dying at home of bowel cancer, used to enjoy watching Tarzan reruns on the children's hour of television. Like a strong green vine, they swung him far away from his death-bed to a world of skinny-dipping and friendly animals and scenic beauty linked to the lost realities of his adolescence in Kansas City. Earlier, when he had still been able to walk without much pain, he'd paced the house for several hours at night, contemplating suicide, I expect, along with other anguishing thoughts, re-grets, remembrances, and yearnings, while the rest of us slept. But he decided to lie down and die the slower way. I don't know how much of that decision was for the sake of his wife and children, how much was because he didn't want to be a "quitter," as he sometimes put it, and how much was due to his believing that life belongs to God (which I'm not even sure he did). He was not a churchgoer after his thirties. He had belonged to J. P. Morgan's church, St. George's, on Stuyvesant Square—Morgan was a hero of his—but when things went a little wrong for him at the Wall Street law firm he worked for and he changed jobs and moved out to the suburbs, he became a skeptic on religious matters, and grad-ually, in the absence of faith of that previous kind, he adhered to a determined allegiance to the social order. Wendell Willkie or Dwight D. Eisenhower instead of J. P. Morgan became the sort of hero he admired, and suicide would have seemed an act of insur-rection against the laws and conventions of the society, interna-tionalist-Republican, that he believed in.

I was never particularly afraid that I might plan a suicide, swallowing a bunch of pills and keeping them down—only of what I think of as being Anna Karenina's kind of death. This most plausible self-killing in all of literature is frightening because it was unwilled, regretted at midpoint, and came as a complete surprise to Anna herself. After rushing impulsively, in great misery, to the Moscow railway station to catch a train, she ended up underneath another one, dismayed, astonished, and trying to climb out from under the wheels even as they crushed her. Many people who briefly verge on suicide undergo a mental somersault for a terrifying interval during which they're upside down, their perspective topsy-turvy, skidding, churning; and this is why I got rid of the bullets for my .22.

Nobody expects to trust his body overmuch after the age of fifty. Incipient cataracts or arthritis, outlandish snores, tooth-grinding, ankles that threaten to turn are part of the game. But not to trust one's *mind?* That's a surprise. The single attribute that older people were sure to have (we thought as boys) was a stodgy dependability, a steady temperance or caution. Adults might be vain, unimaginative, pompous, and callous, but they did have their affairs tightly in hand. It was not till my thirties that I began to know friends who were in their fifties on equal terms, and I remember being amused, piqued, irritated, and slightly bewildered to learn that some of them still felt as marginal or rebellious or in a quandary about what to do with themselves for the next dozen years as my contemporaries were likely to. That close to retirement, some of them harbored a deep-seated contempt for the organizations they had been working for, ready to walk away from almost everybody they had known and the efforts and expertise of whole decades with very little sentiment. Nor did twenty years of marriage necessarily mean more than two or three—they might be just as ready to walk away from that also, and didn't really register it as twenty years at all. Rather, life could be about to begin all over again. "Bummish" was how one man described himself, with a raffish smile—"Lucky to have a roof over my head"—though he'd just put a child through Yale. He was quitting his job and claimed with exasperation that his wife still cried for her mother in her sleep, as if they'd never been married.

The great English traveler Richard Burton quoted an Arab proverb that speaks for many middle-aged men of the old-fashioned variety: "Conceal thy Tenets, thy Treasure, and thy Traveling." These are serious matters, in other words. People didn't conceal their tenets in order to betray them, but to fight for them more opportunely. And except for kings and princelings, concealing whatever treasure one had went almost without saying. As for travel, a man's travels were also a matter of gravity. Travel was knowledge, ambiguity, dalliances or misalliances, divided loyalty, forbidden thinking; and besides, someday he might need to make a run for it and go to ground someplace where he had made some secret friends. Friends of mine whose husbands or whose wives have died have been quite startled afterwards to discover caches of money or traveler's checks concealed around the house, or a bundle of cash in a safe deposit box.

Burton, like any other desert adage-spinner and most individuals over fifty, would have agreed to an addition so obvious that it wasn't included to begin with: "Conceal thy Illnesses." I can remember how urgently my father worried that word would get out, after a preliminary operation for his cancer. He didn't want to be written off, counted out of the running at the corporation he worked for and in other enclaves of competition. Men often compete with one another until the day they die; comradeship consists of rubbing shoulders jocularly with a competitor. As breadwinners, they must be considered fit and sound by friend as well as foe, and so there's lots of truth to the most common answer I heard when asking why three times as many men as women kill themselves: "They keep their troubles to themselves"; "They don't know how to ask for help." Men greet each other with a sock on the arm, women with a hug, and the hug wears better in the long run.

I'm not entirely like that, and I discovered that when I confided something of my perturbation to a woman friend she was likely to keep telephoning me or mailing cheery postcards, whereas a man would usually listen with concern, communicate his sympathy, and maybe intimate that he had pondered the same drastic course of action himself a few years back and would end up respecting my decision either way. Open-mindedness seems an important attribute to a good many men, who pride themselves on being objective, hearing all sides of an issue, on knowing that truth and honesty do not always coincide with social dicta, and who may even cherish a subterranean outlaw streak that, like being ready to violently defend one's family, reputation, and country, is by tradition male.

Men, being so much freer than women in society, used to feel they had less of a stake in the maintenance of certain churchly conventions and enjoyed speaking irreverently about various social truisms, including even the principle that people ought to die on schedule, not cutting in ahead of their assigned place in line. Contemporary women, after their triumphant irreverence during the 1960s and 1970s, cannot be generalized about so easily, however. They turn as skeptical and saturnine as any man. In fact, women attempt suicide more frequently, but favor pills or other methods, whereas two-thirds of the men who kill themselves have used a gun. In 1985, 85 percent of suicides by means of firearms were done by men. An overdose of medication hasn't the same finality. It may be reversible if the person is discovered quickly, or be subject to benign miscalculation to start with. Even if it works, perhaps it can be fudged by a kindly doctor in the record-keeping. Like an enigmatic drowning or a single-car accident that baffles the suspicions of the insurance company, a suicide by drugs can be a way to avoid making a loud statement, and merely illustrate the final modesty of a person who didn't wish to ask for too much of the world's attention.

Unconsummated attempts at suicide can strike the rest of us as self-pitying and self-aggrandizing, or plaintive plea-bargaining—"childish," we say, though actually the suicide of children is ghastly beyond any stunt of self-mutilation an adult may indulge in because of the helplessness that echoes through the act. It would be hard to define chaos better than as a world where children decide that they don't want to live.

Love is the solution to all dilemmas, we sometimes hear; and and in those moments when the spirit bathes itself in beneficence and manages to transcend the static of personalities rubbing fur off of each other, indeed it is. Without love nothing matters, Paul told the Corinthians, a mystery which, if true, has no ready Darwinian explanation. Love without a significant sexual component and for people who are unrelated to us serves little practical purpose. It doesn't help us feed our families, win struggles, thrive and prosper. It distracts us from the ordinary business of sizing people up and making a living, and is not even conducive to intellectual observation, because instead of seeing them, we see right through them to the bewildered child and dreaming adolescent who inhabited their bodies earlier, the now-tired idealist who fell in love and out of love, got hired and quit, hired and fired, bought cars and wore them out, liked black-eyed Susans, blueberry muffins, and roosters crowing—liked roosters crowing better than skyscrapers but now likes skyscrapers better than roosters crowing. As swift as thought, we select the details that we need to see in order to be able to love them.

Yet at other times we'll dispense with these same poignancies and choose only their grunginess to look at, their pinched mouths and shifty eyes, their thirst for gin at noon and indifference to their kids, their greed for the best tidbit on the buffet table and penchant for poking their penises up the excretory end of other human beings. I tend to gaze quite closely at the faces of priests I meet on the street to see if a lifetime of love has marked them noticeably. Real serenity or asceticism I no longer expect, and I take for granted the beefy calm that frequently goes with Catholic celibacy, but I am watching for the marks of love and often see mere resignation or tenacity.

Many men are romantics, likely to plunge, go for broke, take action in a spirit of exigency rather than waiting for the problem to resolve itself. Then, on the contrary, still as romantics, they may drift into despairing passivity, stare at the TV all day long, and binge with a bottle. Women too may turn frenetic for a while and then throw up their hands; but though they may not seem as grandiosely fanciful and romantic at the outset, they are more often believers—at least I think they tend to believe in God or in humanity, the future, and so on. We have above us the inviting eternity of "the heavens," if we choose to look at it, lying on our backs in the summer grass under starlight, some of which had left its source before mankind became man. But because we live in our heads more than in nature nowadays, even the summer sky is a minefield for people whose memories are mined. With the sky no longer humbling, the sunshine only a sort of convenience, and no godhead located anywhere outside of our own heads, every problem may seem insolubly interlocked. When the telephone has become impossible to answer at home, sometimes it finally becomes impossible to stride down the gangplank of a cruise ship in Mombasa too, although no telephones will ring for you there.

But if escapist travel is ruled out in certain emergencies, surely you can *pray?* Pray, yes; but to whom? That requires a bit of preparation. Rarely do people obtain much relief from praying if they haven't stood in line awhile to get a visa. It's an appealing idea that you can just *go,* and in a previous era perhaps you could have, like on an old-fashioned shooting safari. But it's not so simple now. What do you believe in? Whom are you praying to? What are you praying for? There's no crèche on the courthouse lawn; you're not supposed to adhere exactly even to what your parents had believed. Like psychotherapy, praying takes time, even if you know which direction to face when you kneel.

Love is powerfully helpful when the roof falls in—loving other people with a high and hopeful heart and as a kind of prayer. Yet that feat too requires new and sudden insights or long practice. The beatitude of loving strangers as well as friends—loving them on sight with a leap of empathy and intuition—is a form of inspiration, edging, of course, in some cases towards madness, as other states of beatitude can do. But there's no question that a genuine love for the living will stymie suicidal depressions not chemical in origin. Love is an elixir, changing the life of the lover like no other. And many of us have experienced this—a temporary lightening of our leery, prickly disapproval of much of the rest of the world when at a wedding or a funeral of shared emotion, or when we have fallen in love.

Yet the zest for life of those unusual men and women who make a great zealous success of living is due more often in good part to the craftiness and pertinacity with which they manage to overlook the misery of others. You can watch them watch life beat the stuffing out of the faces of their friends and acquaintances, yet they themselves seem to outwit the dense delays of social custom, the tedious tick-tock of bureaucratic obfuscation, accepting loss and age and change and disappointment without suffering punctures in their stomach lining. Breathlessness or strange dull pains from their nether organs don't nonplus them. They fret and doubt in moderation, and love a lobster roast, squeeze lemon juice on living clams on the half shell to prove that the clams are alive, laugh as robins tussle a worm out of the ground or a kitten flees a dog. Like the problem drinkers, pork eaters, and chain smokers who nevertheless finish out their allotted years, succumbing to a stroke at a nice round biblical age when the best vitamin-eating vegetarian has long since died, their faces become veritable walnuts of fine character, with the same smile lines as the rarer individual whose grin has been affectionate all of his life.

We spend our lives getting to know ourselves, yet wonders never cease. During my adolescent years my states of mind, though undulant, seemed seamless; even when I was unhappy no cracks or fissures made me wonder if I was a danger to myself. My confidence was such that I treaded the slippery lips of waterfalls, fought forest fires, drove ancient cars cross-country night and day, and scratched the necks of menagerie leopards in the course of various adventures which enhanced the joy of being alive. The chemistry of the mind, because unfathomable, is more frightening. In the city, I live on the waterfront and occasionally will notice an agitated-looking figure picking his way along the pilings and stringpieces of the timbered piers nearby, staring at the sliding whorls on the surface of the Hudson as if teetering over an abyss. Our building, across the street, seems imposing from the water and over the years has acted as a magnet for a number of suicides—people who have dreaded the clammy chill, the onerous smothering essential to their first plan. One woman climbed out after jumping in and took the elevator to the roof (my neighbors remember how wringing wet she was), and leapt off, banging window ledges on the way down, and hit with the whap of a sack of potatoes, as others have.

Yet what is more remarkable than that a tiny minority of souls reach a point where they entrust their bodies to the force of gravity is that so few of the rest of us splurge an hour of a summer day gazing at the trees and sky. How many summers do we *have?* One sees prosperous families in the city who keep plants in their apartment windows that have grown so high they block the sunlight and appear to be doing the living for the tenants who are bolted inside. But beauty is nobody's sure salvation: not the beauty of a swimming hole if you get a cramp, and not the beauty of a woman if she doesn't care for you. The swimming hole looks inviting under the blue sky, with its amber bottom, green sedges sticking up in the shallows, and curls of gentle current over a waterlogged basswood tree two feet beneath the surface near the brook that feeds it. Come back at dusk, however, and the pond turns black—as dark as death, or on the contrary, a restful dark, a dark to savor. Take it as you will.

People with sunny natures do seem to live longer than people who are nervous wrecks; yet mankind didn't evolve out of the animal kingdom by being unduly sunny-minded. Life was fearful and phantasmagoric, supernatural and preternatural, as well as encompassing the kind of clockwork regularity of our well-governed day. It had numerous superstitious (from the Latin, "standing over") elements, such as we are likely to catch a whiff of only when we're peering at a dead body. And it was not just our optimism but our pessimistic premonitions, our dark moments as a species, our irrational, frightful speculations, our strange mutations upon the simple theme of love, and our sleepless, obsessive inventiveness—our dread as well as our faith—that made us human beings. Staking one's life on the more general good came to include risking suicide also. Brilliant, fecund people sometimes kill themselves.

"Joy to the world . . . let heaven and nature sing, and heaven and nature sing . . . Repeat the sounding joy . . ." The famous Christmas carol invokes not only glee but unity: heaven with nature, not always a Christian combination. It's a rapturous hymn, and no one should refuse to surrender to such a pitch of revelation when it comes. But the flip side of rapture can be a riptide of panic, of hysterical gloom. Our faces are not molded as if joy were a preponderant experience. (Nor is a caribou's or a thrush's.) Our faces in repose look stoic or battered, and people of the sunniest temperament sometimes die utterly unstrung, doubting everything they have ever believed in or have done.

Let heaven and nature sing! the hymn proclaims. But *is* there such harmony? Are God and Mother Nature really the same? Are they even compatible? And will we risk burning our wings if we mount high enough to try to see? I've noticed that woods soil in Italy smells the same as woods soil in New England when you pick up a handful of it and enjoy its aromas—but is God there the same? It can be precarious to wonder. I don't rule out suicide as being unthinkable for people who have tried to live full lives, and don't regard it as negating the work and faith and satisfaction and fun and even ecstasy they may have known before. In killing himself a person acknowledges his failures during a time span when perhaps heaven and earth had caught him like a pair of scissors— but not his life span. Man is different from animals in that he speculates, a high-risk activity.

Tiger Bright

Ringling Bros. and Barnum & Bailey circus still tours America, and all the divorced mothers and fathers are glad because it gives them someplace to take the kids. The notices that it gets are uniformly friendly and noddly, not like sharp sports-writing or theater criticism, and afterwards the press agent sends out a letter of thanks to everybody concerned. But last year, after seven good weeks in New York City and two in Boston, the circus left for points west with some of its same old impudent alacrity. Zacchini, the cannonball, was fired from his X-15 with a tremendous boom, so that smoke filled the back passageways, and, even before the smoke thinned, twenty elephants, chained in pairs, went rushing past, with that middle-aged, big-footed push to their gait, down the ramp to the street, to the circus train, at least fifty horses hard after them, even before all the patrons were out of their seats. There is no sentiment about how a circus leaves town; it shakes off the dust of your burg just as readily as it quits Kankakee.

I worked in the circus for a few months about twenty years ago and have followed its fortunes with a fond, mournful eye ever since from the distance of the civilian world—the world that with such a flourish is left behind. The circus has nationhood, but there has been the question whether it will survive. The Depression, then the Hartford circus fire of 1944, in which a hundred and sixty-eight people died, precipitated bankruptcies and changes of management, and after recovering from these crises the more mundane problems of budget in a swept-wing economy caused the Big Show to forswear tenting in 1956 and resolve to play only arena engagements indoors. Whereas the old circus used to need three trains, leaving at intervals, in order to travel, now that the acres of canvas and poles, the seats, cookhouse, generator wagons, box offices, sideshow, and much of what was the menagerie have been dispensed with, one train is enough. The money saved is more than matched by the loss of so much buoyant tradition and color, but the change may have been necessary in a day when workmen are paid $70 a week instead of $14, as they were in my time, and the youngest dancing girl gets $140, and the greenest clown $165.

Still, the customers keep coming, and in 1967 the heirs and successors of the Ringling family sold Ringling Bros. and Barnum & Bailey for eight million dollars to two pop-music magnates and a former mayor of Houston, who soon got it listed over the counter as a growth stock. Their first act of reorganization was to split the show into two separate circuses which can play simultaneously in different cities, the ultimate plan being to expand to four units, all operating at the same time. Only one of the four would have to be staged new each year, with new acts from Europe and new choreography. This one would appear in New York and Los Angeles and so on, while the others hedgehopped, just as road companies in the theater do, carrying the presentations of previous years to smaller cities. Expenses have been pared so skillfully that the main cost of fielding additional units has become the buying and converting of Pullman cars as the railroads abandon them. Apparently a torrent of children fills all available arenas and halls, and more are being built, so that if there really are going to be four Ringling Bros. and Barnum & Baileys, with twelve rings to fill, the only hitch may turn out to be whether there is enough circus artistry left in the world to display in them. Already, with two shows going, the cream has been spread rather thin.

I spent a week with the Madison Square Garden edition of the show, then another week down in Birmingham, Alabama, with the version that was playing there, remembering all the time the grinding fatigue of the life, yet feeling an extraordinary yearning to be with it again. In Birmingham I sat next to an old acquaintance who had once worked in the menagerie taking care of the pygmy hippo and who felt the same way. His home is ninety miles north, near the Georgia border. He needs a cane nowadays and is feeling poorly, his eyes are going bad on him, he has no teeth and is stout in a petrified way, though he was wearing pants so wide that as stout as he was, they must have been hand-me-downs. He said he hadn't worked in a circus since I had known him—"It takes a mighty good man to work on a circus and travel and all"—but that for the sake of his memories he hitchhiked down every year when the show was in Birmingham. (Yet *I* remembered him as a man tormented continually, frequently raped, prison-style, his arms twisted behind his back, nearly twisted off.)

Before the performance we watched the propmen lug the elephant tubs and the chimp- and lion-act furniture, the rigging boys stunt in the rigging, the clowns' hypertense terrier snort around the clowns' goose as it ate, the Roman-nosed, wooden-looking horses, and the browsing camels, all joints and humps. Then the performance began as if irrevocably, like a giant aroused—old blondes somehow mustering up a dazzle to their faces, a brave workaday walk turning into a glamorous strut. Squally, heavy-beat music was played for the elephants, songs from *My Fair Lady* for the trick dogs; the trainer's whip was a swagger stick. A "March of the Olympiads" fanfare announced the trapezists, and sweet-swaying ice-skating music accompanied their clocked twists. I recognized a few of the old hands, twisty and lame, among the roughnecks backstage. They didn't look strong these days, but they were probably very strong. A circus travels and never stops: this is the point, and it is addictive. The mud, the heat, the privation, the gypsy allegiances and easy goodbyes, the chaotic glory and whirl, all mix together and fix a man into the troupe, and as long as he's traveling he need never stop and take stock; his situation is fluid, in a sense his life is ahead of him; things may look up. Even if he's not young, the ashes of his past are well behind him and he's in new country this week, next week, and forever on.

But there's more to it than that. Twice daily the organization builds to its performances, which are created to convey amazement and glee. Formerly a circus hand might go through the year and practically never see a performance because so much was going on outside the big top. Band music accompanied his chores, but he lived with the herds of horses and a horde of wild characters in the satellite wagons and tents. Now that the performance is all there is, he's with the performers, most of whom really light up and come to life when the show gets under way; and it's contagious. Though they may look as wilted and crumpled and sad over breakfast as civilian folk, every evening their faces spread into the same beaming lines that the children wear, and receiving the cheers of thousands, are lifted beyond the expressions of wonder and childhood to the graceful wide grin of a conquering king. Over the years, their mouths enlarge and their faces grow ever more malleable. A man who has just staked his life on his physical skill isn't modest. He stands in the platinum-colored spotlight used only for danger and princes, and casts his head back, throws his arms wide, his body undulating sensuously as the ovation bathes him, and listens to the crowd rejoice that he is alive.

Women performers aren't quite so dramatic. Rogana is a flawless-bodied tall personage who grips the hilt of one sword in her mouth and balances another by its point from the point of the first, with a tray and six glasses balancing on the second sword's hilt. Meanwhile she climbs a swaying ladder and straddles the top, swinging eerily, poising the swords nearly perpendicularly. After this and other feats, she accepts the applause with reserve, withholding some of herself and looking, despite her long legs and black hair, like Babe Didrikson Zaharias; her face is unfortunately masculine, which may be the trouble. "La Toria," who in fact is Vicky Unus—her father stood on one finger in performances for many years—is another slightly sad athlete. Except for her muscular arms she is slimmer but gawkier and shorter than Rogana, and like an exotic, she paints her eyelids white with streaks of black, though she seems timid and at a loss with men. (Rogana is married to a ringmaster.) Vicky Unus does a brave series of vertical arm twists, fifty-two of them for matinées and seventy-two in the evening, while hanging by one hand from a rope above the center ring. The act, an American invention, is plaintive and arduous, although she looks like a young girl swimming as her legs wrench her body around and around in a sort of scissors kick. She's a small girl built like a big one—rawboned, with a swinging walk, a sharp nose, a gaunt masklike face, but terribly human and touching and feminine because of that jerk her legs make. She tapes her wrist where the rope cuts in, wearing Band-Aids under the tape and sometimes a covering cape. In a way, her stunt and her father's before her seem somewhat the same, perhaps because it is such a short distance from what is compelling to what is compulsive, and they both have managed to stay on the side of the angels in this regard. The great Lilian Leitzel did twice as many twists, varying the number according to mood, suffering more torment from the wounds in her wrist, and, full of fire, eventually fell to her death.

Most performers are Europeans from one or another of a dwindling number of circus families. America has not produced many headliners: just some daredevil types and high-wire men, several great clowns, and a few bravura animal trainers of the Clyde Beatty kind. Without circus parents to steer them, kids here were going to school when they should have been learning to tumble and flip, so that daredevil stunts, animal stuff, and clowning were the only crafts they were still eligible for by the time they left home. Now even the trainers are German and most of the notable clowns have died or retired. Ringling Bros. has started a school for clowns, and scouts seeking young performers who have been painstakingly schooled in the physical arts are going all the way to the Eastern Bloc countries, where the lag of a decade or two has preserved an old-style dedication to the crafts of the past (also they're cheaper to hire). The Silagis, who are Bulgarian teeterboard tumblers, and the Czechoslovakian Poldis are examples. The youngest Poldi somersaults thirty feet into the air from an aluminum swing, a very shy man who locks his heels when he takes a bow so that his legs won't wobble and looks straight out from under his brows at a dot in the audience, as he's been taught to.

The best acts are hard to write about because they are consummate cameos, long practiced, that an imprecise process like writing cannot reproduce. Furthermore, in this milieu all words are considered venal by the insiders—if not hyperbole, then frankly bilge. Inaccuracies puff every newspaper piece, people hardly know the difference between a straight man and a strong man anymore, and especially now, after the circus has endured years of decline, the truly incomparable feats are often not recognized for what they are. The excellence of Tito Gaona on the flying trapeze is not like that seen in a competitive sport, for instance; it is perfection. His triple, done blindfolded, is done in the single tick of a clock. He elaborates on what can be done, and leaps, finally, to the net, springs unexpectedly high to land sitting up in the catcher's swing, does a lazy man's dive, bounces to grab the trapeze again, does a sailor's dive, a dead man's dive, and a duck dive, toying with his body's limberness. When at last he touches the ground, he keeps right on bouncing, as if the very ground had spring. He gets a shrill, steely ovation, and Antoinette Concello, now in her sixties, who was the greatest woman trapezist and who stands below at every performance—a tiny, quick-looking woman with eyes alluringly deepened and darkened and a long sly, survivor's face— smiles at him. He reaches exuberantly toward the crowd for his cheers. He has a huge chest and a broad pre-Columbian face.

There are other young men who may carry the show for the next few years: Emanuel Zacchini, the cannonball, Elvin Bale on the single trapeze, and Gunther Gebel-Williams, who constitutes a circus all by himself and is a Nureyev of show business, a man geared for great fame. It's a question whether he will achieve it— what with the circus's low estate in the world—but in Imperial Rome the crowd's accolade for him would have lapped over the rim of the Colosseum like a tidal wave; he would have been installed in public office. He makes marble steps out of his elephants' trunks and ascends and descends. Obviously if he could afford to have fifty elephants he could lead them all, ride into the jungle, as in some fantasy, and live with them there in his sleek gold boots and open red tunic. With his large mouth, large teeth, young-Satan's grin, and a big cross on his chest that bobs as he runs, he seems almost perpetually elated. His first wife, Jeanette, like a deposed queen, and his second wife, Sigrid, direct high-school horses in adjoining rings, and he stands on the ring curbing just between, ready to dart into the thicket of hooves and plumes to enforce their rule.

While he is waiting his turn, Elvin Bale looks like a cockney sharpster with a beaklike nose and pasted hair, but once in the air he swings on the single trapeze with absorption and even a kind of onrushing joy. He swings higher and higher, as a child would wish to, pulling, reaching for extra height; he has no implements to encumber his act, just his arms and legs. Then, when he is swinging as high as he can go, he delicately lets himself slide backwards head-down, only halting his fall with his bent heels. He varies these heel catches in every possible way, catching the bar on his thighs in the most dangerous dives, letting the force of the swing hold him there, before slipping farther down as the arc of the trapeze peaks and reverses itself. He squints anxiously for an instant as he hangs by his heels, until, finding that he's secure, he spreads his arms, marking the finish of the feat. He pulls himself up and lolls, gazing into the expanse of the crowd, swinging and grinning. His body, which had been red with tension, turns golden in the spotlights.

In the New York edition of the show, the first half displayed mostly the arts, the second half the thrills, and Zacchini and a woman named Marcia who masqueraded as his wife—his real wife was recuperating from a broken neck—closed the performance. Zacchini, like many thrill men, is no more daredevil in manner than an astronaut and is not a promising subject for an interview; he appears to be a quite ordinary bloke except when alone during his bout in space. He is flat-faced, built like a running back, and looks petted and plump like a mama's boy until the trapeze act, when he begins guying himself up to risk his life. His wife, neatly dressed in a suit, pushes her wheelchair to a good vantage point, and he gives her his wedding ring to hold. Watching Tito Gaona work but wincing and covering his ears when the clowns' firecrackers go off, he chins himself on the bleacher piping, stretching his back and neck, stretching even his mouth; briefly his stolid face contorts into the visage of a man fighting for life.

The cannon is a giant slingshot contoured to fit inside a rocket which emits lots of noise. He and Marcia load themselves into the muzzle. His father, Zacchini, Sr., who limps from having once broken *his* neck, stage-manages the buildup and sound effects and watches as they are shot out, separated by an interval of less than a second, soaring so high that they seem to pause in the air— Zacchini's trajectory slightly higher—before following long, logical parabolas down onto a net, landing carefully on their backs, as trapeze flyers do. Always they keep as straight as possible during the flight; they don't ball up. Unlike most performers, their job is *not* to turn somersaults, because any activity in the air might turn them off course; and the more wind resistance they meet, the more they can slow down.

Before the event, the band stops playing, forebodingly, and Zacchini Senior calls out their names in the voice of Abraham standing over his son. A terrifying siren wails, and there is a thunderous explosion and the astounding sight of two bodies propelled half the length of the hippodrome. As they recover themselves and roll out of the net, the band strikes up, the performers who have been watching breathe easier and smile, the crowd is rejuvenated, and since the circus's purpose is to evoke emotions like this, it seems altogether a fitting end. Zacchini walks toward the cheers with his arms raised high, his head back, as dazed as a man reborn from the grave, his face in a kind of ecstasy, and moving as if he were swimming in cream. In a day of casual death everywhere, we are rejoicing *he lives! he lives!*

Elvin Bale, a subtle man, structures his feat, entering it intelligently, whereas Zacchini, brave and plump, following in his father's footsteps, is just shot off, then rises and runs forward to meet the crowd's jubilation—radiant, reborn. Tito Gaona doesn't risk his life comparably on the flying trapeze, but he sprouts wings on his heels, bounding practically into the crowd to take their cheers. Flying is special, classical, the *haut monde,* though sociable at the same time, going from hand to hand. On the street near Madison Square Garden, raggedly dressed, Tito, who is Mexican, looks like one of the Spanish-speaking men who push racks of clothes through the garment center, but as soon as he recognizes me he straightens like a man who knows he's considered to be the greatest trapezist in history.

It would be more fun to announce the existence of all this talent if the announcement would cause a stir. Instead, the circus remains a private passion for children and loyal fans; among sophisticates it occupies a niche similar to that of primitive art. Even more than the theater or sports, however, it is a way of life. The clowns are odd loners, the roustabouts are sometimes headed for prison or fiery ends, the performers are clannish; yet they all team up with a collection of candy butchers, nightclub girls, homeless Negroes and Germans and cowboys and Indians, and put on a permanent itinerant show.

The elephants and the horses are citizens too, and one mark of the circus man is that he can deal with this jumbled constituency. Gebel-Williams, who in Europe directed his own show, is remarkable for his impartiality. He guides his elephants with his voice and hands, touching and steering them, waving some to circle the track clockwise and others counterclockwise. He also touches the people he's talking to, intent and good-humored like a young general who fights alongside his troops. He's remarkable for being ebullient whether in the ring or backstage, taking the crowd's admiration in stride and seeming, as far as an outsider can tell, to live in a state of direct gaiety. He seems not to have the death wish, so his act is not a conquest of that.

Evy Althoff's tiger is nearly as big as the stallion it rides. Like most big tigers, it's a slumbering, deliberate-mannered beast. Evy wears a silver dress with a snaky motif, combs her yellow hair high, and makes abrupt, idiosyncratic, female movements in giving directions, as if she were guiding a lover, although in fact the tiger was trained by Gunther. She doesn't hurry the two animals but fits herself into their sense of time. Both she and the horse serve mainly as stand-ins while the tiger, well schooled but bored, with a peculiarly humpy run which resembles a wolverine's, leaps through an oily flame, picks its way on and off the deadpan horse, and lies down and rolls on request. The story goes that the first several horses died of heart failure while they were being trained, and even this valorous Appaloosa used to be so drenched with sweat after a session that its color changed from roan to gray. Being placed in the cage was bad enough but was nothing compared with *carrying* the tiger—that momentous pounce when the grisly creature landed on its back, sickening the instincts of a million years.

Evy is the same height and physical type as Sigrid, Gunther's second wife, except that her face is more compact, less enlightening. Sigrid is pert, freckled, and communicative, whereas Jeanette, who is Gunther's stepsister as well as his ex-wife, looks like a smoldering ribald beauty. She's a blonde too, with a mocking mouth, chubby nose, large sidelong eyes, a fleshier body, and more of a head of hair. While the band plays *Carmen,* she rides on a black Friesian stallion, which is accoutered in silver and muscled like a war-horse but glossy and curly in the tail and mane.

Gunther has a rounded, big, forward nose, too sensual to fit a clown, white-blond hair that his ears tuck into, flat cheeks, a mobile face—a cloven-hoofed, urchinish, inspired look—and a swaying, slim walk of quick persistence. His eyes are usually wide open, especially at any sign of trouble; smiling, he dodges into a tangle of animals. He wears brief-skirted gladiatorial costumes and does tight turns in stand-up, two-horse Roman riding. When he needs a whip somebody throws him one as he is passing, and he twitches it, so that it clicks rather than cracks. He's not a mystic, not even a specialist, because he meets people just as easily as wildlife; he likes money, golf, cars, rock music, airplanes. The money is here in America, he says; performances are faster-paced and more sumptuous than in Europe, the audiences are younger, and though he has not become a celebrity, the traveling is hectic and he is still busy learning English. It's curious that he isn't more famous—being at thirty-five the world's leading circus star, the best animal trainer alive. It is not as if we manage without heroes nowadays or that our heroes are noticeably above the level of *The Jungle Book*. Perhaps his position resembles that of an Indian scout and negotiator in the years after most people had lost interest in Indians and considered them virtually extinct.

He was born Gunther Gebel, far from the aristocracy of tightly knit German circus families, in a Silesian city called Schweidnitz in disputed territory which was transferred to Poland after World War II. When he was eleven his mother and he fled from the approaching Russians toward the Western armies—his father was not in evidence—and finally reached Cologne, where they lived on CARE parcels and Hershey bars until she got a position as a seamstress with the Circus Williams, a large, war-devastated show which was headquartered there. Though she didn't stay with the show, Mr. Williams, the impresario, who was a splendid stunt man in his own right, wound up adopting the boy. Gunther, keen as the orphan Dick Whittington, learned how to juggle and dance on a wire, flip like a tumbler, ride liberty horses, and swing from a trapeze. At first he spoke a primitive, comedian's dialect of German because of the border region he came from, but he had coordination and presence and soon could do anything. He had a way with animals in particular, so Mr. Williams encouraged his involvement with them: it was a rarer gift. When he grew expert with horses he began training lions, and when he felt easy with lions he worked with elephants, and then on to tigers.

In talking with Gebel-Williams, I suggested the loneliness of his position in those years might have something to do with his extraordinary responsiveness to animals, but he disagreed. Indeed, there is nothing misshapen or compensatory about his skill with them; it is more like an extension of his talent with people. He is charismatic and graceful rather than driven, not even very ambitious professionally. He is inexhaustible and delights in his work, but his talent exceeds his ambition. This might seem to be his weakness if he were set beside the few greats of the past; his strength would be his joy and versatility.

In the postwar havoc Gunther's schooling was hit-or-miss, enabling him to avoid the conventional engineering career he thinks he might have headed for under better circumstances. After five years had passed, his foster father was killed in a chariot race during a performance in London. The next year Williams's only natural son was also killed. Gunther, now seventeen, found himself running a show which traveled all over the Continent and employed more than fifty people. The widow managed business matters and there were family retainers, but Gunther went without sleep, learned to holler orders, hid his uncertainty, and supervised the teardowns, the overnight trips, the struggle to put up the tent the next morning. He was a centerpiece in the performance also, appearing repeatedly, and he married his classy stepsister. Later he encountered Sigrid, who, like him, was not born of the circus elite but was simply a Berliner who came to watch and sat close enough in the crowd. He was like a fish thrown into water; it was the world he had been meant for.

Gebel-Williams is one of the primary trainers, able to prepare an act from its raw beginnings, maybe passing it on to another performer later while he trains a new group of animals. As long as discipline is maintained, the original bunch will keep on doing the chores they have been taught, and if casualties occur the other fellow can insert a yearling or two, which will pick up the cues and gradually reach some understanding of what is expected; their quirks can even be exploited to enhance the act. Generally the group deteriorates to a patchwork, but there is a market for it. Royalties are paid by the secondary trainer to the first trainer or to the impresario who employed him and who still may own the animals he worked with. There may be additional owners, as other animals are acquired along the way, or there may be a succession of trainers, many of whom quit for work that is less dangerous and wearying, feeling that they too are somehow penned in with the cats, a sense akin to what jailers feel. Gunther himself, though he is not punitive with them, says that when he finishes a performance now he closes a door mentally on the tigers and doesn't think about them again; this in contrast to his relations with the elephants, who are uncaged and smarter and with whom he continues to chum.

In America, cat acts are divided between those in which a good deal of fighting goes on—"fighting acts"—and the so-called wrestling acts, where a degree of friendship prevails. The trainer may actually rassle around as if the beasts were sumo wrestlers instead of big cats, stumbling under their enormous weight, demeaning both himself and them. Some movie serials used to feature people who dressed up like Flash Gordon and staggered across the set with four-hundred-pound pets they'd raised from cubs; after a seesaw contest they'd "strangle" the dears. Old World trainers like the Hagenbecks, Alfred Court, and Damoo Dohtre worked equally closely with their animals but employed many more at once, and with refinement—no child's play or muscle stuff. They were likely to mix in smaller cats, such as leopards, or bears and wolves; the more of a stew of forces, the more complications. Mabel Stark was of that genre. At the end of her life she still appeared in the round cage in her Jungle Land amusement park, in Ventura, California at least for the Sunday show, receiving her tigers one by one because one arm hung dead, the other could only be raised as high as her waist, and she could not longer move on her feet except at a wobble. She communed with them, exhibiting them softly and nobly. The fighting showmen, Terrell Jacobs ("the Lion King") and Clyde Beatty, who toured the country through storms of roars, were not really less knowledgeable about the animals they presented, but their style was to cast them as killers, emphasizing the courage and grace of the man, not the beast. Though probably a number of cats rather enjoyed their company, the tumult of scrapping created confusion and quick changes of mood. Make-believe adversaries could turn into real ones if the fun went sour, and with thirty or forty big cats in one cage, the trainer's first job was to head off trouble between the creatures themselves; a whole bankroll could go in one battle royal.

Charly Baumann, another Ringling Bros. trainer, using tigers owned in part by a woman in Germany, gives a smooth, soft-touch performance, although without the fond intensity of some men, who wind up lying down at peace with their cats. He wears an expression like that of a martyr already smelling the flames. (It is not the tigers that distress him, however; practically the only time he seems happy is when he is helping the clowns throw balloons to the crowd.) His trademark is one special tiger which does nothing at all during the friendly bustle of hoop-jumping and pussy-roll-over-and-sit-up-and-beg that the rest engage in. Working with his back to her, eventually he gets too close, as if by accident, and she clasps his shoulders with awkward paws, and licks his neck vigorously and rubs her lips hard on his head (Cats "mark" property by rubbing their lips on it.) This wins applause, but you can tell Baumann doesn't entirely like the procedure by the way he neatens up afterwards. Sometimes she holds him there longer than he wishes; yet he can't be too rough in extricating himself because he is at her mercy and will be so again during the next show. Clutching him, she powders her nose on his head.

Gebel-Williams doesn't go in for this kind of thing. *He* does the licking, if any is done, his hands approximating the slow tugging motion of a tiger's tongue till the cat begins to jerk its head to the rhythm. But he doesn't pretend that tigers are brimstone dragons either. A fighting act can be as much a distortion as sumo wrestling, since it caters to the image of tigerish tigers and ferocious lions that we cherish from childhood. No animal could go through life leading such an existence of smoke and fire without burning out.

Ringling Bros. has hired still a fourth cat trainer—Wolfgang Holzmair from Germany. Appearing on the same bill with Gunther in Birmingham, he furnished an ideal foil for him, not least because he was very good. The two of them sat for each other as health insurance, the one off-duty just outside the door of the cage holding a club while the other performed. Gunther has his own cage hands from the Circus Williams for this if necessary, but Holzmair—like Baumann and Evy in New York City—would have been on his own if he had fallen under a pileup and been mauled.

Holzmair looks like a cut-down Kirk Douglas, with the same challenging chin. He is as heavy as Gunther is light, and works three-quarters naked, wearing slave armlets and leather kilts, an ironic curl to his mouth. He is square-chested, big-backed, a rough playmate, and has the appearance of sleepy fury in the cage, a Wehrmacht contentiousness, so that when he puts on his tux after his act he looks like a bouncer relaxing. But his work is his job, not a daydream, and so he's a little amused by it and does not seem to suffer, as some trainers do (even the mild-mannered Baumann), from the incongruity of striding out of a cage full of lions where he has been braving death and exercising his formidable will, to lay down the whips, the dominance, the belligerence, and defer to the performance director, step around the children in the entryway, sidestep the ballet girls and their husbands, avoid offending police and arena officials, and speak civilly in the dressing room. Some trainers can't. They go off in a corner, shout at the walls and whale about with their whips for half an hour, as if in a decompression chamber.

Lions are different from tigers, more repetitive and predictable. They operate as a gang without many independent characters, so that the trainer, keying himself into the swirl of the group, has fewer variables to keep track of. If he stumbles the whole cage may come down on him, but if he keeps on his feet and stays with the script, his flanks and over-the-shoulder area are more secure than if he were working with tigers. Certain lions are the ministers of war, some are followers, and still others—usually including the males—are noncombatants; the trainer's task is to make the best use of each. But even the ruggedest Amazon develops settled reactions to what the trainer is doing; he can almost depend upon her. In most cases he could work up a lion-lamb Androcles act if he wished, instead of the earthslide-of-roars routine, because for months he has carefully aggravated the warriors. If a lioness is in love with him, so much the better; it will put passion into her raging.

But lions roar too well for their own good and, colored a straightforward, soldierly khaki, are too stalwart-looking to bedeck with hugs. Roaring like motorcyclists, they charge as straight as a white circus horse goes round and round. They're prosaic good citizens and infantry, loyal to friends, martial toward foes. They're like bread and butter, and Gebel-Williams, who learned his fundamentals on them as a boy, finds them a bore. To sit beside him while Holzmair works is like sitting next to a bullfighter watching another fighter whose sensationalized style and whose bulls he abhors.

The fact is that lions and tigers are flesh and blood, not myths, and they can be stopped when they charge by the simple expedient of poking a strong oak stick in their path. If they can't get past that they can't reach the man, and their paws are not faster than his hands, especially when he has a whip. However, tigers also require delicacy. They spit up their food, and will balk and brood. Solitaries by temperament, they seldom defend one another against an attack. Being somewhat faster, a tiger can usually kill a lion of the same weight, though he may take a moment to chew past the mane, but in a brouhaha involving a dozen of each the result will be several dead tigers, as the lions proceed in a pack from one to the next, while the surviving tigers quietly observe. Only the trainer weeps at the result, because tigers, who are so nervous that they are reluctant to breed, will cost him ten times as much to replace as lions would. Lions are pragmatists; tigers are creatures of emotion and mood. Their camouflage of crazy cross-hatched stripes—a knitwork on the head, thick on the back and growing practically mad down on the hips and pant legs—are symbolic of this. Sometimes the spaces between the stripes even have eyes. Tigers are the proverbial hundred flowers. There are no leaders for the trainer to watch; any one of them will stick out a paw and the earth may become his sky.

In Birmingham, Holzmair's lions entered snarling, abused by

the cage hands, whirling in a sand-colored blur: there were so many of them that not until the third show could I count accurately. They were long-striding and masculine-looking like the hounds of hell, magnificent as they loped, roaring like pianos being rolled on a hollow floor. There were seventeen: so much barracks furor and collective noise that they spent the remainder of the day asleep to recover their poise. Lions are generous in using their vocal cords and are most impressive when they are weaving concertedly around a space that gives them room to dash and jump. Holzmair kept them moving, letting the sight sink in, then arranged them on pedestals around the cage by fives, so that the geography of conflict was clear-cut for him. There were five lionesses who never ceased to rev and roar, providing a foundation of dramatic rage for the act as a whole; these were the savage ones, his enemies. Five other, vaulting lionesses did the strenuous chores, leaping through flames and so on, claxoning like engines only if asked to. They were more businesslike and less self-assured, not such ideologues. Stamping his boots, wielding two whips, he could stampede them into wild climaxes if he chose to. There were also five modest cats who were of little use except to add bulk to the act. They beefed up the admirable milling swirl with which he began—the one natural display of lions presented as themselves, like a powerful sandstorm. Once posted on their stools, they didn't move, just pulled in their heads to sullen, intractable humps under the lash. Holzmair kept his back turned to them most of the time, as well as to two tame young cats he never roughed up because they figured in a brief exhibition of wrestling and trust towards the end, when he demonstrated that he knew the sweetness-and-light technique as well as the coercive stuff. He tried thrusting his head into the mouth of one, but the opening as yet was too small for the task; the lion gagged as if it were being doped, and he had to work at the mouth as if he were hollowing a melon. The other lion he carried across his shoulders. Along with handling the fiery hoop, this was apparently his least favorite interlude. The youngster itself didn't like the posture, and grimaced but didn't dare quarrel when Holzmair caught hold of its throat. Like Baumann with his pet tiger, he could hardly control these two, having never dared beat them, and resorted to tidbits to make them move.

With the motorized brigade Holzmair was in command, persuading the toughest of them to charge while he held the flaming hoop, and not only to leap through it but also through a circle he formed by clasping the whip above his head. Whereas Gunther's nakedness, expensively costumed, was sexy, his, clothed like a slave's, set off sadistic reverberations and emphasized the violence of the act—we were supposed to imagine him torn. Yet he was more ferocious than the lions, in fact; they watched him pass with frank apprehension, just as the rest of us might anticipate trouble from a loose lion. His every motion increased the racket; the snarls were a demon's snore. Ears back, faces flat, sweating from their mouths and streaming urine, the lionesses turned themselves into tunnels to roar. Twisting their heads to bellow from new angles, they thudded down off their stools and charged, as big as titans— but so was he. This was man's earliest image of wild beasts and how to undo them; this was how ancient lion tamers sneered and strode. An actor, a primitive, Holzmair carried one stiff prod and one long-distance lash, and most spectacular of all, as a finale he pushed the swarm of them into an ulcerous turmoil and then stood straddling the cage's outlet when the gate opened so that in frantically exiting they had to dash through his legs.

Tigers would fly off the handle if hectored so. Not being creatures of habit, and without the communal bond, they don't weather bullying. Like other cats, they are not overly bright. The reason a house cat cannot be trained to do many things is not only its "independence," it just isn't as smart as a dog. Cats are supremely equipped physically and have a simplified, well-defined personality that enhances their bodies' efficiency. The great cats, too, are miracles of physicality, a special version of the life force continuous since the Oligocene; and Gebel-Williams from boyhood gravitated to an interpretive role, not squashing or putting them down, but drawing them out.

Every part of his act is a refinement of the usual manner in which tigers are presented. When they take their places on the pyramid of pedestals to show off their coats, each tiger does not head for the closest perch, but goes roundabout to the farthest, so that the crowd sees an extravagant moil. While some roll over and over on the ground, others leapfrog across them in a simulation of the way a litter plays; and when they vault between springboards, Gunther varies this familiar maneuver by stationing a tiger in the middle and having the rest alternately bound over it, dart under it and dodge around in front—a playful effect that seems almost voluntary, in which no imitative momentum is set up. He encourages a male to waltz to the band music—a matter of boxing with him in a comradely fashion, using the butt of his whip. Horses and elephants are often forced to dance by disciplinary means, but tigers cannot be handled so easily because if they become fearful or fly into a fury they move faster and faster. He coaxes hard enthusiastic swipes out of one cat, then moves to the largest tiger, which lunges up on its hind legs, topping him by a couple of feet, and roars and lashes at a stick he lifts, jumping awkwardly but awesomely toward him as he backs up. Since the tiger looms grand as a dinosaur, roars like an inferno, and is not laid low as a result, the sight is not offensive as is sometimes the case when trainers stage heroic scenes.

Gunther's tigers are mostly males, because a male, though surly and slow, is bigger—*"more tiger,"* as he says, measuring with his arms. They smell like rye bread smeared with Roquefort cheese, and he chants and sings like Glenn Gould as he works with them, swinging back and forth, drawing murmuring rumbles and air-blast roars. Tigers growl softly but roar far more explosively than lions do, and he spreads his arms wide so that the animals have both of them to keep track of as well as watching his face; it's like having two assistants in the ring. He holds his whips in one hand, butt and lash reversed, and pets tiger chins with the other, grinning like a lapsed angel, a satyr—it's a lean V face, the flat planes cut for mischief and glee, or a big-eyed lemur's, a tree-dweller's face. Singing and chattering, he composes their ladylike lunges into a fluttering of stripes, touching his forehead with his fingers in a Hindu salute to acknowledge applause, and kneels theatrically while the tigers sit. Throwing sawdust on their turds so that he won't slip, he pitches his whip like a jokester, his crucifix bouncing on his bare chest, his eyes big and round, organizing them into a jungle trot. They look bulky as bulls, but when he bats them they rise into a pussy pose, paws up. "Ziva!" he calls, running to one, mimicking the twitch of her white cheeks and black mouth, and stroking her rump. "Hubblebay!" he says, and they all revolve. The band accelerates into a keynote of victory.

Maybe the loveliest moment is when Gunther simply has them walk: not a feat many trainers would consider exciting or could even achieve by the adversary technique. Two leave their pedestals and promenade as they might alongside a water hole. He induces another pair to join them—but counterposed—the two pairs passing in the center of the cage. Then he gets the other four to join in, crisscrossing as in Chinese checkers before lining up in formation like the spokes of a wheel. Round and round they slink, keeping abreast, looking up at him, delaying behind the band to exercise their claws (tigers never "march").

Bidding this group goodbye, he welcomes a middle-aged, equable tiger, redder than most, and fluffing and scratching it, introduces two elephants, an African with tusks and an Indian one without. The Indian voices its aversion in squeals, but the African seems indifferent to the tiger, having perhaps inherited no feelings about it one way or the other. The tiger springs to the howdah that each elephant carries, down to the ground and up again, then leaps between them, back and forth, finally mounting a platform near the roof of the cage, and jumps again onto the African's back. Gunther directs all this choreography only by words, sitting at his ease on the ring curbing and watching. The elephants and tiger mount three pedestals and rotate quietly as he talks to them; he tugs on the African's tusks and feeds it a loaf of Italian bread. The band plays traditional Spartan brass, the tiger mounts the African elephant again, and so does Gunther, his face in a Pan-like grin. He sits on the tiger, and leaning over, tugs its tufted chin, rubs its eyes and lips, and has it roar elegantly into his face. Then he and the tiger drop down to the ground, the elephants leave the cage, and he fondles the cat, tickling its black lips and its orange rump. Then he sits lightly astride its hips and rides it across the stage at a lumbering gallop, a sight not often seen.

Combining the elephants with the tiger is an exploit no rival trainer has managed to duplicate in the six years since Gunther first did it. He himself gave up trying at one point. Unlike horses, elephants are much too powerful to hold still, and the Indian elephant went crazy with fear. Gunther says he probably could train anything, "even mice—only you yourself must a little change." The limitations of a tiger act make it come to seem static and stylized as a Noh play; yet he dislikes training other animals. Bears hold their swinging heads inscrutably low, and have tiny eyes and a locking dentition. If he put lions into his act there would be fights, a challenge which doesn't interest him. Nor does he want to try riding a moose or training hyenas or tapirs. Like a gifted young man at a standstill stage, he seems not to have any plans for what he will do with his abilities, only for what he may do with the money he earns. He has a few scars, for which he blames himself. "You get very close to play, but one time it is not possible." He wears a red robe that says "Animal Trainer," and aimless and ebullient, drives his Toronado around town, honking at friends.

The elephants please him. He has one wise female who runs from a distance and tromps accurately on the teeterboard on which he's poised, flinging him into a somersault to land on her back. "Hup-hup!" he yells, sliding down by way of her trunk and front legs. "The Colonel Bogey March" switches to "Elephant Boogie," and all twenty elephants rush out in a line for the final parade, clutching each other's tails with their trunks. Gunther runs and runs, directing the herd with his hands and voice, sorting them into different rings as they fly by. They curl their trunks in, wave their ears and perform practically on their own while he talks and talks, directing them. His wife, Sigrid, swings on a rope held by two elephants while the others gnomishly do a jig. When Gunther shouts over the waterfall of applause they all heave themselves up on their hindlegs, like whales of the earth, each one balancing herself with her front feet on her neighbor's rear end.

The band slides from minor to major key for the finale; the trombones fluff-fluff, the trumpets blow like blue sky, the elephants stomp like mahogany. Shy-seeming skittering people turn into troupers as the lights hit them. All of the stars come out to recapitulate the evening. Alert showgirls ride by on gray horses, and guys in drag wear flapping shoes that extend out like dachshunds in front of them. Tumblers turn cartwheels relentlessly, and aerialists scramble up ladders, their spangled costumes glittering off the ceiling. And they're all smiling because it's the night of the teardown and they're leaving your town.

Dying Argots

Y ou know what *birling* is—the loggers' sport, begun on the old-time river drives, wherein two men in spiked boots run fast crosswise on a floating log and try to throw each other into cold water by stopping suddenly to reverse the spin. And you know that the outfit of supply wagons that accompanied these rivermen along the bank during a log drive was called the *wangan* (an Indian word); that each man's sack of personal belongings was his *turkey;* and that the previous winter, when he had worked in the woods *falling* trees and sledding them over the snow to streamside, the bunkhouse he had lived in was called the *ram-pasture.* The horses that *twitched* the downed trees out of the forest to the *landing,* where they were loaded onto sleds, and that hauled the sleds, lived in the *horse hovel.* A logger's basic tool for levering logs about—whether on the forest floor, in the sleds, in the river, or finally in the millpond—was of course his *peavey* (really only an improved *cant-dog* with a spike at the end), invented by Joseph Peavey in 1858.

You'll have read *Tall Trees, Tough Men,* Robert E. Pike's lilting account of logging in the Northeast; so in this brief piece about dying argots we can move on to the world of carnivals and circuses, whose glory days are vanishing almost as fast as that craftsmanlike logging done by hand instead of by huge tracked vehicles.

When you stand on a carnival lot, you as a *towner* become also a *mark* (a word that should need no explaining), if it is an old-fashioned carnival, and part of the *tip,* the crowd that gathers in front of each *bally* (ballyhoo) *box* upon which the *talker* talks to try to tip you inside the tent or onto the ride whose attractions he touts. The *glass house* is the Hall of Mirrors. The *ten-in-one* is the big sideshow tent with the *banner line* in front depicting the sword-swallowers, fire-eaters, snake charmers, knife throwers, and "human oddities'' inside. *Crime shows* display police memorabilia; and *peek stores* offer such wonders as a frozen caveman dug out of a glacier, under glass. *Grab-stands* are where you buy fried dough or a hot dog to eat standing up. A *mug joint* takes your picture. *Hanky-panks* are mildly competitive games, like those in a shooting gallery, where somebody "wins" every time—*slum* is what the carnies call the prizes, worth usually five or ten cents. A *flat store* is a *joint* (business operation) where chance rather than skill makes a winner; it might have those wheels with numbers on them that spin like a sort of sandlot roulette. A *gaffed joint* is a game where the operator determines who wins and when; and his *stick* is the accomplice who may befriend a mark to help the *carnie* fleece him. *Grift* is the general term for crookedness on a midway. And the *patch* is the fixer who handles the police.

A&S (age and scale) *men* will guess your age and weight. *Bozo* is the joint where you can throw a baseball at a bull's-eye and dump a clown into a tank of water—a successor, says Arthur H. Lewis in his book *Carnival*, to a crueler turn-of-the-century concession called the African Dip. In the *girl show*, the performer, if she doesn't have to *serve lunch*, will have a *snorting pole*, which she pretends is a man. And a *geek* who ate as well as simply bit off snakes' or chickens' heads was called a *glomming geek* as late as 1970, according to Lewis, though he doesn't say why ("glomming," I think, once meant eating too fast). Brutality did go with the liberty of the midway in the old days.

For the quite different realm of the circus, a good reference is *Wild Tigers and Tame Fleas,* Bill Ballantine's book of memories of working for Ringling Bros. and Barnum & Bailey under canvas more than thirty years ago (as did I).

The performers were called *kinkers* because of their frequent exercises to work the kinks out of their muscles. If they were foreigners—and the best generally were—they were also called *hulligans* (for hooligans), if one wanted to be unflattering. The horses that some of them did acrobatics on were *rosinbacks,* having been sprinkled with rosin to help the feet stick, though the general term for performing horses was *ringstock* (versus baggage stock). The elephants, all of which were female, were rarely called elephants, but *bulls.* The electrician was the *shandy* (from "chandelier") and the sound man the *screechie. Risley,* of course, is the ancient art of foot-juggling, named for a practitioner of the last century. A *perch act* is performed on a high pole; *ironjaw* means hanging by one's teeth.

To join the circus was to *join out.* The *sneeze mob* was the parking-lot crew, who supposedly warned each other by sneezing when they were going through a customer's car and either he or *the fuzz* approached. To *iggy* was to play dumb (ignorant) in such a pinch. Roustabouts were *workhands,* and carried their belongings in *crumb-boxes* ("crumb" for what a flea or a louse looks like). To wash up was to *crumb up,* and washing one's clothes was *boiling up.* The toilet or outhouse tent was the *donnicker,* from seventeenth-century underworld cant: *danna* (ordure) + *ken* (room).

If a circus or carnival ran so roughshod over the towners that it couldn't come back, it was said to have *burned the lot.* But it's important to remember that—like the loggers on a river drive— these troupers and workhands were pariahs in the towns they passed through, and would be gobbled up by the cops if they got drunk and got left behind.

On a circus lot, you as a towner were not ordinarily a mark; no-body was trying to gaff you. But if you stood around and didn't end up buying a ticket, just tried to see whatever was free, you were a *lot louse.* A particular nuisance was called *Elmer,* because that was a likely name for a country bumpkin. Firemen checking for viola-tions were called *Oscar,* as in the alarm call across the *backyard* behind the big top or among the chain smokers of *clown alley: "Have you seen Oscar?"* A fight, on the other hand, was called a *clem,* because the kind of rube who started one might be named Clem (not Elmer or Oscar).

Circuses were never anticountry, however; the very word "clown" comes from *colonus,* Latin for "farmer." And it was in the little towns that circuses might have a *straw house* (extra pay-ing spectators sitting on straw in front of the bleachers). Nor were circus people so hardhearted as not to recognize genuine poverty, the unemployed father with his raggedy brood of hungry-eyed kids. These were not lot lice; somebody would quietly *sidewall* them— sneak them into the big top under the canvas sidewall.

Teardown was what the circus did when it left town. The distance from the lot to the railroad yard was the *haul,* and the train crew was composed of *razorbacks,* from the lifting of wagons they did ("raise your backs!"). A long *run* between towns was a *dukie run,* because the bosses handed out *dukies,* box lunches (from the slang for "hands"). *China!* was the cry when the train rattled into the next town—probably not from the rattle, Mr. Bal-lantine suggests, but from wagon-show days, when the nightlong drive would have seemed like a trip to China.

And nobody wanted to have been left behind.

Two Clowns

Clowning is the one profession in the circus which has no limits on what can be done, and where youth and physique don't count for much. A man may start late in it or may operate in the realm of hallucination if he wants. Usually clowns take a role which is close to the earth—a plowman-pieman-tinker type, a barefoot sprite whose sex is uncertain because he's infantile. He's overly tall or small or in some way out of the running—innocent and light of heart, yet stuck with some disfigurement which is an extension of what the rest of us are supposed to want: a nose with "character," for instance, or tously hair and a fair skin. But these possibilities, ample for the average rather passive though contentious fellow who makes clowning his career, are a trivial detail in the persona of the few great clowns. After apprenticing in paleface as a simpleton for a few years, with a thick, giddy, up-arching, imprinted smile, such men will gradually begin to draw a more scored and complicated personality with the greasepaint, developing a darker, or what is called an "august," role.

Otto Griebling, who is the best American clown, wears a rag heap that has grown so shapeless as to seem mountainous. His nose, instead of bulbous, is bent and decomposing in a face the color of a frying pan. His resentful stare, eaten up with grievances, is as calculating as a monkey's. He plays a bum whose universe has been so mutilated and circumscribed that all he knows is that he's free to sit where he is sitting or walk where he is going to walk, and any impulse we may feel to try and cheer him up is itself cause for outrage, not worth even a bitter laugh. He hasn't lost so much that he isn't afraid of further blows, but as he shuffles along with a notebook, compiling a blacklist, marking people in the audience down, all his grudges blaze in his face. Like a sore-footed janitor (he's seventy-four), he climbs into the crowd to put the heat on selected guests—begins perversely dusting their chairs, or falling in love at close quarters, gazing at some squirming miss with his whole soul, leaning closer still, until, inexplicably furious, he slaps her with his cleaning cloth—she may try kissing him but it won't work.

Now that in actual life his vocal cords have been removed, Griebling has inaugurated a "broadcast," too. Wearing a headset and a microphone, he follows the rest of the clowns, whispering a commentary on their fate, on each mishap. His role is madder, more paranoid and ruined, than Emmett Kelly's famous tramp was; less lachrymose, it fits the times. With faded baggage tickets pinned to his cloak, he tries to powder his scorched face, looks for old enemies in the crowd. Obviously long past attempting to cope, he simply wants revenge; yet he's so small-time that instead of being fearful we laugh at him.

Added to Griebling's troubles is the same seething irritant that seems to bother other clowns. Nobody likes these ovations which are bestowed on the man in the center ring. Suddenly he loses patience, grabs three tin plates, clacks them together, and insists that the audience hail *him*. He juggles perfunctorily, since what he's interested in is not the juggling but the applause, and signals with his hands for a real crescendo. Setting two sides of the arena against each other, he works them up almost to the level the trapeze troupe achieved. But he isn't a bit satisfied. It never quite reaches the imagined pitch. Besides, it is too late for consolation now—too much of his life already has gone by!

Pio Nock is the Swiss master clown. He's old enough to have a daughter who romps on the single trapeze, dangling her yellow hair, wriggling from side to side, looking like butterfat in the strong lights. Nock confronted big cats and the flying trapeze when he was young and now is a high-wire clown, although he does some conventional clowning as well. He plays a sort of country cousin, a man floundering past the prime of life with nothing to show for it except his scars, not even an ironic viewpoint or the pleasure of vindictiveness. Where Griebling stands in baffled fury, past tears or shouting, torn between petulance and outraged astonishment, Nock is a man who doesn't look for root causes, doesn't even suspect that he has enemies or that the odds might be stacked against him. From every misfortune he simply goes on trying to learn. And for this characterization he doesn't rely much on greasepaint or costumes; instead, he makes queer hollow hoots, like the sounds in a birdhouse. As a trademark they have the advantage over costumes that the kids also can imitate them. They troop out of the auditorium parroting him.

Whenever Nock's country bumpkin gets slapped around, he's always willing to forgive the prankster if only the fellow will teach him how to do that particular trick so that Nock will never be slapped around in quite the same way again. Of course, during the show we discover that there are more pranks on the earth than

Nock will ever become proof against. We learn that life has limited its gifts to him to these few satisfactions—after the fact. After all, if the world appears upside down it must be only because he is standing on his head. Punishment follows each blunder; yet when he sees a nice girl (his daughter) up on the high wire, he decides that he wants to make an attempt at that endeavor also. At first the ringmaster stops him, but escaping the ringmaster's grasp, he climbs a rope ladder and in pantomime is instructed by her in the rudiments of wire-walking, cheeping eagerly at every lesson learned. The next thing he knows, he is out on the wire, terrified, alone, all the tips forgotten, whistling if he can. Whistling in the dark, a man in a jam, he teeters, steps on his own feet, gaining experience by trial and error, keeping his courage up with those strange hoots, which seem to epitomize how absurdly fragile life is, how often we see a tragedy in the making, as well as its end. The band plays music representing the wry look we wear while watching a stranger's funeral procession pass.

Nock stumbles on the wire and slips to his knees; wobbling, he looks downward, giving an unforgettable peep of fear. He's a short man with long legs and one of those wedgelike noses that even without makeup poke out starkly. His hoot is really like a sigh distilled—the sigh that draws on one's own resources as being the only source from which to draw. A man in the wrong place, again he jerks and nearly falls, giving his peep of mortality, and casts all his hopes just on the process of being methodical, doing what he's been taught as if by rote, which is what most of us do when we are in over our heads. But now he discovers he's learning! His obtuseness has shielded him from the danger a little, and suddenly he finds that he is getting the knack. He lets out a tombstone-chiseler's hoot. Now comes the moment when he can enjoy himself after having learned a particular dodge.

Pio Nock and Otto Griebling are great stars, and the image they leave in my mind's eye is so vivid and accessible that unlike those performers who do mere heroics, I hardly miss them after the circus moves on.

Should
Auld Acquaintance

Do you remember how funny schoolmasters' names used to sound? They probably still do, but especially was this so at pricey prep schools four decades ago. Poland, Cate, Crow, Bohrer, Suitor, Poor, Cook, Coffin, Hatch, Conklin—these were flesh-and-blood men I knew at Deerfield Academy in central Massachusetts in the late 1940s. Mr. Conklin, with a polished pink pate, was a pretty good geology teacher who ran a dogsled during the winter and whose means of maintaining order among teenage boys was to speak louder, *louder* and LOUDER until the whole Science Building rang with the rage in his tenor voice. Mr. Poland, angularly bony, with crested eyebrows, was an avid bird-watcher long before anybody had thought up the term, and taught biology successfully at nearly a whisper. Mr. Bohrer (in physics) was not boring, but Mr. Coffin taught Latin by rote in a stiff high collar and a gruff dry bark. Mr. Hatch—leaning back in his swivel chair with his feet crossed on his desk—hatched me as a writer by alternating the rhapsodic with the Socratic methods of teaching English and by navy war stories and evocative chat about the nub of ideas and the aims of an artist.

Mr. Crow, a small, bird-boned, feline-mannered historian, was a student of wealth and waxed most eloquent when he got on the subject of the rights of the rich. Mr. Poor carried a clipboard everywhere, hurrying so fast with a posture so straight he looked as if he might topple over backwards. He supervised attendance-taking seventeen times a day and on Sundays sat in the balcony of the church we went to and wrote down the names of boys who fidgeted. Saturday nights in the winter, at the basketball games where the roll call of the school was once again checked, he sat opposite the bleachers to note down (he said) who didn't stand and cheer at appropriate baskets. Mr. Cate, on the other hand, Dickensianly rotund and ruddy, was Deerfield's "greeter." He

greeted the parents, gave them the tour, smiling widely, and tried
to massage them a little as he led them into the big doorless office
of our famously diminutive and intuitive headmaster, located in
the hallway of the main school building, where all of the boys
passed by many times every day.

Frank Boyden (appropriately named, since his life was devoted to raising boys) was a man who trusted the evidence of his
eyes and trusted above all in *character*. He thought he could not
only recognize the nature of it at a glance in a tongue-tied new
boy but mold it almost irrevocably as well. In this latter conceit
he was probably wrong. In the several alumni gatherings I've
poked my head into over the years I've never had the feeling that
we Deerfield graduates are any less grungy, shifty, petty-minded,
and nondescript than any average grouping of men who have gone
to a well-heeled school. A preponderance of us have become simply
company men for whatever company employs us, veneered with a
corporate piety, skin-deep.

The Head, or "the Quid," as we also called him (we didn't
know why, but the name went back to the school's early days when
the students were local farm boys and had to spit out their quids
of chewing tobacco when he came in sight), had a mild-looking,
rather froglike face. He wore wire-rimmed glasses and double-
breasted dark suits with ties the same color. He catnapped more
than he slept, drove a horse and buggy on campus, and traveled by limousine everywhere else. He was whimsical, arbitrary,
or even worse in his treatment of some of the masters, once
firing a bachelor for getting married (bachelorhood was encouraged), and firing my friend Mr. Hatch after twenty-five years' service for suggesting that the older faculty should be covered by a
pension plan. But he was kind to the boys, employing no disciplinary measures beyond a clap of the hands and what we called
his "toilet face" to impose silence on the school when it gathered.
Individually, his appeal was always to our consciences, and somehow it worked. When an errant boy showed up at his desk, he
would peer at him intently, directly into his eyes no matter how
the boy hung his head (the headmaster's phenomenal shortness
was a help in accomplishing this), and blush for and with him,
telling him that he, the headmaster, had been hurt as well as
disappointed by his behavior, until the boy flushed red with shame.

"We are not a high school," he would say at Evening Meeting
if graffiti had appeared on a wall somewhere, and by morning the
anonymous culprit would have turned himself in. We were mostly
good boys, no question about it. When a straw ballot was taken
before the 1948 presidential election, Thomas Dewey got four

hundred and seven votes, Henry Wallace eight votes, Harry Truman only three, and Norman Thomas, the Socialist candidate, one (mine)—a result so remarkably skewed as to prove how astute Mr. Boyden was at picking the sort of conservative body of students he wanted. Indeed, Deerfield still admits no girls, the last of the old-line New England male schools to refuse to go coed. As a result, applications for admission have fallen by 20 percent in the past two years. And yet more present students say they approve of the policy than disapprove.

The profane in my day was represented by "the bank," a board lean-to dug into a bank of earth, out of sight, overhanging the hockey rink. This was where juniors and seniors who wished to smoke were allowed to do so (smoking is outlawed now); and it was a long, cold, conspicuous walk that athletes didn't make, or the designated class leaders, the faculty favorites, or the handful of scholars we had. Those who did venture there were boys as skeptical of the values of Deerfield as I and my closest friends were, but who expressed their independence by the slouch in their walk, by where they walked, and the dirty jokes they told when they got there, dragging on their butts and blowing smoke rings; some had even lost their virginity over summer vacation.

David Dunbar, a young history teacher presently at the school, says he "works on intellect in the morning in the classroom and character on the soccer field in the afternoon." That was Mr. Boyden's theory too. Mr. Boyden coached football and baseball himself, relying on such basics as the off-tackle plunge and the bunt towards first base. The school's library was in an incredibly cramped, squalid basement room, but the gym was immense, a temple of brick where I enjoyed watching high-caliber diving and swimming. He was right that if people don't get a special appreciation of sports in secondary school it's not likely to be made up for during the busier years of college. Also, he insisted we all put our hands in the soil of the potato fields surrounding our campus for a couple of days in the early fall, harvesting five thousand bushels. Even his varsity football team missed practice to dig potatoes, and I'm sure he thought it was one of the distinctions between how he trained us and how his rival headmasters at Hotchkiss and Choate operated, not to mention still more snobbish schools like Groton and St. Mark's. Mr. Boyden, who stayed on as Head for a total of sixty-six years (he quit at eighty-eight) and who had converted Deerfield from a local day school with fourteen students by taking on a good many boarders who had been kicked out of older prep schools (such families are often rich), seemed free of class snobbery with regard to boys of conventionally Anglo-Saxon parentage, but he relished telling us that we had outworked the itinerant Mexican harvesters in the next potato field, as if it weren't just our youth that had accomplished this, but our genes and our breeding.

Though he wanted a kindly tone to prevail, we were boys, and sometimes unkind. One student was turned into a living football on occasion, when two teams vied to push him across a "goal." Another was tied to a radiator, which then was turned on. The boys most rewarded were the big bland presentable ones who took nothing too seriously, said the right things, and went along to get along. At the hymn-singing on Sunday evenings these tallest, handsomest, best-dressed boys sat in the front row of the mass of students in the common room of the Old Dorm, facing a succession of well-tweeded clergymen from comfortable churches, and I suspect that at times we all had the feeling they were placed there to hide the rest of us in our grubbiness, stumpiness, and misshapen, nose-picking inadequacy. The school laid such emphasis on the trappings of idealism—on picking up any papers we saw blowing about, so visitors would get a good impression, on finishing up any job once begun, on sportsmanship on the playing field—that it's odd to realize in retrospect how free of any deeper substance it floated: not charitable, philanthropic, or particularly "Christian." At least I can't remember Christianity ever being preached to us as derived from the Christ who, infusing the work of Tolstoy and Dostoyevski, had quite mesmerized me by that point.

I had happy days there (I used to arrive on the train with my pet baby alligator concealed in a blanket), but should confess that my position at Deerfield was ambiguous enough that in my third year, as a senior, I was assigned to the dormitory corridor apportioned for misfits and known as The Zoo. We weren't such a bad group—my friend Eddy Mumford, the class poet, and me, the class novelist; a boy whose ambition was to run a bus business and who helped buy the local bus line that served Deerfield in his graduation year; another not too out-of-sync boy with a prominent Adam's apple whose passion was photography but who later became a flying instructor; and the scion of one of America's major smokestack fortunes who had not yet found himself. We had three or four heirs of major fortunes in our class, all mildly floundering. I, perhaps, wasn't, being within a few years of publishing my first novel, but I didn't know that then, and for many years afterwards had bad dreams about trying to get into the dining hall in the wrong-colored shirt. (To eat supper one had to wear white.) More important, many of us suffered later on, I think, from a fear of women, a remoteness and intransigence with them and an incomprehension of them, that was due to our not having rubbed shoulders with them in adolescence.

It's unnatural, anyhow, that boys of thirteen or fourteen should be uprooted from home. "Red" Sullivan, a ginger-haired, salty-tongued Irishman with a puckery mouth, was a father figure to the freshmen from broken households and dealt also with the upperclassmen who wanted to smoke. He was thought, too, to be able to talk with the local construction workers and delivery people, "speaking their language." Mr. McGlynn's stock in trade, on the other hand, was his wit. He was a tamed radical but still had a few uncommon ideas, always alert with a verbal conundrum to pose to the boys he liked. Mr. Cook, who called the whole school's roll every evening (sitting on the floor with our legs scrunched into the lotus position, we became expert at inserting our "Here!" with split-second precision into the rush of 419 names), taught French grammar and appeared to be more bored than any man I had ever seen before. Like many of the masters, his face was that of an overgrown boy, though his eyebrows had long since turned bushy and white, but unlike most of them, he had no zeal for the crush of earth, grass, and bodies on the athletic fields or the parade ground of twenty-four tennis courts, or for running back and forth all afternoon till one's face grew gray and gaunt. Mr. Cobb— who like Mr. Cook was married and a relaxed good-fellow—had been an officer in the shore patrol in the navy during the war and "handled" the boys everybody had failed, such as the sophomore who hanged himself from an apple tree by the railroad tracks one morning, wearing only his skivvies, just before the first train went by.

Students at Deerfield now have a freer schedule, I found on a visit last fall—a less narrowly meat-and-potatoes curriculum. Philosophy, art history, religion, and drama are taught. The masters still work under one-year contracts till the end of their teaching lives, but the lawns and buildings look yet more grandiose, and the fields we marched down to en masse with our overcoats draped across our left arms to cheer for the football team have expanded also. I remember wanting to swim the river that borders them but never doing it, a regret that may have fueled some boldness on my part later on. I regret not having been a better friend to a roommate or two, as well; and I regret my failure at a piquant moment when I discovered a skunk wandering around with his head stuck inside a peanut-butter jar, but didn't manage to pry the jar all the way off. I broke the bottom so that the creature could breathe, but let him hurry away still jaggedly collared.

When I go to reunions and stand underneath the big striped

tent, with Malcolm Forbes's hot-air balloon outside giving rides to alumni children, and the crowd of hundreds of grown-ups emitting its primal, involuntary, gleeful sigh as hundreds of lobsters are thrown alive on the coals of a bonfire to writhe and roast, I wonder what we all have learned since, apart from something about the precariousness of life. At best, we know a bit about love and how to work purposefully, but the experiences of adolescence seem random and hazardous in retrospect. I left Deerfield determined to become a writer at all cost, expecting even harder obstacles ahead than there really were, and wanting to be my own man, which also seemed a more difficult feat to attempt at a school like that than it did afterward.

Gods,
Masks,
and Horses

Puppet-carriers, mask-wearers, musicians wanted," the ad in the local paper read. And driving past the farm at any time during the next three weeks, one might have seen wooden horses fifteen feet high being built, a Genghis Khan taller than that, people peeling flagpoles by the dozen, stapling thatching to a series of six-foot movable huts, making yard-long shoes for floating giants out of cardboard, molding a whole variety of masks from many layers of shopping-bag paper steeped and stiffened in wallpaper glue, and drying and painting these.

At the meeting for volunteers for the Nineteenth Annual Domestic Resurrection Circus (each is the "Nineteenth") and the Pageant that follows, Peter Schumann announced, "We will attempt to present a proposal for our domestic resurrection, like always. A destruction will precede the resurrection, because in order to have a powerful resurrection you must have a powerful destruction. St. Francis will be the leitmotif this year, because it is his eight hundredth birthday and he was a bright clear man who set the record straight. The main animal will be the cow. The houses will move and there will be a forest that moves. The houses will have a Garbageman and a Washerwoman inside each of them, and two people and a kid are inside each cow. The armies will move and fight each other until they are all dead and then will get up and go on and hide in the moving forest. We need people on stilts who can fall but then get up and fight each other again. Also we need burnable items that we can use on the big fire."

He spoke in a mellifluous voice, with a light German accent, in short immediate energetic sentences, and wore, as usual, a red strip of bandanna that kept his hair out of his eyes—which look as if they had spent considerable time peering quickly out at audi-

ences from behind a stage curtain. His nose is lumpy, in a bone-
less face, but a fine black beard and wild black hair lend plenty of
force to it, as do his overlarge hands. Yet although he has this face
of somebody who could live by his wits if necessary, two months
earlier he'd walked and danced and marched two miles on twelve-
foot stilts in a Giacometti-style Uncle Sam costume from the
United Nations building up Fifth Avenue to Central Park, as the
definitive figure in the nearly million-soul June 1982 demonstration in favor of a nuclear freeze, with all of his demons, dragons,
birds, and angels around him—perhaps a thousand strong.

It may be that, like me, you enjoy the several light-repertory
companies of puppets who appear on television, but still believe
that life is paired with death, that generous impulses can reverber-
ate into a radiant poignance, that evil is more than merely mischief, that size is of looming importance, and color is seldom so
prismatic as on *The Muppet Show,* and therefore that the art of
puppetry is being only half served. Peter Schumann's Bread and
Puppet Theater is a marvelous corrective, and Schumann—who
operated on New York's Lower East Side throughout the tumult
of the 1960s and now lives in Glover, Vermont—is blessed with a
marbling of talents besides.

At forty-nine, he is working with twenty-foot effigies and
head-sized masks: the monstrous red figure of Yama, the King of
Hell, who has prongs in his forehead and is moved by three or
four strong men; a brown Nature God that resembles a Bigfoot
dressed in cedar boughs; a tall, careworn Madonna-Godface, with
hair woven of milkweed and goldenrod, and a cryptic smile. He
has other gods on tap as well, such as Jesus and the God-king
Uranus, Miss America, Joan of Arc, the Selfish Giant, Janus-faced
Herod, Mother Earth, Atom Bomb—all in the hayloft of the grand
old dairy barn that serves as his museum-storehouse. Genghis
Khan is clothed in fiery streamers and clattering beer cans, and the
several St. Francises are cloaked in pine cones and haloed with
moons. Yet the same day that they and Yama and the Nature God
and the Godface performed, he had the Mosaic God audaciously
appear as a tiny hand puppet talking to Noah from behind three
hand-held clouds.

Schumann's exemplary human beings are his Garbagemen
and Washerwomen, who are mostly worn as masks and puffed
stomachs by assistants and who look like thirty-year veterans of
difficult marriages, of cold northern winters and tedious employ-
ment. They move with a joyless slowness, buttoned into bruise-
colored faces afflicted with stoicism, with the beer bellies, potato

bellies, and bread bellies of defeat, dull labor, and impoverishment.

"Don't run. Never run! You're Garbagemen!" Schumann shouted in rehearsals. Work as such has no nobility in his canon, and for ten years or so the Garbagemen have been carrying out a variety of maintenance and cleanup chores (sometimes very grisly cleanups) in his pageants and circuses. The men of affairs—businessmen, newspaper readers in dark suits and ties—who plague and exploit them, brutalizing even their children, do get some pleasure from "working," but it is only an evil delight. The Washerwomen, with their downcast eyes and dented foreheads, their lantern jaws and mannish noses—who were created as unenviable helpmeets and coequals to the Garbagemen in 1977 at the time of a surge in the Women's Movement—had been preceded by many Gray Ladies who ironed or mopped their way through presentations that he calls "cantatas." Nevertheless, these faces aren't unlike real faces. And the Garbagemen in their humdrum green coveralls, though their duties and personalities have become more benign recently, still wear caps with a small swastikalike insignia on the front, crossed miner's hammers or swastikas with two of the four tails knocked off.

Being out in the country for the past dozen years, Schumann has added more and more animals to his cast. Lovely white oxen haul the Moon or the planet Earth on a farm cart in parades. Then there are rams' heads sculptured in the form of a splendid live ram that the Schumanns keep and that is so old its horns curve in a double curl. But his cows have fearful, goaty physiognomies and horns like ears. Vague, bewildered human faces are painted onto their sides as patches of brown, although—in humorous counterpoint to this dose of despair—when the legs of the two puppeteers manipulating each cow from inside do show, they are wearing skirts.

The Moon is what Schumann keeps up his sleeve to redeem the Earth, after the Sun or his several Godfaces have been destroyed. Wolf-headed fiends and trumpet-mouthed demons strut by on stilts with cymbals and drums during the course of a pageant, and winged crimson lizards fly directly from Hell, while his soldiers and businessmen—zestfully, gratuitously cruel—lay waste the homes of the paired-off Garbagemen and Washerwomen. A whole school bus, built up into the Devil Incarnate, plumes smoke and firecrackers, points its dread finger, and swings its dread jaws. But in the pageants of some years huge white galloping horses struggle against these scenes of butchery, dying glorious deaths.

His herd of twenty or thirty white deer, by contrast, submit as an innocent throng to being murdered; then are resurrected. White birds with wingspans of fifteen feet—each flown by three puppeteers holding long poles—travel fast to fulfill this latter role, crying with all of the vigor of sea gulls and quartering over the outdoor amphitheater, rousting up every dead soul and bringing peace once again, as the Moon on its ox-drawn wagon appears and (clouds and the calendar permitting) the real moon rises from a pine woods opposite the embers of the real sunset.

The amphitheater that the troupe uses each August is a flat-bottomed, horseshoe-shaped, grassed-over gravel pit with sloping sides, as spacious as a football field, and situated in a rolling hayfield across the road from that 1862 dairy barn where twenty years' worth of puppets tumble over one another—heads, hands, ears, and arms. There are packs of ravening beasts with incredible nostrils that can be unleashed and sicked on a unicorn; human skeletons scrimmaging; Death on a horse skeleton; a cluster of gesso-faced Vietnamese women ready for chaining or burning; and numerous "Johnnies," as in "Johnny Comes Marching Home" from war. King George III has a stall. Also a villain named Big Stomach, from *The History of Bread*. Weeping Queens. The Bulb-head Family, from *The Lions of Inflation*. A sepulchral Judge. And you can see the makings of Carl Orff's cantata *Carmina Burana* and Georg Büchner's play *Woyzeck* in puppet versions; of other dramas about El Cid and Goya; and the true-life stories of Masaniello, a Neapolitan revolutionary, and Victor Jara, a Chilean guitarist who after the overthrow of Salvatore Allende in 1973 had his hands chopped off by General Pinochet's police in a soccer stadium because he continued to strum for the masses of other prisoners assembled there, but who then raised his stumps so everyone could see what had been done to him and sang his song in the hush that fell. And of course Uncle Fatso, the Harlem slumlord with thick jowls and a cigar and a whole chorus of rats, thought up in 1966 by East 100th Street kids in New York to represent their own landlords but often used in the years since to stand in for Uncle Sam.

The sculptural, not the intellectual, impact of Mr. Schumann's politics is what is remarkable. After a certain period of drifting when the Vietnam War ended (at Christmas-time in 1966 his masks of the Biblical Mary and Joseph had delivered a bloody doll to the steps of St. Patrick's Cathedral), he has been reinvigorated by what he describes in the title of one of his pageants as *The Fight Against the End of the World*. Indeed, the dangers of a nuclear catastrophe are now so surreal that on that subject conventional wisdom has almost caught up with him. The dangers if not the solutions are as simple as the tableaux he makes of them, and he was no lonely radical as he danced on stilts up Fifth Avenue.

But he is an anomaly at the moment because he is such a happy radical. One knows martyr radicals glumly holding to their sixties tenets in garrets, and "radicals" earning ninety-five thousand dollars a year on a corporate payroll and sleekly cheerful because of it. Schumann, however, with the same fidelity that caused him to hold to the old-line social values of family and children as a centerpiece of his puppetry through an entire generation of nihilism, narcissism, hedonism, and absurdism in the theater, puts on his gala Circus, free to all, in a gravel pit twenty-five miles from the Canadian border, a splendiferous continuous extravaganza for ten hours—morris dancing, fire juggling, Byrd motets, slack-rope walking, a strolling jazz band. Each day of this late-August harvest weekend, six or eight thousand people come and enjoy a corn-and-potato roast, also free, as well as some five hundred loaves of the inimitable heavy sourdough rye bread which Peter himself has been waking up at five-thirty every morning for the previous six weeks to punch and bake, and now spreads with homemade garlic mayonnaise and hands out.

The Circus goes on at 4:00 P.M. with a homemade prayer for peace in eight languages, from Russian and Persian to Schweizer-deutsch. Then nine gorillas vault into the arena—tall, strong men maneuvering on six-foot stilts and evocatively got up in raggedy, black-dyed cotton costumes that project the illusion of wild fur better than fur would. Besides, they have hooked additional stilts to their arms, and by this furry motive power swiftly swing themselves along the way apes do. The stilts brilliantly lift them out of the human realm, and after romping through an animal kingdom of stunts, they raise their lengthy arms in a haunting, mute, emotional salute to the crowd across the millennia from long before Adam and Eve.

There was a Horse Ballet in the 1982 show, with stilts again lending an animal agitation to even untrained human performers, and a "water act" on a surface of black plastic spread on the grass. Several broncos loped into the hippodrome and bucked their cowboys off, and Annie Oakley put on a Wild West Show, issuing her instructions in a flat, energetic, Okie accent, rifle in hand: "I will now remove this radish from betwixt this man's teeth by use of a special ricochet device. Stand still, Bill, or I'm going to make a collander outer yu!"

Sultan Ottoman Sofa, with a harem and entourage, watched

a sword-swallower, then decapitated one of his flunkies who had misbehaved, and had another man divided in two inside a magical box. A "Bengali" put four two-man yellow tigers on seesaws, "saved" some children in the audience when one of these escaped, kneeled gingerly as the same tiger obediently touched his shoulder with its big paw, but hastily stood up and with lots of drumrolls, fed them meat.

Noah paraded with paired frogs, elephants, turtles, skunks, cockroaches, and giraffes to the Ark. And eight gigantic Garbagemen and Washerwomen twenty feet high (each manipulated by four individuals underneath) floated out and did a square dance for a finale, whereupon—as the music changed from fiddle-and-accordion to slaloming brass—Schumann joined them dressed as Yankee Doodle, boogying on stilts as tall as any used on earth to the Dixieland jazz that, in all of his circuses, resurrects the world: "When the Saints Go Marchin' In."

To sketch these highlights, however, leaves out the dragging interludes of antiwar scenarios, where files of children trudged toward the threshold of nuclear war, where soldiers tossed away their guns to obtain haloes, Garbagemen rose in a revolution against plutocracy as personified by the Duke of York, whose facial features were compressed underneath an enormous forehead. Before the Circus, St. Francis had appeared in picturesque but static skits in cedar-slab huts scattered around the field, preaching to the Birds and Fish, to Potatoes, and to Eighteen-year-olds about to register for the draft, and said something about El Salvador. He thanked his Toothbrush, Toes, and breakfast Milk, and, as in the "Canticle of the Creatures" composed by the real St. Francis, thanked his Brother Sun, and finally welcomed Brother Death.

The Not Dangerous (Yiddish) Band played "Wild Night in Odessa." The Mattawee River Theater put on a Welsh folk tale. The Regular Theater did "Mr. Blister and Fatman." The Dragon Dance Theater did a sketch about the Angel Gabriel. A snare drum and the bold toodle-oo of saxophones and trombones had then led people from the sideshows to the circus grounds, and auto horns, doorknobs, copper piping, and a crowhunter's call were pressed into service musically. Somebody's clarinet got considerably pocked by having firecrackers set off in it, and old New York City radicals could see saints of the Movement like David Dellinger slicing bread alongside Schumann in the "Free Bread Store," next to the nail-hung "Hiroshima Memorial." (Grace Paley had pitched her tent in a hayfield in a driving rainstorm the night before.) The Bread and Puppet Theater is the only commune in northeastern Vermont that has actually worked out, so one could notice survivors of all the communes that failed contentedly wandering around: Lost Nation, New Hamburger, Bean Hollow, Toad Hall, Entropy Acres, Mad Brook, Frog Run, Mullein Hill. Why is the Bread and Puppet free? Because it is so radical a concept that the food is donated, the outhouses are dug by volunteers, and two hundred people show up to perform without pay. Elka Schumann is her husband's most devoted assistant, an indefatigable majordomo and *Hausfrau*. Their own cadre of four puppeteers are paid seventy-five dollars a week year-round, and perhaps a dozen former apprentices return each year for two weeks of rehearsal for scarcely more than that: Joanne Schulz of the Ninth Street Theater and On-the-lam Band, back in the city; Genevieve Yeuillaz, a Parisian actress who looks like a younger Godface. Margo Lee Sherman, now a New York actress, plays eighty-seven-year-old Octavia, an inquisitive, myopic lady who is the necessary naysayer, asking desolemnizing questions, such as whether the lepers of Assisi hadn't thought that St. Francis was a little bit *meshuggeh* for kissing lepers. She carries a loaf of Wonder Bread over to Schumann's Bread Store to ask the Director himself—to the audience's delight—why ordinary white bread isn't good enough for him.

When Amy Trompeter, another fifteen-year veteran, who makes masks at the Staten Island Children's Museum, arrived at the farm, she got right back up on stilts, catching the feel and the balance of them, and took up her bugle again. Although she is a shy person with close-set eyes and a tentative voice like a child's, so waiflike she seems to be always looking for another costume and personality to leap into, she was smiling so gleefully that the male puppeteers felt encouraged to come forward and hug her where the wood met her knees. Then she went out and cut fresh field flowers to take into the woods to decorate the memorial hut that she and the Schumanns had built as a home for a benign simulacrum of her puppeteer husband when he'd died of a heart attack at the age of thirty-seven. A pet blackbird sits on his forearm, commemorating his "Blackbird Theater."

Most of the throng who throw themselves into the festivities are not semiprofessional actors from Manhattan and Boston, acting students from Atlanta and Berkeley, or 1960s radicals and 1970s hippies. Even less are they likely to be native Vermonters from around the neighborhood. Instead, like the audience, they are mostly the so-called New Vermonters—educated, city-bred, middle-class people who have moved to the country within the past ten years to get away from the city and participate in the new or fictional Vermont. One meets doctors who wish they were carpenters and carpenters who ought to be doctors, ministers who look like car mechanics and car mechanics with a lawyerly manner, painters who say that their work had been stymied badly, and organic farmers going through the mess of a divorce or on the mend from an operation for cancer. They are people who will fly to Amsterdam or Idaho on vacation and yet suppose, when they get back, that these little communities they return to are true 1920s-type small Vermont towns—that, say, Cabot is different from Browningston or Danville or Lowell.

Peter, who has hiked on stilts in processions in Tunis and Algiers, surely recognizes a genteel fiction when he sees one. But fiction is his business, and Vermont's fictions have been hospitable to him. He, too, taps his maple trees with Elka during the spring, plants a wondrous garden of herbs, corn, and sunflowers, paints meadowy scenes on goose eggs, and squeezes apple cider with liturgical solemnity in a cloud of benumbed bumblebees as the hummingbirds leave the jewelweed to fly south and the leaves change with the first frost of the fall. Snowed-in in his barn, he is likely to construct a sculptural collage of found objects, like "Portrait of a Woman" or "The Snowflake King." He may draw a hundred smiles, or a hundred "Cheap Art" tree-and-clouds on little blocks of Masonite, for which he insists upon charging only fifty cents, and which acquire their effectiveness only when seen in bulk.

Collages, found objects, the idea that an accidental, unfinished, unperfected element is essential in the arts, is part of what Schumann teethed on in Germany and New York. So when these Found People turn up by the many dozens to participate in rehearsals for his evening Pageant, he gives them flags to run with and teaches them to ululate to open the ceremony, and to cry later on like quartering sea gulls surveying the aftermath of a holocaust before rousing the dead, or to blow softly into a Coca-Cola bottle among the horde of souls who, dressed in white, leave this life for an afterlife in a fifty-foot-long blue-and-white cloth ship just at dusk as the moon rises. After a couple of days of blowing into Coke bottles, most people will realize that they are producing a superbly theological sound; that tapping on a string of nails can add an extra dimension to it; that a clarinet mouthpiece stuck into the end of a garden hose emits a sound of such unearthly terror as to befit the trumpet-mouthed, wolf-headed demons who have destroyed the world.

A blue-eyed husky strayed into one of the rehearsals, and Peter, taking note of him among the small golden soldier puppets with chests made out of olive-oil tins, said, "There's a figure that purports to be a dog." The eight St. Francises of the Pageant were shifting position too fast, and he shouted to them that they would have to learn to move with dignity, his megaphone an old dunce cap with the peak knocked off.

"We don't want to hang that picture too long," he suggested when a peaceful scene of Garbagemen-farmers consumed too much time.

"Quiet. The Cows can't hear their cues," he said when the Villagers forgot themselves. His Stilted Army was to fight an army operating on hobbyhorses, but he abandoned the hobbyhorses as antidramatic. "And the battle was too short. Take more time dying!" he said. Then, to his puppeteers managing the Angels: "Keep the wings spread. Don't run faster than your wings!" He scrapped the oxcart that usually pulls the Moon and had the Moon carried on poles because the oxcart looked incongruous beside the fifty-foot Ark transporting the souls.

As for the Circus, "The trick is, the point is . . ." he kept suggesting. And to the band: "One tune for one trick. Don't mix the tunes." The tigers didn't twist enough as they paced and slunk. The two persons inside each painted suit had a rubber hose for a backbone. "The spines are good, but you must do more turns. Your turns aren't good enough. Never turn in the same direction as your partner turns. Hurry up. Faster," he said. Reviewers had accused him of slowing down lately.

The Circus seems to be of secondary interest to him; he leaves a lot of it to the puppeteers to develop, in contrast to the Pageant, which is always about life and death, evil and good way beyond even the momentary influence of single human beings, and which he oversees to the last detail. Helpers who materialize two months beforehand are given short stilts and told to make bigger ones when they have become proficient on those. They are also handed masks, to get the feel of being a Washerwoman or a Garbageman. Stilts will convert anybody into a puppet—stumbling, tripping, relearning how to walk, and then forever swaying slightly in order to keep upright. Equally, to peer through the pinholes of a mask breaks down the preconceptions of a lifetime, which is especially important because part of Schumann's method is never to explain to anybody what he "means." He leaves people to grope toward their own understanding in the darkness of his masks and the fragilities of stilt-walking, or in conferences with one another, of which there are many. Watching the result, he will speed up a sequence or, with a laugh, try to reduce a sideshow's scale. "We can't advocate world anarchy. That's too big a project for us."

"Let's dress that up a bit. Milking. Churning. Genghis Khan! Milking. Churning. Genghis Khan!" he told a group that was rehearsing—beating time with his hands to show how abruptly he wanted the transition made from the pastoral half of the scene to the destruction that would descend.

Teaching some other people to play homemade marimbas in what was scheduled to be a "Symphony," he had them hit the unfamiliar wooden instruments as they wished to for a quarter of an hour, and then came back and said, "Instead of hitting as hard as you can, try hitting them as soft as you can." Meanwhile, several fiddlers and drummers and cornet players and people with flutes and recorders had also been improvising. Each section began to listen to the others and to adapt carefully. He moved around, listening, inserting new themes, ideas, and adjustments, until at last the "Symphony" became a symphony in the same sense that a "God" was a god.

These volunteers making wind machines from a strip of canvas strung on a three-foot wooden spool, painting orange into the outlines for St. Francis's Fish that Peter had drawn, sewing fur loincloths for the stone-age Garbagemen in his *History of Labor,* painting the locomotive that Badmen were going to hold up during the Wild West Show, wore white clothing. White dress in performances lends his troupe a pacifist or an innocent air, as if they were a clean slate to write on. But the white pants, white sheeting, places them at one remove from the rest of humanity too—"like a butcher," said a slightly unsettled psychiatrist sitting on the hillside during a rehearsal, or like members of some vaguely unnerving cult.

Schumann's fidelity to his present puppets is such that whoever operates them doesn't look down on and manipulate them from above or wiggle them on the end of the hand. Rather, he staggers along, gazing up at the looming fringes of the puppet's costume while supporting a pole that by itself may weigh as much as sixty pounds. And loving the proud traditionalism of the art—Indian effigies thirty feet tall, Indonesian, Turkish, Flemish constructions, Japanese Bunraku and Noh theater—Peter is actually glad it's so arduous to dance for a mile on stilts or to heft the heavy poles that hold up Yama or the Nature God (called Marvin by the puppet handlers). It reminds him, for example, of how Papa Manteo's Sicilian troupe, of New York's Little Italy and Coney Island, whom he used to watch performing the many cycles of the Orlando epic, would pilot eighty-pound knights in jubilant sword battles while leaning over from a plank bridge behind and above the stage.

African and Alaskan shamans wore puppet masks. So ancient is the heritage that Peter is like many puppetmasters before him in mistrusting the power of words. Puppets, by simplifying or caricaturing us, stand in for us in tangled and horrendous situations. We make puppets big or tiny, mute or noisy so that their plight can't be ignored. And—though it's partly envy that a puppeteer must feel, comparing the overwhelmingly predominant position legitimate or cinematic theater enjoys, next to his own humble, checkered, belowstairs art—masks and effigies preceded "books" and scripts by an immense interval, and the reason they retain their extraordinary force is that they do reach veins of feeling in us that are deeper than words.

"Puppet theater is of action rather than dialogue," he has written in several of his manifestoes; and when Peter needs a narrator, he likes to employ a stripped-down, deliberately unlovely language spoken by a puppeteer in lifeless tones in order not to vitiate the clarity of what's going on. But his distrust of verbiage goes beyond the milieu of his own performances to make him very difficult for any writer to do justice to. His low esteem for the art of using words combines with a sixties anti-intellectual slant and contempt for the act of analysis and a furious anarchist's scorn for "Madison Avenue" and other stereotypes of interlocking networks of government and "media" power, to make his resistance to being written about nearly impenetrable.

"Governments run our economies but none of them represent us," he says, and after twenty years in America, he still carries a German passport rather than commit himself to a new citizenship. For television his disdain is such that he may not even pick up the telephone to talk to a producer who has called him—he ordinarily bars cameramen—and he allowed the makers of the movie *Hair* to copycat some of his giant puppets rather than dirty his own hands by taking a few lucrative days to duplicate the figures for them. He pays himself the same seventy-five dollars per week as the others, so there is a defensive or protective factor to the extravagantly pie-in-the-face behavior his disciples indulge in when emissaries of the corrupt outside world arrive. If I hadn't lived in the next town and known many of the Schumanns' friends outside the puppet theater, I could not have written about him. Other people who have ventured to ask questions of the puppeteers have experienced the same musk-oxen or lowered-horns defense, but when I mentioned to Burt Porter, the Schumanns' next-door neighbor, how exasperating the process was of walking around and around the little band trying to acquire information, he reminded me that musk oxen are an endangered species too.

Humanity at its best, in recent Bread and Puppet productions, is conceived of as being helplessly, passively pure. In a nuclear age (as opposed to the personalized era of the Vietnam protests), human beings, if they are any good, wait as obliviously as lambs for the inevitable slaughter. Peter's Horses, on the other hand, often resist, and represent vigor, fecundity, and youth. Dancing on his stilts in the raiments of a tall White Angel, he likes to resurrect them after they have been killed. Like Jonathan Swift, whose admirable Houyhnhnms were horses, he finds them a versatile and dependable image to work with. Impressive yet beloved, they seem to have piled up nothing but good will for themselves through the ages. If an Angel of Death rides a horse, the Angel picks up increased bulk and might, but the horse never seems to share in the onus of what the Angel does; from when we first catch sight of it, we know that it had no choice and may itself be forced to join the pyre. And an Angel who comes afterwards to repair the destruction gains in benevolence as well as stature by riding (on stilts) a (two-person) horse.

It's no wonder a puppetmaster should like horses, horses have rolled so many puppetmasters across the world. A horse did Schumann the same favor in Germany and Austria, when he was a young man with just a wagon and a violin. By twenty-one, he had dropped out of two art schools, had studied choreography and the violin, and with some friends he might "construe" a new-sounding music from invented instruments, or do a Dada skit in which he stood on the tail of his wagon holding a stone, then maybe dropped it after half an hour. He admired master painters like Rembrandt and Michelangelo, Matisse and Paul Klee, George Grosz and Wassily Kandinsky—"who was the brain of modern art," he says. "Kandinsky more than Picasso, who was an acrobat, and empty like most acrobats." The expressionist painter Paula Modersohn-Becker and the sculptor Wilhelm Lehmbruck affected him particularly personally, and Ernst Ludwig Kirchner, "who was the most difficult and spiteful of the German expressionists, with mean, wild colors," he adds with some delight. "And Erich Heckel, who was part of him." His own painted landscapes and animals resemble Kirchner's, and his country scenes are a bit like Heckel's. His heads remind one of Emil Nolde's, and, like Edvard Munch, he pictures the end of the world. Expressionist sculpture and painting were nonanatomical, seeking a free, flat spontaneity; and Peter, with papier-mâché as his usual material and polychrome painting overlying that, is only minimally three-dimensional. He is a sculptor against form, a sculptor trying not to be sculptural.

Max Jacob, proprietor of the Hohnsteiner Kasperle puppet theater, now of Hamburg, was a family friend, so Peter spent much time during his teens backstage there. His father was a teacher of literature, a high-school principal, and often read to him the Brothers Grimm, the classic Russians, the Swiss novelist Gottfried Keller, and Rilke's, Brecht's and Hebbel's poetry. Peter also especially liked Kafka's *Amerika* and various nineteenth-century didactic German-language novelists like Adalbert Stifter and Jeremias Gotthelf, who tended to write about peasants and country life, the struggle for a just society, and what Stifter described as the "law of gentleness" (though one notices when Peter mentions authors that have impressed him, it usually turns out that they were read to him, either by his parents or, nowadays, by Elka).

Until he was ten, the Schumann family lived in the Silesian village of Brokau, near the industrial city of Breslau, which was renamed Wroclaw after the end of World War II, when this portion of what had been eastern Germany was incorporated into Poland. During that fall of 1944, his family fled from their home barely ahead of the Soviet army, with the whole horizon ablaze behind them and other frantic refugees clinging to the roof and windows of the last train. He remembers his town on fire and the black smoke and explosions from the inferno of Breslau as it burned.

His mother had baked the rye grain she had saved into hard, long-lasting sourdough loaves, just like the hundreds that he shares out to visitors at his festival now, and they survived on these till they reached Schleswig-Holstein and could live on what grain they were able to glean from the harvested fields—while she knitted sweaters for the winter from wool that Peter, his two brothers, and his sister picked off the pasture fences where sheep had grazed. At the community oven in the new town, she cut miniature suns onto the tops of her loaves to mark them off from other people's. It was a sign of familyhood and survival that he still uses when making bread, except that his suns look like puppet animals, the rays being "legs" sticking off a round body.

The sudden, utter, fiery, fathomless devastation he visits upon his pageant world is thus a repeat of what he actually saw visited upon his own hometown when he was ten, and the image of life on earth being incinerated in a nuclear exchange is not so inconceivable to him as to an American. However, both his mother and father influenced him to become a traditionalist as well as a man of Dada gloom and innovation. Though he will fashion a fiddle from a Mel-Fry Liquid Shortening can impaled on a poplar stick, what he plays on it is likely to be a wedding ditty or a short hymn.

He met Elka in 1956 in Munich, where she was studying on her junior year abroad from Bryn Mawr College. Bryn Mawr is a first-class conventional college, but at that point she had had a singularly unconventional history. She had been born in Russia but deported with her family to the United States across Siberia and through Japan in 1941 when she was five years old—scarcely two weeks ahead of the German invasion of Russia, indeed—which gave her a complex and scary baptism in world affairs rather like Peter's. Her father was an American Communist who had dropped out of the University of Wisconsin a decade earlier to learn arc welding and help the Revolution at its source. He had married an educated peasant woman in the remote city of Magnitogorsk, but had lately taken up the more controversial activity of journalism. Elka did speak German in Munich, nevertheless, because her father had then made a 120-degree political turn, becoming a war correspondent, based in Stockholm, for *Time* magazine, and the magazine's bureau chief in Berlin after the war. Eventually, he was a special assistant to Henry Luce and dedicated a book called *China: The Hungry Dragon* to him, in 1967. He had a reputation as a loner and a mystery man about the *Time* offices in New York, an individual who seemed to have arrived from the Soviet Union with his ideas fully formed, unlike other apostates from Communism like Whittaker Chambers, and who traveled abroad so frequently on closemouthed missions for Mr. Luce or for James A. Linen, the company's president, as to arouse the joking rumor that he might be an intelligence agent, using *Time* as a cover.

He called himself John Scott to distinguish himself from his father, Scott Nearing, an economics professor from Pennsylvania who had been expelled from a brief stint in the Communist Party for contradicting a Leninist theory about ten years before John Scott was in his turn kicked out of Russia. Nearing, instead of turning conservative afterwards, took to the woods of southern Vermont—his "cyclone cellar," as he called it—in 1932, to pioneer the back-to-the-land movement a little later with books like *Living the Good Life: How to Live Sanely and Simply in a Troubled World* and *The Maple Sugar Book*. Though Nearing remained an angry, vocal radical, he tends to be treated respectfully in the memoirs of antiradical intellectuals like Whittaker Chambers and Sidney Hook. Chambers, in his book *Witness*, for instance, describes him as really a "species of Christian socialist." (After John Scott died in 1976, Elka's mother became an evangelizing born-again Christian.)

Several of the Schumanns' friends suggest that while Peter himself supplies the *Weltschmerz* and religiosity of their theater, Elka is more tirelessly, doctrinairely political. Her opinions tend to be black-and-white, spoken in the familiar, certain, brisk tones of naiveté of her father's conservative books and her grandfather's radical ones. Anyway, it was to the pleasantly suburban oasis of Ridgefield, Connecticut (where Luce also lived), but to this pamphleteering, hortatory background that she brought her German husband in 1961. Their first daughter and son had already been born, and by autumn they were installed in New York on East Sixth Street between Avenues C and D, on the Lower East Side—Tamara, Ephraim, and then Solveig stacked up in double-decker bunks and Peter working as a housepainter and church sexton to support them all or making life masks out at Coney Island at five dollars a throw ("Get One for Your Mother").

The starburst of abstract expressionism was around, as well as happenings, junk painting, and a collage art of found objects expressing the glut of a society of excesses. Peter had discovered Franz Kline in Europe, and now was moved by Willem de Kooning. He may have picked up a bit of the prankish quality and the technique of using paint as form (but not the cynicism) of the schools of Robert Rauschenberg and Claes Oldenburg—whose apartment he sublet,

John Cage, Merce Cunningham: it's hard to say just what he learned from whom. Certainly, as Vermont's puppet impresario appearing with his bass drums and pennywhistles, his Celastic dragon and cotton angels, during any neighboring warm-weather celebration from Hardwick's Spring Festival parade to Sheffield's Field Day in September, he adheres to that insistence upon an improvised look. "Art is impermanent," he insists, but unlike those artists of the sixties, he is trying to bring "a spiritual reaction" to the lives of ordinary people, believing that art that doesn't reach them is genuinely incomplete. Street presentations have been his specialty all along, gathering whatever human material was at hand—not only the stray kids who hung out with but occasionally would steal a violin from him, but even the Lower East Side junkies if he had to have ten extra bodies to hold high his puppet poles and get them out onto Second Avenue to sock his agitprop messages to the crowd.

Of course, the paradox is that ordinary people set a higher store on just the kind of polished craftsmanship in art which he deliberately eschews than do people who have more educated tastes. So his charmingly raggedy slapdash animals speaking to us from the Pliocene, and his grotesque Garbagemen with slackened cheeks like victims of Bell's palsy, who represent the ravages of the Industrial Revolution, "reach" mainly people whom he regretfully considers the elite.

Elka had attended the Putney School in Vermont before Bryn Mawr, and for a breather from the city, took a job there teaching Russian in 1963, while Peter did puppet workshops with the students, plus a series called *The Mr. Miller Stories* on a trailer stage that he hauled about central New England. Back in New York again, they found a loft on Delancey Street near the Williamsburg Bridge with a high ceiling, where he constructed his first oversized figures, such as Great Warrior, Yama, and Christ. The building had a cupola on the roof, where a river breeze blew in the summer and his helpers enjoyed smoking marijuana after rehearsals, while watching the police station across the way.

He built a stage of pilfered milk crates and put on shows like *King's Story, The Difficult Life of Uncle Fatso, War Demonstration, Murder Mystery, The Birdcatcher in Hell, Chicken Little,* and *Fire.* In *King's Story,* a good king—a rod puppet in the style of those historically made in Cologne—invites a huge warrior into his kingdom to kill a dangerous dragon, which the warrior does. But the warrior's sword seems to have a life of its own, and the warrior turns on the king, priests, courtiers, and citizens, killing everybody, until he is alone, and the short figure of Death runs out impartially and twists off his hands.

In *Birdcatcher,* a frightened birdcatcher finds himself in Hell, rather than in Heaven, where he had expected to go. But Yama is so pleased by a demonstration of the birdcatcher's professional prowess at netting, shooting, and roasting pheasants and herons that he lets him go back to earth for a second life.

Fire, dating from 1965, is said to be the most dramatic of all the productions Peter has done. With the invariably stately pace he employs—a pace which alters the actors' habits of walking and the spectators' habits of breathing, telling the audience, *I have a story to tell when you have settled down to listen to it*—he portrayed the purposeful burning of a Vietnamese village. The masks of the villagers were antiromantic life masks that he had taken directly from a Chinese apprentice in his theater; and with only these, and a soup tureen, a rattle, a violin, a bare light bulb, and a number of dressmaker mannequins, masked and moved about in such a way that five actors could animate as many as twenty different figures so no one watching could tell which individuals were alive under their costumes and which were not, the rhythms and homely tradition of the living village were conveyed.

Air raids came and then American infantry with weaponry. Finally a fire-colored cloth was spread with exquisite slowness over the residents, who were by now immobilized with horror. There is one survivor, a lovely, long-haired woman whom the conquerors imprison in a cage amid the ashes. They leave her alone for a while, but she slowly and deliberately immolates herself, using many strips of red adhesive tape which she rips off the roll with a crackling sound like flames, gradually covering her body with stripes of fire—and at last her mouth and eyes. The production toured Paris, Nancy, Aubervilliers, and Berlin. In New York City people who saw it can remember stumbling down the stairs into Delancey Street and to the subway, weeping.

Chicken Little was a Candide journey from Adam and Eve to the atom bomb falling. In *Christmas Story,* Herod was featured, with a cigar, big chest, and fists, and a slaughter of the innocents occurred, courtesy of a huge machine gun and several carts into which baby dolls were thrown. In *The Cry of the People for Meat,* Uranus, the god of the sky, and Mother Earth mated and produced the god Kronos, who promptly decapitated Uranus. Kronos and wild beasts created Eden and a man and woman, but soon ejected them. The Vietnam War somehow intervened, and one of the woman survivors was transformed into Christ, to be crucified on the Cross of a warplane's wings.

Sleeping Beauty, The Gray Lady Cantata, The Stations of the Cross, The Dance of Death, The Dead Man Rises, A Man Says Goodbye to His Mother: the titles were handsome, the stories simplified and antiwar, the puppets riveting, and the tempo so majestically slow as to be either disastrous or brilliant. Indeed, when Peter's assistants tour without him, they tend to lose their nerve after the first few weeks and speed up to a safer, less breathtaking pace.

After he outgrew the loft on Delancey Street, the City of New York lent him a defunct courthouse on Second Avenue and Second Street where he could stage events in the hearing room and store his puppets in the detention cells. Later he occupied an abandoned bank building in Brooklyn, which he shared with a sick horse. And he found further space at the "Old Prop Shop" at Joseph Papp's Public Theater, and at the Living Theater, on Fourteenth Street and Sixth Avenue, where he experimented with a cherub motif and a set of scavenged organ pipes, which he passed to the audience to wield and blow into. He performed his dramas too at the "Hall of Issues" at Judson Memorial Church in Greenwich

Village, at St. Peter's, St. Clement's, St. John the Divine, and other churches around the city, and for more than a year at an old vaudeville theater on Coney Island which was loaned to him by Nathan's Famous hot dog company and which had previously housed an animal freak show. There, he spieled or fiddled on a bally box outdoors to get himself an audience, which wandered in and out because he didn't charge for admission.

He worked with street kids for the Parks Department, constructing the long green dragon which undulated through Harlem with a hundred children squealing inside and now delights country kids on the Fourth of July. In 1968 and 1969 he toured Europe with a troupe, doing *The History of Bread* and *El Cid* in Lyon and Zagreb, *The Lions of Inflation* and *The Chapel of the Condemned*. 1968 was a year of revolutionary turbulence in France, and his plays were a hit. Also in Spain; in Shiraz, as the Iranian revolution approached; and in Italy in the mid-1970s, when American experimental theater came into vogue—although the anticlerical students fretted about his religious content.

Bread and Puppet is better known in Europe, where its experiments in improvisation have seemed newer and its traditions older, and the thrust of its satire appears to be directed comfortably back at targets on this side of the ocean. In Europe, Peter—who didn't come to the United States till he was twenty-seven and still speaks mainly German with Elka when they are alone—has sought more success. Flinging his hair back with a jerk of his head, looking out from that bare block of skin between his bushy beard and buccaneer's forelock, lurching with a rolling, fishlike walk that leans to the right because of some back troubles he has been having lately, yet holding himself with a marten's alertness—with his women around him, the look of a Pan about him, and his retinue of male disciples, his stubby big hands for sculpturing God's, Garbagemen's, and Horses' heads in clay for mask-making and hammering those eloquent, suffering rib cages onto enormous horse frames—Peter could be the itinerant hero of an Ingmar Bergman movie. The strenuous demons, haggard peasant women, mystified and tired gods, dogged, loyal animals, and other dramatis personae he employs would intrigue Bergman, just as the simple abridgments of the antique myths and legends they appear in would probably touch him for their repetitiousness—genius in the narrow gauge.

Bergman's response to his own agnosticism is forever to try new stories in a nonstop search for God, while Schumann's is always to repeat the same story, hoping that at last he may come to believe it. When a puppeteer at the first Pageant rehearsal in 1982 asked which of the many gods stored in the barn were going to be used this year, Peter said perfunctorily, "Any gods," and looked for the next question. Bergman would like such single-mindedness or tunnel vision in a hero, but would want a sampling of *temptations* added to the repertoire, at least a Pan or two, from such a Pan-like man, to make the puppet characters more active and more human. Presumably there are no temptations in Schumann's work because temptations, choices, the possibility of human sin, would imply that we have some flexibility, some degree of intelligent responsibility for our behavior—in other words, that there are human beings like you and me and Peter himself living. And such an admission would drastically change his passive, "peasant" picture of mankind—mankind as a sort of sinless, flaccid dairy herd, to be put out to graze and then abruptly, sportively slaughtered.

As a *Flüchtling,* fugitive from the East, and then a teenage Dadaist in ravaged Germany, a sixties rebel in opulently experimental New York, Peter had been juiced with boldness enough to try anything: in physical scale, dramatic collage, religious eclecticism, political acerbity. But, having tried a lot, in 1970, soon after Elka had been mugged in the hallway of their building on Sixth Street, he was pleased to accept an offer to move to Goddard College in Plainfield, Vermont, and practice puppetry on the college's "Cate Farm." (Such sites are likely to retain a vanished farmer's name, in a state that sentimentalizes at the same time as it is destroying its farming heritage.) This was a year when the counterculture was feverishly organizing communes, when hordes of New Yorkers, radical and otherwise, were pouring into upstate New England looking for land. Elka's father, the lone-wolf, wine-connoisseur, Time Inc. troubleshooter and correspondent—who had become such a contrast to *his* ascetic, back-to-the-woods but still Marxist father—also decided to buy a farm in Vermont, "the Dopp Farm," which coincidentally was only forty miles north of Plainfield. With his two hundred and sixty acres he did do one thing differently from the counterculture, however. He set about mining his hayfields for gravel to sell to the contractors then constructing Interstate 91 where it swoops through the town of Glover, thus providing his anticapitalist son-in-law with the supremely suitable stage setting he uses now.

Down at Cate Farm, a commune of thirty or more Goddard students and hangers-on had coalesced around Peter. The college itself was an experiment in education, and he must have encouraged the philosophical and organic-gardening aspects of their living communally. But gradually he found that his unwieldy group was not seriously apprenticed to puppetry; the artistic intent of the project was being subordinated to "swinging." Just as he had shed the streets of Munich for New York in 1961 (had fled the flames of Brokau seventeen years before that), and the streets of New York for Plainfield in 1970, he molted his whole entourage of young people in 1974, leaving Goddard too—which was threatening to disintegrate, his friends among the faculty turning to holistic doctoring and whole-grain bread-baking for a livelihood—and moved north with his family to John Scott's farm.

The first Domestic Resurrection Circus, in Plainfield, had been a resurrection for the Schumann family personally; and Peter had exploited the country landscape well, presenting pageants such as *The Dead Man Rises* across the Winooski River from his audience. Also, he created his first Garbagemen from the model of the college's maintenance crew in their green coveralls and caps, with frigid-seeming Vermont faces and a dairy farmer's matter-of-fact equanimity in the face of pregnancy and birth and death. Handy at any task, these early Garbagemen were rather sinister, compared with the present Glover variety. They never initiated evil doings—evil ideas were the province of the businessmen in suits and ties. But with the broken-tailed swastikas on their cap bills, these country men could be roused from passivity to carry out any ugly job that might be suggested, like throwing babies into wheelbarrows or cleaning out a gas chamber. In the fresh glimpse he had got of his new country setting, he didn't yet see the local people through rose-colored glasses; he could have recognized, for instance, that Vermont country boys would be as likely as any other Americans to perpetrate a My Lai massacre.

Peter leads a hermetic existence, never discussing his work with anybody but his disciples, and one seldom meets him round about northeastern Vermont at the cattle auctions, the hunters' breakfasts during deer season, the demolition derbies at the county fair, where young farmer-loggers batter each other in junk jalopies, or the tent for female mud wrestling, or the old-style girlie shows where "you can watch Sheba marry your next-door neighbor right onstage on the inside," as the barker on the carnie platform likes to proclaim—all places where he could witness passions that would be new to him in the rural context and see new lusts unbuttoned and new faces. So, it was like him not to have learned about stilts simply by attending the nearest circus. Instead, while he was doing puppetry at Cate Farm, a visiting French mime described to him how shepherds in the Les Landes district near Bordeaux traditionally used to stride on stilts over the rolling ground, stopping to rest against a staff with a seat fastened to it. The women herders even knitted in this way. The men held a fa-

mous race from Bordeaux to Marseilles: one young hero is reported to have hiked from Paris clear to Moscow. And thereupon,
Peter says, it occurred to him to adapt the craft of stilt-walking to
puppetry. The accidental quality of his discovery, for a man who
trusts and values accidents, made it feel all the better.

Stilts put Peter and his spectacles into an airier and more dy-
namic realm. His warriors became scarier, his angels more ethe-
real, his gods more awesome and supernatural, at the same time
that his now superabundant menagerie of animal and puppet
masks spread his field of concern to include the kingdom of nature. When he had arrived in Plainfield he had startled and offended the citizenry by parading on the Fourth of July with Uncle
Fatso (that loathsome 1966 Harlem slumlord) dressed as Uncle
Sam, dragging a chainload of agonized newt-headed Vietnamese
ladies behind him. But stilts somehow made even his confronta-
tional protests more metaphorical. Besides, the end of the Vietnam
War, as well as the splendid, irresistible intricacy of the New England seasons, cheered him enough that he gave up the sock-it-to-'em
city style of expression in favor of a milder brand of allegory. For
parades, Uncle Fatso was replaced by the skinny Yankee Doodle
on high stilts whose can-do pep even a Johnny Reb might love.
And having always believed that in an indoor puppet show the
arena of the stage should seem deeper and more spacious than
wherever the audience sits, so that the audience will be over-
whelmed by the figures, how exhilarated he was, surveying these
rolling Dopp Farm fields, where gods, soldiers, and commoners of
every conceivable size could wheel and sail about, to selections
from Bach, Schubert, Mahler, Janáček, and Josquin des Prez, mixed
with prolonged and happy blasts of jazz.

At such a site as Glover it took only a year's isolation before
he couldn't resist inviting the six most faithful of his Goddard
flock to rejoin him. For five years he lived again in communal
fashion with them, thinking up productions like *The Washerwoman Nativity, The Dream of the Dirty Woman, The White
Horse Butcher, In Danger Is Help,* and *The Story of One Who
Set Out to Study Fear.* Finally Elka insisted that the family build
a private house uphill from the original farm buildings—forgoing
the 1980 circus festival in order to do so—which in the summer still
hum with dozens of people rushing in and out, everybody walking
around in that special envelope of privacy that commune denizens
develop, the food the same brown rice, fried squash, and bowls of
cabbage, with the inevitable commune "bug" that flies about and
knocks everybody for a loop for a day or two.

John Bell, a stalwart from the Cate Farm days, lives in the old farmhouse with his wife, Trudi, and plays a mean trombone and guitar in performances, as well as pennywhistle, double bass, and recorder. He is the troupe's electrician, drives the trip school bus, can speak Italian, sing in Yiddish, and tell long jokes in Quebeçois patois, and, ambling on seven-foot stilts in gorilla costume, will balance on his shoulders a ten-year-old boy dressed as a baby gorilla, while hailing the audience with gestures from the forests of the Pliocene. Yet out of costume he would appear to be only a tall, nondescript, self-effacing young man with a permanent expression that looks as if he were about to cry.

Barbara Leber, another trouper from Cate Farm, is a sturdy blonde with the face of Petrushka and a Pinocchio bravado whenever she is "on." She does the preparation painting of backcloths and side scenery and has a gym teacher's manner in ordinary life, but she is wonderfully serviceable in Schumann's productions, able to improvise in dancing style a portrait of a fecund, and then a poisoned, Earth, when ecological poems are read, though she can also prance like a drum majorette in pompoms and bobbysox for "American" scenes. Rather like a vaudeville actress of decades back, she has mastered the flat, exaggerated verbal delivery of a foil in responding to the lines of a script, can do a bellydance for Sultan Ottoman Sofa of the Near East, but later, in the evening Pageant, she high-kicked tirelessly on four-foot stilts to an accordion in a lengthy, charming milkmaid's dance of innocence while leading eight cows downhill toward their eventual slaughter at the hands of the Four Horsemen of the Apocalypse.

Michael Romanyshyn dropped out of high school in Maine a few years ago to adopt the precarious life of a puppeteer. He is Schumann's particular protégé, though more like a regular circus performer now, and is nobody's foil. He does demons, clowns, gunfighters, bumpkins, and fireworks and dragon displays, and tears about the hippodrome balancing a puppet on a twenty-foot pole on the bridge of his nose—claiming, like any good puppeteer, that his purpose is to focus the gaze of the crowd upon the lofty little rag puppet, though in fact he has developed such presence, agility, and speed, such a superstar's physical flair and nose for slapstick humor, that it would be impossible for anybody to watch the puppet instead of him.

These three are ubiquitous. And Joanne Schultz, the soul of the On-the-Lam Band in New York City (where she serves garlic spaghetti before performances instead of garlic-spread bread), is a mercurial personality from the Goddard commune, a dashing would-be actress who returns to Vermont every summer to put her spontaneity at the service of puppetry again. Paul Zaloom is a

Syrian-American comedian from the old commune who comes back from New York's Tribeca neighborhood to beat a sharp snare drum and play master of ceremonies with splendiferous panache. Genevieve Yeuillaz, the Parisian actress whose face resembles the Mona Lisa–like Godface's, flies over for a holiday month to assist with mask sculpture and to dance and run with a flag and project her fine timing and voice. Catherine Schaub, a sleek, very pretty young dancer from France, sews the pole puppets Michael Romanyshyn runs with, and has mastered the craft of stilt-walking nearly as well as Barbara Leber, so that, as the Goddess of Milk and Cheese, she can herd two-person sideshow cows over the pastures with four-foot strides and an insistent stick until a crowd follows wherever she goes. Cate Peck, a Vermont country girl, shaped four fat white horses out of wire and sheeting to haul the cageful of tigers into the hippodrome for the 1982 Circus. Then she roared through a toilet-paper tube into the band's microphone, as the tigers slunk and the trumpets blared, just as she'd used to do when she was five years old, hiding behind her grandfather's easy chair in the parlor.

Andre Mugnai, a Florentine mime, covered his chest with pawnshop medals for the Pageant and led his Foot-Soldier Army against John Bell's Stilted Army in extended identical tableaux of the Battles of Troy, Gettysburg, and Normandy to demonstrate the futility of war. Typically, however, in staging this event, Peter had made no distinction between a war fought to avenge Menelaus's chagrin over being abandoned by Helen of Troy and a war whose purpose was to overthrow Adolph Hitler—just as in an ingenuous sideshow called *A Thousand Eyes for an Eye,* a committee of his puppeteers managed to compare the actions of Israel in Lebanon to those of the Nazis in Europe, while in the next breath they said that the Palestinians who had been displaced from Israel were merely a "wild people."

But all scripts and manifestos receive perfunctory attention. Since nothing significant can be "done" with words, since, furthermore, words are the instruments of corruption in politics and media advertising and seem to stand in opposition to the free flow of spontaneity, words have no interest in this theater. When I asked questions, one participant liked to refer them to her nine-year-old son to emphasize her objection to the idea that it was possible to "think" about such a production; another repeated my queries in singsong mockery. The 1960s' antipathy for reflection is here preserved in amber, and after a couple of weeks of rebuffs, I felt a perverse satisfaction during the last few days before the festival as a succession of young newspaper writers and photographers showed up and stubbed their toes against the silence that they met. I kept wishing for a lightening of the sloganeering, a leavening of Günter Grass's irreverence, the fluidity of the kind of mind which is more fascinated by human beings and acknowledges more possibilities in them for contradiction, rebellion, mystery, and incongruity. But two months later, at Halloween, when I ran into the New York contingent marching in the annual fright-wig parade through Greenwich Village, I was nostalgic. Paul Zaloom in his top hat and tails rat-tatted on a snare drum, Catherine Schaub danced ahead of him on stilts, while the On-the-Lam Band pointed their trumpets at the roofs of the brownstones in "Tiger Rag," "Bourbon Street Parade," and "Jolly Foot Fanfare." Since I was wearing a green "Leaf Man" mask made by Ralph Lee, I was not recognized, and stuck with them affectionately for the sheer pleasure of the sumptuous beat.

Ralph Lee among mask-makers is second only to Schumann in the United States, and it is Lee who runs the Greenwich Village parade. Whereas Schumann looks like a showman when he is putting on a show and like a knotty-shouldered, hambone-handed sculptor otherwise, Lee looks like a puppetmaster always. He has grave bushy eyebrows and a formidable forehead, like an alchemist's or necromancer's, and he looks betranced, preoccupied—more visionary and intellectual than a real intellectual or visionary—as though he might be masticating a fable and rearranging marionettes in the rings and corridors of his mind. Schumann never gets so absorbed as to lose the live-by-the-wits air that he has.

Lee remarked that Schumann's work is "reliably inspiring" (the same words the theatrical director Joseph Chaikin later used, expressing wonderment that anybody's could be nowadays) and doesn't require developed actors—needs amateurs, indeed, who will not infect with foreign stylization the visions he presents, but will embody them. Though Lee's masks are a good deal more polished and ornate, he generously suggested that Schumann's, by their exceptional simplicity and what is deliberately left uncovered or unfinished, demonstrate what is necessary in mask creation and what is not. It's exciting, he added—that mass of faces Peter brings to a scene, indoors or out, and the way he can plunge into the streets with a strong dramatic core in mind and enlist whole crowds of strangers to his cause. His use of music is effective, and he has evolved a theater of masks more than of puppets because he likes choreographing the human body so much. His extraordinary "rootedness," as Lee said, provides him with this sense of simplicity, which at its best is not simplistic but enables him to develop the action with mesmerizing slowness, forcing upon the audience time to remember, imagine or anticipate, until they become his collaborators, a pace which can be breathtaking when the unfolding details are of suffering and death.

His limitations, Lee said, are that "he is stalled in" that one oracular pattern of death and resurrection, an *idée fixe* which repeats and repeats; and that his techniques are better suited to an issue such as the Vietnam War, which can reasonably be portrayed in stark juxtapositions, than to more complicated, "artistic" productions, such as his *Masaniello,* about the seventeenth-century Neapolitan revolutionary who gained a following of a hundred and fifty thousand in ten days and then turned tyrant; or *Wolkenstein,* his tale of a sixteenth-century poet-composer, half of whose soul winds up in Heaven and half in Hell. Another failing is that because his apprentices do most of his Celastic and papier-mâché work, his masks have less intrinsic interest to a colleague—"they're 'School of Schumann' "—than if they'd been done by his own hand. (Celastic is a woven plastic material that has been dipped in acetone.)

The Pageant that August evening was less intriguing and cohesive than others have seemed over the years. Several loyal Schumann fans spoke of it as "tired," "too thematic," "out of control." Nevertheless, nothing remotely like it was being performed anywhere else in the 1980s.

The crowd of thousands, streaming across the grounds after the Circus performance, ate the food provided, sampled the numerous official sideshows and the wares of the free-lance tumblers, mummers, and buffoons. At sunset, led by a jazz band, they massed again in the bowl of the gravel pit and heard a homemade prayer sung by perhaps a hundred people moving in reverse directions but concentric circles around the Godface, down on the floor. Then Andre Mugnai's white-clad, sword-wielding army battled John Bell's red-tunicked, short-stilted battalion up along the rim where they could be seen by everybody, while, close by, there in the pit, a ritual of spring planting was under way. The distant soldiers had drums and trumpets, but a dozen cupid-sized winged angels and their female mentor were dancing slowly to the poignant, penetrating sound of a tiny, dime-store toy piano. As though in a kindergarten commencement ceremony, they stopped once in a while to "plant," but the strange, stunning notes of the Woolworth piano somehow made it all right.

After the Trojan War, the U.S. Civil War, and the Second World War had been disposed of, and the little angels had left as well, Barbara Leber led a herd of cows down into the amphitheater with her milkmaid's magic dance on stilts. Garbagemen and Washerwomen in family couples transporting eight patchwork huts also arrived; and "Marvin," with a decorated forest accompanying him, to give Nature a stake in whatever was going to happen— Marvin's facial features being different from the Godface's because of his deeper tint, innocent mouth, and close-set eyes. Eight St. Francises materialized; and the symphony orchestra, with its marimbas, fiddles, wind machines, Coke bottles, brass doorknobs, and lengths of pipe, sat front and center, with Schumann as director.

Now, at the eight established households, chickens crowed, cows mooed and were milked, newspapers were perused, people went to sleep at nightfall, woke up again when the roosters crowed, and drank coffee ("At night I dream / Of you and cream . . ."). Then the milking, and the newspapers again. Babies were born, and married, in good time, to an accordion jig.

Peter stood up and rang an altar bell and in his loud melodic voice introduced the Household Gods, which were gigantic Garbagemen and Washerwomen floating forth as lightly as balloons to "When the Saints" and other strains of Dixieland. They were respectively the Goddess of Good Humor and the God of Bad Moods, the God of Cleanliness, the Goddess of Messiness, the God of Clarity, the Goddess of Wishywashiness, and the Goddess of Brightness and the God of Boring Stupidity, and they stood behind the homey life-sized households.

All of the St. Francises moved out to chant to the audience (with John Bell and a chorus) part of St. Francis's "Canticle of the Creatures":

Most high and most holy, most powerful Lord . . .

To Thee and Thy creatures we proffer our praise:
To our brother the sun in the heavens ashine,
Who brings us the beauty and joy of our days,
Thine emblem and sign.

We praise Thee, O Lord, for our sister the moon,
For the stars of the night shining sweetly together,
For our brother the wind, for the bright of the noon,
For all of Thy weather.

For our sister the water, so humble and chaste,
For beautiful fire, with his perilous powers,
For our mother the earth, who holds us embraced,
Who delights us with flowers. . . .

These St. Francises and giants were imposing. Moreover, the music of the theological Coke bottles and wind machines, banjos, spoons, and strings of nails denoting time passing was gradually joined by a tattoo of drums which became menacing, and brass and saxes and violins wailing. This broke off. A sweet, soft six-note refrain, begun by the accordion, was picked up by a cello, then the trumpets, then the voice chorus and all of the rest of the ensemble. In its compelling gravity, its inevitability, it soon stopped sounding merely sweet. With repetition it became a clear, relentless, and yet still gentle dirge of death.

Beyond the householders and their new-fledged children, beyond the chickens and cows, and Marvin and his forest decorated with paper stars and streamers, beyond the Godface and the big modest Household Gods, a plume of smoke was rising. Though it was almost dusk by this point, at the far edge of the hayfield the audience now saw indistinctly four huge Horses wheeling toward the amphitheater, with a retinue of attendants walking beside them. The snare drums slid into a kind of playful syncopation, and a brawling cacophony from the brass instruments broke the sweet nostalgia of the insistent refrain. On the four great Horses drawing closer, the audience now spotted individual demon riders gesticulating. A jawed, enormous Dragon appeared behind them, five times as long as each of the Horses, and streaming the slow tower of prophetic smoke.

As when a person, dying, remembers being in love, and playing with his children when they were young, the music was regretful more than fearful, the six repeated notes still sweet with memories. But the drums' syncopation became not simply high-spirited and disruptive, but evil and vindictive. The trumpets' incoherence began metastasizing to the other instruments, passing like a cancer through the orchestra. Like mahouts on an elephant, three energetic demons were seen to be leaping about on top of the Dragon, which was bus-sized, spewing firecrackers, and equipped with fifteen-foot arms that swung and pointed into sections of the crowd.

Yet, as in the course of a disease, the drums and trumpets had moments of remission, when they played in peaceable and even confident-sounding harmonics, before lapsing helplessly into incoherence again. Strings of firecrackers kept going off. The eerie rubber hoses with clarinet mouthpieces were blown. When the Four Horses had arrived, the Four Horsemen in trumpet-mouthed, horned masks leapt down and ran with wide long flags among the householders and their homey world—flags they swung and swung and swung, flattening all of the people, all the animals, all the gods.

There was silence.

Suddenly, then, the horned demon-Horsemen blew fierce whistles and clashed cruel cymbals, dashing about again. All the dead people who had been flattened started up from their deathly positions and slunk and snuck away. Marvin and the Godface and the Household Gods were also removed, and the Dragon, its mission accomplished, backed out of the way. The Horsemen next wheeled their own Horses alongside the forest of decorated trees that could now be seen to have been painted with bogeys, banshees, fiends, imps, genies, ghouls, incubuses, succubuses, Satans, serpents, ogres, Lucifers, sharks, sirens, yetis, trolls, werewolves, and vampires— and set them all on fire. The trees, made of mill ends and cedar bark, crackled quickly; and the Horses, sporting large saddles of hay in which more firecrackers had been seeded, went up in a great brutal blaze, before subsiding to a bonfire.

From above the opposite slope, after an interval, we heard the liturgical tones of the Coke bottles, as well as gull and raven calls and low trombones. In a little while, white Birds of Salvation swept down into the hippodrome and crossed and recrossed it with their raw vigor and ocean cries—not, as in previous years, as though intending to repopulate it, but scouring it for signs of life and to rescue any dead souls that the demons had missed. They then flew off to join the three-masted blue Ark that appeared majestically on the high ground, extending fifty feet, escorted by a swan and other birds. Every human being was enclosed inside, slowly sailing away to a better world to the same lovely, nostalgic, but ominous refrain, adding their voices to the instruments now.

When they had gone, Peter stepped out to the fire, standing with his protégé and chief of the demons, Michael Romanyshyn, to beat out flying sparks and consolidate the fire but prevent it from burning up too fast. Leaning on long-handled shovels, the two of them stared at the flames and coals, warming their exhaustion, murmuring to each other, reassuming the mantle of civility.

Many of the spectators, too, gathered around the fire, looking at the pines on the hill, the clouds, and the three-quarter moon. They began to chat, hug old friends, greet old neighbors. If one knew them, one also saw ex-good friends and wary former lovers meet, as they had probably expected to at this annual event. The maple trees spread out their limbs in puppet shapes animated by the wind.

The puppeteers had headed for the barn, where they folded

their costumes into a dozen of the puppet boxes, which are old-fashioned stout wooden crates such as used to sit on handcarts outside Railway Express offices years ago but are painted, like the Schumann's two school buses, with birds, daisies, and sunflowers. John Bell checked the four Horses left for tomorrow's performance; the day before, a sudden storm had blown down two prop tents and done some damage. Romanyshyn climbed onto the Dragon with tomorrow's smoke bomb.

On the notice board was a schedule of rehearsals for two shows that would go on tour, *Diagonal Man* and *The Thunderstorm of the Youngest Child*. And in the basement of the barn, a number of the other puppeteers were gearing up for Peter's post-Pageant offering, *The Tragedy of the Ineffective Man and the Dream Woman*. More people had lined up to see this bonus playlet than could be fitted on the benches. It was about Michelangelo, and in miniature was a précis of much of the Schumann method. That is, it contained a clichéd idea—that all women are "dream women" to their men—wedded to an outlandish interpretation—that Michelangelo was an "ineffective" man—and sketchy research—that he was mainly heterosexual, not homosexual, and phlegmatic, not mercurial by temperament, and that his periods of productive work composed only a brief portion of his life. As applied to Michelangelo, in other words, it was a nonsense tale, despite a reading of discouraged poems from his last years. Nonetheless, if one paid no attention to the conceit that this was Michelangelo's life story, the puppetry was stunning.

Like all men and women, this individual is born of Woman and is born as a barbarous infant. Two female half-puppets, which had been split longitudinally and then tied together face to face but asymmetrically, were untied by two unmasked, unobtrusive female puppeteers wearing black leotards. From what had been the conjoined belly of the zaftig but asymmetric half-puppets, a whole male puppet with a green head like an alligator's was dumped onto the floor. After this birth, as unceremonious as anybody's, he was naturally suspicious as he crawled about, assisted by the puppeteers, to the creaks of a lugubrious bass fiddle. Presently his green alligator head fell off, revealing the stark and realistic face of a man with a gray crewcut inside. "He Grows from a Beast," said a sign that they held up.

On his knees, he lifted and examined his hands, realized that he was human, and began to read. Soon he progressed from his schooling to becoming a family man and was beset by the responsibilities of middle age. "Tedious Life," the new sign said, as the self-effacing but abrupt, commanding, nurselike puppeteers held out to him assorted tasks that were to be completed. By and by he became an artist, and, placed in a sort of stretcher-sling, was raised on two pulleys, lying facing upwards, and labored intensively with the motions of painting a fresco in concentrated grimness, while the bass fiddle groaned. "Giant Effort and Tragedy," the sign said.

Exhausted, played out, lacking the faintest sense of satisfaction or achievement, he collapsed in the sling. The pulleys jerked. The sling was upended. He was tipped headfirst onto the floor, and his taskmistresses—not without some sympathy—started preparing him for burial. For his sarcophagus, the two mismatched, big-hipped, large-breasted puppet halves were brought forward again. He was placed between them and they were tied together, rather as the proverbial mother-wife or wife-and-mistress combination may enclose a man through life. It was a vivid image, and one remembered him inside the resulting effigy as it was hoisted by pulleys and began to rock. All about, in the meantime, other big-breasted, large-hipped females of a beige color brushed with black had been lowered to the stage, and they likewise began to rock, each—and there were many of them—clasping and suckling a midget man. Some stood cradling the figure baby-fashion against their breasts. Some stood pressing him closely against their legs, his face at vagina level, where he sucked for his own comfort. But this arresting scene did not imply either lasciviousness or any special contentment for the couples, because the "rocking" for all of them was quickly speeded up. It turned so mindless, fast, and manic it was a misery, frightening for the women as well as for the men because it did not stop; it had become part of the rhythm of life and both were imprisoned in the torment of it.

After watching *The Tragedy of the Ineffective Man and the Dream Woman,* we adjourned to a workroom in an el of the farmhouse for a party. The day had been such a success that the On-the-Lam Band was blowing gleeful blasts of jazz whenever Burt Porter's country fiddlers quit playing mountain music for a minute, and various neighbors' kids were setting up loudspeakers for what would wind up as a rock concert. We had a keg of beer, a wheel of cheese, a bin of cookies, pots of rice, potato salad, and refried beans, and platters of fried chicken wings. ("Thank you, Brother Chicken!" shouted Andre Mugnai, the mime from Florence.)

Peter looked done in and flushed. He slumped on a bench way in the back, sipping beer, picking at a plate of food, no longer bothering to push his hank of hair out of his eyes when people congratulated him. A young acting student from Boston sidled near and passionately praised what she had seen, begged to be allowed to participate next year. "Write a letter to us," he said, smiling in fatigue and pointing to a puppeteer who could give her the particulars.

People who had been working with him—a costume designer from Vancouver, a sociology professor from Bremen—glanced wistfully in his direction and, mindful that the last day was tomorrow, picked out a loaf or two of sun-emblemed bread to carry home with them. There were the annual August romances to bring to an end, and a writer friend of mine whose wife had nursed two babies on Bread and Puppet tours abroad, carrying them for miles in a backpack underneath the raiment of Gray Ladies and Godfaces or under dragon skins, pointed out how, even now that they were in their teens, they had distinctly "Bread and Puppet" mannerisms.

A jiggling New York inventiveness was in the room—that city-on-strings that had been so important to Peter in greasing his fluency. In New York it was not just an abstract idea that you whip your act together out of junk and afterwards throw it away. But his old buddies from the radical movement of twenty years ago still had faces that looked to be in the throes of integrity. Earth mothers with sensitive, sisterly husbands who, as it turned out, had had trust funds to live on all along and had moved from New York to northern New England were embracing other earth mothers who didn't have trust funds and still had an eight-hour drive back to the city ahead of them.

Peter was blinking happily to keep his eyes open, scrunched into the corner like a sculptor tired at the end of an opening. I walked over and told him it was a fine party, a fine pageant. "Yes," he said. "And it's not over. It's not just us. The Horses are still burning. They burn a long time. If you look outside you'll see a hundred people still out in the gravel pit talking to each other."

Acknowledgments

These essays originally appeared in many magazines:

"The Ridge-Slope Fox and the Knife Thrower" in *Harper's* January 1977.

"The Courage of Turtles" in *The Village Voice*, December 12, 1968.

"Home Is Two Places" in *Commentary*, February 1970.

"Mountain Notch" in the Sierra Club's Wilderness Calendar, 1981.

"Of Cows and Cambodia" in *The Atlantic*, July 1971.

"Howling Back at the Wolves" in *Saturday Review*, December 1972.

"Lament the Red Wolf" in *Sports Illustrated*, January 14, 1974.

"Thoughts on Returning to the City After Five Months on a Mountain Where the Wolves Howled" in *The Village Voice*, November 9, 1972.

"City Walking" in *The New York Times Book Review*, June 1, 1975.

"City Rat" in *Audience*, March 1972.

"The Threshold and the Jolt of Pain" in *The Village Voice*, October 17, 1968.

"In the Toils of the Law" in *The Atlantic*, June 1972.

"Virginie and the Slaves" in *Travel & Leisure*, February 1976.

"Mushpan Man" in *American Heritage*, January 1979.

"Bears, Bears, Bears" in *Sports Illustrated*, March 26, 1973.

"Hailing the Elusory Mountain Lion" in *The New Yorker*, August 7, 1971.

"The Moose on the Wall" in *New American Review #9*, April 1970.

"A Run of Bad Luck" in *Newsweek*, July 30, 1973.

"Heart's Desire" in *Audience*, December 1972.

"The Lapping, Itchy Edge of Love" dates from 1968 but was never in a magazine.

"The Problem of the Golden Rule" in *Commentary*, August 1969.

"Bragging for Humanity" in *American Heritage*, July 1988.

"Dogs and the Tug of Life" in *Harper's*, February 1975.

"Other Lives" in *Harper's*, July 1973.

"The Midnight Freight to Portland" in *The Atlantic*, February 1971.

"Fred King on the Allagash" in *Audience*, February 1973.

"Walking the Dead Diamond River" in *The Atlantic*, August 1972.
"The Tugman's Passage" in *Harper's*, December 1979.
"A Low-Water Man" in *Sports Illustrated*, March 3, 1975.
"Heaven and Nature" in *Harper's*, March 1988.
"Tiger Bright" in *Esquire*, July 1971.
"Dying Argots" in *Harper's*, January 1986.
"Two Clowns" in *Life*, April 25, 1971.
"Should Auld Acquaintance" in *New England Monthly*, May 1987.
"Gods, Masks, and Horses" in *Vanity Fair*, July 1983.

Grateful acknowledgment is given to the many editors who worked with me.